In an era of corporate surveillanc_, ⌐ ‿ ⌐ ‿ ⌐ ‿
modification, automation, and more, law often seems to take a back seat to
rampant technological change. To listen to Silicon Valley barons, there's
nothing any of us can do about it. In this riveting work, Joshua Fairfield calls
their bluff. He provides a fresh look at law, at what it actually is, how it works, and
how we can create the kind of laws that help humans thrive in the face of
technological change. He shows that law can keep up with technology because
law is a kind of technology—a social technology built by humans out of
cooperative fictions like firms, nations, and money. However, to secure the
benefits of changing technology for all of us, we need a new kind of law, one
that reflects our evolving understanding of how humans use language to
cooperate.

Joshua A. T. Fairfield is William D. Bain Family Professor of Law, Washington
and Lee University School of Law. He is the author of *Owned: Property, Privacy,
and the New Digital Serfdom* (2017). A Fulbright and Fernand Braudel Scholar,
Professor Fairfield was a privacy and civil liberties counsel on intelligence
community studies of virtual worlds, and was part of the founding team of
Rosetta Stone.

Runaway Technology

CAN LAW KEEP UP?

JOSHUA A. T. FAIRFIELD
Washington and Lee University School of Law

CAMBRIDGE
UNIVERSITY PRESS

CAMBRIDGE
UNIVERSITY PRESS

University Printing House, Cambridge CB2 8BS, United Kingdom

One Liberty Plaza, 20th Floor, New York, NY 10006, USA

477 Williamstown Road, Port Melbourne, VIC 3207, Australia

314–321, 3rd Floor, Plot 3, Splendor Forum, Jasola District Centre,
New Delhi – 110025, India

79 Anson Road, #06–04/06, Singapore 079906

Cambridge University Press is part of the University of Cambridge.

It furthers the University's mission by disseminating knowledge in the pursuit of
education, learning, and research at the highest international levels of excellence.

www.cambridge.org
Information on this title: www.cambridge.org/9781108426121
DOI: 10.1017/9781108545839

First published 2021

Printed in the United Kingdom by TJ Books Limited, Padstow Cornwall

A catalogue record for this publication is available from the British Library.

ISBN 978-1-108-42612-1 Hardback
ISBN 978-1-108-44457-6 Paperback

Cambridge University Press has no responsibility for the persistence or accuracy of
URLs for external or third-party internet websites referred to in this publication
and does not guarantee that any content on such websites is, or will remain,
accurate or appropriate.

To Christine, Mary, Maggie, Hannah, and Grace.

Contents

Acknowledgements

This book is the result of many conferences and conversations over several years. I particularly appreciate the editorial vision of Matt Gallaway and Sara Versluis. I am also deeply indebted to the intellectual input of BJ Ard, Kiel Brennan-Marquez, Ryan Calo, Ted Castronova, Bryan Choi, Andrew Ferguson, Cristie Ford, Brett Frischmann, Eric Goldman, Woodrow Hartzog, Gus Hurwitz, Margaret Hu, Margot Kaminsky, Alexandra Klein, Matthias Leistner, Arno Lodder, Russ Miller, Aaron Perzanowski, Joel Reidenberg, Chris Seaman, Andrew Selbst, David Thaw, Ari Waldman, and Elana Zeide, among many others. I am particularly indebted to the European University Institute in Florence, Italy and the Frances Lewis Law Center at Washington and Lee School of Law for grant support, and both the EUI and the Max Planck Institute for Innovation and Competition in Munich, Germany, for research support and a place to write. I owe a debt of gratitude to my research assistants Jessiah Hulle, Patrick Twisdale, and Nathaniel Reynolds for their assistance in the preparation of the manuscript, to Jacob Lester for grant writing support, to my father, John Fairfield, for his tireless reading and commenting on drafts, and to my amanuensis, who listened to every word.

PART I

KEEPING UP: LAW AS SOCIAL TECHNOLOGY

1

Can Law Keep Up?

We need to talk. The future is coming fast, and we need to work together to decide how to meet the challenges of rampant technological progress. Talking is how humans cooperate. Cooperation, through language, is humans' super-power. Language is why humans, and not wolves, run this particular show. But there are two problems. First, we don't yet have the kind of language we need to talk about the problems of the future. Second, you and I don't yet have the kind of language we need to talk about how we will build the kind of language we need. In this book, I will try to build, between us, a language that will let us talk about the problems of the future.

"Wait," one might say. "What's all this about language? I thought this was a book about law!" It is. Law *is* language, a special kind. It is language that states how we have decided to live together. Law is the language that we need to build, to help us cooperate, in order to deal with the rapid changes introduced by technology. We need to develop language to permit us to talk about certain hard problems, and we need to do it quickly. That language is humanity's scratching at the surface of reality, building better social tools to handle what it finds.

The news is full of new challenges: dragnet surveillance,[1] artificial intelligence,[2] autonomous vehicles,[3] biohacking,[4] and 3D printing.[5] If

---

[1] *See, e.g.,* Raymond Zhong, *China Snares Tourists' Phones in Surveillance Dragnet by Adding Secret App,* N.Y. TIMES (July 2, 2019), www.nytimes.com/2019/07/02/technology/china-xinjiang-app.html; Jennifer Valentino-DeVries, *Tracking Phones, Google Is a Dragnet for the Police,* N.Y. TIMES (April 13, 2019), www.nytimes.com/interactive/2019/04/13/us/google-location-tracking-police.html; Kyllo v. United States, 533 U.S. 27 (2001); United States v. Knotts, 460 U.S. 276 (1983).

[2] *See, e.g.,* Janosch Delcker, *Europe Divided over Robot "Personhood",* POLITICO (Apr. 11, 2018), www.politico.eu/article/europe-divided-over-robot-ai-artificial-intelligence-personhood/; Zara Stone, *Everything You Need to Know about Sophia, the World's First Robot Citizen,* FORBES (Nov. 7, 2017), www.forbes.com/sites/zarastone/2017/11/07/everything-you-need-to-know-about-sophia-the-worlds-first-robot-citizen/#24f7c10846fa.

[3] *See, e.g.,* Peter Holley, *After Crash, Injured Motorcyclist Accuses Robot-Driven Vehicle of "Negligent Driving",* WA. POST(Jan. 25, 2018), www.washingtonpost.com/news/innovations/wp/2018/01/25/after-crash-injured-motorcyclist-accuses-robot-driven-vehicle-of-negligent-driving/; Cleve Wootson Jr., *Feds Investigating after a Tesla on Autopilot Barreled into a Parked Firetruck,*

---

law becomes obsolete, lagging behind the ever-increasing rate of technological advances, what happens to individual rights and freedoms? If law
evolves to grant increased flexibility to government, will those broader,
more far-reaching powers upset the balance between citizen and state? Is
there a way that law can keep pace with innovation while protecting and
preserving the freedoms that create the necessary context for innovation?
If law is to do this, it must not only change, but embrace the concept of
ongoing change, interweaving flexibility and resilience with the more
established concepts of order upon which society is built.

With the widespread adoption of any new technology, there is an assumption that the technology has created a space that law is unable to reach.
Money, for instance, has morphed from dollars to checks to credit cards to
cryptocurrencies like Bitcoin, all faster than regulators can react.[6] With
Apple's introduction of end-to-end encryption on cellular devices[7] came
then FBI Director James Comey's claim that the "Going Dark" phenomenon
would leave the public at risk and law enforcement unable to thwart crime.[8] Is
technology doomed to always be regulated by out-of-date rules? Or, worse, is
the world doomed to become lawless, as technology leaves dusty law codes
behind?

The currently accepted narrative is that technology outpaces anti-
quated legal institutions in the blinding rush of progress. Lawyers and
judges are deemed to be at technology's mercy. But there is another

WA. Post (Jan. 24, 2018), www.washingtonpost.com/news/innovations/wp/2018/01/23/a-tesla-owners
-excuse-for-his-dui-crash-the-car-was-driving/.

4 *See, e.g.,* Emily Baumgaertner, *As D.I.Y. Gene Editing Gains Popularity, "Someone Is Going to
Get Hurt"*, N.Y. TIMES (May 14, 2018), www.nytimes.com/2018/05/14/science/biohackers-gene
-editing-virus.html; Antonio Regalado, *In Blow to New Tech, European Court Decides CRISPR
Plants Are GMOs*, MIT TECHNOLOGY REVIEW (July 25, 2018), www.technologyreview.com
/the-download/611716/in-blow-to-new-tech-europe-court-decides-crispr-plants-are-gmos/.

5 *See, e.g.,* Steve Henn, *As 3-D Printing Becomes More Accessible, Copyright Questions Arise*,
NPR (Feb. 19, 2013), www.npr.org/sections/alltechconsidered/2013/02/19/171912826/as-3-d-print
ing-become-more-accessible-copyright-questions-arise; Michael D. Shear et al., *Judge Blocks
Attempt to Post Blueprints for 3-D Guns*, N.Y. TIMES (July 31, 2018), www.nytimes.com/2018/
07/31/us/politics/3d-guns-trump.html.

6 *See, e.g.,* Peter J. Henning, *Policing Cryptocurrencies Has Become a Game of Whack-a-Mole for
Regulators*, N.Y. TIMES (May 31, 2018).

7 Matt Apuzzo et al., *Apple and Other Tech Companies Tangle With U.S. over Data Access*, N.Y.
TIMES (Dec. 7, 2015), www.nytimes.com/2015/09/08/us/politics/apple-and-other-tech-
companies-tangle-with-us-over-access-to-data.html.

8 Hon. James B. Comey, Statement before the House Committee on Homeland Security
(Washington, D.C., Oct. 21, 2015) (available at www.fbi.gov/news/testimony/worldwidethreats-
and-homeland-security-challenges).

story. Law can keep up. Law itself is the social technology of regulating human behavioral change under conditions of technological development. Law is often far ahead of technology. Lawyers and judges must wait to regulate—often for years—until a technology matures. The sense here is that creating law too early will be a mistake. This story tells us that law is capable of being overhauled, that we might create systems that can keep up. However, unless we begin now, we will experience an ever-increasing disconnect between society and its tools, between democracy and technology.

This book examines what happens at the nexus of law and technology. It analyzes the interaction between the two, seeking a framework on which to build a set of principles to guide legal evolution in the coming years. It counters the technological fatalist narrative that law is simply too slow to incorporate technological change. It challenges received wisdom that law must trail technological change, and argues that law plays a critical role in anticipating and guiding, in naming and shaping, technological change.

Upon closer examination, the narrative that law can't keep up turns out to be not true, and is a particular problem tied to the United States—we could regulate these new technologies appropriately and responsibly if we decided to, and many countries do. Rather, the argument that law can't keep up is propaganda advanced by technology companies eager to avoid legal responsibility for the stunning damage their business models cause the surrounding society. Consider the role social media companies play in systematically profiting from compromising democratic elections, for example. The fact that such propaganda succeeds means there is a hole in our collective heads, a problem with how we talk about the problems of the future.

FAILING NARRATIVES

Bad narratives, like the one that law can't keep up, only live because of the absence of better ones. Our dominant narratives, the stories we use to organize meaning in our lives, are failing across the board. Consider the fact that right now, both science and religion are failing. Science fails to convince flat-earthers,[9]

---

[9] Moya Sarner, *The Rise of the Flat Earthers*, SCIENCE FOCUS (Aug. 31, 2019), www .sciencefocus.com/the-human-body/the-rise-of-the-flat-earthers/ (last accessed Nov. 11, 2019); Matt J. Weber, *How the Internet Made Us Believe in a Flat Earth*, MEDIUM (Dec. 12, 2018), https://medium.com/s/world-wide-wtf/how-the-internet-made-us-believe-in-a-flat-earth -2e42c3206223.

anti-vaxxers,[10] and racists.[11] Religion fails to convince an increasing share of the young[12] and highly educated.[13] The question is why our dominant narratives are dying, leaving us at the mercy of the self-serving ad slogans of corporations and clickbait articles as our source of truth.

Religion is failing because religious language often lacks a valid epistemology: a way of knowing what is factual and what is not. As religious communities empty themselves of the young, the tolerant, and the educated at truly startling rates,[14] those communities have come increasingly to understand their myths as representing some kind of pseudoscientific reality. Religion was never intended to tell us how the world worked, only how to orient ourselves within it. By making obviously false scientific claims in religious language, speakers of religious language have revealed that they have no way of determining facts about the world. Consulting one's feelings is not a measure of how the world is.

But if religion fails to convince for lack of valid epistemology, science is failing for a lack of guiding narrative. Science tells us *how* to do things, not *why* or *whether* to do them. As we will explore, scientists won't even admit that they lack a meta-narrative, a guiding story of why they should conduct some experiments over others, a reason to pursue some lines of research over others. The sad truth is that the current meta-narrative of science is that the experiments which scientists pursue are most often in the name of corporate profit, not human thriving—and the two are not at all the same thing. Science's false claims of neutrality: "we're just doing science!" is the same as technology's obviously false claims of neutrality: "we're just building technology!" Facebook is not neutral technology, and atom bombs are not neutral science. They are decisions in a direction. And if we do not straighten out *why* we do science, provide some account for *where we need to go* with scientific progress, we will end up continuing to blindly create technologies that harm our

---

[10] Jan Hoffman, *How Anti-Vaccine Sentiment Took Hold in the United States*, N.Y. TIMES (Sept. 23, 2019), www.nytimes.com/2019/09/23/health/anti-vaccination-movement-us.html.

[11] Angela Saini, *Why Race Science Is on the Rise Again*, THE GUARDIAN (May 18, 2019), www .theguardian.com/books/2019/may/18/race-science-on-the-rise-angela-saini.

[12] *The Age Gap in Religion around the World: 2. Young Adults around the World Are Less Religious by Several Measures*, Pew Research Center (June 13, 2018), www.pewforum.org/201 8/06/13/young-adults-around-the-world-are-less-religious-by-several-measures/.

[13] *In America, Does More Education Equal Less Religion?*, Pew Research Center (Apr. 26, 2017), www.pewforum.org/2017/04/26/in-america-does-more-education-equal-less-religion/.

[14] *See, e.g.,* ROBERT P. JONES, DANIEL COX, BETSY COOPER, & RACHEL LIENESCH, EXODUS: WHY AMERICANS ARE LEAVING THE CHURCH AND WHY THEY'RE UNLIKELY TO COME BACK (2016).

democratic institutions and our long-term chances for survival on a dying planet. In the absence of a well-thought-out reason for our science, a guiding meta-narrative that keeps us alive, the current meta-narrative of our high priests of technology is this: we do whatever we want to, just because we can, hidden behind the propaganda that technology is neutral.

WHAT'S AT STAKE?

Why would I write this book, and why should you read it? Why try to preserve the rule of law in the face of technological change? The answer is that law plays a fundamental role in helping humans adapt to new circumstances. Humans upgrade their ability to cooperate in new circumstances by upgrading their social software, their language of cooperation, their law. The biggest change in our circumstances right now is technology. Law is the discipline that adapts human systems to technological shifts. If we give up on law, especially now, we're going to have a very hard time. Put simply, no state that fails to adapt the rule of law to new technology will survive as a liberal democracy.

Law helps us sort the difference between what governments *can* do and what they *actually* do. Natural sciences technology, or "hard" technology, has always upset that balance by increasing the range of things we can do. Law must adapt, to protect important social values. Consider the development of the sword or spear: with basic technology, we can deprive each other of life and limb. Thus law adapted rules to determine when this use of technology was considered by society to be just (too often, in a war) or unjust (a private murder). The development of a new technology is not enough. We must develop social technology: norms and rules surrounding its use that will help us survive and thrive. Unfortunately, we have moved into something dangerously close to a post-legal era, in which what we can do is very nearly equated with what we should do. Take, for example, the surveillance apparatus used by most modern surveillance states. Law does not seriously constrain states' snooping on their citizens, even when the citizenry is in broad agreement that it should.[15] The *ability* to snoop is equated with its *legality*. This is a fundamental failure of law.

We also need a theory by which law can respond to technology because technology is increasingly putting law directly under attack. Technologies

---

[15] *See* Jonathan Turley, *It's Too Easy for the Government to Invade Privacy in Name of Security*, THE HILL (Nov. 30, 2017), https://thehill.com/opinion/judiciary/362500-its-too-easy-for-the-government-to-invade-privacy-in-name-of-security.

have always caused new forms of politics. The development of agriculture shifted our form of life from herding and hunting to settled life and politics in the same way that the railroad changed the nature of cities and urbanization. Politics is often not pretty, but from its manure springs some greenery of democracy. The difficulty is that if technology poisons the ground, we'll get twisted fruit. If technology is permitted to dominate politics, and if politicians wish to do away with the rule of law, we will see the emergence of very bad societies. If we do not wish authoritarian nationalism to be the dominant political form of the twenty-first century, we are going to have to understand how to help the rule of law survive technological change.

LAW AND LANGUAGE

We can no longer afford to see law as a series of dry and dusty legal codes that, in the face of evolving technology, are already obsolete by the time the laws are printed. That vision of law is just going to have to go. We must learn to see the discipline of law as a method for adapting to technological change, not a series of presently existing rules. We must attend to change in law, rather than its present state. It's like driving a car: many people look at the speedometer to see how fast they are going. That's looking at the law as it is now. But we need to be looking at how fast we are accelerating. That's a different way to look at law, and one that is necessary if law is to keep pace with technology.

In order to accelerate law, we need to understand how law works—what fuel it runs on. Law runs on language. That language is used to create cooperative fictions like statutes, kingdoms, money, days of the week, contracts, and torts, but those are only snapshots of what law is.[16] Law is a series of made-up systems, rules, norms—made up by people trying to cooperate. It is a cooperative fiction created by groups of humans to help them coordinate their actions at scale. Law bubbles up between us; when we interact with each other, we build rules and norms about relationships and resources. These rules and norms expand outward and interact with others, colliding and collaborating. Over time and across geography, rules and norms spread from relationships to communities to jurisdictions and become law.

Language is humans' superpower. Humans took over the planet because they stopped dealing with threats on an evolutionary scale and started solving problems collectively, through language, by upgrading their cultural and linguistic software instead of waiting for a genetic evolutionary upgrade.

---

[16]   YUVAL NOAH HARARI, SAPIENS: A BRIEF HISTORY OF HUMANKIND (2015).

Language is why humans can cooperate in numbers far greater than bees or ants.

Changing our language to develop cooperative symbols like the State of California or the Rule of Law, and cooperative fictions like "all [people] are created equal" or "next Tuesday" help us follow the laws of the State of California, to treat people decently under the law, and to make it to a meeting next Tuesday. We have adapted our language to stay ahead of our shifting technological circumstances since well before nomads became farmers, farmers became town dwellers, town dwellers organized into nations, and so on, and so on. Law is the cooperative fiction that lets us live together productively under conditions of constantly changing technological context. If anything can help stabilize our life together in the face of rampant technological change, it is our superpower.

Developing law requires developing language. So we need a clear idea of what language is, what it does, how it changes, and where it comes from. Language comes from use by a linguistic community located in a context. This apparently simple statement underlies a revolution in how we think about language, rules, and law. This revolution is badly needed. For the moment, law as a discipline has surrendered its essential function—the crafting of beautiful cooperative fictions like "all [people] are created equal"[17]—to become a not particularly useful subbranch of economics and empirical survey studies, as I will elaborate in Chapter 6. There is nothing wrong with the tools of math or microscope, but the legal profession and legal theorists have badly lost their way. They cannot create new and generous cooperative fictions that will help us coordinate in the face of technological change, because they think that their job is to be second-rate economists or laboratory scientists. Understanding the origins and role of language and law in human cooperation and survival may help law as a discipline reclaim its soul.

A CONVERSATIONAL METHOD

Law should be understood as a system for adapting human social technology to human physical technology. Law runs on language, and it upgrades according to the rules of language. So as we discuss those rules and the role they play in the development of law, I would like to *do* so at the same time.

---

[17] Beautiful despite the multiple obvious problems in the original expression. I use "all people" to show that our foundational norms must continue to be updated, that the original expression of a foundational norm cannot be allowed to become a trap.

My aim is for this book to be an example of this method. This book tries to develop language we can use to talk about how to develop the kind of language (law) that will help us survive the future. I will try to state my understanding of how things are and how things ought to be straightforwardly. It is important to me to be clear enough to be understood where I am right, and identifiably wrong where I am wrong. But even if stated forcefully, everything I say here is to be taken provisionally, as an introduction to a conversation. That is because a book is only half a conversation. A book is only paper until read, and the reader brings more than half the meaning to the table. If I mean to say—as I do mean to say—that life-giving language arises from community and context, then I must admit that I am missing your half of the conversation. I wish that this book were closer in form to a conversation, such that you could respond to what I say here, and I could accept your criticism, and we could develop more precise and better language for talking about the issue. That is how we would make progress.

As for my part of the conversation: I'm a lawyer and the William D. Bain Family Professor of Law at Washington and Lee University School of Law, trained at the University of Chicago, with experience in both the law-and-economics and behavioral economics traditions. I have worked in the technology sector while helping to found the language-teaching startup Rosetta Stone. I also have extensive research experience as a legal academic writing about technology subjects, including online communities, the future of property, online currencies, and cryptocurrencies, virtual worlds, mixed and augmented reality, and a host of other technology issues. My prior book showed how norms of private property have been subverted by software developers: you don't really own or control Alexa. For several years I worked with the intelligence community on a range of cutting-edge technology issues and served as privacy and civil liberties counsel for intelligence community studies in online communities. My recent work has focused heavily on privacy and new applications of cryptocurrencies and decentralized ledger technology. I conducted the research for this book in the United States; Munich, Germany; and Florence, Italy, under generous invitations from the Max Planck Institute for Innovation and Competition in Munich and the European University Institute in Florence.

My method in this book is to start a conversation about the nature of law, technology, and language that will help us better understand the problems we face as we try to develop social rules that keep a grip on a fast-changing technological environment. That environment is changing us, and how we interact, and we have the opportunity to shape it in turn. The problem is a hard one, and goes to the root of what law and language are. So in this book you will hear from futurists, computer scientists, legal theorists, economists, historians, cultural anthropologists, philosophers of language, philosophers of science, and even the occasional theologian: the set of people who have been occupied with the question of how we should live together.

And although this book is only one half of the conversation, you will have the benefit of having both my voice and yours in your head as you read. So when you disagree with something written here—*and you will*—it might be useful for you to think to yourself, "the author would probably agree with me. How can my idea build on or improve what was written here?" In short, the inevitable questions and challenges that will arise in your mind as you read these pages are not necessarily a rejection of this book, its contents, or its method, but rather are examples and critically important products of that method.

INTRODUCING SOCIAL TECHNOLOGY

So, I believe that law can keep up. But the kind of law that can keep up will be something that is barely recognizable to us now as law. Once we shift our frame of reference for thinking about law, we can see something fairly simple. Law can keep up with technology because law *is* technology: social technology, but technology nonetheless.

Let me explain. For much of our culture (this definition is not universal, and I will offer better definitions later), technology is the practical implementation of observation-based science,[18] a certain method of cognition given its current form in the early part of the twentieth century (with Karl Popper's development of falsifiability),[19] yet one dating back to the ancient Greeks. For some kinds of science, primarily related to what we traditionally understand as hard technology[20]—physics, electronics, computation, and the like—we use formal modeling and experiments to isolate certain elements of human behavior the way we isolate certain elements of physical interaction, and that is both a strength and a weakness. The strength is that in an experimental mode, we strip the world down to just one thing that we are trying to test. We then jiggle the input and see if it creates any identifiable corresponding jiggle in the outputs of our system. For example, if I want to know whether eating

---

[18] *Technology*, OXFORD ENGLISH DICTIONARY (2018) (defining technology as the "application of scientific knowledge for practical purposes").

[19] *See* Karl Popper, *Chapter 4: Falsifiability*, *in* THE LOGIC OF SCIENTIFIC DISCOVERY 57–73 (Karl Popper et al. trans., 1983).

[20] *See generally* ZHOUYING JIN, GLOBAL TECHNOLOGICAL CHANGE: FROM HARD TECHNOLOGY TO SOFT TECHNOLOGY 19–76 (Kelvin Willoughby & Ying Bai trans., 2nd ed., 2011).

more rich food increases my weight, I might eat more of it for a couple of months and see if I gain weight, then eat less of it and see if I lose weight. If jiggling the input causes a detectable corresponding jiggle in the output, I might call my experiment a success.

That's the kind of science we're used to. But we need to acknowledge that there is a different kind of observation-based science which is equally as valid and in fact dominant in the social sciences (as a result of a fork in the scientific road occasioned by Ludwig Wittgenstein around the middle of the twentieth century—more on this later).[21] The difficulty is that some problems are very difficult to observe because their scale is greater than our measuring tools. Human history is one of the more important of these large observational problems, because by definition we didn't develop certain analytic tools until later in our history. There are two components to this. First, every experiment is a stripped-down model of the world, a friction-free universe whose essential theoretical characteristic is that it is absolutely nothing like the real thing. That is, of course, an enormous advantage to helping determine whether one jiggle creates another. But simplifying the world that way means that experimental results are extremely limited in terms of what they can tell us about practical implementation. Or as the old canard puts it, "in theory, there is no difference between theory and practice. In practice, there is."[22]

What this means is that the simpler the experimental universe is, the clearer the results. Conversely, however, the simpler the universe of the experiment is, the less likely it is to give us immediately practical and useful outputs. For practicality, we need something beyond experiments. We need trial and error, we need actual practical implementation that succeeds or fails in the real world over long periods of time.

More than that: consider looking at a book, like *Harry Potter and the Sorcerer's Stone*, and trying to explain to a Martian what it is. There is an answer: it's a novel about magical children in danger that fits with the *bildungsroman* tradition transposed into the English public school setting— a fairly common genre. But to say those—true—things, you can't use a laboratory, as chemists do, or a logical system, as mathematicians do. You have to interpret culture using tools built by culture. You have to explicate words using other words.

---

[21] *See* ALLAN JANIK & STEPHEN TOULMIN, WITTGENSTEIN'S VIENNA (1973).

[22] This statement is often erroneously attributed to Yogi Berra. *See, e.g.,* NASSIM NICHOLAS TALEB, ANTIFRAGILE: THINGS THAT GAIN FROM DISORDER 213 (2012). In reality, it is an anonymous remark overheard at a conference on computer science, first recorded in WALTER J. SAVITCH, PASCAL: AN INTRODUCTION TO THE ART AND SCIENCE OF PROGRAMMING 507 (1984).

That is closer to what history and law are. There, we use observation-based science, but we are observing one massive and messy field experiment and attempting to extract information from it, rather than stripping the world down to the one thing we are trying to study. And more: we are trying to make sense of the narrative of history, culture, law, and language. We are analyzing the cooperative fictive tools we use to work together using other tools also made of language.

Of course, the approach of history and law has its drawbacks. We can never be sure whether the lessons we are learning from law and history are true. We do not have a chance to go back and run a given battle, or a given parliamentary session, or a given fad or famine again, to see if doing things differently would have a different result. But the advantage of the approach taken by history and law is that the findings are pretty robust. We adopt a certain way of running our society until another way comes along that better addresses the challenges we face. (Like evolution, our science and law does not necessarily get "better" or "worse," it simply addresses or fails in the face of adversely selecting circumstances.[23]) We have a lot of bad laws, and we can do much better, but each law and each legal system has the distinct advantage of having existed within the real world. It is the product of a long process of trial, error, and social competition.

What I want to dispel at the outset is the idea that there is a "real" technology or science, and that disciplines like history and law are somehow either not technology or not science. In particular, if technology as we traditionally understand it is the practical implementation of scientific truth, then law is also the business end, the practical implementation, of social, economic, and psychological truths.

This then leads to a fundamental vocabulary word for this book. Social technology is the practical implementation of rules and norms through human social systems. Families are social technology. Marriage is a social technology. Summer vacations are social technology. Political parties are social technology. Nation-states are social technology. Money is social technology. What binds these together is that they are practical implementations of core insights about groups, individual human psychology, resource allocation, hierarchy of human needs, and so on. They are no less technology for being practical implementations of observations on human wetware and through human social networks than would be hard implementations through silicon chips, forged steel, or smokestack-sporting factories.

---

[23] Thomas Kuhn, The Structure of Scientific Revolutions 205 (1996).

As Polish science fiction author Stanislaw Lem writes, "Technology is the domain of problems posed and the methods of solving them."[24] How we ought to live together is clearly one such problem, and the rule of law is a method for solving it. Law is clearly a technology—a social technology, made up of cooperative fictions and symbols in language, but no less a technology for all that. What is common here is the practical attempt to better human life through implementation of our best guesses about how to respond to what we observe.

Here's an example of what I mean. In his book *Industries of the Future*, former State Department tech advisor Alec Ross compares Ripple, one of the more prominent examples of a cryptocurrency-facilitated money exchange network, to *hawala*, a family-based social exchange system ranging from the Middle East to northern Africa and some parts of India.[25] In Ripple's system, businesses transfer value through one another to avoid the fees and costs of the banking system.[26] Where needed, Ripple uses a cryptocurrency, XRP, to bridge gaps and connect systems.[27] Similarly, *hawala* effects money transfer by paying one member of the network, a *hawaladar*, who then contacts another member in another country and instructs him to pay out the money.[28] Notably, the system works entirely by trust: the honor of the *hawaladar* who receives money is the only bond that secures the right to payment by the *hawaladar* who pays the money out.[29] So which network of trust is the technological one, the one built on a consensus ledger and cryptography, or the one built on honor (itself a social technology), family (same), and social connection?

Nor can we say that we can distinguish between these systems because a system made out of humans is always more primitive and less efficient than a system made out of processors. Consider the example of Amazon's Mechanical Turk. In the Mechanical Turk's system, a large network of humans performs tasks that computers cannot.[30] Mechanical Turk is used

---

[24] STANISLAW LEM, IMAGINARY MAGNITUDE 135 (Houghton Mifflin 2012).
[25] ALEC ROSS, THE INDUSTRIES OF THE FUTURE 118–19 (Simon and Schuster 2016).
[26] *See* Real-Time Cross Border Payments for Banks, Ripple, https://ripple.com/use-cases/banks/ (using infographics to illustrate the reduced transaction costs for banks that use the Ripple Net for cross-border transactions).
[27] ALEC ROSS, THE INDUSTRIES OF THE FUTURE 119 (Simon and Schuster 2016); *see also XRP*, Ripple, https://ripple.com/xrp/ (2018).
[28] *See* Mohammed El-Qorchi, *The Hawala System*, 39:4 FINANCE AND DEVELOPMENT n.p. (2002) (explaining the process of *hawala* in detail).
[29] *Id.* (*Hawaladars* maintain ledgers to track transactions and debts, which can be settled in cash, goods, or services).
[30] *See Amazon Mechanical Turk*, MTurk, www.mturk.com/.

for surveys, businesses seeking a list of all sushi restaurants in Canton, Ohio, people seeking to identify a specific object in a photograph, and so on.[31] Crowdsourcing is a faster way to solve many tasks than computation. That crowdsourcing has become possible through technology does not change the fact that crowdsourcing itself is largely social technology.

The upshot of all of this: I suspect that the idea of social technology (which is itself, of course, a small piece of social technology) will help us understand that we can evolve and update social tech to handle the social problems that traditional hard technology poses. Or to put it bluntly, the question of whether law can keep up with technology is resolved when we understand that law *is* technology.

CAN WE SUCCEED?

We can succeed, but we have to move quickly and understand clearly what we are doing. We are not out of time to make changes to help the rule of law adapt to new technologies, but we are out of time to begin. Already, elections are being tipped by mass robotic social engineering,[32] Twitter drives international policy,[33] and surveillance states track their citizens' locations and internet traffic in massive cross-referencing databases.[34] There is no sign that the pace of technological change will slow. In fact, if progress in miniaturization,[35] sensor profusion,[36]

---

[31] *Id.*

[32] *See, e.g.,* Scott Shane, *The Fake Americans Russia Created to Influence the Election,* NY TIMES (Sep. 7, 2017), www.nytimes.com/2017/09/07/us/politics/russia-facebook-twitter-election.html.

[33] *See, e.g.,* Krishnadev Calamur, *The International Incidents Sparked by Trump's Twitter Feed in 2017,* THE ATLANTIC (Dec. 19, 2017), www.theatlantic.com/international/archive/2017/12/tru mp-tweets-foreign-policy/547892/.

[34] *See, e.g.,* Paul Mozur, *Looking through the Eyes of China's Surveillance State,* N.Y. TIMES (July 16, 2018), www.nytimes.com/2018/07/16/technology/china-surveillance-state.html.

[35] *See, e.g.,* John Markoff, *IBM Scientists Find New Way to Shrink Transistors,* N.Y. TIMES (Oct. 1, 2015), www.nytimes.com/2015/10/02/science/ibm-scientists-find-new-way-to-shrink-transistors.html; Jennifer Chu, *Miniaturizing the Brain of a Drone,* MIT News (July 11, 2017), http://news.mit.edu/2017/miniaturizing-brain-smart-drones-0712?utm_campaign=Wee kly%20Newsletters&utm_source=hs_email&utm_medium=email&_hsenc=p2ANqtz-9yIyIZQfpouXbyCXm3lrFk2QOdVN22Fkvx55efgHsiwXfUYBedb7t8m5vmMo46k_uOlCld.

[36] *See, e.g., Sensor Market Growth Is Driven by Proliferation of Smart Homes,* MARKETWATCH (July 19, 2019), www.marketwatch.com/press-release/sensor-market-growth-is-driven-by-proliferation-of-smart-homes-2019-07-19; Richard Nabors, *Integrated Sensors: The Critical Element in Future Complex Environment Warfare,* ARMY: MAD SCIENTIST LABORATORY, https://madsciblog.tradoc.army.mil/46-integrated-sensors-the-critical-element-in-future -complex-environment-warfare/; *Sensor Market Is Projected to Reach USD 266.27 Billion by 2023,* MARKETWATCH (Aug. 13, 2018), www.marketwatch.com/press-release/sensor-market-is-

genomics,[37] artificial intelligence,[38] DIY biology,[39] and automation[40] continues apace, we will see increasing inability to govern according to the rule of law—unless we do something about it.

Now is the time to use the human superpower—language—that we have always used to update our social software to face new challenges. We have done this before, as nomads adapting to agriculture, as family-based feudal holdings adapting to modern nation-states, as we adapted to the shifts from agrarian to industrial, and from industrial to information economies. (Indeed, we had to invent each of those words' current meanings so the previous sentence would make sense!) We will adapt to the future the way we always have: by coming up with new ways to talk about things so we can have the conversations we need to have. And the most important conversation we can have is a conversation about conversations, about how to talk about what we need to talk about. Law is the language of human coordination. Language is how humans update their

projected-to-reach-usd-26627-billion-by-2023-by-product-type-technology-end-users-demand-and-trends-by-forecasts-2018–08-13.

[37] *See, e.g., A Brief Guide to Genomics*, Nat'l Human Genome Research Inst., www.genome.gov /about-genomics/fact-sheets/A-Brief-Guide-to-Genomics (last updated Aug. 27, 2015); Jackie Drees, *AdventHealth to Provide Free DNA Tests to 10,000 Florida Residents for Genomics Study*, BECKER'S HOSPITAL REVIEW, www.beckershospitalreview.com/healthcare-information-technology/adventhealth-to-provide-free-dna-tests-to-10–000-florida-residents-for -genomics-study.html (July 25, 2019); *Major Investment in Genomics Research Will Improve the Lives of Canadians*, GENOME CANADA, www.genomecanada.ca/en/news/major-investment-in-genomics-research-will-improve-the-lives-of-canadians (Feb. 4, 2019).

[38] Rob Matheson, *New AI Programming Language Goes Beyond Deep Learning*, MIT NEWS (June 26, 2019), http://news.mit.edu/2019/ai-programming-gen-0626; K. K. Rebecca Lai, et al., *How A.I. Helped Improve Crowd Counting in Hong Kong Protests*, N.Y. TIMES (July 3, 2019), www.nytimes.com/interactive/2019/07/03/world/asia/hong-kong-protest-crowd-ai.html; Gabe Cohn, *AI Art at Christie's Sells for $432,500*, N.Y. TIMES (Oct. 25, 2018), www .nytimes.com/2018/10/25/arts/design/ai-art-sold-christies.html.

[39] Alexandra Ossola, *These Biohackers Are Creating Open-Source Insulin*, Popular Science (Nov. 18, 2015), www.popsci.com/these-biohackers-are-making-open-source-insulin; Catrin Nye, *Biohacker: Meet the People "Hacking" Their Bodies*, BBC NEWS (Dec. 5, 2018), www.bbc.com/news/tech nology-46442519; Moa Petersen, *New Way to Pay: Why Thousands of Swedes Are Deliberately Inserting Themselves with Microchips*, INDEPENDENT (June 27, 2018), www.independent.co.uk /life-style/gadgets-and-tech/features/sweden-microchips-contactless-cards-biohackers-dystopian-future-a8408486.html.

[40] *See, e.g.*, Tom Simonite, *Robots Will Take Jobs from Men, the Young, and Minorities*, WIRED (Jan. 24, 2019), www.wired.com/story/robots-will-take-jobs-from-men-young-minorities/?ver so=true; Adam Rogers, *Welcome to Checkout-Free Retail. Don't Mind All the Cameras*, Wired (Aug. 28, 2018), www.wired.com/story/zippin-cashier-free-retail-store/?verso=true; Mattie Milner & Stephen Rice, *Robotic Health Care Is Coming to a Hospital Near You*, THE CONVERSATION (May 7, 2019), https://theconversation.com/robotic-health-care-is-coming-to-a-hospital-near-you-116236.

social software through symbol and cooperative fiction. Learning how we create and innovate language, and especially creating a vocabulary and way of talking about doing that, is going to be our best bet for activating our human superpower, and surviving the challenges of the future together. That is what this book is about. So let's talk.

2

Rates of Change

Technology is the domain of problems posed and the methods of solving them.
— Stanislaw Lem, *Imaginary Magnitude*[1]

Law is an adaptive social technology that helps us cooperate through language, symbol, narrative, and fiction. By "fiction" I do not mean not real. Money, Wednesday, years, California, kilometers, contract law, and legal concepts like "all men are created equal" and the "rule of law" are very real in that they affect our behavior and lives, but they are also obviously made up by humans for purposes of human coordination.[2]

Our goal in developing these cooperative fictions must be to coordinate our efforts to survive and thrive in the face of rampant technological change. This chapter sets the stage for a range of arguments: that law and other social rules are examples of social technology; that because laws are a form of technology, they can be produced more rapidly and more accurately than we are currently doing; and that in order to adapt human society to technological change, we will have to change not only *laws* but the concept of *law* itself.

So, in looking at updating law, where should we focus? Should we focus on bad laws as they are? I could write an entire chapter on terrible statutes that horribly mangle technology policy. (Don't worry, I won't.) Should we focus on good laws, ones that currently handle technology policy fairly well? (There are actually a lot!) My answer is neither: we should focus on the *rate of change* in law.

Consider driving a car. If we are worried about someone chasing us who is driving faster and faster, we should be worried about our zero to sixty, our rate of acceleration. It's not how fast we're going at any given time that matters, it's

---

[1]   STANISLAW LEM, IMAGINARY MAGNITUDE 135 (2012).
[2]   YUVAL NOAH HARARI, SAPIENS 28–32 (2015).

how fast we can accelerate. If we are worried about staying ahead of the heat, our current speed matters less than what happens when we press the pedal down.

With that in mind, we can begin to look at the problem: the rate of change in hard technology is often faster than the rate of change in law. New designer drugs,[3] like bath salts, come out as fast as the last bunch are criminalized. But new laws are often obsolete by the time they are published.[4] If they are not obsolete, their attempts to anticipate the future are often disastrous. There is a rising fatalism about the relationship between law and technology. Technologists are dangerously close to giving up on the importance of laws. And lawyers themselves have noticed law's weakness: technological power often defeats legal rules. Technological power often overwhelms justice in even the most everyday settings, from arrests[5] to the rights that consumers give up by clicking "I Accept" to activate their new software-enhanced purchases.[6]

But there is hope.[7] This chapter explains why. First, we identify the problem: the idea of the technological singularity—the point in time where the

---

[3] See, E. D. Wish, et al., *Drug Early Warning from Re-testing Biological Samples: Maryland Hospital Study*, Univ. of Md. (July 2018), https://ndews.umd.edu/resources/drug-early-warning-re-testing-biological-samples-maryland-hospital-study.

[4] See, *Many Synthetic Drugs Still Legal after "Bath Salts" Ban*, CBS News (Oct. 20, 2015), www.cbsnews.com/news/many-synthetic-drugs-still-legal-after-bath-salts-ban/.

[5] *See* Maryland v. King, 569 U.S. 435 (2013). *See also* David Grossman, *Report: U.S. Police Are Abusing Facial Recognition Technology*, Popular Mechanics (May 16, 2019), www.popularmechanics.com/technology/security/a27493840/police-abusing-facial-recognition-tech/, *citing* Clare Garvie, *Garbage In, Garbage Out: Face Recognition on Flawed Data*, Georgetown Law Center on Privacy and Tech. (May 16, 2019), www.flawedfacedata.com/; Karen Hao, *Police across the US Are Training Crime-Predicting AIs on Falsified Data*, MIT Tech. Rev. (Feb. 13, 2019), www.technologyreview.com/s/612957/predictive-policing-algorithms-ai-crime-dirty-data/.

[6] Jessica Silver-Greenberg & Robert Gebeloff, *Beware the Fine Print, Part I: Arbitration Everywhere, Stacking the Deck of Justice*, N.Y. Times DealBook (Oct. 31, 2015), www.nytimes.com/2015/11/01/business/dealbook/arbitration-everywhere-stacking-the-deck-of-justice.html; Jessica Silver-Greenberg & Robert Gebeloff, *Beware the Fine Print, Part II: In Arbitration, a "Privatization of the Justice System,"* N.Y. Times DealBook (Nov. 1, 2015), www.nytimes.com/2015/11/02/business/dealbook/in-arbitration-a-privatization-of-the-justice-system.html; Jessica Silver-Greenberg & Robert Gebeloff, *Beware the Fine Print, Part III: In Religious Arbitration, Scripture Is the Rule of Law*, N.Y. Times DealBook (Nov. 2, 2015), www.nytimes.com/2015/11/03/business/dealbook/in-religious-arbitration-scripture-is-the-rule-of-law.html.

[7] *See, e.g.*, Nguyen v. Barnes & Noble Inc., 763 F.3d 1171 (9th Cir. 2014) (In this case, the circuit court denied the defendant's motion to compel arbitration. It ruled that "[g]iven the breadth of the range of technological savvy of online purchasers, consumers cannot be expected to ferret out hyperlinks to terms and conditions to which they have no reason to suspect they will be bound." This case provides an example of the type of hope I present in this passage of how law can keep up with technology).

rate of technological change exceeds the human capacity to adapt. We then explore the legal nihilism that arises from embracing technological change without first establishing a comprehensive theory of legal change. Next, we explore solutions. I contend that the idea of the singularity imposes a false kind of technological fatalism which posits that "hard" technology will surpass human social technologies like law. Rather than accepting this as an inevitable trajectory, I attempt to develop a theory of legal change to keep pace with any other technological innovation. The process of law is not static. It is the process of generating rules with pragmatic impact over time in the face of technological change.

EXPONENTIAL CHANGE AND EXISTENTIAL ANXIETY

In 2005, the futurist Ray Kurzweil claimed that "the singularity is near" in a book of that title.[8] (The term is derived from mathematics and describes a mathematical break; a place where some aspect of an otherwise regular function becomes undefined.) Kurzweil argued we are approaching a technological singularity—a point at which technology would advance more and more quickly, until human systems can't keep up anymore.[9] Technology will lead to superhuman intelligence and completely change how humans view themselves. Kurzweil argued that certain kinds of technology progress in an ever-accelerating exponential curve.[10] This is important because accelerating curve projections require different thinking about the middle future than do linear projections. We stand at a place in history where we need to know what a plot of the future looks like. If the future looks like a technological curve that is going straight to infinity and beyond, we need to make one set of policy interventions. If the future looks more like regular plodding progress, we need a different set. Right now we stand at the "knee of the curve," a perceptual point at which the shape of the future is becoming clear.

A standard joke by high school math teachers runs like this: a teacher requires her math students to do twenty problems each night. She also offers an alternative where students can do one problem a night for the first week, with the number of math problems due per night doubling each week. For the first week, students will solve one problem each night. For the second week,

---

[8] RAY KURZWEIL, THE SINGULARITY IS NEAR (2005).
[9] *Id.* at 7.
[10] For those who can take a joke: all I'm saying in this section is that from the perspective of 2020, Kurzweil seems to have muffed something a bit. The project of this book is to figure out what.

two problems each night. Then four problems each night in week three, eight problems in week four, and so on.

After doing a little rough figuring, none of the students take the teacher up on this. They note that the progression runs 1, 2, 4, 8, 16, 32, 64, 128, 256, and beyond. By the beginning of the ninth week, a student who falls for the trap would be doing 256 problems each night, and the class would be far from over. That is the point: it is a dad joke for math teachers. Students do the math, and realize their math teacher is teasing them. Hilarious.[11]

This seemingly hackneyed math joke illustrates the concept of exponential or geometric growth (I use these two terms interchangeably here).[12] At each step, exponential growth multiplies by some constant growth rate. Figure 2.1 shows two exponential curves: the number of math problems in the joke, which is doubled every step (i.e., the growth rate is 2), and the funds in a fictitious bank account with 10 percent compound interest (i.e., the growth rate is 1.10).

The third curve is not exponential. It shows the distance traveled by a rocket accelerating so as to provide its crew with the feel of Earthside gravitation. Every second, the speed of the rocket increases by the same amount. Acceleration is the additive increase in speed, and speed is the additive increase in distance. The acceleration stays constant, so the sensation remains constant.

Note that exponential growth (based on multiplication by a constant growth rate) is not the same as acceleration (based on two levels of addition).[13] With its

---

[11]   This joke is based on the wheat and chessboard problem. One of the oldest versions of the problem explains that the inventor of chess goes to the ruler and asks him to put one grain in the first tile of the chessboard, and double the grains in the subsequent tile each day, until all 64 tiles are done. Originally the ruler laughs it off as a small prize for a great invention, but becomes distressed once the amount begins to deplete his resources. The ending of this version differs, either making the inventor a high-ranking advisor for his wit or executed for his wit. See MALBA TAHAN, THE MAN WHO COUNTED: A COLLECTION OF MATHEMATICAL ADVENTURES, 113–17 (1993).

[12]   See http://mathworld.wolfram.com/LawofGrowth.html and http://mathworld.wolfram.com/GeometricSequence.html.

[13]   Two levels of addition: acceleration is the additive increase in speed, and speed is the additive increase in distance, where by "additive increase" is meant how much is added per step, not how much is multiplied by. For example, if you multiply 40 by 1.10, you get 44. The growth factor was 1.10, the additive increase was 4. If you repeat the same additive increase one more step, you get to 48. But if you repeat the multiplication one more step, you get to $44^{*}1.10 = 48.4$ (an additive increase of 4.4). Holding the multiplication constant (multiplying by 1.10 per step) is not the same as holding the additive increase constant (adding 4 per step).

People with some math background will recognize that I'm using "speed" and "acceleration" here for the first and second derivatives, because most everyone has gut-level automotive experience with speed and acceleration, which are good exemplars of the first and second derivatives.

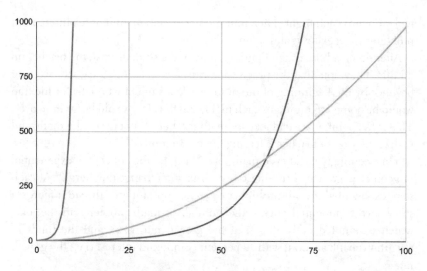

FIGURE 2.1 The comparison of exponential and non-exponential growth.
Teacher's math problems in purple, 10% compound interest in blue, and the
distance traveled (in hectometers) of a rocket undergoing earth-surface-gravity
acceleration in orange. The x-axis represents the number of steps, up to 100. The
first two curves are exponential, the third is not.

constant growth rate, an exponential curve's acceleration accelerates! In fact, the
acceleration of any exponential growth grows exponentially. And the acceleration of the acceleration grows exponentially. Yes, it's turtles all the way down, an
infinite stack of accelerating accelerations. That's why exponential growth, even
if it has a weak growth rate, will eventually explode and head for the stratosphere.

For instance, in Figure 2.1 try to picture how high the interest rate curve
must get by step 100. It's way off the graph, way over the top of the page. It's
even more drastic for the math problems! Note that even though the rocket
acceleration curve starts out way above the interest rate curve, the latter
eventually blows it away. Any exponential growth will eventually outstrip
any linear function (a straight line, so no acceleration at all) or polynomial[14]
function (whose turtle-stack of accelerations of accelerations eventually dies
out). Their accelerations can't take the heat.

---

[14] A polynomial is a sum of one or more weighted powers of x (the number of steps), for example,
$14x^3 + 0.4x^{17} + 32x^{125}$. The degree of a polynomial is the greatest exponent in the sum, so in the
last example the degree is 125. Fact: the acceleration of a polynomial is a polynomial of lesser
degree. In this way, the stack of accelerations of accelerations eventually gets to degree zero,
i.e., dies out, unlike an exponential function whose stack continues infinitely. The yellow
curve of figure 1 is the polynomial $0.098x^2$.

Exponential growth has notable implications for mid-future planning, some of which are aptly illustrated by another math problem, the classic lily pad problem. Imagine a pond with a single lily pad. If ever the pond becomes completely covered by lily pads, the fish will die. Starting with the single pad, the lily pads double every day. On the twenty-ninth day, we find the pond half-covered by lily pads. What is the urgency of doing something about the lily pad problem? The pond is only half-covered, after all. If we view the pond on day twenty-nine with a linear growth model, we think we have twenty-nine more days to solve the lily pad problem because the pond is only half-covered, and it took 29 days to reach that state. But, in fact, in only one more day the lily pads will double and cover the pond and kill the fish. If we view the pond with an exponential growth model, we realize that we are out of time and must act immediately.

If lily pads reproduced linearly, there would be, say, ten more lily pads today than there were yesterday, ten more tomorrow, and so on (day 1 = 10, day 2 = 20, day 3 = 30, etc.), adding a constant amount at each step. In contrast, exponential progressions, when graphed, depict a curve that not only accelerates, but whose acceleration accelerates as time progresses. Such a curve can look quite innocent at first, but then suddenly begin to curve sharply at an increasing rate. At some point, one realizes that the acceleration is passing the point at which one can accommodate it—in our examples, at about week six with the math homework and day twenty-nine with the lily pads.

The development of new technology often follows exponential growth. Moore's Law—the number of transistors in a dense integrated circuit doubles roughly every eighteen months to two years—has held for a shocking fifty-some years.[15] Modern smartphones have the capacity of historical supercomputers.[16] Yet even after many years of explosive exponential growth, the modern world is not incomprehensible to humans. Our problems in regulating technology seem to be failings of political structure, not technology that has escaped human comprehension. I understand that we might view some events in both ways: What do we make of Facebook users not being able to tell the difference between fellow citizens and social-media-targeted AI?[17] Is

---

[15] Although this trend shows some signs of abating, it has been a constant for many decades. As Moore's biographer quoted him as saying, "All good exponentials come to an end." Gordon E. Moore, *Cramming more components onto integrated circuits*, 38 ELECTRONICS 8 (1965).

[16] See Nick Routley, *How the Computing Power in a Smartphone Compares to Supercomputers Past and Present*, BUS. INSIDER (Nov. 6, 2017), www.businessinsider.com/infographic-how-computing-power-has-changed-over-time-2017-11.

[17] Paul Blumenthal, *How a Twitter Fight over Bernie Sanders Revealed a Network of Fake Accounts*, HUFFINGTON POST (Mar. 14, 2018), www.huffpost.com/entry/democratic-bot-

that not a technology-incomprehensibility problem, rather than "merely" a political problem? Maybe.

Exponential growth is not inherently bad. Positive developments can follow exponential growth patterns, too. Kurzweil personalizes his argument with his claim that he could possibly live forever.[18] Imagine that Kurzweil were diagnosed with cancer in his fifties. Is it worth it for him to hang on for five years, or should he make peace and die with dignity? Decades ago, the answer was to gather friends and family and say goodbye with grace. Now, it might be worth hanging on: technology is changing fast enough that a treatment might emerge in the next five years.

Consider the case of William Ludwig, a retired corrections officer who was diagnosed with not one but three cancers: leukemia, lymphoma, and squamous skin cell cancer.[19] In 2010, at age sixty-four, he was on the brink of death after fighting cancer for a painful five years. The increasing toxicity of chemotherapy was doing more damage to his immune system than to the cancer cells. He was seemingly out of options.

Ludwig's doctor proposed that Ludwig be patient number one in a new gene therapy trial. As part of that trial, doctors engineered killer T-cells with an advanced guidance system that upgraded their ability to target Ludwig's cancer.[20] Doctors extracted T-cells from Ludwig, altered them with a HIV-derived virus, and injected the cells with a new gene coding for an enhanced guidance system.[21] The new gene sequence was a true science fiction hodgepodge: a chimera of gene fragments from mice, cows, and woodchucks.[22]

The therapy wasn't a cure-all, and it was very dangerous. Ludwig went into fever seizures as his T-cells, newly able to target cancer cells with precision, destroyed over two pounds of cancer in his body in a matter of days. As of 2018, Ludwig was alive and well, his only suffering a few of the regular changes of advanced age.[23]

network-sally-albright_n_5aa2f548e4b07047bec68023; Nicholas Fandos & Kevin Roose, *Facebook Identifies an Active Political Influence Campaign Using Fake Accounts*, N.Y. TIMES (Jul. 31, 2018), www.nytimes.com/2018/07/31/us/politics/facebook-political-campaign-midterms.html.

[18] Andrew Goldman, *Ray Kurzweil Says We're Going to Live Forever*, N.Y. Times (Jan. 23, 2013), www.nytimes.com/2013/01/27/magazine/ray-kurzweil-says-were-going-to-live-forever.html.

[19] Denise Gradt, *An Immune System Trained to Kill Cancer*, N.Y. TIMES (Sep. 12, 2011), www.nytimes.com/2011/09/13/health/13gene.html.

[20] *Id.*

[21] *Id.*

[22] *Id.*

[23] Jim Kozubek, *This Man's Immune System Got a Cancer-killing Update*, NAUTILUS (Jul. 19, 2017), http://cancer.nautil.us/article/238/this-mans-immune-system-got-a-cancer-killing-

Consider another example: in Alec Ross's 2016 book *The Industries of the Future*, he introduces a chapter on custom genomics by telling the story of Lukas Wartman, an oncologist who survived acute lymphoblastic leukemia three times. As Ross recounts, the survival rate for double relapses was pretty much nil. But Wartman happened to work in an academic cancer research center, and his colleagues co-opted the massive processing power of the center to sequence the DNA and RNA from his cancer cells and compare the results to the same sequences in healthy skin cells. As Ross writes, "It turned out that one of Wartman's normal genes was producing large quantities of FLT3, a protein that was ultimately spurring his cancer's growth."[24] As it so happened, Pfizer had just released a drug that could inhibit the FLT3 protein. Wartman entered remission within weeks of taking the drug, received a bone marrow transplant, and—thanks to being at just the right place and time on the cutting edge of advancing technology—ultimately survived a previously unsurvivable cancer.

Historically, William Ludwig and Lukas Wartman would have died. Yet two different technological advancements came to fruition just when they needed them. Think about the odds of that. Just when you come down with a fatal condition, scientists find a way around it. This happened less often in the past.[25] Today we hear more and more stories about similar situations not only because it makes for good copy (although that's a big part of it) but also because such nick-of-time medical advancements are simply happening more often.[26] More people are alive than ever before in human history. Medical research is advancing at a more rapid pace. This combination of greater world population and rapid medical advancement, on the pure math, shows that there are simply more people who come down with an untreatable medical

update; www.inquirer.com/philly/health/penn-study-points-to-why-t-cell-therapy-fails-in-some-patients-20180430.html.

[24] *Id.*

[25] Even though it is rare, one of the greatest examples of this event in the past is that of the rabies vaccine. While developing the vaccine, Louis Pasteur vaccinated a child who had been mauled by a rabid dog. The child survived, thus providing evidence that Pasteur's vaccination had worked. *See* P. P. Pastoret & B. Brochier, *The Development and Use of a Vaccinia-Rabies Recombinant Oral Vaccine for the Control of Wildlife Rabies; A Link between Jenner and Pasteur*, 116 EPIDEMIOLOGY & INFECTION 235 (1996).

[26] *See, e.g.*, Maggie Fox, *Experimental Immune Treatment Saves Dying Breast Cancer Patient*, NBC NEWS (Jun. 4, 2018), www.nbcnews.com/health/health-news/highly-personalized-treatment-saves-breast-cancer-patient-n879841; Daniel Prosser, *Cerebral Palsy Rates Drop as Medical, Technological Advancements Boost Quality of Life*, ABC NEWS (Jan. 23, 2019), www.abc.net.au/news/2019-01-24/cerebral-palsy-rates-decline-as-medical-care-improves/10742506.

condition, hang on for long enough, and survive because a new treatment or method becomes available.

One might think that even if medical treatments come along at the right time, old age will catch up with us eventually. But that may be changing as well. As biology and nanotechnology converge, there is every likelihood that we will be able to teach human cells to repair themselves for longer periods of time than our frayed telomeres currently permit.[27] The first step to immortality will not look like the Grail in an Indiana Jones movie: one and done. Rather, the first human to become effectively immortal (or at least sufficiently long-lived to make us use the term responsibly) will become immortal by a series of steps, by avoiding death through technology that evolves at precisely the right time to stave off a final ailment. That person may well be alive today. Unlike Kurzweil, though, I have no faith that it is me.

Growth curves can become a serious source of anxiety about the future. This is the source of the all-too-common narrative in Silicon Valley. "Move fast and break things" is a tech-bro byword. Technology runs rampant.[28] And, the theory goes, law cannot keep up. The only thing that can keep us on the rails is more technology. The twin ideas that law cannot keep up and that only technology can solve the problems raised by technology lead to learned helplessness, and to dystopianism. In the privacy context, for example, many technologists appear to have given up.[29] Because technology companies make money on consumers' data, they construct a comforting fiction that law is obsolete and that their customers didn't want privacy anyway.[30] This significantly weakens the concept of privacy. After all, if law can't keep up and technology mysteriously doesn't work (since the advertisers don't want it to), we might as well give in and let Facebook have all our data.

---

[27]   The process of aging is called senescence which is due to separation of germ and soma cells separating. *See* Paul Nelson & Joanna Masel, *Intercellular Competition and the Inevitability of Multicellular Aging*, 114 PROCEEDINGS OF THE NATIONAL ACADEMY OF SCIENCES OF THE UNITED STATES OF AMERICA 12982 (2017). Though telomere reduction, which occurs with senescence, is believed to be a factor in aging, there are some issues with the theory. *See, e.g.*, Geraldine Aubert & Peter Lansdorp, *Telomeres and Aging*, 88 PHYSIOLOGICAL R. 557 (2008); Mirre Simons, *Questioning Causal Involvement of Telomeres in Aging*, 24 AGEING RESEARCH R. 191 (2015).

[28]   *See* David Ignatius, *My Four-Word Wish for Thanksgiving*, WASH. POST (Nov. 20, 2018), www .washingtonpost.com/opinions/my-four-word-wish-for-thanksgiving/2018/11/20/2e39f0a2-edoo-11e8-96d4-od23f2aaado9_story.html.

[29]   *See* Eduardo Porter, *The Facebook Fallacy: Privacy Is Up to You*, N.Y. TIMES (Apr. 24, 2018), www.nytimes.com/2018/04/24/business/economy/facebook-privacy.html.

[30]   *See* Nitasha Tiku, *Facebook Is Steering Users Away from Privacy Protections*, WIRED (Apr. 18, 2018), www.wired.com/story/facebook-is-steering-users-away-from-privacy-protections/.

A note of techno-utopianism animates the more chipper voices in the "only technology can save us from technology" crowd, in which those products which technologists choose to make are supposed to do us only good. At academic conferences, one hears with painful frequency the argument that consumers love advertising because it brings them goods and services. That's simply wrong by itself, but it's also an example of the kind of self-deceiving techno-utopianism I am talking about.

WHAT'S NOT GOING TO WORK: UNDERESTIMATING SOCIAL TECHNOLOGY

The foregoing description should make it clear that some of the standard solutions to this problem are not going to work. Among the technological elites there is a sense that we need only to invent our way out of any social problems we run into. Technology causing you social problems? No worries—the cure is more technology! There is some serious strength to this way of thinking. Why fight about social problems if we can make them go away? Why encourage recycling if we can develop styrofoam-devouring mealworms?[31]

The answer is that hard technologists tend to underestimate the role of social technology. Take the simple "hard" technology of the sword or gun. Those technologies can very much make certain forms of society come unhinged, as each individual becomes able to take others' lives at minimal cost. Humans have therefore developed varying degrees of strict social technology, requiring training, responsibility, and sometimes even some form of government sanction to carry lethal weapons. In short, gun technology might destabilize a society unless the society develops strong social norms, systems, institutions, and even databases to help channel it. Societies that do not develop such strong social technology devolve into warlordism and chaos. The claim that we can invent hard technological solutions to all our problems is nonsense, because one of our most difficult problems is how to organize ourselves in the face of the solutions that hard technology provides us.

An even stronger reason to reject techno-utopianism in the face of the techno-social conflict is to note that there can be no technological solution to the problem and task of honestly expressed human preference. No neural

---

[31] See Yu Yang, et al., *Biodegradation and Mineralization of Polystyrene by Plastic-Eating Mealworms: Part 1. Chemical and Physical Characterization and Isotopic Tests*, 49 ENVIRON. SCI. TECHNOL. 12080 (2015) (mealworms are capable of having a diet that is solely on Styrofoam which is a grade 6 plastic. This type of plastic is of a quality that would be much more wasteful to recycle than it would be to produce. However, because Mealworms are able to consume it, this is theorized to be a potential way to reduce styrofoam pollution).

network can produce a better read on what a human thinks than that human's honestly expressed view. The argument that computers can make better decisions for us than we would make for ourselves is circular. At some point we would still have to agree that the system's decision is in fact better for us, because if we do not, then it isn't. Mind you, big data algorithms may give us much more information that causes us to change our preferences. And technological capabilities may expand our options such that we will express a preference for something that was simply not technologically feasible before. But there cannot be any better model of what humans prefer than humans. And so there cannot be a technological solution to the problem of law: how humans prefer to live and coordinate themselves and their environment.

Techno-utopian thinkers are often eager not merely to render legal mechanisms obsolete, but to actively erode them. Consider the current hype about cryptocurrencies and blockchain ledgers. One reason for the hype is the entirely false sense that regulators will be helpless to regulate blockchains,[32] and that blockchains will erode the power of legal, banking, and finance institutions.[33] Similarly, the excitement about smart contracting—that is, automated software execution of agreements that previously would have taken the form of a binding legal agreement—is generated by the prospect of doing away with lawyers.

This is rank nonsense, and not merely because I am a lawyer and want to keep my job. We execute automated software deals all the time. I bought gas for my car this morning in an entirely automated transaction. But without a legal framework to back them up, electronic contracts concluded by AI are not worth the paper they are not written on. The shifting of resources facilitated by software must take place against the background of a legal framework that recognizes those transfers as legitimate.

I can transfer your wealth to me by reaching into your wallet and taking your money. That transfer is not legally legitimate, and therefore its mere fact doesn't do away with the lawyers at all. We still cannot get away from asking humans whether a given allocation of goods and services is legally legitimate. We cannot escape the question by automating our contracting procedures, or by creating unbanked cryptocurrencies, or what have you. The rules are for *us*.

---

[32] *See* Francine McKenna, *Here's How the U.S. and the World Regulate Bitcoin and Other Cryptocurrencies*, MARKETWATCH (Dec. 28, 2017), www.marketwatch.com/story/heres-how-the-us-and-the-world-are-regulating-bitcoin-and-cryptocurrency-2017–12-18.

[33] There are serious grounds to be excited about blockchain technology: it is a distributed database technology that solves important problems of collective action and deceit in maintaining records in a group context. But the claim that blockchain technology is immune to legal regulation is nonsense on stilts.

They are expressions of our preference for how we wish things to be. Most people, it turns out, don't want others filching from their wallets. Humans must still pick the rules (or if they delegate that to representatives or computers, the rules for picking the rules), even if the rules are automatically and technologically implemented.

Finally, the siren song of techno-utopianism reaches its zenith in a comforting narrative that the rise of automation will not eliminate jobs, but will provide new jobs that need new workers. The prediction has not fared well. Without a developed set of social technologies, there is a real risk that a lot of people will get sucked under by the automation wave. With the right set of social technologies, we might be able to speed up the rate of upskilling for people who lose their ability to earn a living thanks to advances in automation. We can build good social solutions. Reeducation and reallocation of human labor are social systems, and there is no reason we can't help the most vulnerable with those tasks. I'll dig into these ideas later in the chapter, as well as consider how new social technologies might help us stay afloat in the automation age.

What is the alternative? As the technology cycle continues to speed up, we can continue to saddle students with debt greater than the expected return on the knowledge they receive. We can continue to discard highly trained employees as their degree skills age out. We can continue to close sectors of the economy to humans in chunks of 10 percent at a time.[34] We can put truck drivers out of work with self-driving trucks, refuse to help them with food, clothing, shelter, medical care, and retraining, and then put down peaceful

---

[34] Studies posit a range of figures, depending on which aspect of the problem is studied. *See* Erin Winick, *Every Study We Could Find on what Automation Will Do to Jobs, in One Chart,* MIT TECH. REV. (Jan. 25, 2018), www.technologyreview.com/s/610005/every-study-we-could-find-on-what-automation-will-do-to-jobs-in-one-chart/. *See also* Carl Benedikt Frey & Michael A. Osborne, *The Future of Employment: How Susceptible Are Jobs to Computerisation,* Oxford Martin School, www.oxfordmartin.ox.ac.uk/downloads/academic/The_Future_of_Employment .pdf (last updated Sep. 13, 2017) ("about 47 percent of total US employment is at risk" of automation); Melanie Arntz et al., *The Risk of Automation for Jobs in OECD Countries,* OECD iLIBRARY, www.oecd-ilibrary.org/social-issues-migration-health/the-risk-of-automation-for-jobs-in-oecd-countries_5jlz9h56dvq7-en (last updated May 14, 2016) ("[O]n average across the 21 OECD countries [e.g., United States, Canada, Germany, United Kingdom, Japan, and other major economies], 9% of jobs are automatable."); and James Manyika et al., *Jobs Lost, Jobs Gained: Workforce Transitions in an Age of Automation,* McKinsey & Co. (Dec. 2017) (noting that "60 percent of occupations have at least 30 percent of constituent work activities that could be automated," that "[studies] across 46 countries suggest that between almost zero and one-third of work activities could be displaced by 2030, with a midpoint of 15 percent," and that "by 2030, 75 million to 375 million workers (3 to 14 percent of the global workforce) will need to switch occupational categories.").

protests by identifying and arresting protesters through their mobile data and communications activity, and stop revolts with drones.

Giving up on social technology is not a viable human option. We cannot just adapt machines to us. We are going to have to adapt our communities to machines. And we cannot do that merely by adding technology to our communities. Our communities' social norms and structures, their strictures, taboos, and rites of passage, will have to change. Moreover: our methods of changing our rules will itself have to change, a kind of meta-change. Law is our method for changing our rules. And law also provides our mechanism for changing *how* we change our rules. Thus, not only must *laws* change in order for human society to thrive under these conditions, but *law itself*, including many of our reasons for engaging in the exercise of law in the first place, must change.

The conundrum is this: we do not have time to let new norms naturally evolve. It's taken ten years for people to understand at a deep level how rude it is to use a cellphone at the table.[35] It will be another thirty years until it becomes as unacceptable as loudly passing gas in a crowded room. Our current method of norm production, which involves the process of gathering stories from the media, analysis from public figures, and private conversation, results in some communities settling on some rules. Others settle on others. As the legal scholar Bob Cover has noted, these emergent norms then clash.[36] Judges rule that one argument, one rule of social understanding, prevails over another. These norms rise up everywhere and are pruned by the legal system. That is a key part of our process for establishing formal legal rules.

If this is our account of law—and I think it is a relatively sound one—then we need to go looking for law at its root: the communities where people hammer out the rules of living together. That's where law comes from. It bubbles up from interactions between people, rises to become a discussed norm within a community, and from there branches out to encounter and be defeated by, defeat, or incorporate rules developed in other contexts by other communities. We can look there for the wellspring of law—and we can do one better. We can improve law by improving the communities, optimizing them for creating rules that help members thrive.

The old way of doing law, relying on ostensibly representative legislatures to avoid industry capture and lobbying, to work in the public interest, is a failed

---

[35] See Jamie Ducharme, *Using Your Phone at Dinner Isn't Just Rude. It Also Makes You Unhappy*, Time, Feb. 28, 2018, http://time.com/5178352/phone-ruining-dinner/.
[36] Robert Cover, *Nomos and Narrative*, 97 Harv. L. Rev. 4 (1983–84).

enterprise, at least in many former or decaying democracies. But even if we had functioning legislatures to work with, we cannot completely plan and centralize our way out of this problem. Centralized social engineering will not work, because the risk of mass adoption of a suboptimal social technology is too high, and because the coercion necessary to adopt such programs breeds resistance, at least in liberal democracies. So we need to move quickly, but one seductive path toward moving quickly—centralization and mass production—won't work. What is needed is not a system of ideas, since any such ideas will age out, but a system for rapidly producing, prototyping, testing, implementing, and iterating ideas to be adopted more widely, and purely on the measure of their success in increasing human welfare.

A further temptation will be political dogmatism. As society teeters, rocked by technological change, many will succumb to the lure of believing that a given social system (usually communism or capitalism) will save us, if only implemented in pure enough form. But we cannot double down on such systems, much less retrograde "pure" forms of those solutions, no matter their accumulated social capital or theoretical appeal. Both communism and capitalism have failed to solve problems we now face, although on completely different scales, at different times, and for different reasons. We are not at the end of history, we are on its bleeding edge. We will need different economic, political, religious, and above all legal structures. Different, but not radical. Innovative, but not unrecognizable. Widespread, but not centralized. We have no time to abandon the lessons of the past, no time to make continent-spanning mistakes of centralized planning, and no ability to survive if we do not advance the ball.

WHERE WE ARE GOING

In response to Ray Kurzweil's vision of a lily-pad-choked future, I think it may be useful to imagine the future as it will likely turn out. As with everything in this book, I will probably be wrong in some details. But I have an utterly unfair advantage over Kurzweil: he wrote in 2005, concluding that technology would soon escape human comprehension, and I am writing fifteen years later, when things haven't changed all that much.[37] Because of my unfair advantage, I think that assuming that some things will take more time than Kurzweil thought they would is a responsible move. Similarly, my bet is that an author

---

[37] Except, perhaps the worldwide rise of authoritarian nationalism, which is a more complicated history to tell, especially as it relates to technology, which I discuss in chapter 8.

fifteen years from now will have amazing stories of technological progress to tell, but will not report a technological singularity.

Whether our slower-than-predicted stroll toward the technological singularity is thanks to human intransigence and incompetence, or factionalism, or responsible management of the rate of technological change can be reasonably debated. But my prediction is that humans have more time in a recognizable middle future than Kurzweil and the singularitarians believe. I think the year 2050 will happen, and that life will not be at all the same, but will in some instances be pretty recognizable.

In short, the future will be both more alien and more familiar than we think it will. One way to think about this is to call to mind the impact that geolocation technology has had on the world we know.[38] Fewer people get lost now.[39] Smartphones really help with navigation, and that is revolutionary.[40] Yet the modern world with its ubiquitous geolocation technology would still look pretty familiar from the perspective of twenty or thirty years ago. In one sense, the world has changed completely. On the other hand, a time traveler from 1990 would recognize Main Street USA without a feeling that she had stepped into *Back to the Future Part II*[41] (which itself did not posit much in the way of futurism, except for that cool hoverboard, for which I am still waiting).[42]

---

[38] See Pattrik Perez & Chelsea Cunningham, *A Woman's Phone GPS May Have Helped Save Her Life after Falling off a Cliff Near Pennybacker Bridge*, KVUE News (Nov. 17, 2018), www .kvue.com/article/news/local/a-womans-phone-gps-may-have-helped-save-her-life-after-falling-off-a-cliff-near-pennybacker-bridge/269-615228161; Paul Tassi, *How on Earth Did "Pokemon Go" Make Almost $800 Million in 2018?*, Forbes (Jan. 5, 2019), www.forbes.com/sites/insertcoin/2019/01/05/how-on-earth-did-pokemon-go-make-almost-800-million-in-2018/#3fd143699967 (discussing the massively successful geolocation smartphone game Pokémon Go).

[39] Adam Skolnick, *Racing across Antarctica, One Freezing Day at a Time*, N. Y. Times, Nov. 29, 2018, available at www.nytimes.com/2018/11/29/sports/antarctica-ski-race.html.

[40] See, Trevor Mogg, *Google Maps Tests Features That Will Help Drivers Avoid Crashes, Speed Traps*, Digital Trends (Nov. 8, 2018), www.digitaltrends.com/mobile/google-maps-testing-crash-and-speed-trap-reports-in-navigation/.

[41] *Back to the Future Part II* (Universal Pictures et al. 1989).

[42] Recent events give me hope. John Porter, *Second Attempt to Fly Hoverboard across English Channel Scheduled for Weekend*, The Verge (July 31, 2019), www.theverge.com/2019/7/31/20 748325/flyboard-air-channel-crossing-second-attempt-bigger-refueling-boat; Stuart Dredge, *Hendo Hoverboard: Where We're Going, We Don't Need Roads ...*, The Guardian (March 6, 2015), www.theguardian.com/technology/2015/mar/06/hendo-hoverboard-arx-pax-20 15-back-to-the-future; *see also Nike Hyperadapt*, Nike (n.d.), www.nike.com/us/en_us/c/innov ation/hyperadapt (advertising the Nike Electric Adaptable Reaction Lacing shoe, which was inspired by the "self-lacing Nike sneakers" portrayed in *Back to the Future: Part II*). *But see also* Geoffrey A. Fowler, *Nike's Self-Lacing Shoes Stopped Lacing. Blame the Internet*, Wash. Post (March 14, 2019), www.washingtonpost.com/technology/2019/03/14/nikes-self-lacing-shoes-stopped-lacing-blame-internet ("I don't recall the shoes in 'Back to the Future 2' using an app

So, more to give you the shape of my thinking than to attempt any real prophecy, I posit some changes that I think will certainly take place, in three rough groupings: near, middle, and far future. My goal is to generate both a sense of hope—there is still time!—and a sense of urgency. In particular, proceeding as we have been is not a value-neutral decision. Should we continue on without serious course correction, we will severely compromise our continued existence as a species.

NEAR FUTURE: STILL WAITING TO MEET GEORGE JETSON

In the near future, technology may not progress as quickly as we think it will. My youngest daughter plays computer games sometimes. When she sits down to play, she will often complain after about half a minute. The computer is simply too slow for her. It won't load fast enough, download fast enough, connect fast enough, do what she wants it to do fast enough. The funny thing is that she is my youngest daughter, and I remember when my oldest, nearly a decade older, had the same complaints. The amount of time before my daughter complains about how slow the computer is is a *constant*, even though Moore's law has held that the number of operations per second that a chip can perform has followed exponential growth throughout most of recent history.

When we consider the near future, two things are true: things are changing faster than ever, and they are not changing fast enough. Never mind the *Jetsons*, we're just now getting to electric cars.[43] What this means is that human expectations continue to outstrip technological performance. At no time in the near future will computers or automated production systems act fast enough to satisfy our desires. I doubt I'll see George Jetson's flying car in my lifetime.[44]

Why does exponential technological growth only deliver linear increases in human capability? My daughters' problems with waiting for computers to load

to operate . . . . Staying in our lives after a purchase gives a manufacturer new opportunities to make money, be it from our data, advertising, in-app purchases or services.").

[43] Tabbit Wilberforce et al., *Developments of Electric Cars and Fuel Cell Hydrogen Electric Cars*, 42 INT'L JOURNAL OF HYDROGEN ENERGY 40 (2017).

[44] Will we see personal flying vehicles and flying cars on the market in the next decade? Sure. In some iterations they already exist. But a pragmatic flying car that is affordable to the everyman like Jetson and can be parked in a residential neighborhood is definitely far off. Gideon Lichfield, *When Will We Have Flying Cars? Maybe Sooner Than You Think*, MIT TECH. REV. (Feb. 13, 2019), www.technologyreview.com/s/612891/when-will-we-have-flying-cars-maybe-sooner-than-you-think ("After decades of promises, personal air vehicles are finally getting close to commercial reality—but you still probably won't own one").

and my own reverse future shock about the Jetsons have a basis in mathematics. Consider the well-known traveling salesman problem.[45] A salesperson needs to visit ten cities, and wants to know what route to take to keep her gas costs and travel time the lowest. She wants to travel to each city exactly once, and return home. For up to three cities the problem is trivial. With four cities she has to compare three possible circuits (abcda, abdca, and acbda). From there the number of possible circuits to examine goes through a combinatorial explosion—exponential growth. (By the way, if at each step she just goes to the nearest city remaining to be visited, she will probably not pick the best route.)

This is called a hard nondeterministic polynomial problem (or NP-hard problem). No one has been able to come up with a computer program that solves this problem. All solutions become exponentially slower as the number of cities increases, and nearly all computer scientists believe that there is no more efficient solution possible on a digital computer.[46] It is an NP-hard problem because even if someone were to provide us with a solution (say someone gave our salesperson an itinerary and claimed it was the shortest), it might take just as long to solve the original problem as it would to verify whether the answer was correct.

Solving her problem with a few cities is possible with a lot of computing power and some good algorithms. But consider a problem of thousands, or tens of thousands, or hundreds of thousands of cities. (Hundreds of thousands of cities may seem like a stretch, but the traveling salesman problem stands in for a huge range of optimization problems, many of which have this many factors.) Let's say that our salesperson actually has the massive supercomputers necessary to calculate such a route. Now, let's *double* her available computing power. What is the impact on her ability to calculate an optimal route? *Maybe* she can add one city. And I say *maybe* because the difference between 2,000 cities and 2,001 cities is preposterously huge in terms of the number of routes she may take between all the cities.

Many of the most important and most basic human social problems are problems of optimization, and thus are NP-hard problems. We try to allocate resources between humans to incentivize work and creativity, but show compassion to those who do not have enough. We try to allocate social resources between guns and butter. We have the temerity to do things like try to model an economy of billions of daily decisions. These

---

[45] GREGORY GUTIN & ABRAHAM P. PUNNEN, THE TRAVELING SALESMAN PROBLEM AND ITS VARIATIONS (2007).

[46] A polynomial is the sum of weighted powers of x. A polynomial function will be eventually far outstripped by even the smallest exponential function, where the variable is in the exponent. So: 3^x will eventually massively outstrip x^{1500} as x increases, for example.

are the problems of law, of social technology. Humans and human problems will always be among the most wildly difficult optimization decisions, and so even vast increases in computing power will produce only baby steps of change.

Another factor in our slower-than-expected sense of near-future change is that our perception is not linear, meaning that we perceive a nonlinear stimulus linearly. Experimental evidence shows that our sense of sight and brightness is logarithmic.[47] Something that appears to be twice as bright to us is actually many times the intensity as measured scientifically.[48] Similarly, when we think one noise is twice as loud as another noise, an instrument will measure it as many more times intense.[49] That is why we measure loudness in decibels—a logarithmic scale.[50] This logarithmic perception permits us extreme adaptability, because we can perceive with useful distinction both the very soft and very loud ends of the sound spectrum. There's also evidence that this is true of our sense of mathematics. Many cultures first evolved a logarithmic style of counting, in which we do not count one, two, three but instead count one, two, many, family, herd, horde.[51]

So even if technology changes at mind-boggling speed, humans are likely to be able to cope. Indeed, human perception and cognition seem well conditioned to handle technological change, given that we have accommodated enormous technological change with aplomb thus far. Or, more puckishly: humans will, at least for the near future, still be bored with experiences produced by Moore's Law–level exponential increases in technological capability.

Boredom is very good news. Boredom indicates an excess of cognitive capacity over and beyond the drain on brainpower caused by technological shifts.[52] When we are bored with something, we realize that we have a handle on it. It does not pose an existential threat. Given all the talk about the coming robotic singularity,

---

[47] A logarithm "undoes" an exponential function. For example, the logarithm of 10^{33} is 33. $y=\log(10^x)$ is $y=x$. The growth was exponential, but the logarithm is a straight line, $y=x$.

[48] VINCENT P. COLETTA, PHYSICS FUNDAMENTALS, 630 (2008).

[49] *Id.*, 401.

[50] With β representing the intensity level, *Io* representing the lowest sound intensity perceptible, and *I* representing sound; the logarithmic scale for measuring sound is: $\beta=10\log(I/Io)$.

[51] See, Peter Gordon, *Numerical Cognition without Words: Evidence from Amazonia*, 306 SCIENCE 496 (Oct. 15, 2004).

[52] See, Maggie Koerth-Baker, *Why Boredom Is Anything but Boring*, SCIENTIFIC AMERICAN (Jan. 18, 2016), www.scientificamerican.com/article/why-boredom-is-anything-but-boring/ (the article explains how James Danckert, a cognitive neuroscientist at the University of Waterloo in Canada, studies boredom. Although a universally accepted definition is contested, boredom is commonly believed to be a mental state absent of stimulation and thus one that leaves the individual craving for relief).

I take enormous heart in how bored my daughters are, and indeed how bored most children of their generation seem to be with the absolutely insane increases in technological capability, particularly automation, miniaturization, and ubiquitous computing that have altered the techno-cultural landscape within their lifetimes. I don't mean they are digital natives in the sense that they are particularly good at these technologies. I merely mean that their cognitive model takes the increase in technological capability entirely in stride.

MIDDLE FUTURE: JOHN HENRY VERSUS THE MACHINE

Things will not go on this way forever. I think it is merely reasonable to guess that they will go on this way longer than Ray Kurzweil or the other singularitarians think they will.[53] Eventually, though, we are going to have to come to grips with the fact that we are automating many procedures that used to provide humans with a claim on shelter, food, and water. That is, we are delegating to robots many of the tasks that humans use to earn a living. Historically, this arrangement made some cruel sense: growing the food, building buildings, and providing for the common defense, as well as many other tasks, simply had to be done. The current order ties food and shelter to producing something of use to the community, getting money for it, and then purchasing what the worker needs.

A recent study by the Brookings Institution predicts that in the next few decades, approximately 25 percent of US employment will face "high exposure" to automation, and another 36 percent will experience "medium exposure" to automation.[54] About a year ago, a close friend of mine wanted to start a business. His plan was to buy a road tractor (the large trucks that pull semi-trailers) and

---

[53] Kurzweil, *supra* note 8.

[54] *See* Mark Muro et al., *Automation and Artificial Intelligence: How Machines Affect People and Places*, Brookings Institution: Metropolitan Policy Program (Jan. 2019), www.brookings.edu/wp-content/uploads/2019/01/2019.01_BrookingsMetro_Automation-AI_Report_Muro-Maxim-Whiton-FINAL-version.pdf. *But see* Kai Fu Lee, *Estimates of Job Loss Due to Automation Miss One Big Factor*, QUARTZ (Nov. 28, 2018), https://qz.com/work/1477807/how-many-jobs-will-be-automated-most-predictions-miss-one-big-factor/

"Predicting the scale of AI-induced job losses has become a cottage industry for economists and consulting firms the world over. Depending on which model one uses, estimates range from terrifying to totally not a problem.

Since 2013, the most cited predictions include a study from Oxford University that predicted 47% of US jobs could be automated within the next decade or two; an Organization for Economic Cooperation and Development (OECD) report that suggested just 9% of jobs in the United States were at high risk of automation; PwC research that found 38% of jobs in the United States were at high risk of automation by the early 2030s; and a McKinsey report that found around 50% of work tasks around the world are already automatable."

a car trailer. His business model was to take online transport contracts to deliver cars that people had purchased online. It makes sense—everyone buys more and more stuff online, so why not cars? The demand was there, the opportunity was there. Why not go for it?

My younger brother is a roboticist, one of the lead engineers on the Google autonomous car project (now spun off in a company called Waymo). The biggest problems for autonomous vehicles are the unpredictable pedestrian-filled city centers.[55] Long, straight stretches on the interstate are much less of a problem. Long-haul truck driving is therefore not a skill with a very long shelf life.[56]

Despite the challenges of autonomous urban driving, even taxi drivers—already rocked by sharing economy apps[57]—are likely to completely vanish, as will their Uber-driving competitors, in the face of cars that can drive themselves.[58] We have automated the job of driving. Those jobs are not a good bet, going forward.

The automation trend is fundamentally retooling the work landscape.[59] Take my own profession, law. In the middle of the Great Recession, the number of LSAT test-takers and law school applicants sharply increased.[60]

[55] See Timothy B. Lee, *Pedestrians Are a Hard Problem for Self Driving Cars—here's one solution*, ARS TECHNICA, July 30, 2018, https://arstechnica.com/cars/2018/07/new-software-gives-self-driving-cars-intuitive-understanding-of-pedestrians/.

[56] Maury Gittleman & Kristen Monaco, *Truck-Driving Jobs: Are They Headed for Rapid Elimination?*, ILR REVIEW 19 (June 17, 2019) ("We estimate that between 300,000 and 400,000 workers are currently employed as heavy truck drivers in the long-haul segment of trucking, the segment most likely to adopt level 4 automation.").

[57] See, e.g., *Our First-Quarter Update on Business Travel Spending and Trends*, CERTIFY (Apr. 30, 2018) ("Uber and Lyft are still dominating traditional business traveler ground transportation services, with the ride-hailing companies taking 71% of all ground transportation receipts and expenses. Rental car companies secured 23% of the market, and taxis held on to the remaining 6%. That's a huge shift compared to last year when ride-hailing accounted for only 59% of business travel, and with rental car and taxi companies holding on to 31% and 10% of the market respectively.").

[58] Nick Bastone, *Elon Musk Says Tesla Will Roll Out 1 Million Robo-Taxis by Next Year. Here's How He Plans on Doing It*, INC.COM (Apr. 23, 2019), www.inc.com/business-insider/tesla-is-taking-direct-aim-at-uber-and-lyft-with-plans-to-roll-out-one-million-robo-taxis-by-next-year.html; Faiz Siddiqui & Greg Bensinger, *As IPO Soars, Can Uber and Lyft Survive Long Enough to Replace Their Drivers with Computers?*, WASH. POST (Mar. 29, 2019), www.washingtonpost.com/technology/2019/03/29/even-with-ipo-billions-can-uber-lyft-survive-long-enough-replace-their-drivers-with-machines/.

[59] Josh Dzieza, *How Hard Will the Robots Make Us Work?*, THE VERGE (Feb. 27, 2020), www.theverge.com/2020/2/27/21155254/automation-robots-unemployment-jobs-vs-human-google-amazon?utm_source=pocket-newtab (algorithms detect and root out moments of human rest and respite).

[60] Rebecca R. Ruiz, *Recession Spurs Interest in Graduate, Law Schools*, N. Y. TIMES (Jan. 9, 2010), www.nytimes.com/2010/01/10/education/10grad.html.

This was hardly unusual—for past downturns, it had been a wise tactic to ride out a recession while getting an education and thus graduate with more marketable skills into a reenergized job market. For this reason, law schools, business schools, and medical schools were considered "recession resistant"— a downturn in the economy often meant an uptick in students.

Unfortunately, those who hid from the Great Recession by going to law school graduated three years later into a collapsing legal services market.[61] What happened? The economic downturn caused corporate clients, the mainstay of big law billables, to reevaluate their payment models. Clients became much less willing to pay high prices for relatively inexperienced attorneys to do large amounts of fairly routine work. Law firms responded with a mix of strategies. Partners did more legal work and perhaps less rainmaking, and more work was farmed out to low-paid contract attorneys. But by far the biggest change was automating a large portion of the work once performed by newly minted attorneys.[62]

For example, even twenty years ago, document discovery was a rite of passage for young attorneys. New hires would often be shipped out to a warehouse of documents to sort through hundreds of thousands of corporate records. Their goal: find and identify those documents relevant and responsive to a party's litigation discovery request. Attorneys would mark some documents for production to the other party, others as irrelevant, others as nonresponsive, and still others as protected from disclosure under attorney work product and attorney-client privilege. The sorting process could easily consume months of time. For this and other repetitive and routine legal tasks, a firm could bill young attorneys out at quite a high rate while paying them a lower one. As a result, each new hire was a profit center for the firm, and hiring rates were correspondingly high.

But the downturn in the legal services market sent law firms scrambling to replace inexperienced associates with lower-cost and more profitable alternatives. An already developed trend toward electronic discovery (warehouses were already being replaced by terabyte hard-drives) merged with the exploding field of machine learning tools to automate a large part of the discovery process. Now a machine learning program could be trained to a high degree of

[61]   See Jordan Weissmann, *How the Job Market for Law School Grads Crumbled (and How It Could Come Back to Life)*, THE ATLANTIC, Feb. 5, 2013, www.theatlantic.com/business/arc hive/2013/02/how-the-job-market-for-law-school-grads-crumbled-and-how-it-could-come-back -to-life/272852/.

[62]   *See generally* Asma Khalid, *From Post-It Notes to Algorithms: How Automation Is Changing Legal Work*, NPR (Nov. 7, 2017), www.npr.org/sections/alltechconsidered/2017/11/07/5616319 27/from-post-it-notes-to-algorithms-how-automation-is-changing-legal-work.

accuracy in a relatively short time by a relatively small team of contract attorneys. Close cases, comparatively few in number, could be kicked up by the algorithm to a human for a determination, and the result then fed back into the algorithm for it to properly sort such future cases.

The once-majestic herds of profitable young associates who used to graze the document warehouses of the world have been hunted to the brink of extinction by law firm human resources departments. Or, to say this without *The Far Side* touch, law firms greatly reduced the hiring of young associates because they had automated their work and because clients would no longer pay as much for their services.

From long-haul truck drivers to newly educated lawyers, automation is making jobs go away. Algorithms now regularly outperform doctors in making diagnoses and radiologists in reading x-rays.[63] Pick a regular, routine task, and someone is working on how to automate it. This process creates some jobs, sure—the jobs of automating other jobs, which snowballs into the elimination of even more.

This isn't by itself the end of the world, or even necessarily a bad thing—*if* we reconsider the basic logic of production and incentives to map to the new reality: humans will produce less and less, and automated processes will produce more and more.

The Engine of Capitalism

A human should not work a task just to work. If a machine can do a task better, at a lower cost, than a human, it probably should. This process is nothing new: water and windmills grind flour more efficiently than human muscle power, and horses or oxen with plows turn earth more efficiently than humans with hoes. We wanted the product of the task, the end result. The problem is that as a culture, we continue to insist on the opposite: humans who do not work, even when that work is useless and inefficient, are penalized by being refused food. That's a stance we will need to update.

There is a growing crack in one of our most powerful pieces of social technology—the incentive/production engine at the heart of capitalism. The labor part of capitalism is easy: no work, no food. It incentivizes humans to produce. The core mechanic of the labor side of capitalism is that those who don't produce don't get resources to live. It was a highly productive piece of

---

[63] See Ivana Bartoletti, *Algorithms May Outperform Doctors, but They're No Healthcare Panacea*, THE GUARDIAN, July 26, 2018, www.theguardian.com/commentisfree/2018/jul/26/tech-healthcare-ethics-artifical-intelligence-doctors-patients.

social technology, particularly compared to communist and authoritarian nationalist systems. It had an advantage in incentivizing production because humans were the producers, and because survival and profit are powerful human motivators.

But the very strength of the capitalist motivational engine is the part of the social technology that is wearing down with age. When humans stop producing—when labor's share of the economy shrinks to vanishing—the heart of capitalism stops beating. When humans don't produce, when humans *can't* produce in competition with machines, it does no good at all to threaten them with starvation, homelessness, and the like. Taking away long-haul truck drivers' ability to eat because they can't beat self-driving trucks is like refusing to feed your cat because it doesn't speak a foreign language.

The production-incentive structure only fails for one side of capitalism. Capitalist structures reward workers and owners. Workers are getting less as work is automated. But ownership has not been reformed in any serious way, and indeed life is increasingly bright on the ownership side of the street. Owning robots that produce is a great way to make a living, and recent scholarship shows that capital's—ownership's—share of the economy grows both as a function of wealth concentration due to falling demographic growth and as a function of the automation of production.[64] So owners will do fine in this world of automated labor. But those of us who work for a living will be out of luck. As in the old song of John Henry, we can work against machines until our hearts give out, but it's useless. The whole point of automation is the same as mechanization: the machines do these jobs better than we do.

The usual pat response to all of this is to claim that new jobs will appear out of nowhere. Yet I'm not the first one to note that the newly empowered "creative class" heralded in Silicon Valley seems to work at Walmart. Yes, it is clear that some new jobs will arise, and retraining will be a critical part of helping people keep up as entire industries are automated out of existence. There will be no large loss without some smaller gain, and using that gain effectively will be important. So we should talk about retraining and upskilling, as well as ways of building social technology that help with those processes. But I do not want us to fall into the trap of complacency like tech propagandists do: the current scale and accelerating speed of job automation is going to change the social symbol of labor within our cultural constellation of meanings. We will not so much be retooled as transformed.

Automation will change the nature of work, and that change is going to be permanent and accelerating. It's not just that the experience of work will shift,

[64] Thomas Piketty, Capitalism in the 21st Century 25 (2014).

but that its cultural meaning—what it means to work, to not work, what "work" is, and so on—will change. And that's good. If we don't think about how we link work and life, we are in for a long and horrible period where few people work, fewer people own everything that produces, and the masses are left to scrabble for scraps.

Rethinking Retraining and Upskilling

Retraining and upskilling offer easy and hard versions. The easy insight is that we must direct a lot of resources toward helping people learn new skills and new jobs. But already this is more complicated than it sounds. One thing that *won't* work is to chase after quick blips in the job market. This is the version of upskilling popular with businesses and the tech media: they want public money to finance the skills they need so they can pay lower wages and get jobs done that they need done now. For example, if there is high demand for Python coders, we might be tempted to open Python coding classes for out-of-work truck drivers, lawyers, or coal miners. But by the time people are trained in those skills, they are often just a few years from obsolescence, and the entire process must begin again.

The model of finding a place in the economy that needs skilled labor, training people to meet that need, and ranking them for employment according to their performance on set criteria will not only miss the moving target of a rapidly developing economy but also, because of knowledge monoculture, produce worse outcomes. Humans do not think or create alone, so cultivating many people all trained to the best standard will simply result in teams of people with overlapping and redundant skill sets instead of the diverse cognitive toolsets necessary for innovation. This affects testing and training policy. Measurement of skill on any single metric or even a range of metrics (say, by testing people and hiring those who test the best) will create teams of people who all tested well—who all overlap.[65] These "best" teams—best precisely because they have all excelled at the same standard—will substantially underperform teams that include members with diverse cognitive toolsets, even if those toolsets are considered less valuable for a given task at hand. (More on this in Chapter 9.)

Instead, we will need to teach people how to become lifelong learners—that is, to have the basis for learning whatever new skills will be needed as they are needed. Learning how to learn will be more important than any specific skill.

---

[65] Scott Page, The Diversity Bonus: How Great Teams Pay Off in the Knowledge Economy (2017).

Meta-learning tools like epistemology, philosophy, study skills, statistics, and so on will be significantly more important than learning C# or a specific software development environment. Those will be important, of course, but they are extremely time-limited in value. Even a PhD in computer science now has a knowledge shelf life of about a decade. We can study for five years to learn technical knowledge that is good for ten, at a price tag only repayable after a lifetime of work, or we can go about revising the way we deliver and price skills. The current model is simply not going to survive: as the experience of law students in the Great Recession showed, it's not sustainable.

Moreover, we must teach students a range of subjects and develop diverse cognitive toolsets, including those that do not seem directly related to technological progress. Having philosophers and historians on software development teams would, I suspect, have given us a much less dystopian present, just as economists, technologists, and cultural anthropologists have given us a clearer view of law. Far from needing to channel everyone into the same STEM curriculum, we need people to invest in diverse cognitive toolsets, and to help companies understand the improvements that cognitive diversity brings to their bottom line.

We might even consider policy reforms to make that happen. One thing we do to encourage diversification and innovation in business is provide legal tools that insulate against the chance of failure. Bankruptcy law, for example, encourages innovation because people can take a risk without losing their home if it doesn't pan out—as indeed the overwhelming majority of new businesses do not. Similarly, low education costs can make the risks of investing in a diverse cognitive toolset more attractive. In countries that make education a priority, students are not forced to shoulder massive financial burdens, which raises rates of innovation and entrepreneurialism. Countries like those in northern Europe, where education is broadly available, have seen strong payoffs from their education policy: people can study different toolsets and start innovative businesses without fear that they will starve if they fail. It is worth noting that the United States, where education costs are ruinous, performs well on tests of innovation (patent grants or startups per capita, for example), but benefits—quite intentionally on the part of the tech industry via the H-1B visa program—from low-cost public education by hiring those educated in other countries at cheap rates. In that sense, the US's innovation success also depends on low-cost, high-quality advanced education—just not that of its own citizens.

Bringing education costs under control, if that's a path we are interested in following, would be a book in itself. But there are a few low-hanging fruit. One very possible avenue is to separate the functions of educational institutions:

imparting knowledge, training students how to use that knowledge, and credentialing. Some knowledge is easy enough to teach and test. Factual, substantive knowledge fits in this category. For my discipline, law, that's the easy stuff: What *is* the law? This could be taught by YouTube or app, frankly. But other knowledge is meta-knowledge: understanding how to use and manipulate what one knows. Credentialing, meanwhile, is about providing employers information about the student, rather than providing students with information about the subject. Grades are a very old social technology that does both: they tell a story about the student's mastery of material, but also a story about the qualities of the student herself, of her diligence, performance, intelligence (if there is a single such thing worthy of a single word, which studies doubt), and so on. Letters of recommendation speak to questions of relationships, teamwork, and so on.

Each of these functions of educational institutions could be delivered separately (e.g., Silicon Valley has moved toward offering jobs to people who can verifiably solve certain hard problems—their own credentialing), and the separation could provide some serious efficiencies. Divorcing factual knowledge delivery from meta-knowledge and credentialing would be particularly useful. Distance and mass learning can work for substantive knowledge delivery. It does not work for meta-knowledge and credentialing, which require working with the structure of the subject and working with the individual to produce results.

In short, then, retraining for specific skills demanded for today's economy will be less effective than teaching students how to acquire the skills that will be demanded tomorrow. To create a workforce with the cognitive diversity to innovate, education costs and methods must enable students to take risks. The current system, at least in the United States, of high-cost, short shelf-life knowledge fosters risk aversion, and has forced the technology industry to import educated labor from countries with more effective policies.

Inventing Social Technology for Reskilling

Thus far we have simply talked about tweaking things as they are: trying to deliver knowledge needed for tomorrow's skills as a way of fending off the specter of automation. But retraining and upskilling will need to be supported by strong social technology as well. Consider a marriage: the new couple is (often and optimally) supported by social admiration, surrounded by a helpful community, and even supported financially as they embark on creating a new household. (It all sounds terribly quaint, doesn't it?) The point is: the social technologies that surround a new stage in life can do much to shape our willingness to do something, and even the success of the enterprise. The same goes for the social encouragement and support of learning new skills to stave off automation-driven obsolescence. Compare a graduation ceremony and celebration to the often bleak occasion of trying to obtain the skills to begin a second, third, or fourth career. The first is inspiring, the second depressing. The former is celebrated and supported by the community with congratulations, gifts, and admiration. The latter is often cast as a personal failure, since retraining is often associated with joblessness, as if the automation of an industry casts a moral pall over the former workers in that industry.

There is no reason obtaining a skill is laudable at twenty-two and embarrassing at forty-two, no reason that students should be encouraged to seek meta-knowledge skills in college, but not for their third career. So a second element for upskilling and retraining would be to frame them as cause for cultural and community ceremony, support, and celebration. These are not psychological niceties. Our mental images matter, and it is only when our mental model of retraining changes from misery and joblessness to possibility and prosperity that workers will actively seek the experience instead of clinging to vanishing industries and clamoring for subsidies and defensive regulations to keep things the way they were. When upskilling is supported by social technology as strong as that underpinning marriage, we will begin to see people learning skills with the kind of energy and ferocity necessary to support an effective workforce under conditions of constant and unpredictable technological change.

In the middle future, then, we will have to develop new forms of social technology surrounding education, community, relationships, and the nature of life together in a political body. I have in all honesty only the beginnings of an idea as to what forms that social technology will take. I do fear that without a developed community and language about how to build the social technology we need at the speed we need, we may experience serious social discontinuities. In a nod to the fact that all writings are a product of their time, I might as well admit that I am concerned about what I see in Western democracies at the moment, and am very interested in the discussion about what to do about it. So, if pressed, I would admit that I think we can build much better political technology than that presently used.

I've got no dog in this fight other than to cheer it on. Fine: my own guess, which I offer for the sake of transparency, would be that private property and the free market are good ideas as long as we are careful with them, and that what is needed are tweaks to stop financial markets from dominating political ones, revision of the first-past-the-post voting system to improve pluralistic representation, strong regulation to keep the markets open and fair, and a lot of technology to make voting provably fair and easier to access. But what is important is that we continue to iterate our social technology. The enemy here is not any particular political party or platform, but stagnation in the development and implementation of beneficial social technology.

Unsurprisingly, political dogmatism, tribalism, and nationalism are the villains of this piece. The war on science and education is particularly distressing. Science is not neutral. It encodes bias.[66] But that is a reason to value, not discount, the scientific method. The scientific method leads us to use observation-based science to detect bias in scientific claims, not to raise non-evidence-based biased claims against solid peer-reviewed and widely accepted science. We will dig into these ideas in Parts II and III of this book.

On the other hand, readers who detect a certain Burkean conservatism in these arguments are not wholly wrong, either.[67] A good way to lose the plot is to forget the lessons of history and law. So I suggest that rapid, experimental, iterative change based on previously established experiential success stories is the way to move social technology forward. This does not mean that sometimes breaks with the past aren't necessary. But we often find that successful breaks with past practice are not truly full breaks, but rather the emergence of another trend that has long been detectable in history and culture. In looking for cultural and legal norms to iterate in the future, history should serve as our seed catalog, sounding board, and testbed.

FAR FUTURE: FROM HUMAN-MACHINE CIVILIZATION TO MACHINE-HUMAN CIVILIZATION

It is well worth investing in good social technology that helps our communities do a better job of crafting governing rules. The task of deciding what rules we should live by in community will be one of the longest-lived human jobs. Deciding how we wish to live, and how we can best live together, will be one of the remaining things we must ask of a human instead of a machine. In short, there is one thing that robots will not be able to do: they will never be able to simulate the output of human decision and preference processes better than humans can. It's a matter of definition. Consider asking a system, "what do humans choose under these circumstances?" There is no better way to get an answer than to ask a statistically valid bunch of humans.

---

[66] CAROLE J. LEE, ET AL., *Bias in Peer Review*, 64 J. OF THE AM. SOC'Y FOR INFO. SCI. AND TECH. 64 (2012).

[67] Ernest Young, *Rediscovering Conservatism: Burkean Political Theory and Constitutional Interpretation*, 72 N.C. L. REV. 619 (1994).

That means that even when robots have taken over all conceivable tasks, up to and including writing books like this one, robots will still only imperfectly simulate a human's choice. We will always have one last thing to do, which is to be ourselves. The danger is that the job of being human might come to be of no interest to machine-human civilization. If that happens—that is, if automated processes become indifferent to our outputs as humans—then the last job will be done, and the human race will not matter. But until that time, and especially if we manage our path so as to create a human-machine civilization that cares deeply about finding out what humans need and want, then we will have a job to do for a very long time indeed. We will need to be ourselves and to express our preferences as honestly as we can.

After everything else is automated, and if we have guided our culture to still care about the job of being human, our task will be to answer how we would like to organize ourselves in response to particular contexts. If there is kindness in this, humans might do quite well. If there is no kindness, it is possible that we would do quite badly. To be clear, the danger is not Skynet. The toasters will not rise up against us. Rather, what is quite likely to happen is that the productive intelligences that we will have used to strip humans of their claims to food and shelter will be extremely competent and indifferent to our welfare. Our welfare is the output of human preferences, our sense of what raises our utility or lowers it. If human-machine civilization converts to machine-human civilization without a guiding principle of care for human welfare, then we will rapidly find ourselves both unable to produce, because we cannot out-compete artificial intelligence producers, and unable to make demands on resources except for a very narrow class that has retained legal ownership rights over the distribution of goods and services—if the productive AIs are not indifferent to law, a human social construct, as well. In other words, the only term that will matter in *machine-human civilization* will be the first.

HOW WE CAN FAIL

Social technology stagnation in the face of rampant hard technological change poses important problems for the far future. Nobel Laureate Enrico Fermi, during a marathon bull session at the Los Alamos Laboratory discussing the question of extraterrestrials, famously asked, "Where is everybody?"[68] If the universe is teeming with life, as the math suggests it must be, why hasn't any of it contacted us?

---

[68] *See* Kevin Loria, *Here's Why It's So Weird That We Haven't Found Aliens Yet*, Bus. Insider (Jun. 10, 2015), www.businessinsider.com/how-the-fermi-paradox-works-2015-6.

The answer seems to be that space is too big and time is too long. Faster than light travel is quite probably impossible. And even assuming other civilizations haven't contacted us because they have faster than light travel, emanations from civilizations *can* travel at least as fast as the speed of light—our radio signals, for example. We've heard nothing so far. This probably means that civilizations periodically arise out of the mathematical vastness of the universe, but die off before they are able to talk to each other.[69]

Why might that be? One common answer is that at the kind of timescale we're talking about, entire cultures die off in the briefest flash. Given the threats we're now facing, it seems reasonable to consider rampant uncontrolled technological change as a plausible candidate for what might cause a civilization serious harm. So the stakes of adapting our culture and law to our technological capability are pretty high. If we do not figure out how to adapt human social forms to rapid technological shifts, we may not get a second bite at the apple.

We are playing for all the marbles. There are mistakes we can make (cooking the planet, for example) that will cause us as a species to stop shouting into the dark, to stop being the sole source of intelligence-generated radio waves we've ever seen. Any science fiction movie is a good candidate. I think one really good candidate for an event that causes us to stop shouting into the dark is that we fail to keep up with technological change when we could have done so. If things come off the rails, if there is a discontinuity in the smooth acceleration of social and hard technologies side by side, we enter the realm of the boring end of the world. This is hardly the stuff of sci fi. As T. S. Eliot wrote, "This is the way the world ends / Not with a bang but a whimper."[70]

The goal of this book is to conceive of law as an adaptive social technology that seeks to stop things from flying off the rails. The goal is to keep us alive, and keep us thriving. The goal is to keep human expression of preference a vital part of machine-human civilization. The goal is to keep us shouting into the dark for a long time.

HOW TO STAY ON THE RAILS

The question is whether we can rework how we think about social technology in general, and law in particular, in time to iterate it and progress it fast enough to keep up with hard technological change. It is possible. To do so, we need to

---

[69] *See* Kevin Loria, *There's a Compelling Explanation for Why We've Never Found Aliens—and It Could Mean Humanity Is Doomed*, BUS. INSIDER (Jun. 25, 2018), www.businessinsider.com /climate-change-could-answer-fermi-paradox-2018-6.

[70] T. S. ELIOT, THE COMPLETE POEMS AND PLAYS 1909–1930 59 (2014).

do something that has been alien to many conceptions of law: embrace change.

The conversation we need to have will focus less on the fact that laws *do* change and more on reconceptualizing law *as* change. Instead of focusing on how laws change, and on charting that path, we ought to see what we do as lawyers, lawgivers, and lawmakers (and all of us are, since all law is created by everyday human interactions) as focused on the principles of guiding that change, of managing change and the speed of change, of figuring out how to create communities of people who generate life-giving rules more quickly and responsively to changes in their environment.

More specifically, I am interested in viewing law as the discipline of developing social technological tools to help humans coordinate in the face of hard technological change. The focus here therefore is on the means of developing the language of law, rather than on any given rule. Change needs to enter the core of law, rather than lurk at its periphery. It needs to be the core of the philosophy of law, not an exception. I would like to see rapid and controlled legal change become central to the project of law. We need new vocabularies, not new rules.[71] We need new ways of talking about the problems of the future, not solutions expressed in the old languages. With a shift in the entire vocabulary of law, unsolvable problems can become nonproblems. For example, business scholar Shoshana Zuboff gives as an example the question, how many hours should a child work in a factory?[72] The way to answer that question is to unask it. It's a ridiculous question, because we have established different and more developed values for children. Having unasked the question, we can focus on other, more productive ones. Generating that shift, generating new entire vocabularies for talking about law, should become law's central project.

To do that, we need to change our conception of what law is. We can do that because a concept, or a conception, is precisely what law is in the first place. "Law" is a word, expressed in the English language, which entered that language during a time when parts of England and Scotland were under Danish rule. The part of the island subject to Danish laws was termed the "Danelaw," and traces of that history are still found in place names with a distinct norse air to them. "Lag" in Old Norse became "Lagu" in Old English, and eventually, "law."[73]

---

[71]   *See* Richard Rorty, Contingency, Irony, and Solidarity (1989).

[72]   *See* John Naughton, *"The Goal Is to Automate Us": Welcome to the Age of Surveillance Capitalism*, The Guardian (Jan 20, 2019), www.theguardian.com/technology/2019/jan/20/s hoshana-zuboff-age-of-surveillance-capitalism-google-facebook.

[73]   *See*, Edward Zimmermann, *The Public Prosecutor System in Germany*, 3 Law Mag. & Rev. Monthly J. Juris. & Int'l L. Both Branches Leg. Prof. Home & Abroad 4th ser. 640, 644 (1874).

Even a single word can trigger complex conceptual frameworks, and that is what "law" does. "The Law," at least in the modern quasi-democratic framing of the idea, is a social construct, a cooperative fiction, a conception, a piece of social technology maintained and defined by a professional class. What the law "is" might be usefully described as a half-constructed, half-evolved language comprising cooperative fictions held in the minds of attorneys, judges, juries, outlaws, executioners, journalists, and layfolk. That conception invokes endless smaller pieces of social ritual and technology. The "courtroom drama" ritual that infests police procedurals is one such example. A deposition is another constituent piece of social technology: a particular form, format, pattern, and duration of recorded conversation, selected (again by both rational impulses and evolutionary pressures) for its value in flushing out and locking down the testimony of one party in a dispute.

Language plays a leading role in the development of the law.[74] First, law might be accurately described as a system of social software that runs on words. Those words have been retooled for the occasion, narrowed, made precise, and shaped into terms of art. It would be a mistake to think, for example, that the words "good faith" as drafted by an attorney in a contract would have much at all to do with the general society's view of the words "good" or "faith." And with this insight we can name one basic means by which law changes: as the meaning of legal terms of art change, and as the frameworks and structures within which the terms are change, so the meaning of the law, its method of application, indeed, the rule itself, changes. To lawyers this will all be familiar. To the layperson, the idea that a court might import a legal test from a completely different area of law, or reverse a prior decision without changing the dominant phrasing of the governing legal test at all, might seem odd. An example of the former would be the widespread use, across almost every legal context, of legal tests like "reasonableness" (which means? What a reasonable member of the community would think, of course!). An example of the latter would be interpretation of the commander-in-chief clause of the US Constitution, which states that the president is commander in chief of the Army and Navy, but doesn't mention the Air Force. Yet for obvious enough reasons, no court would hold that the words "Army and Navy of the United States" don't include the Air Force.

---

[74] The other major component to legal rules is force, either the soft force of incentives or the traditional force of the group (as enacted by a police force, for example) to enforce its rules. That social component of law changes too, of course. How could it not: the kind of force with which police routinely did their jobs twenty years ago has become obsolete thanks to the invention of the smartphone.

Law is a social technology that itself develops social tools. It is a language about language. It is self-referential and recursive. Recursive language defines itself in terms of itself. The standard math joke is to provide a definition of recursion as "*see* 'recursion.'" Self-referential language is similar: it talks about itself, although not solely in terms of itself. This is all easy to see in normal, natural language: we talk about whether things are "fair," and in doing so we use language like "just" or "equal," which recursively draw their meaning from words like "fair." Law also uses language self-referentially: lawyers talk about what "fair" or "just" mean all the time. We often experience this as a deepening of the meaning of a word through its use in specific use-contexts: "fair" gains meaning through justice done in specific cases.

These attributes of the natural language of law are directly opposed to some key characteristics of formal languages, the foundations of math and computer science. Formal languages, like those used to build various formal logics, are alien to the language of the law, for a very specific reason. Legal language must reason about itself, from outside itself. Formal logic systems cannot. Consider, for one last bit of math, Fermat's Last Theorem. In 1637, Pierre de Fermat, a French lawyer and mathematician, proposed that no three integers a, b, and c satisfied the equation $a^n + b^n = c^n$ for any integer value of n greater than 2. You might recall the Pythagorean theorem from geometry, in which $a^2 + b^2 = c^2$ for a triangle with sides 3, 4, and 5, for example. What Fermat conjectured was that there was no such equality for any power greater than 2. There was no Pythagorean theorem to the third power or higher.

It took hundreds of years to prove that Fermat was right, and the math of that proof is over my head. But what I want to do is use Fermat's Last Theorem to show something about math and computer science, and by extension formal (logical) languages. Let us imagine a computer scientist who wants to disprove Fermat's theorem. All she would need is any set of numbers a, b, and c, in which $a^n + b^n = c^n$, with n >2. She might choose to brute force the issue by writing a computer program that simply checks different arrays of numbers. Let's try our good old 3, 4, 5 right triangle: $3^3 (27) + 4^3 (64) = 91$. The cube root of 91 is . . . 4.5 and change. Not an integer.

But our computer scientist, undaunted, leaves the program running. She codes the program so that if it finds a solution, it should print the solution and stop. If it doesn't find a solution, it should continue with another set of numbers. She calls this her Fermat Brute Force (FBF) program.

Here's the problem: such a computer program might run forever. In fact, given that mathematicians now have proven Fermat's Last Theorem, we know that *no* combination of integers will fit the bill. Such a computer program *will* run forever, because it can never accomplish its task. Or, as is familiar enough to all computer users, the computer will "hang." The program will run in perpetuity, never stopping, always checking.

Fair enough. But say our computer scientist decides to write a program to check programs like FBF to make sure they won't hang. Such a program might say: "Check [program X]. If [program X] will hang, report back: HANG. If [program X] doesn't hang, report back: SAFE." But in checking FBF, our program Check [FBF] has to reference FBF. It has to run FBF. And if it does, the checking program will itself hang. In short: there is no way to do math except to do the math. There is no way to check a program other than referencing, or emulating it. And any emulation of a program that will hang will itself hang. This is, in short, why we cannot have perfect bug-checking software: the only way to check if a program will hang is to run it, and if we do, our checker will also never report back. It needs to recurse, but because it's a formal language, it can't. This is computer science's famous "halting problem."

This is not to say we cannot solve problems like Fermat's Last Theorem: we can, by using language *outside* the formal system. A formal system, no matter how powerful, will always have blind spots, true statements it cannot reach by application of its own logic. And those blind spots will emerge when the formal system references itself. In fact, one cannot see those blind spots *until* a formal language has enough complexity and power to be able to describe itself. But as soon as it can, pools of truth emerge that the formal system will never reach. This is what Kurt Gödel referred to as "incompleteness." Any formal language with enough power to describe itself must be incomplete. For any formal logic or language, there are true statements that the logic of that language cannot reach. For that, one must rely on outside language, on other formal logics, and most of all on the natural language discussions that generate formal logics.

This is why, by the way, all the trendy legal papers arguing that we ought to reduce law to a coded formal system are nonsense: it's demonstrably impossible. Law must be general, self-descriptive, and self-referential: able to address all problems and contexts. It is not, and cannot be, a formal logical system, because every such system develops blind spots when powerful enough to describe itself. If formal languages are consistent but incomplete, the natural language of law must be complete but inconsistent, capable of formulating different systems and logics to cover blind spots, at the cost of more than occasionally contradicting itself.

The natural language of law follows a markedly different path than that of formal languages and logics. Law develops tools using language and adds those tools to a set of social practices, a social conception of living under "the law." By studying how the language of law has been constructed and evolved, we ought to be able to get some understanding of the mechanisms by which this social technology is adapted to new circumstances. Once we know what we are dealing with, we can then begin to talk about ways to either energize the dynamic processes of law or discuss areas where we may need to break with tradition, to adopt new means of inquiry from other successful scientific fields (and here I expressly include the fields of linguistics, behavioral economics, and sociology, all of which seem to me to have serious claims in the space) and speed things up.

We need to develop language to allow us to talk about and address the demands of the future, and we need to do it quickly. In order to understand each other, and to understand the problems we face, we have to build the language we need.

3

Technology Law

Law is the projection of an imagined future upon reality.
— Robert M. Cover, *Violence and the Word*[1]

My claim is that law can keep up with hard technology. This chapter shows how it has done so in the past, and suggests some mechanisms for doing so going forward. Throughout, I argue that providing coordinating language to help humans navigate a shifting technological landscape is much closer to the central project of law than our current thinking about law might suggest. Handling technological change by developing new language and symbols is a major part of what law does.

Of course, in talking about how law has traditionally handled technological change, I have to admit that past performance is no guarantee of future returns. The mechanisms of law that create coordinating language in the face of technological change might now be failing after thousands of years and multiple technological revolutions. But perhaps not. By showing how law has successfully stayed ahead of technology, I hope to shift the burden of proof to those who claim law can't now do what it has always more or less successfully done.

And that is a burden that cannot be sustained. Their best evidence is obsolete statutes: statutes that have lost their meaning due to technological shift. There is no denying that there are many such out-of-date rules. But as we will explore, claiming that law cannot evolve by pointing to obsolete rules still in the lawbooks makes as much sense as denying the theory of evolution by pointing to extinct species in the fossil record. Like any evolving system, the fact that the landscape is littered with extinct ideas is evidence in favor of a successful dynamic process, not evidence against it.

---

[1] Robert M. Cover, *Violence and the Word*, 95 YALE L.J. 1601, 1604 (1986).

We've seen the argument that law can't keep up with technology fail many times before. It is just that—an argument, not a fact—made by those who, ironically enough, wish to avoid the very law they claim can't touch them. Napster argued it, before reality—and copyright infringement lawsuits—set in.[2] For virtual worlds, academics talked about a "magic circle" that should keep real world law out of virtual communities and online spaces, but of course that was also a bust.[3] And most recently, cryptocurrency enthusiasts claimed that *they* had finally created a technology no law could touch[4]—until they learned that the FBI and FinCEN *could* touch them for their Darknet drug deals, and the banking regulators knocked on the doors of the crypto-currency exchanges, copy of the Bank Secrecy Act in hand.[5] In short, the statement that "law can't keep up" is not a fact, but an argument, and except in very limited circumstances,[6] is a fairly silly and self-serving assertion that has failed over and over again.

DO SEARCH BOTS DREAM OF ELECTRIC SHEEP?

Let us begin with an example of law handling technological change. One of my favorites is a story of how an ancient law against bothering sheep came to be the law governing internet web crawlers and Google's search bots.

In the late 1990s, CompuServe had a problem. It had grown to be one of the largest online service providers in the United States, and its many users were plagued by unwanted emails, spam, from an advertising outfit called Cyber

---

[2]   *See* A&M Record, Inc. v. Napster, Inc., 239 F.3d 1004, 1014 (9th Cir. 2001) (Napster claimed that due to how the technology worked, it did not perform copyright infringement, rather its users did.) The Court held that Napster was liable for Contributory Infringement and affirmed an injunction against it. *Id.* at 1029.

[3]   Joshua A. T. Fairfield, *The Magic Circle*, 14 VAND. J. ENT. & TECH. L. 545 (2012).

[4]   *See* Sheng Zhou, *Bitcoin Laundromats for Dirty Money: The Bank Secrecy Act's (BSA) Inadequacies in Regulating and Enforcing Money Laundering Laws over Virtual Currencies and the Internet*, 3 J. OF L. & CYBER WARFARE 103 (2014).

[5]   *See, e.g.*, Norman Roos, *New FinCEN Cryptocurrency Guidance Clarifies Applicability of Anti-Money Laundering Regulations to Virtual Currency Business Models*, THE NAT'L L. R. (May 23, 2019), www.natlawreview.com/article/new-fincen-cryptocurrency-guidance-clarifies-applicability-anti-money-laundering; Steve Hudak, *FinCEN Fines BTC-e Virtual Currency Exchange $110 Million for Facilitating Ransomware, Dark Net Drug Sales*, FINANCIAL CRIMES ENFORCEMENT NETWORK (Jul. 27, 2017), www.fincen.gov/news/news-releases/fincen-fines-btc-e-virtual-currency-exchange-110-million-facilitating-ransomware.

[6]   Such as a limited "sandbox" period for a new technology, during which regulators might forbear for a while to let the technology develop. Note, though, that this argument often is misappropriated by tech lobbyists to argue for perpetual regulatory paralysis rather than limited forbearance.

Promotions.[7] To solve the problem, CompuServe turned to the old law of trespass.[8] Under that law, if you step on someone else's land without permission, you're liable. If someone enters your land without permission, you don't have to prove that they did any damage.[9] To protect the sanctity of property and the owner's right to exclude interlopers, a claim of trespass can succeed without proof of harm. It's simple. If you come on the land, you're liable.

Convincing a court to apply the old law of trespass to the new practice of email spam took some good lawyering. Indeed, the law of trespass to land was not a great fit for spam. Do mail carriers trespass on your land every time they deliver the mail? When the FedEx delivery guy shows up, can he not come up to your door to deliver the package? What about junk mail? Does it not get the same privileges even if it is a pain to throw it all out? Suppose a company sets up a server and invites the world to send emails to it. How would a potential sender know to what extent they are allowed to do so before they are a trespasser?

All of this is to say: the law of trespass was not a shoo-in. We could have refrained from applying any law and simply let advertisers spam CompuServe users. We could have asked the legislature to draw up a law regulating spam. Eventually, in fact, they did the latter.[10] It did not do much good—just take a look at your spam folder.

The better option is to adapt an old law with some similarities to our new situation. Law progresses by analogy, not formal logic: by relating old stories to new contexts. In this context, the courts grappled with the problem of applying trespass to land to what was essentially a trespass to personal property—the servers. So they adapted the law. Instead of holding that any contact with a server is a potential trespass, they used a twist on trespass law called trespass to chattels.[11] In traditional common law, one party was not permitted to trespass on another's land. But what if one party didn't actually trespass on the land, but instead bothered, say, someone's sheep? That is, what if they interfered with a person's personal property? The law termed personal property "chattel," and developed a theory that if one person "trespassed" on another's chattel by bothering their sheep or otherwise interfering with the owner's rightful enjoyment and possession of it, then the owner had a cause of action called trespass

---

[7] CompuServe Inc. v. Cyber Promotions, 962 F. Supp. 1015, 1017 (S.D. Ohio 1997).
[8] *Id.*
[9] *Id.* at 1023 ("[D]amage is assumed where there is a trespass to real property ...").
[10] *See* CAN-SPAM ACT of 2003, 117 Stat. 2699 (2003).
[11] *See, e.g.,* RESTATEMENT (SECOND) OF TORTS §§ 217–218 (1965), and W. PAGE KEETON, PROSSER AND KEATON ON TORTS § 14 (5th ed. 1984).

to chattels. (We can see law's evolution here too: the idea of trespass shifted from land to other property.)

Trespass to chattels had become nearly obsolete by the late twentieth century because its big brother, a cause of action called "conversion," had taken over the field.[12] When someone messes with someone else's personal property, the owner either wants it back (it's not damaged) or doesn't (it is damaged). If someone took your personal property without your permission, you can get it back with a common law cause of action called "replevin." If you don't want your stuff back, and instead you want money, you can force the defendant to buy the goods in an action called "conversion."[13] Trespass to chattels falls in between: the person has interfered with your personal property enough that you could bring a lawsuit, but not so much that you want to invoke the "you broke it, you bought it" rule of conversion.

Trespass to chattels required greater proof and reaped less damages-wise than an action in conversion. It fell into disuse.[14] That is, until courts started looking around for a way to remedy the harm that spammers caused to the systems they spammed. They decided that trespass to chattels—the old law of sheep-bothering—struck the appropriate balance of interests and was rhetorically convincing.[15] Servers were personal property—chattel. Spam "bothered" them. After all, spam caused processing load. That might impede server function if spamming reached high enough volumes.[16] On the other hand, email systems are set up to receive email, just like a mailbox is setup to receive mail. Getting a few letters in your mailbox is not an interference with your use and enjoyment of the mailbox; that's why it is there. Stuffing the mailbox with so many junk letters that no legitimate traffic can get through would be another matter.[17]

The newly born law of cybertrespass then branched out, adapting to new situations that seemed similar enough to make the comparison worthwhile. For example, when one party sends a program to another's website to repeatedly query a database, that can cause a lot of server load. In one case, auction aggregator site Bidder's Edge gathered information about auctions from around the web and put them all in one place.[18] Auction site eBay did not like that arrangement, because it wanted people to come to eBay's website

---

[12]   *See* W. PAGE KEETON, PROSSER AND KEATON ON TORTS § 14 (5th ed. 1984) (discussing how conversion has replaced trespass to chattels as a cause of action, resulting trespass to chattels being referred to as the little brother of conversion).
[13]   *Id.* at § 15.
[14]   *Id.* at § 14.
[15]   *See Compuserve,* 962 F. Supp. at 1019.
[16]   *See* School of Visual Arts v. Kuprewicz, 771 N.Y.S.2d 804 (Sup. Ct. 2003).
[17]   *See* Intel Corp. v. Hamidi, 30 Cal. 4th 1342 (2003).
[18]   Ebay, Inc. v. Bidder's Edge, Inc., 100 F. Supp. 2d 1058, 1061 (N.D. Cal. 2000).

(and see eBay's advertising, and give eBay their traffic data) instead of using the aggregator.[19] But eBay had no claim to the raw facts of its auctions. Instead, eBay used a cybertrespass claim: Bidder's Edge bots routinely "scraped" or "crawled" eBay's website—repeatedly querying eBay's database in order to keep the auction aggregators accurate.[20] The result slowed eBay server performance and frustrated customers who were unable to get their own queries in edgewise amid the storm of automated requests.[21] A federal court in California therefore decided that Bidder's Edge interfered with eBay's interest in its servers, and that such use caused damage to eBay.[22]

In *CompuServe v. Cyber Promotions* and *eBay v. Bidder's Edge*, two different courts brought the law of trespass, which was firmly rooted in the physical properties of real space, to less tangible cyberspace. They did not stray too far, however. Trespass to chattels, unlike trespass to land, requires some demonstration of harm to the property, however slight.[23] Standing on the shoulders of a previous court's decision that electronic signals are tangible enough for a trespass,[24] both decisions reasoned that there was some physical harm to the server: valuable space was taken up and processing speed slowed, which impaired the value to the owner in serving actual customers.[25]

Soon after, cases popped up in which the physical servers were being used irritatingly, but not enough to diminish their value to their owners. First, after Tickets.com repeatedly pulled event information off Ticketmaster's website, the court evaluated a claim for trespass in line with *eBay Corp. v. Bidder's Edge*.[26] Many facts were similar. Tickets.com was compiling information about how to buy tickets for as many events as it possibly could.[27] It used web crawlers to pull the information off Ticketmaster's event pages to compile on their own website and link back to the original event page.[28] Tickets.com was not making the sale, but Ticketmaster objected to the fact that Tickets.com would deep link straight to the event page, bypassing Ticketmaster's home page and directories (and its

---

[19] *Id.* at 1062.
[20] *Id.*
[21] *Id.*
[22] *Id.* at 1071.
[23] *See, e.g.,* RESTATEMENT (SECOND) OF TORTS §§ 217–218 (1965); W. PAGE KEETON, PROSSER AND KEATON ON TORTS § 14 (5th ed. 1984).
[24] *See* Thrifty-Tel, Inc. v. Bezenek, 54 Cal. Rptr. 2d 468 (Ct. App. 1996).
[25] *See* Bidder's Edge, 100 F. Supp. 2d at 1071; CompuServe, 962 F. Supp. at 1028.
[26] *See* Ticketmaster Corp. v. Tickets.Com, Inc., No. CV997654HLHVBKX, 2003 WL 21406289, at *3 (C.D. Cal. Mar. 7, 2003).
[27] *Id.* at *1.
[28] *Id.* at *2.

advertisements).[29] Was Tickets.com impairing the use of Ticketmaster's servers? The court said no. Not only was there no real burden on the servers, but its actions were not even interfering with their basic function. A trespass to personal property needs to show that something was done to that property beyond its ordinary use that further impaired its function.[30]

In a case called *Intel Corp. v. Hamidi*,[31] the California Supreme Court added another twist to the emerging law of cybertrespass. A disgruntled former employee had sent emails criticizing Intel to all its employees.[32] Although he sent emails on just six occasions, he sent them to tens of thousands of employees at once.[33] Intel did not love the emails, which caused conversation between employees on company time.[34] Intel tried to block Hamidi, but he evaded the then-crude spam filters by switching computers.[35] The lower courts felt that Intel's interest in its employees working with company computers was compromised by intrusive distractions like this, and upheld the trespass claim. A lower court felt that Hamidi disrupted Intel's business in using its own property, and that was harm enough.[36] On appeal, however, the Supreme Court of California reversed.[37] Intel's servers were not noticeably burdened by the emails.[38] Ultimately, what was objectionable was not the quantity but the employee-distracting content.[39] The harm was not to the property trespassed upon or its function. However, if the quantity were large enough that it measurably slowed the servers, that would be a different matter.[40] The California Supreme Court struck a balance. Hamidi was permitted to send a few emails to Intel employees. But if he sent too many, the court would count that as interference with Intel's use and enjoyment of its servers, and would order Hamidi (or spammers like him) to stop.

We have evolved from the law of sheep-bothering to the law of web-crawling. A rule that was used to keep farmers from harassing each other's livestock is now used to keep roaming artificial intelligences from download-ing databases. This law is not finished. Serious questions remain. For

---

[29] *Id.*
[30] *Id.* at *3.
[31] Intel Corp. v. Hamidi, 30 Cal. 4th 1342 (2003).
[32] *Id.* at 1349.
[33] *Id.*
[34] *Id.*
[35] *Id.*
[36] *Id.* at 1350.
[37] *Id.* at 1357–58.
[38] *Id.*
[39] *Id.* at 1359.
[40] *Id.* at 1381–82.

example, my university does not maintain its own email servers, it runs its email through Microsoft Exchange. If a cybertrespass claim were to crop up, does an administrator need to own the server to assert the claim, or may they merely have rented the processor cycles that are being abused? It seems like an easy call; courts going forward should have no problem extending cyber-trespass to cloud-computing models. Just like a renter is entitled to claim trespass against an interloper,[41] so a cloud computing customer is entitled to claim cybertrespass even if they themselves do not maintain any physical server.

This kind of reasoning is, again, analogical. The idea is that there is nothing new under the sun, that old stories can apply to new contexts. This adaptation through analogy, through story, is what law does. It engages in a series of decisions that function as experimental steps for the overall project of law, testing each case against the relevant need. The trick is to serve current needs while providing a structure that supports continuous adaptation. Each step is linked to the past for credibility and stability but adapts to future situations. From land to sheep to email to web-crawling robots, we tweak the law thoughtfully and creatively, keeping what works and discarding what doesn't.

In such a system, it is not accurate to state that law lags technology. We may even say law *anticipates* technology. The oldest cases routinely provide the narrative from which we decide the newest technological issues. Certainly when we worked out the rules for scaring livestock nobody could have foreseen the problems created by wide-ranging search bots operating on a global electronic communications network. But the law of trespass to chattels embeds good intuitions about balancing one person's ownership with another's casual interaction. It is fine if you pet my dog, just don't pet him so much that his hair falls off! It's fine if you link my content, just don't give my server the Internet hug of death.[42] When it comes to interacting with the personal property of others, some contact is fine, even necessary, as in the case of the mail carrier and the mailbox. But the idea that scale can lead to damage is a response to human incentives to abuse the property of others. Although the technology has changed from sheep to robots, in this respect, humans have pretty much stayed the same.

---

[41] *See* RESTATEMENT (SECOND) OF TORTS § 329.
[42] A hug of death can occur when a posting on a website leads to exponential traffic and overwhelms the website. For an example, see Thibaud Jobert, *Story of a Reddit Hug of Death and Lessons Learned*, MEDIUM (Sep. 27, 2016), https://medium.com/codingame/story-of-a-reddit-hug-of-death-and-lessons-learned-3565bb8a6793.

THERE IS NOTHING NEW UNDER THE SUN

Using analogical reasoning and narrative, we often use the oldest cases to solve the newest problems. Why? What do these rules show? For one thing, it's a legal jungle out there. A common law rule that has survived significant technological upheaval is resilient. It does not stand athwart technological change. It provides a cognitive/logical framework for accommodating change, a workable legal solution at lower cost than technology-specific legislation. It allows human values to persevere and human rules to remain recognizable across time while permitting flexibility in adapting those rules to the new markets occasioned by technology. It saves a lot of time teaching people, because the new rules are actually old rules.

Let's take a very simple example: the law of how we get stuff. The first case that most law students study in Intro to Property, *Pierson v. Post*, looks at the law of capture.[43] It's a rule that every four year old can recite: "I had it first!" But why? Why should the person who gets something first have a superior claim to a person who will put it to more productive use, or who will value it more, or even who needs it more?

The law of capture is not a law we apply to mature property systems. You can't yell "dibs" on a house as you enter a gated community. Someone already owns that, and they weren't the first possessor either. Even many governments, the source of all title, often weren't the first possessor. They took the land from someone else.[44]

We don't usually ask who captured something first. Unless, of course, the thing was previously unowned. Look around. Why would something be unowned? As legal scholar Saul Levmore points out, perhaps a thing is unowned because we have not propertized it yet. It isn't useful yet.[45] Consider the airspace over your home. Since Roman law, landowners supposedly owned their land *cuius est solum, eius est usque ad coelum et ad inferos*.[46] The sole owner owned the land to the heavens and to the center of the earth. All that changed with aircraft.[47] There was no reason to control air traffic routes until airplanes were a thing. Or the satellite routes that spin over your property. Or spectrum. Until the radio and its massive popularization as

---

43 Pierson v. Post, 3 Cai. R. 175 (N.Y. Sup. Ct. 1805) at 179.
44 *See, e.g.*, Johnson v. M'Intosh, 21 U.S. 543, 5 L. Ed. 681 (1823).
45 *See* Saul Levmore, *Property's Uneasy Path and Expanding Future*, 70 U. Chi. L. Rev. 181, 186 (2003).
46 "Whoever owns the soil owns everything up to the sky and down to the depths." Black's Law Dictionary 1834 (9th ed. 2009).
47 *See, e.g.*, Peter H. Sand, Jorge de Sousa Freitas & Geoffrey N. Pratt, *An Historical Survey of International Air Law before the Second World War*, 7 McGill L. J. 24, 25 (1960).

the primary means of communicating information (the internet still runs on it, at least the mobile version)[48] there was no need to allocate bandwidth. With technology came the need for property.[49] And then the land rush was on.

We see land grabs across the technological spectrum. Do you know someone whose Gmail account is just their name? They got the address early. Someone whose Twitter handle is just their name? Same deal. As the internet expanded, entrepreneurs grabbed domain names that reflected companies' protected trademarks. The companies, most notably McDonald's, had delayed entering a forum that they thought might just be a fad.[50] They paid the price by having to clear squatters off their digital land.[51]

We replace Wild West land grabs with mature land title systems—all of which often overlay on other, older conceptions for how to use and care for land.[52] Which, then, is the "core" of property? None, really. Land grabs get a resource newly developed by technology into operation as quickly as possible, and land title systems make sure that the developed resource can pass to the highest value user for minimum transaction costs through the market mechanism. Property seen this way is a method for bringing the fruits of technological development into rapid production and eventual introduction to markets.

The capture rule makes appearances in old and new stories. Land development in the American West was spurred by a capture rule: the Homesteading Act[53]—which you may recall from the Laura Ingalls Wilder books[54]—followed by a title rule: the everyday title deed that you use to buy and sell your

---

[48] See *Verizon Turns on World's First Commercial 5G Network in Sacramento*, N.Y. TIMES: BUSINESS DAY MARKETS, Dec. 17, 2018, https://markets.on.nytimes.com/research/stocks/news/press_release.asp?docTag=201810010730PRIMZONEFULLFEED7395382&feedID=600&press_symbol=283359.

[49] See Saul Levmore, *Property's Uneasy Path and Expanding Future*, 70 U. CHI. L. REV. 181, 186 (2003).

[50] See, e.g., Joshua Quittner, *Billions Registered*, WIRED (Oct. 1, 1994), www.wired.com/1994/10/mcdonalds/?pg=4&topic= (discussing how the author Joshua Quittner purchased the domain name mcdonalds.com while writing this article for Wired about how big corporations were neglecting to register their domain names; he compares himself to "McPrometheus" having stolen the "McFire").

[51] See Frederic M. Wilf, *Law (or the Lack of It) on the Web: A Primer for Financial Services Technology Manages*, in FINANCIAL SERVICES INFORMATION SYSTEMS 373 (Jessica Keyes ed., 2000).

[52] Johnson v. M'Intosh, 21 U.S. 543 (1823).

[53] GENERAL HOMESTEAD ACT, c. 75, 12 Stat. 392 (May 20, 1862), repealed by Pub. L. 94–579, Title VII, § 702, 90 Stat. 2787 (Oct. 21, 1976).

[54] See generally LAURA INGALLS WILDER, THE LITTLE HOUSE ON THE PRAIRIE (1932) and its sequels.

home. If oil lies under two neighbors' land, who gets it? We use the law of capture when we find new oil deposits—the first owner of land above who extracts the oil below owns it.[55] We use it for asteroids. The US Commercial Space Launch Competitiveness Act[56] was signed in 2015, permitting commercial miners to appropriate whatever resources they can extract from the Moon, asteroids, or other celestial bodies. In short, the law of capture is an intentional attempt to kickstart technological exploitation of newly discovered or developed resources.

My point here is less one about property and more about how law develops. It is a series of negotiated approximations. A language is worked out that governs an area of law—in property, the question is how to allocate scarce resources in groups—and as the circumstances change, the language mutates while remaining rooted in the past. Law reasons analogically within groups over time. The groups keep what works and discard what doesn't. The narratives generated by law provide examples that are the foundation for new decisions. When asteroid mining was developed, we didn't have to reinvent the book—we went to the old law of capturing foxes, or oil, or what-have-you, to understand the rules we were going to use in space. This is why it's a little bit silly to say that technology outpaces law—law is a set of narratives that creates a language for talking about what we might do when new things come up.

Law adapts past rules to new cases by deciding which stories apply best. From the very first cases students read in law school to the highest echelons of practice, law is deeply involved with the art of the new. New cases are studied carefully because they set precedent. New technologies are promptly the source of heated litigation. Old cases are prized and studied, as we've been doing, not because they are currently relevant but because they provide examples of toolsets, logic, compelling stories, and techniques used to successfully adapt human systems to technological ones.

Some rules get left behind in technological foment. But this is very different from saying that law in general cannot handle technological change. To use an evolutionary analogy, saying that some species cannot handle an asteroid impact does not indicate that life cannot handle even the most rapidly changing ecosystem.

Rules that fail to provide salience in the face of technological change cease to have meaning, and thus pass away. Those that continue to provide guidance

---

[55]   *See* Bruce M. Kramer; Owen L. Anderson, *The Rule of Capture—An Oil and Gas Perspective*, 35 Envtl. L. 899 (2005).

[56]   US Commercial Space Launch Competitiveness Act, Pub. L. No. 114–90 (Nov. 25, 2015).

have force. A legal rule that survives, that continues to influence human action, has some characteristic that helps it do so. Most often, this is marked not by a rule's reaction to change, but by its ability to anticipate and embody change.

WHAT HAS BEEN DONE WILL BE DONE AGAIN

By "anticipate and embody change" I do not mean that law prophesies particular technologies or futures. Rather, it expects that change will occur and isn't stymied when it does. I invite us to challenge received wisdom that law must trail technological shift. Law instead plays a critical role in anticipating technological change. Law can keep up. In fact, I argue that what makes law "law" is its ability to survive and regulate human behavior despite technological change.

In other words, law is law only as long as it stays relevant in the face of technological change. The law that not only keeps up, but anticipates technological change by providing a compelling, multifaceted story with multiple applications, is the law that rules. Adapting to change is law's function, and it has successfully done its job for thousands of years. We can see this by looking at how law anticipates and handles emerging questions of technology using principles of narrative and analogy.[57]

Law works the way language works: by using old words to create new systems of meanings. For example, how should the culture of the 1850s United States have solved the question of what legal regime is best for human chattel slavery? Our solution is very different from what would have been (and was) proposed at the time. Today, law has answered the problem of human chattel slavery not by determining the best way of doing human chattel slavery, but by creating systems of symbol and meaning in which it is impossible not to understand that all humans are created equal, and that every person has equal rights under the rule of law. When we create new law through narrative, we start by speaking metaphorically. The statement that "all people are created equal" is a good example. It's obvious that all people are not equal, and it is not at all clear they were created. But through use, we add to our meaning of equal the idea of "equal" contained in the sentence "all people are created equal." Now *equal* means legal and dignitary equality. A language system, a system of symbols and understanding that is grounded on the idea that all people are

---

[57] Although the examples I use here are primarily from the common law tradition, the insights are applicable to civil law jurisdictions as well, simply recast through different cultural institutions, some of which I discuss later in this chapter and chapter 8.

equal under the rule of law, grows into a system of thought that makes human chattel slavery impossible to countenance.[58] By changing our language, we changed the meaning of *equal*; we made a metaphorical statement ("all people are created equal") that had never been true in human history into a literal one.

Philosopher Richard Rorty made this case cleanly. The way to advance our ability to deal with problems is not to solve the issues that are presented to us in current language; it is to develop new languages of working and living together that make the problems solvable, or even the expression of the problem unthinkable. The question, "what is the best legal regime for human chattel slavery?" *goes away* in any system grounded on the cooperative fictions of the rule of law. Or, as Rorty instructs us: "[T]hink of the history of language, and thus of culture, as Darwin taught us to think of the history of a coral reef. Old metaphors are constantly dying off into literalness, and then serving as a platform and foil for new metaphors."[59]

Again, we can see this in the law by taking a look at the driest and dustiest cases, the ones that start pretty much every law school class, and examining how those cases have continuing salience today—not because of the specific rule they hand down, but because they provide a rich and adaptable vocabulary for future courts dealing with new cases, and because they demonstrate how commonly the law is tasked with managing how we adapt our social technology to our physical ones.

In Contracts, for example, students often begin with discussion of *Hawkins v. McGee*,[60] the infamous "hairy hand" case. The case is famous both because of its common use in legal education and because it made it into movies like *The Paper Chase* and *On the Basis of Sex*, which is as close to being in law school as some people ever want to be. As the 1929 case lays out, George Hawkins' palm was badly burned when he was a child, leaving serious scarring.[61] Dr. McGee guaranteed Hawkins' father that he would make the boy's hand a "one hundred percent good hand" by way of skin graft.[62] Because

---

[58] There were then, as there are now, counternarratives. We have evolved new forms of slavery through public and private for-profit prisons, for example, or the recurring practice of jailing debtors. *See, e.g.,* MICHELLE ALEXANDER, THE NEW JIM CROW: MASS INCARCERATION IN THE AGE OF COLORBLINDNESS (2010).

[59] RICHARD RORTY, CONTINGENCY, IRONY, AND SOLIDARITY 16 (1989).

[60] Hawkins v. McGee, 84 N.H. 114, 146 A. 641 (N.H. 1929). The "hairy hand" is only referenced in a subsequent case, McGee v. United States Fidelity & Guaranty Co., 53 F.2D 953 (1st Cir. 1931).

[61] *Hawkins*, 146 A. at 642.

[62] *Id.* at 642–43.

Dr. McGee took skin from Hawkins' chest, his palm grew thick hair, which was (quite understandably) distressing for Hawkins.[63]

Oddly, the case is an exceptionally boring one for experienced lawyers. The case stands for the proposition that if someone breaches a contract, the victim of the breach can get her "expectation" damages—that is, the difference between what the breacher promised and what the victim of the breach actually got.[64] In *Hawkins*, the difference was between the hairy hand that Hawkins got and the "one hundred percent good hand" that McGee promised him. Lawyers can take the fun out of anything.

What's interesting about the case is not the measure of contract damages for which it is known in law books. The case is interesting because it does not really reflect the realities of contracting at all. When was the last time your doctor signed a contract with you promising you a one hundred percent positive outcome on a medical procedure? Here's a hint: never. Even when doctors do make mistakes—bad ones—the legal system does not address these errors through contract law.[65] Instead, a patient who has been harmed brings tort claims for a doctor's malpractice. The argument in a tort case is not that the doctor failed to live up to her contractual promise, the argument is that the doctor failed to live up to a professional standard of care.[66]

Dr. McGee made the unwise promise because he wanted to try out a new technology. He wanted to attempt a skin graft.[67] Because it was a new procedure, Hawkins' father was unwilling. It was only Dr. McGee's promises that won him over.[68] Today, *Hawkins* would take a different legal pathway, one based on hospitals, trials, training, and standards of care. The case is an example of how new technologies make demands of the law by requiring immediate, at first provisional, then slowly and over time iteratively rules

---

[63] Daniel P. O'Gorman, *Expectation Damages, the Objective Theory of Contracts, and the "Hairy Hand" Case: A Proposed Modification to the Effect of Two Classical Contract Law Axioms in Cases Involving Contractual Is Understanding*, 99 KY. L.J. 327, 329 (2011).

[64] *Hawkins*, 146 A, at 644 ("As a general rule, the measure of the vendee's damages is the difference between the value of the goods as they would have been if the warranty as to quality had been true, and the actual value at the time of the sale, including gains prevented and losses sustained, and such other damages as could be reasonably anticipated by the parties as likely to be caused by the vendor's failure to keep his agreement, and could not by reasonable care on the part of the vendee have been avoided.") (quoting Union Bank v. Blanchard, 65 N. H. 21, 23, 18 A. 90, 91 (1889)).

[65] *See*, Theodore Silver, *One Hundred Years of Harmful Error: The Historical Jurisprudence of Medical Malpractice.*, 1992 WIS. L. REV. 1193 (1992).

[66] *See, e.g.*, Peter Moffett & Gregory Moore, *The Standard of Care: Legal History and Definitions*, 12:1 WEST J. EMERG. MED. 109 (2011).

[67] *Hawkins*, 146 A. at 643.

[68] *Id.* at 642–43.

better adapted to the fit of technology to human circumstance. What is exciting about *Hawkins* is that it shows us how rules come into being. It's not just a technology case, it's a case about how law grows and merges at the edges for new medical techniques. More, it's a case about how stories can mean multiple things at different times, yet still retain impact and persuasive power as a core part of a language dealing with the issue the story means to address.

Consider the 1854 English case *Hadley v. Baxendale*,[69] another staple of contracts case law. In *Hadley*, the owners of a mill contracted with a railroad company to ship a replacement crankshaft by a certain date because the mill's crankshaft had broken.[70] The owners needed the shaft to keep their mill running, but (the court concluded) they didn't inform the railway company that the mill could not run until the new shaft arrived. They did not inform the railway company that they had no spare. The shaft took a long time to get there, and the mill owners lost quite a lot of money because the mill was out of commission.[71] The question in the case was whether the railway would be liable for the extended damages that arose as a consequence of its breach of contract.[72]

If we want to take all of the fun out of the case, it stands for the simple proposition that damages for breach of contract will be limited to those damages which flow foreseeably from the breach.[73] Or, in *Hadley*, the railway operator was not liable for damages from the mill's inoperation, because the mill operator had not informed the railway of the potential for this consequence.

Here again, the interesting part of the case is how it develops a story, a set of vocabulary, that can be slotted into many different language systems. It's a story about the development of new technology, and law's reaction to it. *Hadley* took place at a time when railway technology was just beginning to knit the United Kingdom together.[74] The railway companies were privately owned, but provided critical infrastructure for the country. Imposing liability on a private operator of infrastructure was somehow different than applying it to

---

[69]   Hadley v. Baxendale, 9 Exch. 341, 156 Eng. Rep. 145 (1854).
[70]   *Id.*
[71]   *Id.* at 146.
[72]   *Id.* at 147.
[73]   *Id.* at 151 (holding that damages should be limited to the amount that may "reasonably be supposed to have been in the contemplation of both parties, at the time they made the contract, as the probable result of the breach of it."); *see also* RESTATEMENT (SECOND) OF CONTRACTS § 351 (1979).
[74]   See *generally* Richard Danzig, *Hadley v. Baxendale: A study in the Industrialization of Law*, 4:2 J. LEGAL STUD. 249 (1975).

an individual private operator (say, a carriage driver) who failed to get a package to its destination on time. The law had to come to grips with the power of private companies to run critical facilities. It did so by limiting the responsibility of the infrastructure provider, termed a "common carrier,"[75] because if that carrier were limitlessly liable for all damages that flowed from its operations, it would cease to perform that role. So courts used a rule that would require parties that were uniquely susceptible to particular damages to disclose that fact to the common carrier, permitting the carrier to then decide whether to shoulder that risk or require the customer to seek independent insurance for the high-risk transaction.

Hadley v. Baxendale is still very relevant today, not just for its rule on foreseeability of damages, but for the deal it strikes between private ownership of key infrastructure and the public interest. It is, for example, the core dispute underlying net neutrality, the idea that internet service providers should act like railways or the mail. Most people think that the deal should be the same: internet service providers should have to carry all information on equal terms—they should be "common carriers," too—and in return the law might give them some protection for liability for carrying that traffic.[76] The story fits, because the problem is universal. How do we deal with private ownership of critical flow infrastructure? We make the infrastructure providers carry traffic equally, in return for limited protections from liability so that they can carry out that role for society.

Law is like Darwin's coral reef. The edge of a coral reef is alive and growing. The bulk of a reef is ossified. As humans encounter new people and situations, they develop new understandings, new rules for how the relationship is going to work out. As things progress, larger groups draw on language and rules of behavior developed between individuals and smaller gatherings to establish norms and rules of behavior between members of the broader community. After a while, a given set of understandings becomes so universal that we

---

[75]   The development of Anglo-American understanding of "common carriers" goes back to 1670, when English Lord Chief Justice Hale wrote that the *jus publicum*, or common interest, shared in English ports superseded private interests in the same ports. *See* Matthew Hale, *A Treatise in Three Parts, in* 1 Collection of Tracts Relative to the Law of England 1, 72 (F. Hargrave ed. 1787). Since Hale's time, the "common carrier" doctrine expanded statutorily to include public services ranging from railroads, e.g., the Interstate Commerce Act of 1887, to internet service providers, e.g., the Telecommunications Act of 1996. For a brief history of the term "common carrier" in Anglo-American jurisprudence, see generally Phil Nichols, *Redefining Common Carrier: The FCC's Attempt at Deregulation by Redefinition*, 1987 Duke L.J. 501, 506–14 (1987).

[76]   That this is not necessarily the thinking applied to net neutrality in the United States is explored in chapter 8.

instead consider them basic elements of human care and decency. As things become more standardized, they ossify—forming a scaffolding for future growth. Perhaps a legislature wants to tweak the basic common understanding, or perhaps they just want to standardize it across their jurisdiction. The rule becomes part of statutory law. This pattern, from informal agreement to formal agreement to common understanding to legislation, can describe a large part of our lawmaking process.

THE LAW OF HORSES AND OTHER OLD STORIES

An early cyberlaw conference was trolled by one of the country's most prominent judges. In a now famous speech, Judge Frank Easterbrook addressed a 1996 University of Chicago Legal Forum symposium on "Property in Cyberspace" by arguing that courses on law and information technology were unlikely to teach students much, and that "no one at this symposium is going to win a Nobel Prize any time soon for advances in computer science."[77]

Judge Easterbrook made his point in his trademark bare-knuckled style by claiming studies of law and computers were about as interesting as "The Law of the Horse," a course on every law involving horses.[78] He claimed that students were better off studying (and by extension, academics were better off developing) rules of general application—property, torts, contracts—than taking a focus-specific course on law and technology.[79] He counseled caution in the face of technological change. Judges, he said, must mostly do nothing when confronted by technological questions they know nothing about. In discussing how judges could barely regulate copying machine technology, he despaired of wisely regulating technology around the then-emerging internet:

> If we are so far behind in matching law to a well-understood technology such as photocopiers—if we have not even managed to create well-defined property rights so that people can adapt their own conduct to maximize total wealth—what chance do we have for a technology such as computers that is mutating faster than the virus in *The Andromeda Strain?*[80]

Many scholars have taken a run at the "Law of the Horse" speech. Certainly it has not proven prescient about whether information technology would change the shape of the law—it has. Nor has it aged well regarding the value of

---

77 Frank H. Easterbrook, *Cyberspace and the Law of the Horse*, 1996 U. CHI. LEGAL F. 207, 207 (1996).
78 *Id.* at 207–08.
79 *Id.* at 208.
80 *Id.* at 210.

studying law as it develops in response to technology. An entire field of data privacy now stands where once there was next to nothing. But the compelling thing about the Law of the Horse speech, and what drives me to trot out this topic yet again, is how close its author got to understanding how law can and does accommodate technological change.

His ideas were: first, the study of law, technology, and their interaction is not useful. Judgment of history: by and large, wrong. Second, the study of general principles of law is better than studying the specific characteristics of specific technologies. Judgment of history: right. Third, law can never keep up. Judges cannot (and should not) come up with rules to govern new technologies.[81] Judgment of history: the jury is out. A lot of people, both technologists and jurists, believe this. I don't.

Law keeps up because its most successful principles are the ones most easily adapted to new contexts. The rules of broad application apply broadly, if you will excuse the tautology, precisely because they apply broadly. That concept, that a rule is of broad application is what makes a rule successful in the face of technological change, goes to the heart of what makes a successful legal rule. Rules that apply narrowly do not survive technological change; they are locked to their circumstances and the specific technological incidents that spawned them. The tragedy of the Law of the Horse speech is that Judge Easterbrook accurately described the mechanism by which law accounts for technological change—patient and humble iteration of existing legal principles based on multifaceted and rich narratives—but in the next step despaired that law could perform in the coming decades what it had successfully done over the prior centuries.

Judge Easterbrook incorrectly believed that "law and computers" was dilettantism, similar to studying "the law of the horse." He thought we should study law, pure and simple, not law and technology.[82] Of course we should study law, pure and simple. But *all* law is technology law. Horses are technology. Railways are technology. The internal combustion engine is technology. Planes are technology. Maglev trains, hyperloops, and autonomous cars are or will soon be functioning technology. Law will be perfectly capable of dealing with the questions of liability in an autonomous car crash.[83] I expect

---

[81] *Id.*

[82] *Id.*

[83] High-profile cases of autonomous and semi-autonomous vehicles causing injury or even death to riders and pedestrians are on the increase, but the question of who is liable in these circumstances are not always clear under existing tort law. *See, e.g.,* The Associated Press, *California Regulators Nix Rules Limiting Carmaker Liability,* ASSOCIATED PRESS NEWS (Dec. 1, 2017), www.apnews.com/ce707c88718446c5b9b93b318oc70e6e/California-regulators-

the judge in such a case not to throw up her hands and do nothing, but to roll up her sleeves and pick guiding principles drawn from old and rich narratives that have proven useful in the past and which still seem to offer insight in the face of technological shift.

THE LIFE CYCLE OF LAW

This process of applying old narratives to new cases stands at the very center of the law. Law helps us adapt to change by balancing sameness and newness, by balancing theme and variation. Too much sameness, and human systems become stale and ineffective. Too much variation, and there is chaos. Good law, like good music, must have a balance of stability and innovation. The cost of too much instability is uncertainty in human ordering—a major purpose of law is to provide predictability in human interaction. But the cost of too much stability is stagnation. Markets stagnate when legacy power-holders use market share to dominate future developments. Human relationships stagnate as power differences lock in and create class and caste effects.

If law is a system for adapting human behavior to technological change, then to say that law is being left behind by developing technology doesn't make any sense. What is really meant is that some rules have gone away. That does not mean that a society whose technology is accelerating is becoming lawless. We can rewire the natural pathways of the law so that the language of law more easily encompasses new questions raised by technology. Law's identity is inextricably tied to adapting with change. It not only responds to change, but walks alongside it.

I have compared the development of law to that of a coral reef. There is also another metaphor I find to be useful. In his seminal article *Nomos and Narrative*,[84] Yale law professor Bob Cover developed the idea that law grows

nix-rules-limiting-carmaker-liability; Peter Holley, *After Crash, Injured Motorcyclist Accuses Robot-Driven Vehicle of "Negligent Driving,"* WASH. POST (Jan. 25, 2018), www .washingtonpost.com/news/innovations/wp/2018/01/25/after-crash-injured-motorcyclist-accuses-robot-driven-vehicle-of-negligent-driving/?utm_term=.32d40c95a4e5; Cleve Wootson Jr., *Feds Investigating after a Tesla on Autopilot Barreled into a Parked Firetruck*, WASH. POST (Jan. 24, 2018), www.washingtonpost.com/news/innovations/wp/2018/01/23/a-tesla-owners-excuse-for-his-dui-crash-the-car-was-driving/?noredirect=on&utm_term=.c631f9939730; Ian Bogost, *Can You Sue a Robocar?*, THE ATLANTIC (Mar. 20, 2018), www.theatlantic.com/technology/archive/201 8/03/can-you-sue-a-robocar/556007/; Dan Strumpf, *Liability Issues Create Potholes on the Road to Driverless Cars*, WALL ST. J. (Jan. 27, 2013), www.wsj.com/articles/SB10001424127887323854904578264162749109462; California Department of Motor Vehicles, Report of Traffic Collision Involving an Autonomous Vehicle, 2014–2018 (Dec. 3, 2018), www.dmv.ca.gov/portal/dmv/detail/vr/autonomous/autonomousveh_ol316+.

[84] Robert M. Cover, *Foreword: Nomos and Narrative*, 97 HARV. L. REV 4 (1983).

organically, drawing an analogy to biologically diverse systems. Law is not made by legislatures, he wrote; it starts growing in relationships, then unfurls throughout communities, and spreads to whole jurisdictions. So to say that law lags technology ignores the first stirrings of law already in place. As soon as technology emerges and evolves, humans have ideas about how to arrange the use of that technology within human relationships. Many of those ideas are terrible. Think about the norms in bars about Google Glass: so-called "glassholes"[85] thought it was okay to wear their recording glasses in the bathroom. More than one got punched in the face.[86] Many rules and norms, like not wearing perpetually recording eyewear in intimate settings, are fairly reasonable. What most people consider to be the heart of law—the activity of courts and legislatures—is the process of weeding out the terrible rules. But there is no such thing as technology use unconstrained by human rulemaking. As soon as the tech is here, we have ideas about how we should use it.

Rules of law pop up like weeds. Every time two people hammer out a new rule or norm to help them live together, a rule is generated. Millions of experiences yield millions of rules. The problem is not how to generate new rules, but how to select for the ones that should survive and become generalized. Some rules may work, but we may not know why. Different rules may evolve in different jurisdictions based on different experiences for solving similar problems. In this way, law lives and evolves like life. As Oliver Wendell Holmes famously wrote, "The life of the law has not been logic, it has been experience."[87]

This helps us see that law is created not in courts, but in communities. As Cover writes,[88] courts do not create law, they select which law must be killed off:

> Judges are people of violence. Because of the violence they command, judges characteristically do not create law, but kill it. Theirs is the jurispathic office. Confronting the luxuriant growth of a hundred legal traditions, they assert that this one is law and destroy or try to destroy the rest.[89]

As Cover describes it, communities are greenhouses, fecund with law. The rules worked out in these communities work well within a limited space, but

---

[85] *See, e.g.*, Dana Schuster, *The Revolt against Google "Glassholes,"* N.Y. Post (July 14, 2014), https://nypost.com/2014/07/14/is-google-glass-cool-or-just-plain-creepy/.

[86] Nick Bilton, *Why Google Glass Broke*, N.Y. Times (Feb. 4, 2015).

[87] Oliver Wendell Holmes, Jr., The Common Law ¶ 1 (1881).

[88] Robert M. Cover, *Foreword: Nomos and Narrative*, 97 Harv. L. Rev. 4 (1983).

[89] *Id.* at 53.

they may not translate well to other contexts. They may serve as poor rules of general validity; that is, they may not sufficiently sort cases contemporaneous with the decision. Or such locally generated rules may not translate well temporally: they may not stand the test of time, and thus should be killed off. The institutions of law, courts, judges, and lawyers alike respond to: "the need to suppress law, to choose between two or more laws, to impose upon laws a hierarchy. It is the multiplicity of laws, the fecundity of the jurisgenerative principle, that creates the problem to which the court and the state are the solution."[90] This yields Cover's definition of law, which is expressly futurist: "Law is the projection of an imagined future upon reality."[91] Law is an expression of the past, in terms of what survives the jurispathic process, and it is a projection of the future, in which lawyers, judges, and legal systems select rules of law that may survive this future-casting. A holder of the law-killing office should select not merely which rule should survive to resolve the current conflict, but which law demonstrates the characteristics of resilience that will permit it to adapt, mutate, evolve, and survive to handle future conflicts.

If an idea has a practical impact on human behavior, it may be said to matter. If you hold a belief that has absolutely no effect, the world in which you do not hold that belief is indistinguishable from a world in which you do. How do we know what the law is, apart from how humans under the law act? If there is a set of words on the page that changes no set of human behavior, do we call it a law? If law is a set of rules intended to shape human behavior, then I do not think it is inappropriate to say that a law must be an idea that has a practical impact on what people actually do. Those rules that do not affect human behavior are not laws, whatever their abstract philosophical claims. They are code without a computer. They are proclamations in a language no one can read.

A child gets this pretty quickly. If one parent makes a rule to not wipe dirty hands on clothing, but another parent does it a second later without reprimand, then perhaps that is not the rule after all. Repeated breaches without practical consequence mean that the rule no longer influences the child's behavior. The rule is dead. Meanwhile, when the child wants to play on the swings on the playground, she knows to wait her turn and count to a hundred. And the other child knows she has to get off at one hundred. Rules that influence behavior are rules, rules that influence nothing are not.

A significant number of obsolete statutes still on the books do not influence any human behavior because of technological advances, and that number is

---

[90]   *Id.* at 40.
[91]   Robert M. Cover, *Violence and the Word*, 95 YALE L.J. 1601, 1604 (1986).

increasing by the minute. These rules have not stood the test of time. They are obsolete, because they regulate ways of being and doing that we do not use anymore.

When my German friends heard I was a lawyer, they gave me some legal books in German that collected crazy US statutes that no longer make sense. The title of the book is *Nackt duschen ist streng verboten,*[92] which translates to "Showering naked is strictly prohibited." You may have heard of rules requiring someone to walk ahead of your horseless carriage with a lantern so that your horseless carriage will not scare real horses.[93] But perhaps you did not know that in South Carolina, minors are prohibited from playing pinball.[94] In Tennessee, clergymen, atheists, and those who have participated in duels forfeit their right to hold public office.[95] In the United Kingdom, it is still illegal to enter the Houses of Parliament in a suit of armor.[96] Rules like these may be on the books, but they no longer regulate human behavior. (Except when they do: an 1835 law banning carriages from sidewalks was recently used in the United Kingdom to prosecute a man who drove his Segway on the sidewalk; the court deemed it a "carriage."[97]) We should understand these rules as the waste, the byproducts, the miscues, the flops of an experimental local process. They are no longer laws, they are Edison's broken light bulbs. They are not the way things work; they are the ways that do not work, that no human thinks works, that no human acts on.

Those rules are not law, they are law's runoff. They clog up law books (and too many law classes) but do not pragmatically affect human behavior. We should not mistake the waste for the product, the residue for the process. To say that law cannot produce rules adapted to technological shifts based on the

---

[92] ROMAN LEUTHNER, NACKT DUSCHEN IST STRENG VERBOTEN: DIE VERRÜCKTESTEN GESETZE DER WELT (2009).

[93] *See, e.g.*, the Locomotives Acts of 1860s in the United Kingdom, where a pedestrian had to walk in front of a vehicle waving a red flag or carrying a lantern to warn others, or individual state statutes, like Alabama's Code Title 32 Motor Vehicles and Traffic § 32–5-240(a)(1) ("All vehicles, including animal-drawn vehicles and those for which special permits have been issued under authority of Section 32–9-29, not otherwise specifically required to be equipped with lamps, shall at the times specified in subsection (a) of this section be equipped with at least one lighted lamp or lantern exhibiting a white light visible from a distance of 500 feet to the front of the vehicle and with a lamp or lantern exhibiting a red light visible from a distance of 500 feet to the rear.").

[94] S.C. Code § 63–19-2430 (2012).

[95] Tenn. Const. art. IX.

[96] Louise Scrivens, *Changing the Flaws in London's Laws*, BBC NEWS (May 10, 2005), news .bbc.co.uk/2/hi/uk_news/england/london/4527223.stm.

[97] *See* Alastair Jamieson, *Segway Owner: I'll Fight in the High Court for My Right to Ride*, TELEGRAPH (2011), n.p. (available at www.telegraph.co.uk/motoring/news/8276240/Segway-owner-Ill-fight-in-the-High-Court-for-my-right-to-ride.html).

existence of obsolete rules is like arguing that a factory cannot produce cars because of the evidence of spilled oil.

Laws can even come back from the junkyard. Different rules have worked well in different contexts over the course of human experience. Often, like the law of trespass to chattels we talked about earlier, a rule can be retrofitted, can come back from near or complete oblivion once the rule once again runs on human minds.

In sum: law is born naturally, and is selected for salience in the face of technological change. And law dies when it no longer meaningfully influences human behavior—most often when it can't keep up with technological change. So technological change kills lots of laws, but only the weak ones, so to speak. We might say that technology is the shark eating the sick and decaying matter of the legal ecosystem, keeping it in balance.

STAYING ALIVE: THE ELEMENTS OF RESILIENCE

How does law stay ahead of technology? A good case does not show us what the law *is* in a moment of time, but offers a compelling narrative and flexible vocabulary that seem to human judgment relevant and applicable to future cases. That is why many cases in law school textbooks exist not to demonstrate what the law currently is, but how it changes in the face of something new. The law is not really a system for describing rules. The law is a system for guiding change through analogical reasoning: talking about how this is like that. It does so by offering rich, resilient, memorable, adaptable narratives that speak to different constellations of human needs. The most effective stories are often resilient, the main characteristics of which are *human, humble, experimental, iterative, diverse,* and *viral.* The following pages discuss each in turn.

To start, it's worth noting the characteristics that successful rules do *not* share. Successful rules are rarely narrowly defined statutes tailored to the characteristics of a particular technology. Rather, they are broad and analogic, providing decision-makers with flexibility and adaptability.[98] Successful rules are not technologically savvy. They look to human incentives rather than technological truths. A successful rule responds far more to how humans will use or do use a technology than to any deep understanding of how the technology operates.

One example of this comes from our discussion of the law of cybertrespass. More than one technologist has said that trespass makes no sense as applied to

[98] Of course, decision-makers have to be able to run with it, a different part of the legal system, but still subject to the same rules.

electrons.[99] There is nothing really "there," they say, so claiming that electrons "step" on someone's server is nonsense. It's even more nonsense when we consider that most servers are now virtual: there's no actual physical property (or, more accurately, the server processes are distributed among multiple locations, and consist in operations, not as definable specific physical property) to trespass on! But a successful rule does not give credence to the technologist's claims of what a technology "really" is. What matters is how humans use it. If one person abuses the freedom to send email to servers by soaking up bandwidth, processor cycles, or even attention, we treat that in a similar way to the trespasser who misuses another's land or personal property.

What makes these stories resilient is that they respond to human incentives rather than technological features—in the case of cybertrespass, the eternal incentive to use and misuse someone else's property. Many modern "Internet of Things" devices, for example, have hidden Bitcoin mining capacity. Your toaster or fridge may quietly activate this capacity, soaking up your electricity and bandwidth to mine Bitcoin for the appliance's manufacturer.[100] That is a bleeding edge technological context. But a very old rule—the law of bothering sheep—handles it perfectly well.

Human

Law must respond to human needs. It is a human system and responds to human concerns. To the extent that law does not meet human needs, it should be discarded. This is usually not a contested definition. We may fight about whether more wealth or more distribution is generally a good idea, or whether to serve human interests in the short term or the long term, but the idea that law ought to make humans' lives better is not deeply debated.[101]

If we don't pay attention, though, we may find that legal or digital constructions like corporations or artificial intelligences might supplant human interests within our legal system. Already, corporations have done enormous damage to rule by the people, of the people, and for the people. Artificial intelligence need not become sentient and spawn terminators to pose a threat to the human-centered nature of law. Artificial intelligence will be competent

---

[99] *See* Dan L. Burke, *The Trouble with Trespass*, 4 J. OF SMALL AND EMERGING BUSINESS L. 27 (2000).

[100] JOSHUA A. T. FAIRFIELD, OWNED 74 (2017).

[101] I recognize that an anthropocentric view of law might seem to exclude animal or environmental interests. It does not. Our relationship with our ecological context is important to our long-term wellbeing.

for most human tasks long before it is sentient. As discussed in the previous chapter, the danger is not that artificial intelligence will be hostile. Rather, we should fear that it will become competent to perform our tasks while being indifferent to our welfare.

Furthermore, it is also important to place humanity at the center of the legal debate because what is *human* will change. I speak of this in a broad and a narrow sense. In the narrow sense, and over a long time horizon, the convergence of nanotechnology and genetics will permit manipulation of what humans are, so we will have to define, through law, the very stuff of our being.[102] Our aspirations will literally become ourselves. But in a far more meaningful sense, technological affordances do not merely satisfy human desires—they shape and fulfill them. Affordances to build social networks lead to reconnected friendships but also to divorces thanks to affairs with old flames. Affordances to communicate instantly and constantly build not only connection but constant surveillance. In a very real way, to be human is to be defined by what we can do. As technology expands what we can do, it will change what we are. Even if we take an expansive view of humanity for both of these measures, that humanity will change as we develop our ability to augment and alter ourselves genetically and technologically, and that humanity will change as our affordances force us to make new decisions about what we *should* do with what we now *can* do, humanity must be the yardstick by which we measure law's accomplishment of its goals.

Humble

Law that adapts well is humble. It takes one case at a time, one issue at a time. This prevents overreach. Because cases are tied to facts, we are able to get rich contextual information for determining the better rule. Rules divorced from context make basic mistakes. Theory kills. Legal rules divorced from their lived context miss common-sense outcomes. This is perhaps a function of cognitive load. We do not see many elements of a situation without a specific factual scenario in which to ground it. Once we see how things play out, we are able to make wiser decisions.

This goes doubly for technology regulation. The first attempt to set rules for when police can access email communications, the Stored

---

[102] *See* DEUS EX, ION STORM (Eidos Interactive pubs. 2000) (Set in the year of 2052, the story follows an FBI-like agent with superhuman abilities by nanotechnology. The series delves into the concept of what is human in later installments).

Communications Act, is a dumpster fire. It is based on the technological realities of BBSs (electronic bulletin board systems) of the 1980s. The law assumes that any email you read and then leave on a server is like a letter you have read and thrown into the trash: free for police to read without any constitutional protections. Given modern cloud computing, where our most private communications are stored encrypted by online service providers, that law is massively, obviously, and disastrously stupid. What sounded like a good idea at the time has turned out to be hilariously wrong.

It is important not to mistake humility for paralysis, though. The lesson is not that we should not act. The point is that rules divorced from lived experience or the actual context that caused humans to think those rules were a good idea turn bad quickly. Humility accepts the need to make a prompt decision. In fact, keeping a rule humble, tied to its origins and context, without immediately generalizing it, may enable us to act quickly without destabilizing other areas of law. We must be cautious, though: most claims for humility in regulating technology are actually disingenuous claims by technology lobbyists that want no law constraining their clients' damaging actions whatsoever.

Experimental and Iterative

Adaptable law is experimental. A rule is rarely right the first time, and no rule is entirely right. No rule is exempt from tweaking, reconsideration, and careful thought in the light of new technology or new contexts. Consider the law of cybertrespass. Trespass to land was not quite the right rule in *CompuServe*,[103] so judges further adapted the theory to trespass to chattels in *Intel v. Hamidi* and *Bidder's Edge*. And even now, the *Bidder's Edge* rule has difficulty with cloud computing and distributed resource systems. To succeed, law must borrow, tweak, and innovate.

Innovation may seem like a tall order in a system ostensibly governed by precedent—by past cases. This appears to be a system governed by the past rather than the future. Not true, says the astute observer. Judges routinely write new opinions using old words. They take prior opinions, cut them up, hash up the quotes and citations, and claim that they have changed nothing while concocting a new regime out of old cloth. The form of the legal opinion is perhaps the best example of remix culture available. Citing precedent is setting the tune of one opinion to the beat of another. It is a mashup of

---

[103]   See CompuServe Inc. v. Cyber Promotions, 962 F. Supp. 1015, 1017 (S.D. Ohio 1997).

policies, reasoning, and legal maxims, built out of distinct blocks from prior legal work. When successfully done, the finished product is in significant part new, yet without ever entirely breaking faith with the past.

Successful technology law is also iterative. We take each version and build on it. Again, consider our discussion of cybertrespass. Each rule not only innovates starting from the prior rule, but uses that prior rule as a point of departure. It was not clear at the outset that the law of trespass was applicable to networked systems. However, once CompuServe invested in that step through its holding, it became more reasonable for other courts to consider adapting other versions of trespass to tweak the rule. Cases are path dependent, each built on the next. Path-independent law can adopt radically new solutions, but does so at the cost of discarding all the information encoded in prior rules. New laws that adopt radically new approaches to govern new technologies often fail spectacularly. Laws which represent a path-dependent iterative and experimental walk across the data retain the wisdom of old rules while adapting it to novel contexts. Even if a given case represents a wise outcome, and even if it represents a significant departure from precedent, it is still dependent on that precedent to test the rule across contexts and time, to provide a contrasting set of facts that exposes certain incentives or features of the rule, or even simply to help humans come to accept the rule as a broad norm. The simple passage of time may give a rule the patina of legitimacy necessary for it to become a foundation stone rather than a capstone.

One note of particular importance about iteration: legislatures do not do this well. Legislators are rewarded with votes by constituents for splashy initiatives, and with cash by lobbyists for legislation that serves corporate interests. Legislators, therefore, are not rewarded for the painstaking work of tweaking, perfecting, and operationalizing the groundbreaking work of others. The Stored Communications Act is still law, although it is universally acknowledged to be badly broken.[104] Technology law books are laden with out-of-date statutes whose pernicious effects reduce and threaten innovation, and all to purposes that have no bite twenty years after the passage of the rule. Yet it takes a crisis of national proportions before Congress seriously considers revising a statute instead of trotting out something new.

---

[104] *See, e.g.,* Gabriel R. Schlabach, *Privacy in the Cloud: The Mosaic Theory and the Stored Communications Act,* 67 STAN. L. REV. 677 (2015); William J. Robison, *Free At What Cost?: Cloud Computing Privacy Under the Stored Communications Act,* 98 GEO. L. J. 1195 (2010); Stephen Juris, *Information Gathering for the Google Age: Some Notes on the Stored Communications Act,* FORBES (Feb. 8, 2012), www.forbes.com/sites/insider/2012/02/08/infor mation-gathering-for-the-google-age-some-notes-on-the-stored-communications-act /#1257f5aa7a42.

How do we get iterative law? We can sunset technology laws, requiring legislatures to revisit them. We can produce technology rules via the common law process, in which judges address new questions of technology as they arise, selecting from among rules brought by litigants for the court's consideration, and then encouraging the rewriting of those rules by later courts, who can refine, elaborate, or overturn them. We can encourage legislators to write technology legislation in human terms rather than by reference to specific technological features. If they do not, those features will inevitably change, rendering the rule obsolete. Technologists have at least one non-trivial reason to buy into an iterative system. A rule that is badly broken can be upgraded by iteration. This prevents long-standing errors in regulation, which rack up transaction costs for industry players.

Diverse

If we are to use Bob Cover's organic metaphor to describe the origins of law, and if it is useful to describe the effects of both judicial decision-making and technological advance as twin adverse selectors of legal rules—the one by killing rules off in court decisions, the other by rendering them obsolete and thus of no pragmatic import—then we might also find salience in the meta-phorically biological origins of law in our discussion of the requisite charac-teristics of resilient technology law.

Consider the Tasmanian devil. A strange communicable cancer is killing off the population.[105] Because the devils are a small, inbred population, millions of years of evolution are at risk.[106] With a larger, more diverse population, maybe some devils would have a slight resistance to the cancer, which thanks to adverse selection would eventually become a common and stronger trait in the population.

Monoculture—the fact that all devils are too much alike—is killing the Tasmanian devil. Deadly monoculture can occur in law, too. Law must come from diverse sources. Even if there were no art or science to building the correct rule or selecting against it, a rich field from which to draw improves the odds that *some* legal rule will survive and thrive. Even raw diversity, that is, diversity without direction or reason, provides strong protection against the dangers of monoculture. It is much less likely for one single pernicious use of

---

[105] *See* Erica Rex, *For Tasmanian Devils, Hope against a Wily Cancer*, N.Y. Times (Nov. 17, 2018), www.nytimes.com/2008/11/18/science/18devil.html.
[106] *Id.* ("We'd predicted they'd be vulnerable to viruses" because they are an inbred population, Dr. Woods said. "That what got them was a cancer took everyone by surprise.").

technology to run up against a single weakness of all rules if the relevant rules are different.

The trend toward harmonization and globalization of law increases the chance of a single, catastrophic failure. Take, for example, the anti-spam regimes in the United States before the federal CAN-SPAM Act.[107] States had different laws governing spam: some requiring honesty, others requiring prompt cooperation with a recipient's desire to opt out. Some laws imposed a slap on the wrist, others felonies. Thanks to the passage of CAN-SPAM, which eliminated these state laws in favor of a single federal one,[108] spam became safer to send, more profitable, and all the more common in your inbox.

In killing diversity, we develop monoculture. In depending on monoculture, we increase the risk of catastrophic system failure. When that system is our social system of governance, catastrophic failure is democratic failure. Whatever your political persuasion, you should not be sanguine about the system falling apart. Monoculture creates that problem. Diversity can help address it.

If one takes rule construction to be more than blind chance, then diversity matters doubly. Local contexts yield diversity of experience, which in turn encodes information in the specific rule that can be critical in the overall determination of the better rule. Studies consistently demonstrate that diverse groups process information more carefully.[109] They correct errors more assiduously. Group members take opposing viewpoints more seriously when they come from a differing perspective. Perhaps most importantly, diverse groups serve as better rule generators because, while similar group members hold similar information, diverse group members hold different information.

Think of it like a cooperative game of Clue (or Cluedo across the pond). Some players have the best information available. They know that the crime was committed by Colonel Mustard in the library. They have the very best education available. They know more than anyone else. Some people, though, have a different perspective. They do not have the best information available.

---

[107]   Controlling the Assault of Non-Solicited Pornography And Marketing Act, 15 U.S. Code §
        7701 (2003).
[108]   *Id.* at § 7707(b) (preempting certain state anti-spam laws); *see, e.g.,* Omega World Travel
        v. Mummagraphics, 469 F.3d 348 (4th Cir. 2006) (ruling that CAN-SPAM preempted an
        Oklahoma anti-spam email statute). *But see* White Buffalo Ventures v. University of Texas at
        Austin, 420 F.3d 366 (5th Cir. 2005) (ruling that CAN-SPAM did not preempt the University
        of Texas's spam-blocking policy because UT fit within an ISP exception of CAN-SPAM).
[109]   SCOTT E. PAGE, THE DIFFERENCE: HOW THE POWER OF DIVERSITY CREATES BETTER
        GROUPS, FIRMS, SCHOOLS, AND SOCIETIES (rev. ed., 2008).

In fact, they have less information than other players. All they know is that the crime was committed with the candlestick.

If we are putting together a team to solve the crime, do we use only those with the best information? If we do, the crime will remain unsolved. Or do we create a diverse team with a range of perspectives? If we do, the crime will be solved (as long as the members talk to each other and share a goal of catching the killer). Diversity is not merely a question of warm feelings. Some solutions cannot be reached by homogenous groups of people that all share sterling credentials.[110]

This leads us to a final dimension of diversity: consultation. I name it last because it is the most dangerous. This book demonstrates why the writing of technology law cannot be left solely to technologists. For one, many technologists think law is something that will "wither away" with the coming of novel technological solutions. For another, a common technologist mindset is that law is merely a cost to doing business, not an affordance that can speed technological innovation. Finally, technology-specific regulation fails. Thus, the extent of the technology lobby's legal creativity is directed toward how to remove or evade law, rather than how to develop good rules. The practice of tech-industry consultation in the drafting of technology law is too often used as a fallback position from the perspective that technology industries should write the rules themselves, under the nonsense concept of self-regulation. When the fox cannot convince the hens to let him write the rules, he feels that he should at least be consulted. If industry lawyers cannot write the law through self-regulatory rules, the argument goes, then the rules should be created by technology lobbyists in a consultative process.

That is *not* what I mean by consultative. Consultative means that relevant groups should have a voice, and must be able to contribute input to a *diverse decision-making body*. Consultation in particular does not mean that the consulted body should have a controlling voice in decision-making. The consultative voice would become the majority voice, crowding out alternative perspectives, purging "less constructive" (read: less reflective of industry views) approaches, and, like our Cluedo example, the crime would remain unsolved.

For consultation to work, consultation cannot threaten diversity. For it to work, technologists and lawyers must both learn humility. They have pieces to the puzzle, not the whole picture. One way of forcing humility is to ensure that no dominant paradigm has a dominant decision-making role. Participants must convince and persuade, parse and correct errors, compromise and learn, in order to reach a rule.

[110] *Id.*, 10.

Viral

Lastly, if law is to keep pace with hard technology, we must increase the speed of legal decision-making. An important part of that project will be to increase law's velocity of adoption. We should consider how viral a law is, how fast it convinces populations to adopt it. If we were to talk about a legal rule as a disease, we would talk about how infectious it is. Effective laws spread quickly to many jurisdictions, providing both economies of scale and resilience against jurispathic judges. A rule that has spread to multiple jurisdictions increases its chances of survival; if it is overruled in one jurisdiction, it nevertheless may mutate and find an update from a clever judge in another. The most successful rules find a home in other legal ecosystems, often attracting their own distinct set of underlying principles and commitments from foreign jurisdictions, making the rule more and more robust to any particular adversely selecting principle or context.

The more convincing a rule is, the greater its velocity of adoption will be. Convincingness comes in several flavors. A rule can be convincing because it is understandable to the average person. It may well be better than a more sophisticated rule that nevertheless leaves the average person incapable of complying with it. A rule can be convincing because it resonates with common sense and experience. In this sense, users adopt the rule more quickly because it is merely a version of a rule they already follow. A rule can be convincing because it has a wide installed base. That is, the rule may simply be widespread, and as rules of decision go, it is often better to go with a common rule than a perfect rule.

These elements have a complementary effect so that when a new rule offers a common-sense tweak on an old rule, is intellectually defensible, and provides tangible benefits to the upgrade, the rule tends to propagate to new jurisdictions. When it tracks human intuitions closely and offers human explanations for its determinations, the rule is accepted with less friction by its user base—the people who must put the rule into practice.

One way to increase the adoption velocity of a rule is to package it as a story. Stories invoke principles without triggering an instinctive resistance to rules. Consider the sudden prominence of "Joe the Plumber" in the 2012 US election. The story became a microcosm for the policy issues, something people could relate to using the narrative reasoning tools of human intelligence. People can agree about the outcome of a story, even if they would strongly disagree about why if the rule were cast in abstract and political terms. This is why politicians and prophets speak in stories: the story has authenticity that the abstract principle would not. Storytelling contextualizes a rule, which both helps it remain memorable in the user base (the brains of the people who will apply it) and helps the rule evolve. A story can be adapted, retrofitted, retconned to fit with a slightly different theme, linking cases together. A rule can only be adopted, discarded, or adapted. A story, however, contains truths that can contribute to the formation of many different rules. As those rules iterate in the hands of experimenting judges, the stories can shift position like faces on a Rubik's Cube, forming parts of new patterns and a more complete whole.

Adoption of the new rule should cause minimum damage to the installed base (what we already know is right). Changes should have high adoption velocity and low adoption resistance. The population must be susceptible to memetic infection. There's a reason we make technology arguments to technologists and property arguments to Americans and teach students using analogy.

We know a great deal about how to make ideas viral. The question is why we cannot do with law what we already do with cat videos. Making ideas infectious is nothing new. Gossip spread through medieval towns like wildfire. What is new is the speed with which we can now communicate social technology to one another, and the raw number of people we have working on common human problems.

COMPARING COMMON AND CIVIL LAW

You may have noted that the many examples and cases in this chapter draw largely from the common law tradition. I am a US lawyer and legal academic. The story of the evolution of law, and how it bubbles up from individual interactions to groups to communities and then, through the decisions of judges who decide which rules live and which die, to nations and rules of generalized law, holds true in common law jurisdictions.

Common law jurisdictions, in which judges decide rules based on prior cases, generally hold sway where the British Empire once ruled. This ranges from New Zealand to the United States, and includes India, South Africa, Australia, and myriad other former members of the British Empire, in addition to the United Kingdom itself. There is, of course, another broadly successful worldwide tradition of law: the civil tradition. Examples are found around the world, but its origins are also in Europe. French and German law, although distinct legal traditions, still together share some characteristics that set them apart from the common law and as members of a communal legal tradition. Also in this tradition are Japan, the US state of Louisiana, and numerous

African countries (Japan post–World War II follows roughly in the German civil law tradition, and many former French colonies follow the French Napoleonic Code tradition).

Some of the characteristics of the civil code system are a reliance on a code of laws rather than case authority. German and French law comes in large heavy-bound books of coded law, not in the libraries of cases to be found in a common lawyer's library. Those codes are read by judges in a much more narrow interpretive tradition. Civil law judges often see themselves as merely applying the words of the code. The civil tradition is often seen as more rigid and inflexible, and certainly civil-trained lawyers are much more likely to view the law as consisting of what the law *is* rather than what it should be, which they take to be the sole purview of the legislature.

But that surface view is deeply misleading. Law must have flexibility built into the joints, or it instantly becomes obsolete. Codes in the civil law tradition are very different even from codified statutes in the common law tradition. There is a sense of breadth in the principles. The first principle, for example, of the German Grundgesetz, the German Basic Law, is "Die Würde des Menschen ist unantastbar": "The dignity of mankind is untouchable." In the common law system, what we might see as a laudatory background principle may not even appear in the code—"all men are created equal" is background, not foreground, to the United States Code. And it is simply fact that currently, Europe has a far better reputation for human rights than the United States. Maybe, if one intends to build a nation on the rule of law and respect for the rights of citizens, one ought to do it the civil tradition way.

Civil lawyers benefit from broad interpretive frameworks—entire sets of lenses for interpreting and looking at law, such as the "proportionality principle" that pervades civil law traditions. It is in these interpretive tools and perspectives that the necessary flexibility for law to adapt to new technological cases arises. For a civil-trained judge to apply what the law is, she must first determine what law applies—what bucket the untyped basket of facts that appear before her fall into. Civil law judges will often claim that they are merely applying the law as if the fit between the law and the facts before them were a foregone conclusion, but that is not at all true. The work of fitting novel facts to preexisting codes is done by analogizing prior cases to the current one. Murder via a sword is analogized to murder with a gun, to murder by hacking someone's implanted 3D-printed medical augmentation. And so on: new technology is fitted into the current understanding by a process of interpreting the broader language of the code and its underlying interpretive structures in a way that is far more flexible and powerful than the interpretive tools brought to bear by common law judges, who are very likely to throw up their hands and apply statutes, for example, far more rigidly, less humanly, and with a smaller range of interpretive freedom. A common law judge presented with a statute often believes she has nothing else to say but to apply the words of a statute. A civil law judge, who will often believe the same thing, nevertheless has a far more powerful range of flexible interpretive tools to understand the backdrop, meaning, purpose, import, and function of a statute than does her common law counterpart.

Civil law traditions also have very different paths for getting new technological information into the law. Where common law jurisdictions foster a careful anti-intellectualism and contempt for expertise, civil law jurisdictions tend to trust and use expert knowledge. Where a US law might be designed by technology industry lobbyists because eggheaded academics aren't expected to know their fields, it is often true that legal reform in Europe is guided by expert institutes, where people who are at the top of their fields work out potential paths for legal reform unguided by the profit motives of one of the regulated parties. This means that the mode by which new technological traditions enter the legal bloodstream occurs in a slightly different way. For example, in Germany, it is fairly common that academics write treatises, gathering cases and explaining how the cases fit under specific code sections and interpretive principles. Judges then soberly cite these treatises, secure in the belief that they have merely applied the law as it is. But that is, of course, not at all what is happening.

The civil law tradition is not monolithic of course. Scholars routinely point out that there is as much or more difference in legal traditions between northern and southern Europe as there is between common and civil law traditions generally. But this, too, is a strength, not a weakness. The civil law tradition provides a vector, a set of understanding intuitions about the law, along which influences can travel. The European Union has proven a fertile ground for technology regulation not least because its member states come at problems with such widely varying precommitments. That diversity should sound familiar: it is the diversity that renders legal judgment resilient in the face of changing circumstances.

I do not mean to suggest that the civil law tradition is identical to the common law. New contexts work their way into the civil law tradition along different paths—such as from national foundations like the Max Planck Institute,[111] the expertise of academics, and a bent toward relying on technocratic expertise—rather than the US pathway of introducing technological

---

[111] Portions of this book were written on sabbatical as a guest researcher at the Max Planck Institute for Research on Innovation and Competition.

shift into law through the arguments of two interested and opposed parties. There are strengths and weaknesses to each approach. A real risk of the common law system is that the real party in interest may never be in the room. When Google and the US government collude over geofencing warrants, the people who are most affected, the citizens against whom such warrants are illegally applied, do not first appear. Rulemaking by common law is a series of dyads, pairs of opposed interests, which is catastrophically poorly suited to multi-stakeholder decision-making processes. And as mentioned earlier, what passes for multi-stakeholder consultative processes in the United States has, for different reasons, devolved into rank fox-henhouse self-regulation.

And there are real weaknesses to the civil law tradition. Chief among them is a congenital flaw in civil-trained lawyers: that they by training refuse to ask what the law *should* be, and assiduously hide their thought processes and analysis when they are inevitably faced with such questions. I have taught both lawyers trained in the civil law and lawyers trained in the common law. My common law–trained students struggle to interpret a system of laws as an integrated and organic whole, with counterbalancing interests and interpretive methods. My civil law–trained students have been failed by their training in matters of imagination. Ask a civil law–trained student a question, and she will think that she can simply look up the answer.

But these weaknesses are also profound strengths. A common lawyer's willingness to ask what story comes next, what narrative ought to proceed from the current story, perhaps makes up for some of the chaos of the method. And a civil lawyer's highly honed lack of legal imagination is counterbalanced by her commitment to the rule of law, to the idea that what happens outside the framework of law is, in fact, illegal and corrosive to democracy and the rule of law—a problem that will quite likely damage the standing of the United States and United Kingdom, the core common law jurisdictions, beyond the ability to repair on the world stage.

What this means is that both methods have interesting avenues for bringing law to new technological contexts, and both methods of training have unique cultural affordances that bear on the necessary theme and variation of adapting human social systems to new situations. Some of the current best successes come from a combination of these methods. For example, although most EU countries follow civil law traditions, the historical involvement of the United Kingdom in the EU left a mark on the EU courts themselves, which follow a common law model. This creates an interestingly layered cake, in which technology cases that follow established precepts (such as murder-by-hacked-pacemaker) are effortlessly handled by individual countries' civil law courts

under their rich interpretive traditions, but really novel technological cases—
such as the impact of the United States' illegal mass surveillance programs, as
revealed by Edward Snowden, on the robust privacy protections offered the
EU, or the implementation of the new "right to be forgotten" under EU law—
are kicked up to a layer of common law courts at the EU level so that they can
be decided comparatively quickly.

In short, for purposes of the conversation of this book, the divide between
civil and common law traditions is less a barrier to the kind of legal reform we
are talking about here and more an opportunity. In later chapters we will see
why it is so very important to bring many different communities of meaning to
the table to build the kind of language we will need to talk about the problems
of the future. The civil-common law divide is an opportunity: it represents two
different and deeply thought-out legal and cultural traditions that each have
avenues and ideas to bring to bear on how to update the language of law in the
face of technological change.

REDESCRIBING LAW

We have reviewed some of the oldest cases to identify and understand the
characteristics that allow the social technology of law to anticipate and adapt
to technological shifts. All law is technology law. Law is born in communities,
and is the human response to new technologies and emerging markets. Law
dies when it is killed by courts or technological obsolescence. Resilient rules
survive and adapt not by prophetic insight about the direction of technological
development, but by offering enduring insight about human nature.
Technology law is never about technology, it is about humans. And that will
be true going forward, no matter how fast technology develops.

For law to meet the challenge of accelerating technology, it will need to
change some core principles. To the extent that we think of law as rules, we
must reconceive it as a way of guiding change in rules. If we had thought of law
as top-down, we must work to understand that it is bottom-up. Where law was
once a function of power asymmetry between ruling and ruled, it will now
need to evolve flatter hierarchies: we will need to adopt legal rules because
they cause more humans to thrive, not merely because they serve the best
interests of the rich and powerful.

The key to creating better law, faster is to improve our ability to generate the
language of cooperation in individual interactions, small groups, large groups,
and nation-states. These groupings evolve law from smaller groups to larger
contexts, generating ideas for how we should live together and deciding which

idea produced from which group ought to expand and govern more interactions, and which ought to be consigned to the dustbin of history.

To do that, we must improve our ability to cooperate. Cooperation is
humans' evolutionary advantage. As we'll explore next, groups of humans
cooperate at a larger scale than almost any other creature on the planet. We
do so through a very specific ability, an inborn instinct that prewires us to
communicate with each other using systems of sounds and symbols: language.
Since law is language, the honed language of how humans live together, we
cannot talk about how to improve our ability to cooperate through law without
understanding language itself.

PART II

RUNNING ON WORDS: LAW AS COOPERATIVE FICTION

4

Language, the Human Superpower

Imagine what a difference it makes if one thinks of the heart as a pump rather than a furnace, the eye as a receptor rather than a beacon, the atom as the irreducible unit of matter rather than a miniature planetary system. Imagine what it could mean to a program of research if one thinks of the relation of the egg and the sperm as an act of conquest or as one of attachment, of viruses as warriors or as part of a system of locks and keys. Consider the impact of viewing the market as governed by an "invisible hand," one's body as a "temple," language as a set of "games," society as an "organism," a "code," a "text," or a "field."

— Lawrence Rosen, *Law as Culture: An Invitation*[1]

Imagine looking at an anthill. What will strike you is that the ants are working together. How? Millions of years of evolution have developed ants, bees, some wasps, and others into what we call *eusocial*: that is, they work together, even at serious personal cost.[2] Eusociality has costs because it sometimes pits the interests of the individual against the interests of the group. But if a species can pull it off, the ability to cooperate provides a very nearly insurmountable advantage over groups that do not cooperate. This is what E. O. Wilson, a leading researcher on cooperation, eusociality, and evolution calls the iron rule of genetic social evolution: "selfish individuals beat altruistic individuals, while groups of altruists beat groups of selfish individuals."[3]

There is another eusocial species that has dominated the world because of its ability to form groups that cooperate: humans. But where ants cooperate by hundreds of millions of years of evolution of instincts, humans have evolved the ability to cooperate through fictions: advanced abstract

---

[1] LAWRENCE ROSEN, LAW AS CULTURE: AN INVITATION 131 (2006).
[2] *See* Bernard J. Crespi & Douglas Yanega, *The Definition of Eusociality*, 6 BEHAV. L ECOLOGY 109, 109–15 (1995).
[3] EDWARD O. WILSON, THE SOCIAL CONQUEST OF EARTH 243 (2012).

language. And not just any language: languages that permit the creation of abstract cooperative symbols and fictions—gods, tribes, churches, kingdoms, republics, subreddits—that themselves can be further adapted to new contexts.

"Human beings create cultures by means of malleable languages," writes Wilson. "We invent symbols that are intended to be understood among ourselves, and we thereby generate networks of communication many orders of magnitude greater than that of any animal. We have conquered the biosphere and laid waste to it like no other species in the history of life."[4] As we'll explore, *Homo sapiens'* superpower is the ability to create cooperative fictions—narratives—developed through language, that permit hundreds of millions of us to work together.

Humans are eusocial. We, like ants and bees, are super-cooperators. Unlike ants and bees, our competitive advantage is that we can upgrade our cooperative ability through language. As historian and philosopher Yuval Harari notes, bees cannot guillotine the queen and declare a republic.[5] Our ability to cooperate depends on our ability to create and believe in collective fictions, like money, capitalism, firms, human rights, and the State of California.[6] And the most evolved form of language we use to coordinate leaves behind the language of gods and kings, and has stood for something else entirely: the Rule of Law. Law is a refined version of human language eusociality. It is the language about language, the rules about rules. It is that system that is under assault—no wonder the humans are scurrying around like someone just kicked the anthill.

A BRIEF NON-HISTORY OF LANGUAGE, CULTURE, AND LAW

Some 30,000 years ago, the smaller-brained, weaker-bodied, and warm-adapted *Homo sapiens* replaced the bigger-brained, stronger, and cold-adapted *Homo neanderthalensis* on the Neanderthals' very own frigid homeland turf of Europe. How did this happen? For millennia, the various species of the genus *Homo* had followed the normal rules of evolution: evolving, living in small populations for a few hundred thousand years, and then dying out. But about 70,000 years ago, something happened that led to a massive expansion of *sapiens* across the world, taking *sapiens* from the middle of the food chain to masters of the world in a shockingly short period of evolutionary time. Well before the Agricultural

---

[4] *Id.* at 13.
[5] *Id.* at 133.
[6] Yuval Noah Harari, Sapiens: A Brief History of Humankind 113–16 (2015).

Revolution, our ancestors radically altered the world's ecology, and other species the world over, including our Neanderthal cousins, had no time to react. Genetic evolution was just too slow.[7]

I've already let the answer slip, of course. Humans are not world masters at strength or even intelligence.[8] What we *do* is *cooperate*. And while ants and other eusocial creatures cooperate using instincts honed by million years of evolution, we developed the ability to cooperate by *language*, which we can modify and upgrade to permit new forms of cooperation to help us cooperate even better. The discovery, or perhaps the evolution, of the ability to cooperate via abstract thought—fictions—is the single most important event in the history of our species. If anything is going to save our bacon now, it is this: the most important social technology of all, the core competitive advantage that gave us our existence as a species.

We don't exactly know when or how it happened. The origins of language are so hard to determine, and so fraught with political landmines, that they have been broadly taken off of the table by scholars. The reader can understand why: discoveries about an original proto-Indo-European language were used to support the vicious eugenic and racist idiocies of fascist Germany.[9] Because tongues rot, we have too little information about the physical changes that enable language. Because *Homo sapiens* either exterminated or interbred with (evidence shows it was mostly the former and a little the latter) close cousins like Neanderthals, we have no idea what non-*sapiens* language might have looked like.

What we do know is that between 50,000 and 70,000 years ago, humankind went from being an obscure primate, largely confined to sub-Saharan Africa, to a world-dominating species, present on every continent.[10] Anthropologists and archeologists call it the great leap forward.[11] Humans went from the middle to the top of the food chain. Where once tribes of *Homo sapiens* had lost out to the stronger and better cold-adapted Neanderthals, now *Homo sapiens* wiped out (and, at the end, interbred a little with) Neanderthals on their home turf of Europe.[12]

We can rule out some theories about what prompted this great leap forward. It wasn't fire. *Homo erectus* had command of controlled fire, and for long

---

[7]   Slow in comparison to our lives as human beings.

[8]   Yuval Noah Harari, Homo Deus: A Brief History of Tomorrow 132 (2017).

[9]   *See, e.g.,* Handbook of Language and Communication: Diversity and Change 638 (Marlis Hellinger and Anne Pauwels eds., 2008).

[10] *Id.*

[11] *See, e.g.,* Jared Diamond, The Great Leap Forward, in Technology and Society: Issues for the 21st Century and Beyond 15–23 (Linda S. Hjorth et al. eds., 3rd ed. 2008).

[12] *Id.*

enough that fire played a serious part in our evolution.[13] When we worry about whether technology affects our evolutionary path, consider that it is quite likely our oversized and energy-sucking brains evolved only because we were able to extract many more calories from cooked meat and plants. Indeed, our digestive tracts appear to have grown shorter at the same time we increased calorie load, freeing up even more calories for our energy-hog brains.

Tools didn't spark the leap. *Homo heidelbergensis*, the progenitor species of Neanderthals and possibly *sapiens*, used thrown spears with knapped stone-tipped points 400,000 years ago.[14] Nor was the spark basic "ostensive" language, the ability to call out "Lion coming." *Homo neanderthalensis* had language, and recent studies confirm that some species of apes and monkeys use specific words and phrases with unambiguous meanings.[15]

Even culture can't be it, at least not on its own: abstract designs and other indications of culture predate the great leap forward, were lost during an extended drought, in which *Homo sapiens* populations were reduced to near-extinction levels, and were then rediscovered and finally became widespread during *Homo sapiens'* exodus from the African continent on its way to conquer the world. Yuval Harari, author of the award-winning *Sapiens*, has called this the Cognitive Revolution,[16] but it was not an advance in intelligence. We don't know what intelligence is, or how to measure it, and there is little indication that an individual *sapiens* was more intelligent or capable than an individual Neanderthal, for example.

The cognitive revolution was quite likely a revolution in cooperation, based on many of these factors: mostly on language, but also on other social technology—culture, art, the ability to create abstract symbols that served as

---

[13] See, e.g., Kim Luke, *Humans Used Fire a Million Years Ago*, U OF T NEWS, UNIVERSITY OF TORONTO (Apr. 2, 2012), www.utoronto.ca/news/humans-used-fire-million-years-ago (citing Francesco Berna et al., *Microstratigraphic Evidence of In Situ Fire in the Acheulean Strata of Wonderwerk Cave, Northern Cape Province, South Africa*, 109:20 PROCEEDINGS OF THE NATIONAL ACADEMY OF SCIENCES (2012).

[14] Zach Zorich, *The First Spears*, ARCHAEOLOGY, March/April 2013, www.archaeology.org/issues /81–1303/trenches/523-south-africa-earliest-spears.

[15] Not only do species related to humans possess the ability to produce and understand specific words, but even small mammals, such as wild dwarf mongooses, have specific calls. See Katie Collier et al., *Wild Dwarf Mongooses Produce General Alert and Predator-specific Alarm Calls*, 28 BEHAVIORAL ECOLOGY 1293 (2017). (This study analyzed the vocalizations of wild dwarf mongooses belonging to seven different groups. The sounds the mongooses made were recorded and the stimuli that caused the response was noted. The result showed five main types of responses, three of which were non predator-specific alarms and two were predator-specific alarms. Of the two predator-specific alarms, one was for aerial stimuli, while the other was for terrestrial stimuli.)

[16] Yuval Harari, *supra* note 6, Part One: *The Cognitive Revolution*.

cooperative fictions. Based on experiments comparing chimpanzees with two-and-a-half-year-old children (whose levels of intelligence tested similarly in solving physical and spatial problems), the children trounced the chimpanzees when it came to social tests: watching a demonstration, following gaze, and understanding others' intentions.[17] As E. O. Wilson puts it: "Humans, it appears, are successful not because of an elevated general intelligence that addresses all challenges but because they are born to be specialists in social skills. By cooperating through the communication and reading of intention, groups accomplish far more than the effort of any one solitary person."[18]

SOCIAL INTELLIGENCE AND THE SOCIAL BRAIN

Language, community, and intelligence seem to be bound together in ways that we are just now learning about. In a range of tests, researchers are finding that "what distinguishes people is their ability—even their need—to jointly attend with other people to what they are doing. People are built to collaborate."[19] This is known as the social brain hypothesis: the idea that "the driving force of the evolution of human intelligence was the coordination of multiple cognitive systems to pursue complex, shared goals." As cognitive scientists Sloman and Fernbach put it, "Living in a group confers advantages, as we have seen with hunting, but it also demands certain cognitive abilities. It requires the ability to communicate in sophisticated ways, to understand and incorporate the perspectives of others, and to share common goals."[20]

Humans are remarkably savvy at causal thinking. Our minds pay attention to cause and effect. If I throw a small spear at an animal, I may soon be trampled by the herd, but if I can increase the impact of the spear—say, by adding to its mass—one antelope, coming right up! If someone ate smelly meat and got sick the next day, it's probably best to avoid the meat. And when I pass this information along to my neighbors (or, more likely, while working *with* them to hunt and prepare food), I do so by telling them a story. "We tell stories about the past—we reminisce and romanticize," write Sloman and Fernbach. "We tell stories about the future—we predict and fantasize. And we tell stories about the present—we construct who we are and daydream. All of this is about identifying causes and foreseeing effects. How did we come to be? Where are we going?"[21]

[17] WILSON, *supra* note 3, 227.
[18] *Id.*
[19] STEVEN SLOMAN & PHILIP FERNBACH, THE KNOWLEDGE ILLUSION 117 (2017).
[20] *Id.* at 112–13.
[21] *Id.* at 66.

It is a narrative that holds things together. The interaction of what we call "consciousness" and what we call "language," goes pretty deep. Think about what kind of day you're having right now. That's a story. Think about how this week has gone. That's a story. Think about who you are, where you've been, and where you're going. They are all stories. They don't recount everything that occurred—that would be too complex and time-consuming. Instead, they distill and recount the bits that matter to us.

Consciousness is a social narrative device. It evolved within the framework of needing to know what other humans were going to do. Our internal experience of narrative, of rationalization, of telling stories about what it is that *we* do and why, is at least in part an extension of our experience of narrative, of rationalization, of telling stories about what it is that *other* humans are doing and why. Our narrative self is an outgrowth of our need to narrativize others, to predict accurately, to plan our moves in a part-cooperative, part-competitive culture.

We do not and cannot think alone. There is a reason that solitary confinement drives humans mad, and that babies who are not held and physically nurtured experience a failure to thrive. We think together—we cannot think otherwise. We think through our languages, our communities of meaning. We think through our family languages (some family languages are gentle; some are unbelievably violent), through our religious languages (same), through our political languages (even more of the same) and so on.

We have no choice: the nature of human eusociality via language is that we radically partition knowledge. Each one of us knows a tiny amount of information; we store about half a gigabyte worth of data in our brains.[22] We draw on the knowledge of others every time we get into a taxi, start a car, pull on clothes woven by machines so complex none of us understands all of them, and most of all, turn on a light switch, an act of social sorcery drawing on an entire universe of human knowledge. Wonderful experiments have established what is called the illusion of explanatory depth: we think we understand things like toilets and zippers until we are asked to explain to someone else how they work.[23] This form of information cooperation is what permits us to advance: we can rely on others' thoughts and competences, and don't have to figure things out from scratch every time.

The information that permits human civilization to function is stored across a vast network of languages and conversations, from pillow talk to office meetings to professional conferences to national dialogues on race and

---

[22]   *Id.* at 25.
[23]   *Id.* at 6–8.

gender. We rely on mechanics to fix our cars and doctors to fix our bodies. More than that: we rely on doctors to generate language to talk about new ways of testing and healing, new protocols that we know nothing about, but which improve our health.

The modern environment is a testament to the knowledge of others. We move in a world shaped by other people who have already embedded their knowledge and purpose into the objects they leave behind: woodworking knowledge embedded in furniture, civil engineering knowledge in the very streets. The information we rely on is stored in the objects around us. Doctorates in electrical engineering and materials sciences are stored in the turn of a car key.

We can sometimes figure out how things work because they have been designed to reveal to us how they work. Apple has made its entire computing empire on this principle. And when objects do not reveal the information they encode, such as my own law school, which as a matter of urban legend chose to have all the doors open the wrong way as an obscure metaphor for the law, the result is maddening. My family just rented a van for a week's vacation; it took forever to figure out the poorly designed and counterintuitive controls. Clearly some engineer understood her own machine so well that she could not be bothered to communicate its operating information through design to the customers. Perhaps you can relate.

Every street is information: it goes somewhere. Every door is information: it leads somewhere. A lock is a conversation between the owner and a would-be intruder: "Keep out!" A doorknob, meanwhile, is an invitation: "Come in!" The reason that we understand so much less than we think we do is that we must. We must understand how to use the fruits of other people's understanding. To function, we must be proficient in Apple or Android operating systems, or Spanish, or using plumbing. Go to a country where the plumbing standards are different, and you'll understand. We literally cannot use the bathroom in a modern context without relying on information from thousands of different sources, embedded in the design.

"The nature of thought," write Sloman and Fernbach, "is to seamlessly draw on knowledge wherever it can be found, inside and outside of our own heads. We live under the knowledge illusion because we fail to draw an accurate line between what is inside and outside our heads. And we fail because there is no sharp line. So we frequently don't know what we don't know."[24] In other words, our thinking is inside out about our thinking inside out. Humans do not think from the inside, or individual, out, we think from

---

[24] *Id.* at 15.

the outside, or group, in. This allows us to efficiently share experiences and information and organize communal memory. It is the seamless transmission of knowledge that allows us to pursue common goals.

But perhaps you've already spotted a few difficulties. This illusion of knowledge means that we do not see the error in our own arguments, or the limits of our own knowledge that our arguments reveal. Almost everything we need to know to make an informed decision—whom to vote for, for example—is contained in someone else's head. We are left to make the best decision we can, based on our methods for determining whether to trust what someone else says.

And this is why groups, and how groups talk, determine our thinking. The stories we tell are "intimately tied to a community's belief system."[25] When a community aligns with a particular story, they are accepting the attitude implied by the story. Think, for example, of a community whose stories focus on the golden rule of "do unto others," as opposed to a community who ascribes to narratives of "an eye for an eye." The members of each group, in listening to, retelling, and contributing to these stories, are aligning and identifying with the details, the slant, the purpose and moral. It's a smooth, highly efficient process for communicating information and declaring common values, but it's very seamlessness can lead a presumption of accuracy or omniscience. It can erase complexity or vital contradictions (how, for example, do we do unto others when someone has caused harm?). As Sloman and Fernbach write,

> Instead of appreciating complexity, people tend to affiliate with one or another social dogma. Because our knowledge is enmeshed with that of others, the community shapes our beliefs and attitudes. It is so hard to reject an opinion shared by our peers that too often we don't even try to evaluate claims based on their merits. We let our group do our thinking for us. Appreciating the communal nature of knowledge should make us more realistic about what's determining our beliefs and values.[26]

Indeed, the problem is worse than Sloman and Fernbach imagine. It is not merely that we let the group do our thinking for us, it is that the language of the group, the way it addresses a given task and context, constrains how we *think* about problems. Politicians know this; it is why they go to such great lengths to create phrases like "death panels" or "marriage equality." These phrases stand in for entire ways of thinking about a debate. By adopting the term, one adopts

---

[25]   *Id.* at 67.
[26]   *Id.* at 17.

the framework, one chooses a social-cognitive way of approaching the problem. This is why the most vociferous battles are over how we talk about things, from the much-maligned political correctness movement to right-wing hysteria over the "happy holidays" greeting.

What this means is that we have been looking for, and measuring, human intelligence at the wrong level. "[T]hinking is a social entity that takes place in a group and involves teams," write Sloman and Fernbach. "Once you accept that we live in a community of knowledge, it becomes clear that most researchers have been looking in the wrong place for a definition of intelligence. Intelligence is not a property of an individual, it's a property of a team."[27]

JUSTIFICATION AND ARGUMENTATION: THE YOU AND I IN TEAM

There is good evidence for the social intelligence hypothesis. Experimental results seem to confirm that human rationality—the mental processes that generate reasons for what we believe and what we do—does not serve some abstract goal of helping us see the world clearly, whatever that means, but instead to generate reasons that persuade others in our group, or secure our place within our group. Our rationality is social, not empirical.

Cognitive scientists Dan Sperber and Hugo Mercier have gathered a range of experimental and theoretical evidence that strongly supports the hypothesis that reason is itself social.[28] They distinguish between what they term "intellectualist" and "interactionist" views of reason.[29] On the intellectualist account, reason exists to help us make better decisions. On the interactionist account, reason exists to help us find reasons that secure our place within the community, and help us share cognitive labor with others in that community.[30]

There is very good evidence in favor of the social—interactionist—view of reason, and against the hypothesis that we reason rationally as individuals. In particular, experimental evidence shows that individuals do not carefully evaluate their own reasons for their actions, but instead gravitate toward easily socially defensible rationales.[31] Many studies confirm that the reasons people

---

[27] *Id.* at 212.
[28] *See* HUGO MERCIER & DAN SPERBER, THE ENIGMA OF REASON (2017).
[29] *See id.*
[30] *See id.*
[31] Richard Nisbett & Timothy Wilson, *Telling More Than We Can Know: Verbal Reports on Mental Processes*, 84 PSYCHOLOGICAL R. 231 (1977).

produce for their actions and decisions are geared toward establishing and maintaining reputation, rather than logical rigor.[32]

Sperber and Mercier argue that while the experimentally revealed mechanisms of individual reason are not particularly well adapted to achieving correct results, they are admirably adapted to solving two problems in group dynamics: cooperation and communication. They argue that the human capacity for reason focuses on *justification* and *persuasion* in order to address these problems.

The first difficulty may have already come to mind the minute I mentioned eusociality. The key problem with human eusociality is the danger of cheating, free riding, loafing, or what behavioral economists call defection.[33] Defection is a constant risk when humans try to cooperate: one roommate doesn't do his share of the dishes; one factory owner decides to skirt environmental laws to make a profit; one person at the party contributes one-tenth of the price of a pizza but eats half. In econ-speak, these are called collective action problems: everyone in a group would be better off if everyone pitched in, but each individual person would be better off if she slacked off and let the others do the work. This is the core curse of a eusocial species made up of individuals.

Experimental evidence shows that humans provide reasons that *justify* themselves in the eyes of others, rather than reasons that can be parsed from the experiment. For example, in one experiment, subjects were asked to fill out a questionnaire. In the next room, they then heard the sounds of something falling, and the voice of someone in distress, presumably trapped by the fall.[34] When the subjects were alone, they went to help out.[35] When the subjects were with someone else (a patsy placed by the researchers) who shrugged and kept filling out the questionnaire, most subjects did not go to help out.[36] Yet when these subjects were asked why they did not go help out, they did not cite the presence of the other person (the patsy) in the room.[37] In other words, they produced (and believed) reasons for their actions that had little to do with the patterns their experimenters were easily able to discern.

---

[32] *Id.* at 233.

[33] *See id.* at 180–83; See also, Elizabeth Hoffman et al., *Behavioral Foundations of Reciprocity: Experimental Economics and Evolutionary Psychology*, 36 ECON. INQUIRY 335 (1998) (The study looks to, among other factors, the effect of defection on individuals and how people tend to look to strategies that serve their own interests).

[34] Bibb Lantane & Judith Rodin, *A Lady in Distress: Inhibiting Effects of Friends and Strangers on Bystander Intervention*, 5 J. OF EXPERIMENTAL SOC. PSYCHOL. 189, 191 (1969).

[35] *Id.* at 193.

[36] *Id.*

[37] *Id.* at 197.

Another example: subjects were asked which of two movies they wanted to watch, a sad-clown movie or a comedy.[38] The movies were playing in two cubicles, separated by a partition. In both cubicles there were two chairs, and another person (again, a research patsy) was sitting in one of the chairs.[39] One of the seated watchers wore heavy metal braces. The other did not. No matter what movie the person with braces was watching, participants made up reasons to avoid sitting next to the disabled person. But they reported (and believed) completely different reasons for their actions, relating to their love of comedies, or what have you.[40] Again, people produce and believe reasons for their own decisions and behavior that are socially acceptable and easy to justify. They are not, however, particularly accurate.

Why should our capacity for reason evolve to find socially justifiable reasons over logically sound ones? Sperber and Mercier argue that this is because our reason operates in community, not solo.[41] Socially justifiable reasons help convince others in our group that we are not free-riding, that we are acting in a justifiable manner, consistent with the norms of the group.[42] Justifiable reasons secure our place within the group, and secure our share of the valuable products (safety, food, roads, walls, and so on) that the group produces. Consider a roommate who doesn't do his share of the dishes in a given week. If he states the truth, that he would rather spend his time doing something else, he may be excluded from the group and miss out on the cheap rent of a shared apartment. If he offers a better justification, that he was very ill, perhaps he can retain his share of the group benefits.

But, you say, I've had that roommate! He had another excuse the next week too. (The more honest among us can admit we've been that roommate.) Here justification bears even more fruit. Offering the justification lays down a track record, against which he can be measured. If another roommate gets sick, perhaps the original slacker will be expected to pitch in extra, or be revealed as someone who does not truly follow group norms. Or if the slacker is sick by chance every single time it is his turn to do the dishes, again, the group can detect the defection. The giving of justifiable reasons therefore secures the person's place within a group, but also allows the group to detect defection, and over time to exclude free riders, loafers, slackers, and so on.

---

[38] Melvin L. Snyder et al., *Avoidance of the Handicapped: An Attributional Ambiguity Analysis*, 37 J. OF PERSONALITY AND SOC. PSYCHOL. 2297, 2299 (1979).

[39] *Id.*

[40] *Id.* at 2301–02.

[41] MERCIER & SPERBER, *supra* note 28, at 127 ("To put it in more sociological terms: Reasons are social constructs.").

[42] *See id.*, at 183–86.

The second challenge of group dynamics is less noticeable, which is not coincidental but rather indicative of its very essence: We're biased. We have a preference for our own ideas. (And yes, even though our ideas are not even ours! Remember, we are not necessarily rational in the way we pride ourselves on being.) Human reasons have been experimentally shown to be quite biased in favor of the speaker's position, what the literature broadly calls confirmation bias, and what Sperber and Mercier call *myside bias*.[43] If reason were an individual capacity evolved to help individuals make better decisions, humans' systematic myside bias would be a serious flaw. If I am convinced there is no man-eating tiger outside the village, and only pay attention to facts that confirm my hypothesis (I don't see the tiger right now, tigers generally don't hunt humans, tigers are scared of fire), and discount surprising or disconfirming information, I am more likely to get killed.

But there are others in the village, and this is where Sperber and Mercier's theory of argumentation and persuasion comes in.[44] What is important, in their view, is that each hypothesis get a full treatment. The selfish, confirmatory, myside reasoning of one passionate speaker ensures that at least one person in the community has staked their reputation on a given theory, and thus is highly motivated to find all of the reasons for it (although not against it) that they can. And so on for other theorists. In short, myside bias may improve group reasoning more than it damages individual reasoning. If one sees intelligence as a property of a group, a group of myside reasoners may, collectively, think through things based on a richer set of arguments.

All of which is to say: a range of well documented bugs in human reasoning may turn out to be features if one views human reason as a social activity rather than an individual one.[45] If one sees the human capacity for reason as adapted to help solo thinkers find solutions, one must explain away a lot of discrepancies. But it is very possible to see individual human reason as admirably adapted to helping humans take a place in a group and contribute to the group's thinking.[46]

And experimental evidence supports this conclusion. In one famous and often replicated experiment, called the Wason selection task, subjects were given four cards with a letter on one side and a number on the other. They could only see one side, however, like so: [E] [K] [2] [7]

---

[43]   *Id.* at 218–19.
[44]   *See id.* at 12, 194–99.
[45]   *Id.* at 76.
[46]   *See id.* at 243–44.

They were then given a rule: "If a card has a vowel on one side, then the number on the other side is even."[47] The subjects were then asked which cards they would need to turn over to verify that the rule was true or false. Go ahead. Try it. Which cards would you flip over to confirm or falsify the rule?

If one of the cards you picked was the 2 card, you're in good company: most people do. But you'd also be wrong: The rule says only "If there is a vowel on one side, then there will be an even number on the other." It doesn't say "If there is an even number on one side, then there will be a vowel on the other." It's kind of like answering yes to the following scenario: "If it is snowing, then it is cold outside. It is cold outside. Is it necessarily snowing?"

But later researchers noticed something very interesting. When asked to reason individually, only about 20 percent of subjects got the Wason selection task correct. Yet when subjects were placed in small groups and asked to discuss the problem, about 80 percent of groups got the answer correct.[48] The answer, by the way, is E and 7, because *If* [vowel] *then* [even number] says only that. It doesn't say "*If* [even number], *then* [vowel]." So flipping the 2 card over, even though it feels relevant, doesn't help you decide if the statement "*If* [vowel], *then* [even number]" is true. Our rule didn't say anything about *If* [even number]. Or, in the notation some people use for logic: A → B (read "A implies B" or "if A, then B") does not mean B → A (read "B implies A" or "if B, then A"). If you want to understand the problem a bit more intuitively, Sperber and Mercier are there to help with a causal example.[49] Consider the statement: "*If* [it is snowing], *then* [it must be cold outside]." That does not logically lead to "*If* [it is cold outside], *then* [it must be snowing]."

Most people only see this underlying problem with the logic if they talk it out in groups. That is, even when each member of a group was much less likely than a coin-flip to get the answer, when groups were permitted to argue and reason their way to a solution together, they quadrupled their chances of success. Group intelligence can be much greater than the sum of we the individual parts. And it is the very nature of at least some core functions of our intelligence to reason in such groups, for the benefit of the group.

THE IRON RULE OF SOCIAL EVOLUTION

The emerging evidence about human eusociality challenges long-standing assertions about human behavior and evolution. We are coming to recognize

---

[47] P. C. Wason, *Reasoning about a Rule*, 20 QUARTERLY J. OF EXPERIM. PSYCH. 273 (1968).
[48] *Id.*
[49] MERCIER & SPERBER, *supra* note 28, at 39–43.

that intelligence and rationality have much deeper social links than previously understood. But these insights alone do not explain how *Homo sapiens* rose to global predominance and overtook Neanderthals. *Sapiens* was not the only tribal creature; nor, as we've noted, was *sapiens* the only one to use language. Given the placement of the hyoid bone and the appearance of the FOXP2 gene, which Neanderthals share with humans, it seems likely that Neanderthals had language.[50] Recent studies show that monkeys share facts of the world around them (mostly, things to do predators and invaders) with distinct and unambiguous words and phrases. And Neanderthals even cooperated: their specialty was big-game hunting on the mammoth steppe.

In other words, we weren't the only creatures to cooperate. But something was different about our cooperation. E. O. Wilson gives us the iron rule of genetic social evolution: "Selfish individuals beat altruistic individuals, while groups of altruists beat groups of selfish individuals."[51] In short, if one group of *Homo* outcompetes and outlives another group of *Homo*, there is every reason to believe that the reason lies in superior cooperation and organization.

It turns out that there's a natural limit on cooperation, one that both *sapiens* and Neanderthals would have encountered. British anthropologist Robin Dunbar postulated from his study of primates that there is a natural mathematical limit to the size of a group that can cooperate based on personal knowledge alone.[52] Families cooperate (or don't) because they know each person personally. Microsoft does not. Dunbar posited that the number of deep social relationships maintainable by one person maxes out at 150,[53] called Dunbar's number—and no, Facebook has not helped us raise that number.[54] This is why small firms struggle to grow to bigger ones: they must transition from a group of people who cooperate because they know each other to a group of people who cooperate because of a common commitment to an abstract legal entity (say, Microsoft) and process (say, an assembly line), where each person works and cooperates based on an abstract cooperative fiction, like a firm, and not any other given person.

This is Homo sapiens' superpower: whereas chimpanzee bands max out at around one hundred members, humans can cooperate in the hundreds of

---

[50] WILSON, *supra* note 3, at 221.
[51] *Id.*, at 243.
[52] R. I. M. Dunbar, *Neocortex Size as a Constraint on Group Size in Primates*, 20 J. OF HUMAN EVOLUTION 469 (1992).
[53] ROBIN DUNBAR, GROOMING, GOSSIP, AND THE EVOLUTION OF LANGUAGE 69 (ill. ed. 1998).
[54] R. I. M. Dunbar, *Neocortex Size as a Constraint on Group Size in Primates*, 22 J. OF HUMAN EVOLUTION 469 (1992).

millions because of common commitments to cooperative fictions, consensual hallucinations, commitments to things like Mother Russia, Microsoft, the international banking system, or the Categorical Imperative.

It is this capacity for advanced language—the ability to conjure up and talk about abstract, shared concepts—that gave our ancestors their competitive advantage. "Language was the grail of human social evolution, achieved," writes Wilson.

Once installed, it bestowed almost magical powers on the human species. Language uses arbitrar[y] symbols and words to convey meaning and generate a potentially infinite number of messages. It is capable ultimately of expressing to at least a crude degree everything the human senses can perceive, every dream and experience the human mind can imagine, and every mathematical statement our analyses can construct.[55]

No species on earth—except *Homo sapiens*—pledges allegiance to the flag of the United States of America, trades valuable goods or services for intrinsically worthless scraps of paper, or recognizes a co-religionist from dress alone. And, most of all, no chimpanzee has ever refrained from mobbing and murdering foreign chimpanzees purely on the grounds of "we hold these truths to be self-evident, that all chimpanzees are created equal."

So why and how did *Homo sapiens* come roaring out of sub-Saharan Africa 70,000 years ago, and in the next 40,000 years conquer the entire earth before history even began? We can tie all of these points—about abstract language, culture, cooperation above Dunbar's number, and even the Great Drought hypothesis—together with an insight drawn from the development of computer networks known as Metcalfe's law. Metcalfe's law states that the effect of a telecommunications network is the square of the number of connected users.[56] Consider: What is the use of a telephone if no one else has one? What is the use of the internet if no one else is connected to it? As more people get telephones, it becomes more valuable to have a telephone. As more people use the internet, the internet becomes more valuable. As more people contribute to mining Bitcoin, the more secure the system becomes. Or you might choose to learn a language like Mandarin, Spanish, or English, because of the huge numbers of people who speak it.

Advanced language is a telecommunications system. Through it, abstractions can be passed from one group to another, through cultural vehicles, intermarriage, or simple linguistic exchange (about which much more

---

[55] *Id.* at 228.
[56] *See, e.g.*, James Hendler, *Metcalfe's Law, Web 2.0, and the Semantic Web*, 6:1 J. OF WEB SEMANTICS 14 (2008).

below). The point is: the value of a system of abstract language grows at *at least* the square of the number of users of abstract language.

What we know is this: 70,000 years ago, the human conquest of the world started. And it is connected with the development of cooperative fiction in abstract language, as well as with increases in human populations, in a positive feedback loop. The flashpoint seemed to hit when human populations recovered after the Great Drought, such that the network effects of abstract language began to be felt. As human populations increased, our capacity to cooperate above Dunbar's number through cooperative fictions increased and became more valuable. As more humans joined language networks of culturally exchanged meaning, the value and power of the cooperative fictions they generated grew, increasing the ability of human groups to add even more members to a culture, a tribe, a group of humans cooperating. As Sloman and Fernbach write: "As groups got larger and developed more complex joint behaviors, individuals developed new capabilities to support those behaviors. These new capabilities in turn allowed groups to get even larger and allowed group behavior to become even more complex."[57]

Lastly, recall our discussion of Raymond Kurzweil and exponential progressions. Any exponential progression will swamp linear progression given time. Although the 40,000 or so years of the great leap forward are an eyeblink in evolutionary history, the introduction of the tiniest curved progression explains the explosive conquest of earth by a once-unremarkable primate. Once cooperative fictions began to circulate among growing populations, even a little tiny bit, *Homo sapiens* jumped from just another primate in danger of dying out to the top of the food chain and unquestioned dominance of the world.

WHAT IS LANGUAGE?

The broad consensus is that the great leap forward had to do with advanced language, at least in important part.[58] We need to speak, therefore, with some

---

[57] SLOMAN & FERNBACH, *supra* note 19, at 117.
[58] *See, e.g.*, PAUL EHRLICH & ANNE EHRLICH, THE DOMINANT ANIMAL: HUMAN EVOLUTION AND THE ENVIRONMENT, 74–76 (2008); Terence Davidson, *The Great Leap Forward: The Anatomic Basis for the Acquisition of Speech and Obstructive Sleep Apnea*, 4 SLEEP MEDICINE 185 (2003); Andrey Vyshedskiy, *Language Evolution to Revolution: The Leap from Rich-vocabulary Non-recursive Communication System to Recursive Language 70,000 Years Ago Was Associated with Acquisition of a Novel Component of Imagination, Called Prefrontal Synthesis, Enabled by a Mutation That Slowed Down the Prefrontal Cortex Maturation Simultaneously in Two or More Children – The Romulus and Remus Hypothesis*, 5 RESEARCH IDEAS AND OUTCOMES (2019).

precision about language, to talk about what "advanced language" means, because it is the center of this book. Law is language used in a certain way: to promote cooperation, whether that be through top-down governance or peer-to-peer contract. But to understand why law is important and how it can keep up with technology, we need to understand the phenomenon it is based on: language, and particularly the kind of language that lets humans cooperate in multi-million-member groups. That kind of cooperation is not only what sets us apart as a species, but it is also the only way we are going to have a snowball's chance in hell of surviving the next hundred years.

There are two layers to language, which has been the cause of some confusion. First, there is the inborn human capacity for language, the hardware, so to speak, and the patterns that this capacity leaves in our speech: nouns (or noun-ishness), verbs, the organization of the world into subjects, objects, actions, and the like.

Second, there is what we use our capacity of language to build—its software. (This is merely an analogy, but one that helps us understand one distinction.) So, just as computer hardware is a series of silicon/electric on-off switches that store zeroes and ones, but we can run changing patterns on that hardware that have next to nothing to do with the hardware layer, like a video game, or a movie, so human language seems to come in a layer of the ability, which follows certain tendencies, and the words and ideas we create with the capacity of language, which are another matter entirely.

Here is an example of what I mean. Consider words like "run." If I say, "I run every morning at 6 a.m.," the word "run" is a verb, of course. Many languages have verbs or verb-ish sorts of things. Indeed, the "actor-object-action" pattern is a basic way we view reality: given pictures of a ball, a table, and a person putting it on the table, humans will focus on the person as actor, the ball as object, and the action of putting.

This is the hardware layer. When one is interested in the "noun-ishness" or "verb-ishness" of language, then one is talking about our linguistic hardware. Linguists such as Noam Chomsky and Steven Pinker have long advocated for a "language instinct," an evolutionarily evolved predisposition to develop language along certain rough lines.[59] They have some good evidence. For example, when enslaved Africans and other individuals in the Caribbean who spoke wildly different languages developed a common communication framework, called a pidgin, it did not contain linguistic markers common to most languages. But the *children* of those people developed the pidgin into a creole, which did

59   STEVEN PINKER, THE LANGUAGE INSTINCT (1994).

show all of the common markers of a natural language.[60] Something happened when the mishmash of words developed as a pidgin was run through the children's linguistic software.

But Chomsky goes too far, positing a "universal grammar," which is generally now conceded to be an exaggeration. What seems to be the case is that humans come with very few true instincts—a baby's instinctual seeking of its mother's breast is one of the few—but a lot of "prepared learning."[61] So, for example, humans learn to be afraid of snakes very quickly compared to other equally dangerous animals. We are prepared to learn it. We learn from our environment, but we are primed to do so by our genes.

Chomsky's basic theory—that all a child needs to know of a language is stored in a language ability, which contains all language within it—has deep flaws, but a more charitable reading, that we are predisposed to organizing the world in certain ways, thus leaving trace patterns in language, is fairly reasonable. Consider the entire range of models possible, with language-as-genetic capability at one end, represented by Chomsky, and language-as-entircly-learned behavior, represented by the views of the chief behaviorist, B. F. Skinner. E. O. Wilson grants that even these opposing models get something partly right—although Skinner's is more so. "[T]here does appear to be a biasing epigenetic rule for word order embedded in our deeper cognitive structure, but its final products in grammar are highly flexible and learned," Wilson writes. "The multiplicity of pathways in the evolution of elementary syntax suggests that few if any genetic rules guide the learning of language by individual human beings."[62]

So much for the hardware, the "verb-ishness" of the word "run." If one considers the basic human pattern of looking for an actor, an object, and an action, the "verb-ish" word is the third slot, just as actor and object are other slots.[63] But into that slot, we can load anything we can dream up. Because here is the second layer of languages: the word "run" has over 645 meanings, from "run a program," to a "salmon run," to "run up a bill," to "run a bath," or to have a "run of bad luck."[64] Where do these meanings come from?

---

[60] *Id.*

[61] WILSON, *supra* note 3, at 233–35.

[62] *Id.* at 235.

[63] *Id.* at 235.

[64] *See, e.g.*, Simon Winchester, *A Verb for Our Frantic Times*, N.Y. TIMES (last updated May 28, 2011), www.nytimes.com/2011/05/29/opinion/29winchester.html (discussing that the word "run" will have at least 645 definitions in the upcoming edition of the Oxford English Dictionary, according to the dictionary's chief editor).

One place they do *not* come from is the outside world. This is often called the "correspondence," or "ostensive," theory of language. The earliest and incorrect theories of language thought that words drew their meaning from the fact that they corresponded to some object or action or actor or whatever outside the speaker. Many philosophers and scientists saw the early rituals of language-teaching (a parent speaking to a baby, pointing: "Cow!" Baby: "Cow!") as being the whole of what language is. They were wrong.

The problem with the "correspondence" theory of language is that it can't manage to explain "hello," much less "liberal democracy." The kind of language we are seeking is the kind that talks about things that do not exist outside of the language itself—the cooperative fictions we are all looking for. Where does "hello" come from? Perhaps fitting for the subject of this book, it arose in a community of people seeking to use a new communications technology, the telephone. Its usage grew alongside adoption of the telephone, and its ubiquity today—now that "hello" has jumped the barricade from use as a telephone greeting to a general greeting—is entirely thanks to the spread of the technology, and its use in the community. It's a great example of language adapting to new technological affordances.

Meaning comes from communities, context, and use. For example, in Germany, where I am writing a part of this book, people in the north say "Moin moin" as a greeting. In the south, people say "Servus," or "Grüß Gott." In the northeast (and increasingly among friends countrywide), one often hears the simple interrogative "Na?" or the always-useful "Hallo." Why do people say "hello" differently? Because different communities adopt different greeting rituals. In southern France, a greeting is often accompanied by a triple kiss on the cheeks; in New York, sophisticates usually do a single or double peck to signal they are part of the same class and club. In New Zealand, if one is Maori, a warm and intimate greeting is the *hongi*: a touching of the nose and sometimes forehead for the exchange of breath. The point is: a community needs to complete a task (greeting). They negotiate a way of doing things and what to say merely by doing and saying these things. Or as the most important philosopher of language, Ludwig Wittgenstein, noted: meaning is use.[65]

We will discuss Wittgenstein's thinking more extensively in later chapters, but a summary is helpful here. What Wittgenstein meant by "meaning is use" is that the only meaning of a word is its public use by a community, within a context, with reference to a task. If I privately decide that "yes" means "no,"

---

[65] LUDWIG WITTGENSTEIN, PHILOSOPHICAL INVESTIGATIONS 5 (G. E. M. Anscombe trans., 3rd ed. 1974).

that doesn't change the meanings of those words, and if I say yes when asked if I want to order a pizza (or sell my farm, as in a well-known contracts case),[66] I will not be later allowed to argue that I secretly meant no. For lawyers, this is the root of the well-known objective theory of contract: the agreements made in contracts do not mean what the contracting parties secretly believe they mean, but rather mean what the words mean to the public.

When we use words, we are asking other people to act on them despite the fact that they might understand the words we use slightly differently than we do. You say to-may-to, I say to-mah-to, but still, just one red fruit. (Does the word "fruit" sound strange here? That's because different linguistic communities lump tomatoes into "vegetable" or "fruit" categories depending on whether one is a nutritionist or a botanist, and depending on the task: a nutritionist is making a salad, a botanist is categorizing plants. Would the botanist's tomato pie qualify for a county fair dessert competition? You'd have to ask the judges.)

Most of the time we do not notice these mismatches, because most of the time there is only one object answering to the description, and any of the descriptions will do because it is obvious to our inborn social modeling software that the other human expects us to hand something over. There is a red round plant-based object to hand, and sure, it answers to the description of "vegetable" for some purposes, so why be obtuse? This is because, as philosopher Richard Rorty instructs, following Wittgenstein, it is better to think of language as a set of tools, not as a mirror of the world.[67] Language is how we collaboratively build the world around us. Rorty writes, "To think of language as a picture of the world—a set of representations which philosophy needs to exhibit as standing in some sort of nonintentional relation to what they represent—is *not* useful in explaining how language is learned or understood."[68]

Language does not live in our heads (despite our tendency to subvocalize); it lives between us. When I say something is a "good idea," I am making a bid in a linguistic negotiation. I am asking the person I am talking to to include this idea under the heading of "good." What is "good?" What a nonsense question! It is the set of circumstances in which humans use the word. Philosophers have wrecked themselves on these questions for hundreds of years, before they learned to unask the question: "good" has many different meanings, depending on the context and community in which it is used. But

---

[66]   Lucy v. Zehmer, 196 Va. 493 (1954).
[67]   Richard Rorty, Philosophy and the Mirror of Nature (30th anniv. ed. 2009).
[68]   *Id.* at 295.

when we change our view of what is good by, say, removing the practice of chattel slavery from the category of "good," that change is a real and permanent one. Human chattel slavery is not good. Anyone unclear? Anyone disagree? Anyone not understand? Of course, one can scrape the bottom of the internet to find someone who holds any opinion, but would you accept that use of the word "good" as including human chattel slavery? Of course not, which means that their bid to use the word in that context fails. That's what I mean when I say that words' meanings shift and are determined by their use within linguistic communities.

Words' meanings drift, but they are not unconstrained. For example, different languages have different ways of organizing color names (although, as above, there are some discernible patterns). If I spoke a language (Language A) that divides colors into just "light" and "dark," and I used the word "light" to describe something that was "dark," I would be wrong. If I then used a different language (Language B) that has ROYGBIV vocabulary for color (as in English), and I described something as "yellow" when it was clearly "red," I would be wrong, even if both would be "light" in Language A. These words have meaning precisely because they cannot be used at the speaker's whim: they must be part of a community of meaning. It is not how one speaker uses words that matters, but how different communities use words in different contexts.

This, then, shows us the critical features of the kind of advanced language that helps us cooperate over Dunbar's number, that helps us generate the cooperative fictions that help us work together. It is *public*: spoken, living between people, not owned by any one mind. It is *negotiated*: each use of a word is a bid to have that meaning accepted by the community of meaning. It is itself a social ritual, which does not necessarily describe reality at all, but which prescribes that certain words are used in certain contexts. And it is *constrained*, because it is shared with other minds, and has no meaning when not used to secure their understanding. In short, it is a network, which has all of these characteristics.

What this means is that language is upgradable and swappable. We can take one linguistic idea (say, "slavery is part of the natural order") and replace it with a better one: ("all people are created equal"). We can swap out our software without having to swap out our hardware. Whereas bees and ants have to wait another 200,000 years to evolve a response to a threat, humans can upgrade their language in a blink of evolutionary time. This is why humans wiped out almost all of the large animals they encountered outside Africa. In Africa, large mammals had been around *Homo sapiens* long enough to be wary of the cooperative little primates. But the megafauna of Australia had no time:

they were up against creatures that could literally evolve in days or weeks by talking about it. And so everywhere that humans spread after the great leap forward, they eradicated every other *Homo* cousin and decimated the megafauna.

When we try to figure out how to talk about language, I think that it is a useful metaphor to consider languages to be alive. I do not mean languages like French, but local or personal languages like that spoken by your family or closest group of friends on a subject you all know well. If you have a romantic partner or partners, consider the private language that has evolved between the two (or, kids these days, more) of you. Local languages are like that, full of in-jokes, references to "that time when . . .," and in particular, peculiar uses of normal words. Certain phrases, whether religious, or philosophical, or passed down from prior generations, or said by wise-eyed kids, become widespread, repeated and reified by others in the linguistic community. Languages grow, change, mate, reproduce, and divide.

I am not one for metaphysics, and I have never observed anything supernatural, but since part of what this book is about is the power of narrative to help us see patterns at the appropriate level, one might consider these kinds of languages to be like spirits, or pagan gods: small, rich, quick-witted household languages for families and friends; the specific and precise languages of commerce, trade, and profession; and large, stumbling, and powerful national languages, laying waste with broad strokes and crashing into each other with blind atavistic fury. When we look at language through the lens of the appropriate metaphor—and please understand it is a metaphor—our eyes are drawn to what is undoubtedly undeniable: how we talk to each other contains the information we are looking for when it comes to how and whether we can cooperate.

THE QUESTIONS WORTH ASKING

Language is humanity's superpower. Not just simple, referential, "cow!" language—the ability to make a reference that another speaker can understand. Macaques can do that with a specific screech that means "lion!" Ostensive language—"lion!"—is the least that language can do. Rather, humanity's unique superpower is that we can cooperate using abstract cooperative fictions like gods, money, and nation-states, things that obviously do not independently exist (for some values of the term "exist") but nevertheless serve a critical role in helping humans work together at the multi-million-person scale.

Moreover, humans can use old words in new ways, and can speak new systems of language into being, rendering old problems less solved than moot. Recall our answer to the question of human chattel slavery: there *is* no best way to do human chattel slavery, except to rewrite the network of symbols we use until all speakers understand that all people are created equal. New systems of language do not solve problems, they render them obsolete. "How many angels can dance on the head of a pin?" is not a problem to be solved under modern quantum physics, it is merely not a question worth asking. And in exactly the same way, new paradigms of physics will less solve the intractable questions of today than make it obvious they were terrible questions to begin with.

As humans grew in number after the Great Drought, humanity benefitted from a virtuous cycle, a positive feedback loop between the human ability to use cooperative fictions to cooperate and the number of humans who could cooperate using the same or similar cooperative fiction. More humans joined a cultural-linguistic exchange of cooperative fictions, which meant that better cooperative fictions could be generated. And this, in turn, drew even more humans into the cooperative fictions of tribe, religion, political party, subreddit, or Westphalian sovereign state that have turned into the mega-fictions of the twenty-first century. We adapt and build cooperative fictions that add even more minds to a linguistic network of meaning. Those extra minds build better cooperative fictions, and the cycle continues.

That process describes all areas of human linguistic cooperative endeavor, including and especially law. Law, as we discussed in previous chapters, is the social technology that helps us anticipate and adapt to technological shifts. Like all language, law recursively develops new language and symbols to help us handle technological change. Law grows between us as our response to how we want to live together. It is refined eusociality. Law is the discipline of how to work together to talk about what language we need to help us cooperate better. If we're going to make it, there's good reason to think it will be thanks to our most important cooperative fiction: the Rule of Law.

But there is another area of cooperative linguistic endeavor that is also closely related to the survival of the human species in the face of technological change: the language of science itself. Science is our attempt to talk to each other about how to solve certain problems. This understanding—that science is itself a series of stories, a way of talking, a set of vocabulary and social rituals shared among people in a given field that helps speakers solve certain problems—has the potential to help us see precisely what goes wrong when technologists mistake propaganda for universal truth, and to help us see what has gone wrong with the language of science generally, including its derision of law and language. Or, as we will next examine: Why is it that the language of science fails to convince even as the method and results of modern science are our only chance for halting our extinction as a species?

5

What Went Wrong with Science?

We are accustomed to think of myths as the opposite of science. But in fact they are a central part of it: the part that decides its significance in our lives. So we very much need to understand them. Myths are not lies. Nor are they detached stories. They are imaginative patterns, networks of powerful symbols that suggest particular ways of interpreting the world. They shape its meaning.

— Mary Midgley, *The Myths We Live By*[1]

The previous chapter is a story about how Homo sapiens migrated from sub-Saharan Africa and conquered the world. There is some reason to think that advanced language had something to do with the ability of *sapiens* to cooperate in large groups, and given the research I have done, I think the story has much to recommend it.

But here's the point: perhaps you have reached this point in this book and you disagree strongly. Maybe I have some details wrong, or maybe time has taught us. E. O. Wilson's earlier work found no evidence that Neanderthals had art. But a recent study now dates at least some of the haunting handprints on cave walls to Neanderthal communities, rather than *sapiens* ones. Maybe some other information will come to light on linguistics, culture, art, or what have you. Maybe my story needs revising.

But even if it's revised or rewritten, it will still be a story. All statements of meaning are stories. We cannot avoid it. It is one of the features of how humans live in society: we parse experiences into stories and tell the stories to each other. The stories mutate and change as they pass from one person to the next: I promise you, not even the stories of physicists overlap entirely. We do not store collective experiences in raw form—we can't, there's no central brain of experiences. What we do when we try to work together, as I am trying

[1] MARY MIDGLEY, THE MYTHS WE LIVE BY 1 (2011).

115

to work together with you to understand how law can keep up with technology, is we tell stories. There's just no other way.

Sometimes our stories are bad ones—we've already touched on a few, and we'll talk about a lot more here. This book is about creating and telling good stories; the ones that help us cooperate and thrive. But before we can talk about building better language, I'd like to talk about what happens when we ignore stories and discount the power of narrative. I want to talk about what's gone wrong with science and technology.

Science and technology, as fields, claim an exemption from stories, as if stories do not matter, but more often those claims of value-neutrality hide something that I would very much like to surface. Consider a scientist's claim: "Stories, bah! I look at facts." Really? What is a fact? It is a tying together of relationships—a "state of affairs," a *story* about which facts ought to be described when any are described at all, and what relationships between facts matter enough to be observed. "The cup is on the table" is a fact, if the cup is indeed on the table, but so are an infinity of other relationships. Look around whatever space you find yourself in currently. How many facts are there? In how many arrangements? How many infinities of facts could one fit into the smallest perceptible space? As the philosopher and novelist Robert Pirsig puts it, "We take a handful of sand from the endless landscape of awareness around us, and call that handful of sand the world."[2]

Furthermore, if science is about value-neutral facts, what of our current scene? Fake news. Brexit. Anti-vaxxers. Flat-earthers. Holocaust and climate change denialism. QAnon conspiracy theorists. Pizzagate. Chemnitz. Election hacking. The party of crooks and thieves. The domino-like collapse of liberal democracies and the rule of law in the Philippines, Brazil, the United States, and Hungary in the face of authoritarian nationalism. Why do science, truth, moderation, and cooperation seem to be losing ground on every front? If science is about facts and only facts, why doesn't science just "win"? Why doesn't science convince?

For one, we do not see science for what it is: a language (or more accurately, multiple languages) developed between members of a community to address certain problems that the community wants to resolve. Science is a language, spoken by different communities in different contexts and for different goals. It's no different from the other languages, except in its rather obviously silly chauvinistic claim to somehow *be* the world, rather than a series of approximate conversations that offer tools with more or less power to solve problems

---

[2] Robert M. Pirsig, Zen and the Art of Motorcycle Maintenance (1974).

and accomplish tasks. Science doesn't offer a view of the world, it offers a series of conversations about the world.

One of the problems with modern science—indeed, the problem that I think is preventing basic scientific principles like climate change or the effectiveness of vaccinations from taking root—is a matter of tribal language. We think with our group. Some tribes simply refuse to believe statements made in the language of another tribe, no matter how provable the facts may be. Of course, the obtuseness of climate change denialists and anti-vaxxers is also to blame (not to mention the forums and voices which are megaphones for disinformation), but scientists also need to think hard about why they are not being heard.

The problem is deeper than realizing that some people don't understand the words used by another tribe; if that were the case, we could inoculate against conspiracies with a simple vaccination schedule of translated definitions and facts. Rather, scientists do not see that science is guided and shaped by narratives. They refuse to have anything to do with the "unscientific" realm of story and narrative. And this means that we can't see where science is getting the story wrong.

To understand this flaw, we need to delve into the narratives, not the methods of science—the goals, contexts, and communities of scientific and technological progress. Some of these guiding narratives are wildly off-center. My hope for science, as with my hope for law, is that we will be able to develop language to talk about these problems so that science can continue its usual path of providing increasingly useful stories that permit us to act and work in the world.

THE SCIENTIFIC CONVERSATION

We understand and explore our world through constructs of language—stories we tell one another about how things are and how they work. What, then, is the scientific narrative? How does science work? I could give you a definition: "A discipline, field of study, or activity concerned with theory rather than method, or requiring the knowledge and systematic application of principles, rather than relying on traditional rules, acquired skill, or intuition."[3] Or is it "knowledge or a system of knowledge covering general truths or the operation of general laws especially as obtained and tested through scientific method; such knowledge or such a system of knowledge concerned with the physical world and its phenomena"?[4] We could be here all day. Let me tell you a story instead.

[3] OED.
[4] Merriam-Webster's (11 ed.).

In the early twentieth century, a group of European philosophers and scientists wanted to put all of scientific inquiry onto a solid footing. They were tired of incursions from metaphysics that were making a muddle of scientific processes and understanding. They believed that the only truths worth paying attention to were those derived from closed logical systems (like math) and those derived from empirical observation. They developed the concept of verifiability: the idea that only that which can be proved to be true should be the subject of scientific inquiry. The Vienna Circle verificationists told a story: that facts must be proven true before they can be taken seriously.

The problem with verificationism is that a theory can never be verified completely. The next experiment might show what we thought was true was in fact false. Someone might come up with an experiment that shows what we thought was true actually isn't. So philosopher of science Karl Popper developed a better narrative: falsifiability, or the idea that a statement or theory is understood to hold as long as the next experiment does not show that it is false.[5] Falsifiability successfully overcame the Vienna Circle's verification principle and is now the now widely accepted gold standard of scientific experimentation. It's one of the most important elements in the narratives that govern the scientific method.

Scientific falsifiability wasn't ironclad, either. Popper's falsifiability predicts an experience of science in which facts are added cumulatively to the store of knowledge as they are tested. But philosopher of science Thomas Kuhn, looking at the history of science from the outside, noticed that this was not how science progressed at all.[6] Scientific revolutions came in fits and spurts, when a new paradigm, essentially a new story, a new dominating metanarrative, came to command a critical mass of the members of a particular scientific linguistic community.[7] Just as Aristotle's physics was superseded by Newton's, which in turn was superseded by Einstein, and that in turn by Planck's quantum mechanics, so the metanarrative of science itself has gone through a series of changes. The best scientific theories of an age upended those of a prior age, and were in turn themselves upended. Albert Einstein rewrote how we understand physics, but he died still not able to come to grips with quantum mechanics, swearing that "God doesn't roll dice."[8] Sorry, Al, she does.

---

5   *See generally* Karl Popper, Chapter 4: Falsifiability, in THE LOGIC OF SCIENTIFIC DISCOVERY 57–73 (Karl Popper et al. trans., 1983).
6   THOMAS S. KUHN, THE STRUCTURE OF SCIENTIFIC REVOLUTIONS (2 eds. 1970).
7   *Id.* at viii.
8   Albert Einstein, *Letter to Max Born*, in THE BORN-EINSTEIN LETTERS (Irene Born trans., 1926) (writing "Jedenfalls bin ich überzeugt, daß der nicht würfelt," which translates to "I, at any rate, am convinced that [God] does not throw dice").

Kuhn told a story in which science progressed from paradigm to paradigm in moments of revolutionary linguistic shift, when a community would start to talk about the core problems of its discipline using different examples, different core statements of the problem. This framing narrative, involving the use of the paradigmatic situations and problems that a given narrative of a scientific field was meant to solve, was a better description of how scientific communities worked together and progressed than was Popper's falsifiability. Indeed, when a new paradigm first entered scientific communities, it was not falsifiable, nor was the prior narrative. Rather, the new way of talking about the field's problems opened up more research opportunities, provided a way forward, often at the expense of essentially leaving out once-important questions (as Newton did with gravity, for example).

It should come as no surprise that when the challenge to falsifiability came, it came through the disciplines of narrative and history. Kuhn's account of how science progresses was expressly Wittgensteinian and linguistic. A "paradigm," as made famous by Kuhn, was part of a common language that permitted scientists to talk to each other: the "shared elements [that] account for the relatively unproblematic character of professional communication and for the relative unanimity of professional judgment."[9] And the shift from one scientific paradigm to another was marked by a crisis consisting of scientific-linguistic Babel: the "proliferation of competing articulations, the willingness to try anything, the expression of explicit discontent, [and] the recourse to philosophy and to debate over fundamentals."[10] Indeed, Kuhn noted that there are "significant limits to what the proponents of different theories can communicate to one another."[11]

The idea is that each iteration of scientific theory—indeed, each iteration of our theory of theories—is a less-wrong approximation. Scientific truth is a series of consensual hallucinations, agreed-upon untruths that are nevertheless *right-er* than any other theory humans have come up with.[12] They are both wrong and right at the same time. It is this feature that is their source of strength, not weakness, as one sometimes hears from Facebook culture warriors who claim that evolution is "just a theory." With Inigo Montoya, we say: "You keep using that word. I do not think it means what you think it means."

So the narrative of verifiability gave way to the narrative of falsifiability. But as we've already noted, verifiability—the theory itself—cannot be verified.

9 THOMAS KUHN, SECOND THOUGHTS ON PARADIGMS, 297 (1974).
10 KUHN, *supra* note 6, at 91.
11 *Id.*
12 *See* Nick Huggett, *"Zeno's Paradoxes"*, THE STANFORD ENCYCLOPEDIA OF PHILOSOPHY, https://plato.stanford.edu/cgi-bin/encyclopedia/archinfo.cgi?entry=paradox-zeno.

And falsifiability cannot be falsified, and was in turn challenged by Kuhn's historical narrative of scientific revolutions. These are all narratives—fireside tales spun to help scientists, and us, understand why certain patterns of observation, description, experimentation, and group discussion (peer review) help us to discover useful tools and processes.

These guiding narratives of science have different features that make them worthwhile: verifiability tells us to look for evidence, and was part of an important attempt to purge science and philosophy of the metaphysical entities that had plagued them. Focusing on what is real, what works, what makes a difference are important parts of the verificationist narrative. Similarly, falsifiability has an important narrative role. Falsifiability provided a structure for overturning established scientific theories. It established all theory as provisional, not so the shape of the earth could be questioned by flat-earthers, or its age by fundamentalists, but so that it could be revised as we get better dating tools and methods. Falsifiability noted that there is always room for another experiment—that out of the infinity of facts of a given experiment, we cannot be certain of causes; we can only substitute smaller infinities of facts for larger ones, and narrow our search. And Kuhn's historical treatment of paradigmatic language-shifts in scientific communities helped account for the sine-wave of revolution and workaday science.

Science is a linguistic conversation among groups of highly trained speakers. Science is guided by narratives, adopted by the most people, about how the discipline works. Some words have a guiding role on the scientific endeavor. Verification, falsifiability, and other, later narratives of science each played important roles in guiding the scientific community. These narratives of science have helped scientists phrase questions, decide what was worth looking into, and guided them away from fruitless research. The argument, often heard, that verifiability and falsifiability are "unscientific" because they do not meet their own criteria is a prime example of the muddle-headed thinking that now pervades technological progress: technologists too often ignorantly deny the importance of narratives while advancing narratives that are toxic to continued human thriving.

Furthermore, it is only by looking at patterns, at examining science from the perspective of history and narrative, that we can hit on the useful insight that science is a series of evolving conversations and shifting narratives that guide its activity. The scientific narrative is just as subject to change as any other area of human endeavor.

Reminding ourselves of these points helps us think and speak differently about science. We can think, for one, about why the anti-vaxxer isn't hearing us. They are part of an alternative narrative ecosystem, or informational sphere, or linguistic community. Science has more weight than its output alone: it represents a linguistic community loyal to empirical observation, to certain methodologies, and the scientific conversation. Science provides a way of knowing and talking about the world that can threaten political power. Authoritarian regimes, for example, need their truth to bend toward political expediency. So they systematically co-opt and foster distrust in institutions that do not share an allegiance to their regime. The war on science is like any war; propaganda and information technology are used to attack facts and truth.

We won't win the hearts and minds of civilians by the simple reassertion of facts. Even time is against us. With the internet, a lie can get around the world seven billion times before the truth can get its pants on. Rather, science needs to talk differently.[13] I'm not saying its facts should stop being facts. But it must stop presuming that facts are just facts. If a person doesn't understand science, yes, that might be because they don't understand the scientific use of terms like *theory* and *statistical probability*. But explaining things that people might not know is perhaps less effective than building trust and appealing to values and emotion.[14] This is a conversation about *why* not *how*. It sounds like a story, not an operations manual.

REDUCED TO REDUCTIONISM

With the clarifying image of science as a series of shifting conversations and guiding narratives, I'd like to consider a dominant theme in the scientific metanarrative: reductionism. Broadly, reductionism is a dog's breakfast of intuitions that some sciences are "purer," "more basic," or "more elementary" than others.

Scientists attach a strange weight to studying phenomena at the smallest unit measurements available: sociology reduced to economics, economics reduced to individual psychology, psychology reduced to neuroscience, neuroscience reduced to biology, biology reduced to chemistry, chemistry reduced to physics, physics reduced to mathematics.[15] This explains the

---

[13] For an example, *see* Anne Applebaum, *Italians Decided to Fight a Conspiracy Theory. Here's What Happened Next*, WASH. POST (August 8, 2019), www.washingtonpost.com/opinions/global-opinions/italians-decided-to-fight-a-conspiracy-theory-heres-what-happened-next/2019/08/08/ca950828-ba10-11e9-b3b4-2bb69e8c4e39_story.html.

[14] Tim Requarth, *Scientists, Stop Thinking Explaining Science Will Fix Things*, SLATE (April 19, 2017), https://slate.com/technology/2017/04/explaining-science-wont-fix-information-illiteracy.html.

[15] See MIDGLEY, *supra* note 1, at 88.

strange metaphors scientists use to describe the difference between reductionist disciplines, which are described as "hard" (think chemistry, physics, and
mathematics), and those that study patterns, which are called "soft" (think
history, sociology, psychology). Why in the world would one use words like
"purity" and "hard" and "soft" to explain scientific fields? The "soft" sciences
are considered to be "superficial, amateurish, non-serious, because they fall
short of the ultimate explanation."[16] Where does the name-calling and contempt come from? Certainly not from results: as this book argues, sociologists
and historians have done more to understand human patterns than have
physicists, by a long shot.

In her book *The Myths We Live By*, the philosopher Mary Midgley traces
this reductive habit of studying phenomena at their most basic level to the
Enlightenment. "[T]he Enlightenment notion of physical sciences was
imperialist from the outset," writes Midgely. "This science was associated
with two strangely ambitious claims, infallibility and the formal unity of the
whole of thought."[17] We can map from Galileo and Descartes onward the
effort to reduce science to a single model, to science's aspiration to be
a hegemonic theory of all that is, an explanation of everything all at once.
It's obviously not: there are gaps between fields of science that we can and will
fit entire other fields of science into. Yet an Enlightenment addiction to
thinking that there is one field that could explain all others, and indeed
explain reality itself, has led scientists to stack disciplines reductively—and
profoundly unscientifically—according to the theory that the disciplines that
deal with reality at its most "basic" or most "elemental" can encompass all the
others. We can and should question the application of those words, too, and
whether we would consider quarks and atoms more basic than markets,
politics, or romantic poetry if it were not for the tropes of scientism.

Trying to understand love or other facts of subjective human existence by
reducing it to physics is like trying to study ocean currents by studying water
molecules. This profoundly anti-scientific narrative of reductionism is found
throughout the structure of scientific study. Neoclassical economics is an
example particularly ripe for criticism: economists believe in a crippled
Homo economicus, an entirely self-interested actor who betrays the tribe
whenever possible for her own self-interest.[18] Although we know that "no
one is an island," the core crazy assumption of neoclassical economics is

---

[16] *Id.* at 36.
[17] *Id.* at 33.
[18] Chris Doucouliagos, *A Note on the Evolution of Homo Economicus*, 28:3 J. Econ. Issues 877
     (1994) ("The neoclassical economists' Homo Economicus has several characteristics, the most
     important of which are (1) maximizing (optimizing) behavior; (2) the cognitive ability to

that we are: we are atoms, alone, individual economic actors who take what we can in a market of such individuals. Economists screw up, of course, when they define rationality as the desire to operate solely in one's own self-interest, rather than that of the group.[19] Economic experiments show beyond any shadow of a doubt that it is often to the enormous benefit of everyone in a group to forego individual self-advantage and work together—as you may recall, this is E. O. Wilson's iron rule of social evolution.

This is just one example; once you see the problem, you'll see the crack in almost every scientific discipline. We do not see the metanarrative behind why physicists claim to have a better understanding of love than novelists, or why economists make foolish and obviously observably wrong statements about human rationality. This is why we need to delve into the relationship between science and its guiding metanarratives: into the reasons *why* we perform science, rather than merely how.

When it comes to the study of patterns there's little hope in a reductive approach: to study patterns, we are going to have to look up, metaphorically speaking, not drill down. Studying the chemical properties of water helps only a little with understanding why ocean currents are collecting a massive plastic vortex in the Pacific. Drilling down into biology, chemistry, and physics will not help solve our current problems of the pace of technological development, or explain the worldwide collapse of liberal democracies in the face of authoritarian nationalism. Complex patterns require complex analysis; in matters of politics and law, physicists need not apply. As we climb the ladder, without judgment, from simple to complex, from physics to chemistry to biology to neurology to psychology, economics, sociology, linguistics, cultural anthropology, and eventually law, we find that the patterns become clearer, more subject to study, and more susceptible to coherent and useful explanation. Physics cannot itself tell us why to study physics—other than the personal satisfaction and testimony of physicists, which is pretty solid grounds to believe they're having fun. But it doesn't tell us where our time is best spent, what thoughts open us to more possibilities, and most of all, how we can talk to one another in a productive way.

In *The Myths We Live By*, Midgley demonstrates how the Enlightenment is itself a myth—"a partial truth based on an imaginative vision fired by a particular set of ideals," which created its own myths, including those that

---

exercise rational choice; and (3) individualistic behavior and independent tastes and preferences.").

[19]   *Id.* ("(1) [A]gents may not act individualistically, and (2) agents' tastes and references are neither exogenous nor independent.").

pursue the "lure of Reduction—the pleasure of claiming that things are much simpler than they seem."[20] Midgley rightly reasons that the problem is not the *existence* of myths or ideals or other imaginative outputs: our fictions are powerful and necessary; they shape our activity. "What is needed," she writes, "is that they should be conscious and openly expressed for discussion."[21]

Reductionism argues otherwise with a sleight of hand. It denigrates and disposes of narrative while refusing to see that it too is a fiction that guides our activity. Once we begin to see this, we can spot all sorts of other troubling myths that steer our not-at-all-neutral or omnicompetent science.

MYTHS OF PRODUCTIVITY AND PERFORMANCE

The path of science and technology is anything but neutral. It is guided by half-cloaked narratives. Sometimes those narratives are easy to suss out: for example, Big Data is paying for a lot of US senators' reelection campaigns, and in return it expects to be able to continue to exploit users' data without meaningful consent or redress.[22] That is part of the broader story of how wealth is used to destabilize democracy, and although it is pernicious (more on that later), I would like to talk about more subtle effects here.

For example, have you ever noticed that almost all scientific research is focused on increased productivity and efficiency? We could have other goals than maximizing production. Our current science claims to prefer performativity: that which "works," although as we have noticed, lots of things work, yet few are considered valid subjects of scientific inquiry (myths and legends, for example: of course they are not "true," but that has never been their point).

As the philosopher Jean-Francois Lyotard writes: "It was more the desire for wealth than the desire for knowledge that initially forced upon technology the imperative of performance improvement and product realization."[23] And once that cycle started—in the first industrial revolution of the eighteenth century—once scientific principles required increasing amounts of high-powered equipment to demonstrate validity to the linguistic community of scientists, "this equation was discovered: no technology without wealth, but no

---

[20]   MIDGLEY, *supra* note 1, at xii.
[21]   *Id.* at 56.
[22]   *See, e.g.*, Herb Jackson, *Facebook a Big contributor to the Committees in Congress that Will Question Mark Zuckerberg*, USA TODAY, April 4, 2018, www.usatoday.com/story/news/polit ics/2018/04/04/facebook-gave-most-contributions-house-committee-question-zuckerberg-also-got-most-contributions-fac/486313002/.
[23]   JEAN-FRANCOIS LYOTARD, THE POSTMODERN CONDITION 45 (1979).

wealth without technology."[24] In short, our engine for creating science — and it is not the only one possible — was to create products, and use the surplus to pay for further development of more products. Thus,

> [c]apitalism solves the scientific problem of research funding in its own way: directly by financing research departments in private companies, in which demands for performativity and recommercialization orient research first and foremost toward technological "applications." . . . The prevailing corporate norms of work management spread to the applied science laboratories: hierarchy, centralized decision making, teamwork, calculation of individual and collective returns, the development of saleable programs, market research, and so on.[25]

Lyotard puts it bluntly: "Technology is therefore a game pertaining not to the true, the just, or the beautiful, etc., but to efficiency: a technical 'move' is 'good' when it does better and/or expends less energy than another."[26]

A science built solely on the guiding narrative of productivity is a very small science indeed. As Lyotard explains, "Research sectors that are unable to argue that they contribute even indirectly to the optimization of the system's performance are abandoned by the flow of capital and doomed to senescence."[27] This, in turn, feeds back into the education system: "The desired goal becomes the optimal contribution of higher education to the best performativity of the social system. . . . [U]niversities and the institutions of higher learning are called upon to create skills, and no longer ideals."[28] This is not good at all, since it is good ideals and normative commitments — persuasive cooperative fictions that cause humans to work together and to thrive — that we badly need if we are to cooperate to solve the problems that come at an increasing rate.

I should add at this point: I only criticize capitalism because it is the worst form of economic organization, except for all the others that have been tried from time to time.[29] I do not advocate for any other twentieth-century-ism. But some fairly important cogs have broken or are about to break in the capitalist machine that has lifted many out of worldwide poverty, made a vanishing few obscenely wealthy, and decimated the middle class throughout the developed nations.

---

[24] *Id.* at 45.
[25] *Id.* at 45–46.
[26] *Id.*
[27] *Id.* at 47.
[28] *Id.* at 48–50.
[29] To steal Churchill's trenchant take on democracy.

Our scientific focus on productivity and efficiency is the result of a given social pattern of doing things. The point is not that how we do things is bad: it has gotten us this far. But it is important to understand that certain things that appear to be givens about science and technological progress—and chief among them the myth that technology must serve performativity and productivity—need to be held loosely in our minds. We give lip service to sustainability and equilibrium, at least as part of environmental language, but as soon as we cast equilibrium in economic terms, it becomes stagnation, lack of innovation, and so on. These are not scientific terms; they are the framing terms of science as it is currently practiced by a worldwide linguistic community. Increasing our awareness that the core myths of science do not share any special imprimatur—they are just as made up as any other cooperative fiction —will help us make the changes we need to make if we are to study how to thrive with as much or even more ferocity than we have studied how to produce.

HUMAN-SHAPED SCIENCE

A second, and even more subtle guiding influence on our science to date, and one that is already changing with serious beneficial and baneful consequences for human well-being, is what I will call *Zufallssinn*, based on the work of Fritz Mauthner, a philosopher of language.[30] *Zufallssinn* means, literally, "random sense," both in the meaning of the senses, and in the meaning of our own sense of intelligence. What Mauthner meant by *Zufallssinn* was that science is human-shaped. We experiment by observation, fine: but what we observe is determined by our eyes.

Consider a red, white, and blue flag. If you're an American, you might instantly picture the American flag. If you're in the Netherlands or France, you might be imagining their respective tricolors. You already understand the problem that E. O. Wilson describes to help us ponder:

> [T]he seeming obviousness of human nature: an insect flying by would perceive different wavelengths, and break them into different colors or none at all, depending on its species, and if somehow it could speak, its words would be hard to translate into our own. Its flag would be very different from our flag, thanks to its insect (as opposed to human) nature. "This is the

---

[30] Mauthner lived at the turn of the twentieth-century; Ludwig Wittgenstein, the most important twentieth-century philosopher of language, owed him an enormous and largely unacknowledged debt.

ant flag; its colors are ultraviolet and green" (ants can see ultraviolet, which we cannot see, but not red, which we can).[31]

Sure: we build tools to let us see magnetic fields (which birds can sense but we can't), or ultraviolet light, or very tiny particles, but the problem remains: we are interested in a tiny fraction of the universe, the part that matters to fairly small primates on a fairly small ball drifting in a void, the immensity of which we have no real way to grasp. There are no human scientific experiments that take one million years to complete, because that is off our scale of time. There are no human scientific experiments that operate at an interstellar, galactic, or intergalactic scale, because it is off of our scale of space.

And it turns out that this really matters. Consider, for example, that linguist Steven Pinker believes that our sense of space, time, and causation come preloaded in our consciousness. And modern physics shows that almost all of our natural sense of space and time is a useful approximation at the scale of human life on planet Earth, but really, really wrong when applied to the universe. (For example, very nearly all depiction of time in science fiction movies with faster-than-light travel is utter magical thinking.) Some errors about the fundamental nature of the universe are built into our cognitive structure. It would almost be impossible to function as a human if we could not distinguish between space and time, and most of our minds are taken up with causation: if I do this, what happens? Yet our notions of space and causality are also deeply skewed. Our sense of these things is an evolutionary "close enough for purposes of survival under conditions on Earth."

Our wiring has betrayed us on all fronts. Space, time, and causation are illusions caused by the fact that we are so very small and crammed so very tightly together on a cosmologically microscopic speck of interstellar dust. Newtonian physics makes sense to us because of our surroundings and evolution; general and special relativity take training precisely because we are wired wrongly. Noted British philosopher and mathematician Bertrand Russell made this point in a wonderfully simple book on relativity. In it he told the following story (and let me emphasize that it is only a story): imagine that we took an engineer and left her rationality intact, but otherwise removed her memory and all preconceptions based on the world. Then imagine we took her out at night, in a hot-air balloon, drifting over the Atlantic. Below, imagine that all she could see upon waking were ships, moving slowly on the dark waters, and that the only way the ships could communicate was by sending up fireworks. In that environment, floating in the dark, lit only by flashes from far-

---

[31]   EDWARD WILSON, THE SOCIAL CONQUEST OF EARTH 206 (2012).

away slowly moving objects, Russell said, we might have developed a more intuitive sense for how space, time, and causation work. As Russell writes:

> What sort of picture of the world will you form? You will think that nothing is permanent: there are only brief flashes of light, which, during their short existence, travel through the void in the most various and bizarre curves. You cannot touch these flashes of light, you can only see them. Obviously your geometry and your physics and your metaphysics will be quite different from those of ordinary mortals.[32]

What do we do when we find out our evolved intuitive senses of space and time cause our science to be too narrow? We develop words like "spacetime" and "relativity" to talk about a different way of conceptualizing things that avoids the limitations of our evolved intuitions. We come up with new language.

Or, to take another example: Euclid's geometry includes his Fifth Postulate (here I will use Playfair's postulate, which is easier to describe), which says that given a line and a point not on the line, only one line passes through that point and does not intersect the line (i.e., only one line will be parallel). The problem is, this postulate is an assumption about the world in which the geometry is to be performed: it is an assumption that space in that world is flat and two-dimensional. But spacetime isn't flat at all: it is best described as curved. And if reality is curved, then infinitely many (or none at all, depending on the curve) lines can be drawn through a point without intersecting an original line. These geometries—hyperbolic geometry and elliptic geometry among them—are much less natural to us. Because local space does not appear curved to us, our perception misled us as to even the basic nature of geometry for far more centuries than were necessary. Even our geometry, then, is human-shaped.

MACHINE-HUMAN SCIENCE

The fact that our current science is human-shaped matters. On the one hand, it helps us see the limits of the problems we select to work on. The problems humans choose to work on may not be the problems we need to work on to keep ourselves as a species alive, such as climate change. Moreover, the fact that our science is human-shaped is about to change. Artificial intelligence is already changing the kind of science we are doing, and the kind of hypotheses we pose.

---

[32]   BERTRAND RUSSELL, ABCs OF RELATIVITY 11 (4th ed. 1985).

The story of the development of chess algorithms gives us a good view of the process of the integration of machine-human problem-solving. Purely algorithmic attempts to solve chess mathematically proved computationally difficult: there are still just too many permutations. On May 11, 1997, IBM artificial intelligence Deep Blue finally beat Gary Kasparov.[33] At that time, Deep Blue still relied heavily on its own "intelligence": mathematics, statistics, and so on. But the next decade showed a sea change in artificial intelligence methods, such that by 2012, a strange kind of hybrid machine-human intelligence dominated chess play.

The past fifteen years have seen an unprecedented expansion of this new kind of artificial intelligence, one based on a computer examining millions of cases of what humans do, rather than the computer figuring out what to do based on its own internalized formalized rules. AI problems that had gone unsolved for decades suddenly became solvable: teaching a machine to recognize cat videos, take dictation, or drive a car. Machine intelligences learned to do those things from us. What changed was the amount of raw data now recorded, stored, and made available to machine learning algorithms for them to learn. All the data produced on every piece of paper in the world at the turn of the millennium is now a tiny fraction of the amount produced in a month in 2008, in a week in 2012, and very soon sometime in the next decade, in a day. The explosion of the Internet of Things, as well as the smartphone revolution, which caused humans to carry powerful computers with geolocation, motion detection, microphones, and cameras throughout the "real world," had the side effect of multiplying the data produced by those sensors. Social media had the side effect of categorizing and storing the choices, the infamous "likes" of billions of humans. And while no human can make use of that colossal stream of data, machines can.

After the explosion of what is now called Big Data (the fact that this term sounds old and buzzword-y is because these techniques have supplanted almost every other way of doing things), numerous very hard problems of AI became solvable. The one we experience most on a daily basis is voice-to-text and Google Translate, both based on "deep learning."[34] The idea of "deep

---

[33] Bruce Weber, *Deep Blue Escapes with Draw to Force Decisive Last Game*, N.Y. TIMES (May 11, 1997), www.nytimes.com/1997/05/11/nyregion/deep-blue-escapes-with-draw-to-force-decisive-last-game.html.

[34] Y. Wu, M. Schuster, Z. Chen, Q. V. Le, M. Norouzi, W. Macherey, M. Krikun, Y. Cao, Q. Gao, K. Macherey, J. Klingner, A. Shah, M. Johnson, X. Liu, L. Kaiser, S. Gouws, Y. Kato, T. Kudo, H. Kazawa, K. Stevens, G. Kurian, N. Patil, W. Wang, C. Young, J. Smith, J. Riesa, A. Rudnick, O. Vinyals, G. Corrado, M. Hughes, and J. Dean, *"Google's Neural Machine Translation System: Bridging the Gap between Human and Machine Translation,"* CoRR, vol. abs/1609.08144, 2016, https://arxiv.org/pdf/1609.08144.pdf.

learning" is simple at core (although staggeringly complex in execution): feed machine learning algorithms colossal datasets. Then use the patterns learned from those massive datasets to sort through the staggering amounts of data produced by our civilization to find trends too big for us to see.

The problem of teaching computers to recognize, transcribe, and translate human speech—the languages we have been talking about here—is particularly revealing. A machine learning algorithm does not learn to "think," it learns how *we* think. And it learns how we speak not by examining how one person speaks (the speech-recognition engines of the late '1990s were atrocious: they attempted to learn the individual characteristics of the user, and they never got anywhere), but by ingesting exabytes of data about how we speak. Every use of a word is fodder for machine learning algorithms.[35] The algorithms learn how to use words not by referring to their internal machine-logic dictionary of what words mean, but according to highly developed learning algorithms that have examined the millions of different ways and contexts and structures in which words are used. A traditional computer needs to know what the definition of a term is, as well as rules of grammar, the exceptions to the rules of grammar, and so on. A machine-learning algorithm just needs to know how we use words—just as Ludwig Wittgenstein predicted.[36]

Computers that learn from us beat computers that work things out purely according to machine logic. As I write, the best results in chess are no longer from very smart computers, but are from machine learning algorithms that form part of hybrid machine-human teams, where the machine has learned every game ever played, and millions more, spinning out ideas for novel situations.[37] Humans curate these inquiries, pointing out likely avenues, and un-sticking the machines when they get trapped at local maxima.

To recap: computer scientists first taught computers to perform certain tasks by providing them with rules and definitions. But for the harder questions— translating language, or identifying cat videos as cat videos on YouTube, or figuring out in a fraction of a second which advertiser will get the most bang for the buck out of putting an ad under our noses— we turned to feeding machine

---

[35] Jordan Valinsky, *Facebook Will Pay You up to $5 to Record Your Voice* (February 21, 2020), www .cnn.com/2020/02/21/tech/facebook-voice-recordings/index.html (discussing exceedingly modest payments to users for recordings of their voices).

[36] *See* Olivia Goldhill, *Google Translate Is a Manifestation of Wittgenstein's Theory of Language*, Quartz, Feb. 13, 2019, https://qz.com/1549212/google-translate-is-a-manifestation-of-wittgensteins-theory-of-language/.

[37] *See, e.g.*, Emerging Technology from the arXiv, *Deep Learning Machine Teaches Itself Chess in 72 Hours, Plays at International Master Level*, MIT Technology Review (Sept. 14, 2015), www.technologyreview.com/s/541276/deep-learning-machine-teaches-itself-chess-in-72-hours -plays-at-international-master/.

learning algorithms with our own lifeblood: the recorded information of what we think, how we use words, how we act, and what we decide.

And that balance is now shifting. In a sense, we have taught machine learning algorithms what we know, and they can see it in ways we cannot. The amount of data far surpasses any kind of human comprehension. And algorithms that can see those patterns allow us to do the kind of science — or art![38] — that was originally beyond our human capacity.

This is something quite different from prior tools, which extended our senses. In the case of the microscope or telescope, the tool extended our senses, but not our guesses as to what science was to be done. Those tools expanded human science, and elaborated on human goals. We used the tools to human ends.

Human-machine science is increasingly becoming machine-human science. The orthodoxy of scientific hypothesis testing is giving way to a science that listens very carefully to the suggestions of machines. The metanarrative — the "story of how we do it" — of some kinds of science is changing. If you are older, you might, like me, remember that "data driven" science was at one time frowned upon. Starting from your data to form hypotheses was seen as exactly backwards: one must first form a hypothesis, then test it against the data.

But now, there is no advanced science that is not data driven. Consider some statements by leading geneticists on how their science has been completely transformed in the past fifteen years:

> One of the big changes in science . . . has been the move away from a very focused, targeted, hypothesis-driven approach, the "I've got this idea, I design the experiment, I run the experiment, and decide whether I was right or wrong" model.
>
> It used to be that you had to have some plausible idea about *why* a gene might do something — that you could imagine some sensible-sounding biochemical pathway which could link the gene to a disease or trait. The time it took to sequence genes and the limited computing power available meant you had to be quite sure you were going to find something before you dedicated all that expensive lab and analysis time.
>
> Now you just collect a lot of data and let the data decide what the hypothesis should be. If you look at 10,000 genomes of people with a disease and 10,000 without, you can use an algorithm to compare them,

---

[38] Gabe Cohn, *AI Art at Christies Sells for $432,500*, N.Y. TIMES (October 25, 20108), www.nytimes.com/2018/10/25/arts/design/ai-art-sold-christies.html (discussing the sale of an AI-generated artwork).

find the differences and then work out which genes are linked to the disease, without having to think in advance about which ones they might be.[39]

The metanarrative of science continues to change: now, instead of verification or falsifiability of human hypotheses, many advances follow suggestions made by machine algorithms that comb through more data than any human can imagine. The hypothesis and confirmation are often the same: some pattern found in the data.

MACHINE-LED SCIENCE

What role is left for humans in such a science? Note, I do not suggest these developments are bad, in some Luddite sense. Rather, we must carefully examine what will happen when the problems to be studied are selected by machine learning algorithms, and the results are only confirmable by machine learning algorithms, if at all.

This is called the "black box" problem.[40] Here is the difficulty: imagine that we ask a machine learning algorithm to perform some arbitrarily hard task. The usual one is to ask a machine to estimate what the return on investment is for putting a targeted advertisement in front of a consumer, given that consumer's purchase patterns, web browsing, social media, and Internet of Things data. From those, other data—called "features"—can be extracted: income, class, sex, race, sexual orientation, national origin, age, geolocation, and so on. Every piece of information can yield insight to a machine learning algorithm. It does not care whether the connection makes sense, merely that it exists. Assume, for example, that the distance an employee drives to work is the best way to predict employee turnover, or that the purchase of those little felt "footies" for furniture is the best indication of loan repayment. The algorithm engages in no hypothesis testing. No one thinks, "ah, maybe driving distance is an indication of employee dissatisfaction," or "maybe people who buy felt footies are neurotic about taking care of their property, and likely to be similarly neurotic about paying back debt."

Those are explanations, but there is no reason to think they are correct ones. All that the machine learning algorithm knows is that the data field "bought felt footies" is more often correlated with "successful loan repayment" than other fields. All the algorithm knows is that a significant percent of the time, employees with longer driving distances have higher turnover. Not why.

---

[39]   Tom Chivers, *How Big Data Is Changing Science*, MOSAIC SCIENCE (October 2, 2018), https://mosaicscience.com/story/how-big-data-changing-science-algorithms-research-genomics/.
[40]   A black box is a complex device that the user finds unexplainable.

In the case of felt footies and driving distances, humans can automatically generate stories, because we are dealing with one feature. But now comes the rub. If one wants to predict loan repayment or employee turnover, or the future chance of committing a crime based on past history, many features may be positively correlated with the outcome. At a certain point, human scientists (rightly) became certain they could not generate convincing causal stories for the highly accurate predictions of their algorithms. They know the predictions are accurate, but they haven't much of an idea why.

Often the work of a data scientist is to prune the decision trees, like a bonsai artist, cutting off the computer's use of new features once the information gain drops below a certain and often arbitrary threshold. Often we limit the number of features because of human limitations, not machine ones. A machine can always find another feature that helps it predict its output variable slightly better. Maybe number of feet walked per day (extracted from personal fitness trackers) and number of sleep disturbances per night do not have a huge impact on loan repayment, but enough to make predictions slightly more accurate. The algorithms I have personally observed in action were trimmed at seventeen to twenty-five features, based on a floor set for purposes of human interpretability.

What this means is that there is an inverse relationship between machine learning accuracy and human interpretability. We have no idea why the most accurate machine learning algorithms work, other than that they have discovered features that in weighted combination most accurately predict their output variables (without overtraining, which we don't need to go into here).

The relationships between features and output variables found by the machine learning algorithm often have no human explanation at all, or one that is so attenuated that any explanation feels like writing fiction. In one machine learning exercise, which I observed as a privacy and civil liberties counsel, the data scientists attempted to learn which persons were leaders in virtual worlds, like World of Warcraft and Second Life. Out of all the features that the machine learning algorithms sussed out, the top information gain for one of the worlds was whether the person's avatar wore black pants.

Why? I could tell you a story. But any story would be just that, a story, and not one based on any confirmable context. The real answer is nobody knows, and nobody can know, because of the scientific method used: massive machine-detected correlation across many, many features. All the machine knew was that of all the features fed into the machine learning program, the information gain of the field "pants color" was the highest.

This has two fairly unsettling implications. The first is that we are now using tools to research questions that are not focused on hypotheses dreamed up by humans; the second is that the results are accurate, but we cannot explain why. In the experiments with which I am most familiar, the problem was serious: the output reports were intended to guide policymakers, but no one can know why sufficiently well-fed machine learning algorithms burped out a given result. A machine learning algorithm can tell you which customers are worth targeting, but not why. It may tell you who is most likely to commit a crime, but (and this gets scary) the police running it wouldn't be able to give a good answer why—and probably wouldn't like the answer much if they could.[41]

Accuracy and human interpretability are rapidly diverging in the most important areas of scientific inquiry. Demanding decisional transparency from algorithms—as many of the best minds in law have done—is more than a little naive. The point is that algorithms cannot explain themselves, they have no explanation, merely features and information gain. And there is no explanation to be given, merely correlations. The only way to confirm the output of an algorithm is to run it on the same data, which, mathematically, will yield the same results.

Data-sharing for purposes of algorithmic verification is extraordinarily rare, because the companies who train these AIs know that their training data is the lifeblood of their competitive advantage. Facebook makes money because it has more training data about what you will buy. Data is literally AI food: countries and corporations are well aware that raw data amounts result in AI dominance, and so they don't share. Coca-Cola will reveal the secret of its prize formula, or Kentucky Fried Chicken its secret recipe, long before Google will let anyone—*anyone*—get near the data and algorithms underlying its PageRank algorithm. And because these algorithms update constantly based on new data, a machine learning algorithm may be impossible to test except at a given moment in time, which is often not useful.

Moreover, the entire process of falsifiability in data science does not follow normal rules. One algorithm, trained on one dataset, doesn't really falsify another algorithm, trained on a different one. Certainly, there are coding errors and other basic data science sins. But once the algorithms are

---

[41] Since machine learning algorithms learn from humans, there are real problems when an algorithm learns discrimination from us. In the case of algorithmic predictive policing, police behavior often creates the pattern the computer finds. Consider the question, "to which neighborhoods should police be sent?" Well, if an algorithm looks at arrest records, it finds the neighborhoods where most people were arrested—which is problematic for all sorts of obvious reasons, not least of which the history of individual and structural racism in policing. So our algorithm will find that the most arrests occurred in minority neighborhoods, which means that more police should be sent there now, which means that more arrests will continue to happen in those neighborhoods.

responsibly sicced on a rich dataset, there is no way of saying the system is wrong. How would one disconfirm a finding? One would have to find another inexplicable weighting of features, usually using much the same algorithm on an even richer set of data features, that increases accuracy in prediction of output variables. But then the original algorithm hasn't been disconfirmed, merely improved upon, and the new algorithm is every bit as inexplicable as the old. On the contrary: imagine we have two algorithms, trained on different sets. Algorithm A reaches 70 percent accuracy; Algorithm B reaches 65 percent accuracy. Data scientists do not then say that A has falsified B merely because it is more accurate. And here's the trick: *combining A and B into an even less comprehensible and explainable mess is very likely to increase A's accuracy.* Better algorithms don't falsify worse ones — worse ones are often the best way to improve better ones.

The human high priests who tend to the machines can formulate careful prayers, and can confirm miracles of accuracy, but they cannot tell anyone why the features help predict the output variables. At the level of the sophisticated machine learning algorithms that now control the stock market, where speed and accuracy matter far above explainability, no one has the faintest idea *why* any given 100+ features predict which stocks to buy and sell, and when, only that they do. Human intervention is reserved to pulling the plug when an AI runs into an ahistorical event, called a "black swan," something the algorithm has not studied, and therefore responds incorrectly to, or falls into a trap. A great example of this is Knight Capital's berserk stock-purchasing AI, which caused serious damage before being deactivated after just a few minutes of operation.[42]

We are now quite far progressed into nonhuman science. The hypotheses-generation and confirmation roles of humans are an ever smaller proportion of the process, and often human involvement is limited now to a failsafe role, and to limiting the feature sets — that is, telling the algorithms to be less accurate so that we can follow along — where human explainability is particularly important.

And here we can begin to talk frankly about some of the real dangers of artificial intelligence. Forget the Terminator movies. The danger is not that AI will think like we do, and will hate us. The danger is that AI will be simply a different intelligence, competing for some of the same resources. Edsger Dijkstra, one of the founders of modern programming languages, put the problem neatly: "The question of whether a computer can think is no more interesting than the question of whether a submarine can swim."[43] Swimming

42 Jessica Silver-Greenberg & Ben Protess, *Trying to Be Nimble, Knight Capital Stumbles,* N. Y. TIMES DEALBOOK (Aug. 2, 2012).
43 Edsger W. Dijkstra, *The Threats to Computing Science,* Speech delivered at the ACM 1984 South Central Regional Conference (Nov. 16–18, Austin, TX), www.cs.utexas.edu/users/EWD/transcriptions/EWD08xx/EWD898.html.

is a way of doing a task, among many ways, and machines perform these tasks differently. In the same way, the question of whether machines will think as we do when they perform tasks we perform is a bit silly: a Google self-driving car certainly does not experience road rage, highway hypnosis, or consciousness, for that matter, but it drives. It is competent to do a task that previously only humans did, although it performs the task in an entirely different—and inexplicable—way.

The danger is that AI will become *competent* and *will have different, nonhuman objectives.* Superior competence and divergent goals is an existential threat to any intelligent species that comes in second place. There is no reason to think that in 40,000 to 30,000 BCE in what would become Europe, *Homo sapiens* hated Neanderthals, or that in east Asia, *Homo sapiens* hated Denisovans. In fact, in both cases, genetic evidence showed that the species more than occasionally made love not war.[44] But the newfound cooperative competence of *Homo sapiens,* combined with lack of adaptability in Neanderthal and Denisovan culture, led to those species vanishing in an evolutionary moment.[45] As Yuval Harari points out, we don't hate cows, either, but our goals diverge from theirs, and we raise, slaughter, and eat them in their billions.

HUMAN-MACHINE CULTURE

While we are still training AI based on our own output, that is, while our data (and as a result our values) are still the primary input to machine learning algorithms, we desperately need to clarify and develop our goals. We need to think very hard about what we are training AI—using our daily exabytes[46] of Twitter, Facebook, Google, Fitbit, smartphone, Alexa, and Siri data—to do.

It only takes a bit of poetic license to describe the current AI ecosystem as one in which AIs hunt human economic surplus for food. Here is how it works: some time ago, my mother was searching for plane tickets for a family trip. She wanted to know if my wife and I were able to come along, and contacted me in some distress, because when she searched different sites for tickets and googled her destination, the prices kept going up, and seats were vanishing on the relevant planes very quickly. She needed to know right away, therefore, if my wife and I were able to come. I asked her to clear her cookies and start

---

[44]   *See, e.g.,* Ann Gibbons, *Oldest* Homo sapiens *Genome Pinpoints Neandertal Input,* Science, Mar. 28, 2014, http://science.sciencemag.org/content/343/6178/1417; Maria Martinon-Torress et al., Homo sapiens *in the Eastern Asian Late Pleistocene,* 58 Current Anthropology S434 (2017).

[45]   Yuval Noah Harari, Sapiens: A Brief History of Humankind 16–19 (2015).

[46]   An exabyte is one quintillion bytes, or 10^{18} bytes.

a different browser, and suddenly all the missing seats were again available on the planes, and the prices were much lower. (By the way, this is an old story: given the sophistication of tracking technology these days, clearing your cookies and changing browsers likely wouldn't work anymore.)

What was going on? By comparison shopping, my mother was demonstrating that she was indeed very interested in purchasing—which made the price go up, not down, of course. And each time she revisited the online ticket purchase site, she demonstrated to the site's resident pricing programs that she was even more likely to pay a higher price. For an AI, the right price for a good or service is the very maximum you would be willing to pay for it: the price at which, if the AI raised the price by one more cent, you would decide not to purchase. At that point, the AI has found the price that is "all you can pay."[47]

The finest minds of a generation of researchers and programmers have been involved in teaching algorithms to price products and services at the "all you can pay" point.[48] That is why, when you go to a webpage, a high-speed auction for your eyeballs can take place: AIs already know what you, or people sufficiently economically like you as to make no difference, are willing to pay for a good or service, what the hit rate is, and thus what to pay for an advertising impression.[49] Trillions of dollars have been poured into this effort to extract every last dime from consumers.

That's bad, because trade creates wealth. If I want a bicycle and am willing to pay $100 for it, and you have a bicycle, and would be willing to take $50 for it, and I buy it from you for $75, we both go home and tell our families what a great day we had! I got a bicycle cheap! You got a great price for your bicycle! In such a case, we have split the surplus of the trade: you got $25 more than you would have taken in a pinch, and I paid $25 less than I would have paid if I absolutely had to.

This is precisely the surplus that algorithms are trained to hunt. An algorithm is fed on data: data from purchase patterns, data from social media, data from geolocation information, data from internet of things devices, data about friends' data. The more data an algorithm eats, the better it can extract trade surplus from human consumers.[50] The more value it extracts, the more profit

---

[47] Anna Bernasek & D. T. Mongan, All You Can Pay: How Companies Use Our Data to Empty Our Wallets (2015).

[48] *Id.*

[49] *Id.*

[50] And the reach is expanding. For example, a proposed algorithm model adjusted auto insurance rates individually according to collated consumer data. "[The] model seemed to determine how much a customer was willing to pay—or overpay—without defecting, based on how much he or she was already forking out for car insurance. And the harm would not have been equally

the firm it serves makes, the more data it gets, either because the firm extracts it directly (the Google/Facebook model) or because the firm has even more money to buy access to data. The algorithms that survive are the ones that have ingested the most data, and extracted the most surplus.

This is a natural consequence of our priorities. We have decided that earning profit by extracting surplus is one of the ways we would like to get ahead, and so we have fed the world's data to algorithms to teach them how to feed on consumer surplus. Although I think we might have better priorities, my point here is merely to indicate that our values are being taught to AI, not in the way we teach them to other humans, but purely through the training methods we currently use to teach AI—ingestion of our own data.

Beyond what we intend to teach AI, we also are teaching it a number of other unpleasant truths about our values and ourselves. For example, assume an AI is looking for good credit risks on home loans. For reasons of historical discrimination, certain minority groups may appear to be bad credit risks: their terms have been historically far worse than those offered to majority appli-cants. Worse terms equals greater default risks, and the problem compounds when AIs learn to look at communities. Well, we don't want racist AIs, so let us say we remove the "race" field—that is, tell the AI to make its determinations of output variables on every feature other than race. This is, after all, what we do for human firms: race is not a legal consideration.

But it doesn't work. The historical discrimination is there, in the data, and machine learning algorithms are the very best tool we have for sussing out subtle patterns. Historical racism has left a massive data trail, and so the algorithm will learn that people in certain neighborhoods, zip codes, from certain schools, with certain income ranges, who eat at certain restaurants, or who are physically geolocated at certain places of worship and not others on Sunday (or Saturday, or Friday), or what have you, are the "worse credit risks."[51] In fact, the only thing we do by removing the overt race field, is encourage the AI to build the same data back by use of proxies: datafields that alone or in conjunction give the same information gain as the field the AI was forbidden to use. AIs trained on the historical data of a racist society will find race to be pertinent, no matter how

distributed.... This is different from so-called dynamic pricing, where prices change so often that people can end up paying different amounts, like with airfare, because they bought at different times. Personalized prices are instead set by something that's specific to you." Maddy Varner & Aaron Sankin, *Suckers List: How Allstate's Secret Auto Insurance Algorithm Squeezes Big Spenders*, THE MARKUP (Feb. 25, 2020), https://themarkup.org/allstates-algorithm/2020/02/25/car-insurance -suckers-list.

51   Kaveh Waddell, *How Algorithms Can Bring Down Minorities' Credit Scores*, THE ATLANTIC (Dec. 2, 2016), www.theatlantic.com/technology/archive/2016/12/how-algorithms-can-bring-down-minorities-credit-scores/509333/.

many fields we forbid it from using. The only thing we will accomplish is to bury the discriminatory decision-making forty-two fields deep in a decision tree, where the information gain is distributed among many different seemingly innocuous categories that serve to reconstruct the information gain of the original discriminatory category. The black box will protect it from scrutiny.

If we had wanted to design a system to exacerbate and perpetuate economic inequality and structural racial (or sexual, or national, or whatever) discrimination, all the while hiding what we were doing deep in a computerized process that no one can explain or pinpoint, we could not have hit upon a better method than using machine learning algorithms run on our own historical data, especially if the AI has been superficially sanitized by removing obviously discriminatory fields like race or sexual orientation. And we built all of this just to deliver internet ads.

Like all parents who see their sins reflected in their children, we are going to have to do better, and to teach our AIs to be better than we were, and even better than we are. That will not be a matter of how to train AIs, but a matter of what to train AIs to do. If we don't want AIs to be racist, sexist, economic vampires, we will have to code them differently. We will have to tell them to do as we say, not as we once did and too often still do.

As the process of the transfer of doing science from human to artificial intelligence continues, the last and lasting contribution humans will make to science will be values: the cooperative fictions we have been talking about this whole time. By values, I do not mean specific ones. I mean, rather, the goals that humans set: what humans want. A machine cannot fulfill this role, because it is a definitional one: what humans want is what *humans* want; it is not even what a machine thinking on behalf of a human should think it wants. Even after science is nearly entirely conducted by machines—from data gathering and analysis to hypothesis generation, to experiment design, to conducting experiments, to analyzing data—humans *must* still be involved with which experiments we conduct, with what we research, and why. What humans want—human values—will be the last task that humans serve in a science that will be almost entirely conducted by AI, because it will be the last thing that humans *can* do in the face of systematic AI competence in previously human fields of endeavor.

SCIENCE'S COLLAPSING METANARRATIVE

Science does a reasonable job of approaching many challenges we face— challenges of how to do something. Want to go to the moon? Ok, we'll build the Apollo Program. Want to defeat smallpox, polio, measles? Ok, create a vaccine. Those are "how" answers. Science sets the format for an experiment, the social ritual of laboratory, experiment, and peer review. But science does a terrible job of resolving *why* we want to solve the problems we choose to solve. Those reasons must be based on us. Should we spend research dollars on guns or butter? Only we can answer questions of our priorities.

But the conversation about *why* to do things has been sidelined as fuzzy moral thinking. Just as nuclear engineers have sounded silly—and for good reason—when they claim that nuclear power will usher in an age of cheap energy, and gloss over the unimportant detail of mutually assured destruction, so Mark Zuckerberg sounds like an idiot when he defends raking in advertising money while simultaneously destroying America's liberal democracy.[52] Scientists lose not because they have the wrong answers, but because they are researching the wrong questions.

Science is currently guided by unacknowledged myths. The projects we choose have only loosely to do with ensuring human thriving, and many of them significantly increase human suffering. The current meta-narrative of science emphasizes production, profit, and efficiency: the unacknowledged myth that capitalism coupled with coercion must be the basis of our security. At best, much of the output of modern science and technology promotes productivity that benefits a very few humans, deepens inequality, and fails to deliver much of what people want or need. We may expect this trend to increase as more robots take more jobs from humans and AI reproduces our negative values and exploits our data, including "all we can pay."

Our discussion of *why* remains barren because it has been sown with the salt of scientism. Any claim that we ought to direct scientific research toward goals other than productivity and profit are met with claims that such goals are fuzzy or unscientific. Of course, the goals of increasing production and profit are also profoundly unscientific. Production is a proxy, and a really bad one, for any human goal. As Yuval Harari writes, Singaporeans produce, on a per capita basis, far more per year than residents of Costa Rica. Costa Ricans are far happier.[53]

Science is collapsing and failing to convince because it refuses to have anything to do with the "unscientific" realm of cooperative fiction, story, and

---

[52] *See, e.g.,* Evan Osnos, *Can Mark Zuckerberg Fix Facebook Before It Breaks Democracy,* THE NEW YORKER, www.newyorker.com/magazine/2018/09/17/can-mark-zuckerberg-fix-facebook-before-it-breaks-democracy (Sept. 17, 2018); Steven T. Dennis & Sarah Frier, *Zuckerberg Defends Facebook's Value While Senators Question Apology,* BLOOMBERG, www .bloomberg.com/news/articles/2018-04-10/facebook-s-zuckerberg-warned-by-senators-of-privacy-nightmare (April 10, 2018).

[53] YUVAL NOAH HARARI, HOMO DEUS (2015).

narrative. Scientists (and by this I mean with full irony the people who speak the language we accept as "science" even though those same people often see what they are doing as discovering reality instead of speaking a language) too often do not see that science is guided and shaped by narratives. Science proceeds by observation of facts: fine. But which facts? Why those? Scientists miss the fact that they are directing their instruments and hypotheses at some subset of infinity facts, and there is always a reason why.

Robert Pirsig's fictionalized autobiography, *Zen and the Art of Motorcycle Maintenance*, does a great job of asking (not so much of answering, but who am I to judge?) the critical question, "what are scientific theories?" At one point his son asks him if he believes in ghosts. Pirsig responds:

> The problem, the contradiction the scientists are stuck with, is that of "mind." Mind has no matter or energy, but they can't escape its predominance over everything they do. Logic exists in the mind, numbers exist only in the mind. I don't get upset when scientists say that ghosts exist in the mind. It's that "only" that gets me. Science is only in your mind too, it's just that that doesn't make it bad. Or ghosts, either. . . .
>
> Laws of nature are human inventions, like ghosts. Laws of logic, of mathematics are also human inventions, like ghosts. The whole blessed thing is a human invention, including the idea that it *isn't* a human invention.[54]

Well, perhaps the difference is that the ghosts of science *work*. Ghosts like verifiability and falsifiability and peer review cause us to conduct experiments and mathematical proofs in ways that have systematically yielded useful results. But cooperative fictions *work* too.[55] Money is a cooperative fiction, a consensual hallucination, but it certainly has an impact on most people's behavior. Cooperative fictions help us to create orderly societies and cooperate with each other in ways that have systematically yielded useful results, too. E. O. Wilson identifies the creation myth, for example, as a "Darwinian device for survival."[56] It may not be true, but it works, in that it causes a group of people to form an identity, and cooperate at rates not sustainable even by the most widespread social insects. The point is, science is a lot closer to "just what's in our heads" than we think it is. Hypotheses come from the same narrative-generating linguistic features as the rest of our stories.

Science is guess and check, and most thinking about science is the theory of how to check. I want to talk about the theory of guessing: What tasks do we choose for science, and why? What is the measure of science? Its pragmatic

---

[54] PIRSIG, *supra* note 2, at 36–37.
[55] HARARI, HOMO DEUS, *supra* note 53, Chapter 4.
[56] EDWARD WILSON, THE SOCIAL CONQUEST OF EARTH 9 (2012).

ability to produce? Why not its ability to sustain, to satisfy, to create conditions for human survival and thriving?

Science needs a better guiding narrative, or it is going to get us killed. Doing things just because we can (or, more likely, for science's unacknowledged motives), can no longer be our way of thinking about what projects we fund, what programs PhD candidates enter, what tasks are given priority and precedence at conferences, what is published, what is read, what is cited. The entire social apparatus of the scientific community has got to change, and we have got to change how we talk about science and scientists.

THE NARRATIVES WE NEED: VIABILITY AND THRIVING

Thus far we have taken two critical steps. First, we have identified that scientism's claims of neutrality for science and technology are false. Facebook is anything but neutral. Second, we have discovered that these false claims of neutrality are cover for the shadow guiding narratives of scientism: maximization of production, performativity, and profit. Those are bad and distant proxies for human well-being. When our scientists and technologists work toward those goals, they do not serve humanity well. It is clear that a new narrative for science is necessary, a new way of selecting the why of science, not the how. We need better stories of *why* that inspire scientists to figure out how to stop mass disease and save the planet, rather than alleviate symptoms and maximize factory production.

Thus our third step, pursued here, is what narratives we ought to use to guide science instead.

I want to be clear about two points: first, this discussion is not science's job to answer, at least not alone or as science as we tend to think of it. Rather, we are moving into tasks of law, into the questions and conversations of how we want to live together, and why that way. Much of science and technology has been plugging its ears on this subject and pretending that what it's doing is not a decision in a direction. "Because we can" *is* an answer. Usually, it's not a very good one.

My second note is the same with which I prefaced this book. We do not think alone, and thus any individual answer is both informed by other voices and limited by a lack of them. The ideas here don't come from a vacuum, nor are they by any means the only way to put things. But I think they have much to recommend them, and so I humbly but heartily offer them here. I'm happy to be wrong if it means a better answer keeps us alive. I propose to supplement the laudable practicality of verifiability and the developmental soundness of falsifiability with an equal principle for cooperative human endeavor—including science: *viability*.

Viability is simply this: that the core principle of life appears to be, from the best scientific evidence we currently have, a function of what *is*. I only get to write this book because I am alive. You only may choose to read it (thank you!) for the same reason. Each of us is the result of billions of years of organisms who *were*, and who passed on the capacity for being to their descendants. The only reason science, music, art, mathematics, comic books, and pizza exist is because living beings have made them, living beings have conceived of them. The only reason answers exist is because of questions; and questions because of minds. If we think that thinking and wondering are any good at all, then we will wish to preserve wondering and thinking. And the only way to do that is to preserve our viability.

I first mentioned viability in chapter 2, when I said that the purpose of our law, our conversations about how to cooperate to solve the problems of the future, has got to be to keep us alive, to keep us asking questions. Any answer to the questions of the future that stops us from asking any further questions because we are all dead is a really bad answer. And narratives—cooperative fictions—that do help us stay alive are, to this way of thinking, better than the cooperative fictions that do not. Viability is a way of evaluating stories.

I come to viability from a number of angles: some may be convincing to you, some may not, and both paths can help us learn what is going on. The first is Descartes's observation, *cogito ergo sum*. This is less a statement of truth than it is an axiom. Because I am thinking, I must take the fact of thinking for granted: this subjective experience that cannot be confirmed by science is nevertheless the ground subjective fact of science. Consciousness, and thus reason, is a subjective experience, not an objective one, and that subjective fact is the ground of all further discussion. I can easily doubt whether I think or exist—there is good evidence against both hypotheses—but I am going to have to take the phenomenon of thinking for granted if I am going to think about anything, including the fact that "I" as a whole probably do not exist, and that my "thinking" may be caused by something else entirely.

Once we think that thinking is a reasonable basis to do anything, the next question is what we ought to think about: toward what end should our thoughts be directed? This is a selection of metanarrative, or goal: *why* we are doing anything at all, instead of just breathing and noticing the beauty of the world (which is one hell of an attractive alternative)? There are many to choose from. I choose the metanarrative of *thriving*. The goal that appears most convincing to me is that humans not only live, and dominate or are dominated by others, but live happily, peacefully, and in beauty. The domination narrative has much to recommend it: Sparta creamed Athens in the Peloponnesian War, and authoritarian nationalism worldwide is prevailing over liberal democracy. But I choose human thriving purely for this reason: that humans both individually and collectively prefer to thrive. Domination is merely a goal to that end, a goal that mirrors the tragedy of individuals' place in society: sometimes the best way to get ahead, at least in the short-term and short-sighted sense, is to hurt others.

There are other meta-narratives to human thriving. Nietzschean overcoming to achieve maximum potential, for example, or Christian salvation through faith and regeneration. To me, however, human thriving captures what we ought to be about.

One proxy for human thriving is the economic concept of utility. Imagine that we could measure how much circumstances, experiences, and products were worth to people in some abstract sense: that's at least a rough cut at how economists use utility. But here we are on very thin ice: utility provides a useful way to talk about measuring and optimizing human thriving, but too often utility is merely a fancy way of talking about money. This is because of the problem of interpersonal comparison of utility. Imagine that my laptop is stolen: I have suffered a significant loss because it has important files and I need it to work and it is expensive to replace. However, perhaps the thief has a starving child he needs to feed. Which of us values the laptop more?

The only way we really have to compare the utility of goods and services is for people to express how much they want something in a sale. If the thief had offered me money for the laptop, we could know: do I want the laptop more, or the offered amount more? If I accepted the purchase for $1,000, we would know that the laptop was worth *at most* $1,000 to me (maybe I would have accepted less), and if the buyer offered $1,000 for the laptop, we would know that the laptop was worth *at least* $1,000 to him (maybe he would have paid more). Utility is a great concept and helps us get at the problem of optimizing human thriving, but it has huge problems: it requires money to measure, and not everyone has money. What happens if I need a pill to live (say, for example, that I have been bitten by a zombie), but Bill Gates wants it just in case? He can outbid me, but then we would be confident that overall human thriving has been reduced. If I have very little money because I am poor, then most goods and services are like this.

Very well, but perhaps the concept of utility can benefit from a little polishing, to get rid of its dependence on money to solve the problem of interpersonal comparison of utility. Here, I rely on the thinking of Nobel laureate and poverty economist Amartya Sen, who transformed our understanding of utility. First, Sen dismantled the matter of interpersonal comparison of utility by noting that it is a small quibble that prevents economists from seeing or addressing huge problems. He did so with a story, a familiar fable about the mad Roman emperor Nero, who supposedly set Rome on fire and fiddled as it burned (whether this story is historical doesn't matter: stories can be truthful without being literally true). We can imagine that Nero enjoyed the experience—that might be why we call him mad. We can also state confidently that his subjects enjoyed the experience significantly less. And although an economist would say that we have no way of comparing Nero's utility with that of his scorched, dying, and desperate subjects, any human would say that this kind of thinking rightly gives economics a bad name: it's an incorrect way of viewing the world. It does not fit the observations. It is bad science. We can say with absolute confidence that a society in which the 1 percent fiddle while the world burns is a worse world than effortlessly imaginable alternatives, and that it is neoclassical economic orthodoxy that is helping the Neros set fire to the planet.

Having rightfully restricted the problem of interpersonal comparison of utility to a small subset of cases, Sen replaced the theory of *utility* with that of *capability*. We should not measure the productive output of a society as a proxy for whether its citizens are thriving, because many may be miserable and a few so rich that the extra wealth means nothing. Instead of looking at how much humans produce, we should look at how much they can actually *do* with the output of society. Rights and freedoms mean nothing if one lacks the *capability* to use them. The right to vote, for example, means nothing if one lacks a means to get to the polls. The right to work means nothing if one has no skills that cannot be better performed by a machine. Capability is, in this sense, the ground of freedom: the ability to do something is a necessary precondition for the legal permission to do that thing to make any difference in a life. This is why, for example, drugs are not forbidden until they are invented, and why property rights in stars are a whimsical (and legally nonbinding) matter.

But capability does not solve our problems entirely. Let us say that you and I both agree, using Sen's most well-known example, that output and productivity and wealth maximization do not do anything if they do not provide many humans with many capabilities, like owning a car to be able to exercise the right to vote. Let us leave theory behind for a moment. Hundreds of millions of people have been lifted out of poverty in Sen's home country of India (and China, and worldwide) by the expanding network of global trade, the falling costs of transportation of goods, and the vanishing costs of delivering electronic services. These people drive cars, including to go to the polls, eat more meat, and so on. They have more capabilities. They are happier, and their employers are happier, and the people they sell goods and services to are happier, and the people they buy goods and services from are happier.[57] But you see the problem: this is not viable. On the day I wrote this paragraph, scientists from around the world warned that the world has about twelve years to turn climate change around before the global ecosystem suffers catastrophic and irreparable worldwide change.[58] All these happy people driving happy cars are not helping. Of course, neither are the factories in the United States and China that churn out toxins: it is not poor people's fault. But nevertheless, just as maximized utility threatens capability, maximized capability threatens viability. And so just as utility is a powerful but limited tool, so capability is both very useful and decidedly limited. This is how structured thinking works: each useful concept brings us closer, and gives us better ideas, but we only approach truth, never capture it.

In the same way that capability is the ground of freedom, viability is the ground of all endeavors. We cannot do anything if we do not exist. Here, a thought experiment (i.e., a narrative wearing a white coat) might help. Imagine a perfectly designed experiment: it is designed to falsify a null hypothesis, and is carefully tuned to observe facts that serve some pragmatic end. However, the lab is built on a fault line, and the experimental procedure sets up vibrations that might cause the lab to collapse at any moment. Is that good experimental design? One would not get funding for this experiment if one disclosed the risks, and for good reason, but what is interesting is that the normally foolishly cold-hearted logic of the dominant technological narrative yields to a sense of ethical responsibility.

An experiment is a question. One goal of any art of asking questions (and that is all the scientific method is) must be to keep asking questions. Any question that stops further questions is a bad question: it is a dead end. The first amazing thing about the world is that it exists at all. But the more wondrous thing is that anyone or anything wonders about it. As Ludwig Wittgenstein wrote: "It is not *how* things are in the world that is mystical, but *that* it exists."[59] Just as subjective minds cannot deny the existence of subjective minds, so scientific questioners cannot do good science if they threaten future questions.

There is an old science fiction story I read when I was a child. In it, a scientist discovers a way to cause a chain reaction among iron deposits in

---

[57] Being poor in an already developed nation is a different matter.

[58] Jonathan Watts, *We Have 12 Years to Limit Climate Change Catastrophe, Warns UN*, THE GUARDIAN (Oct. 8 2018), www.theguardian.com/environment/2018/oct/08/global-warming-must-not-exceed-15c-warns-landmark-un-report.

[59] LUDWIG WITTGENSTEIN, TRACTATUS LOGICO-PHILOSOPHICUS 89 (C. J. Ogden trans., 1922).

the earth's crust, which would destroy the planet. The story consists of the scientist's ruminations about whether he should write up the report, because he knows that once the technology has been developed, it will be used by someone, somewhere. He has been ruthlessly bullied all his life, bereft of close contact, and despised. At the end of the story, his house is vandalized by what we would now call trolls.

He writes the report.

The point is not "don't harass mad scientists," it's that different kinds of societies will produce different kinds of science, and toxic societies will produce toxic science. Jean-Francis Lyotard writes: "[I]t is impossible to know what the state of knowledge is—in other words, the problems its development and distribution are facing today—without knowing something of the society within which it is situated."[60] Science is limited by what we see, by what we hear, by what we think, by what we can build tools to help us see, hear, and think. It is inevitably colored by our internal models of perception, not least of which is the question of what we perceive is worthy of scientific investigation. Viability, and with it its obverse, nonviability—the sense that certain cooperative fictions, certain goals, certain metanarratives of science are going to get us all killed—must be the gold standard for a new conception of what science ought to be doing.

[60] JEAN-FRANCIS LYOTARD, THE POSTMODERN CONDITION 13 (1979).

6

Law's Fruitful Fictions

Narrative is affirmed, not merely as a significant new field of research, but well beyond that as a central instance of the human mind and a mode of thinking fully as legitimate as that of abstract logic.

— Fredric Jameson, *foreword to Jean-Francois Lyotard,*
The Postmodern Condition[1]

The language of science is failing because it refuses to consider the essential question of why we do science. It wants only to talk of how. That doesn't mean it isn't driven by whys. Behind any action is a why, even if that why is as circular as "because I can." Any action (and that includes nonaction) is a decision in a direction. Whatever consciousness may be, our lot is doomed to carry it about.

Is it science's job to answer why? No. But it needs to stop pretending that it operates without aim or intent. It needs to recognize the indelibility of aim and intent, and to listen to the voices that talk about the whys.

At this point, you likely see where I am going. The oldest, most important technology we have is language. Language lets us upgrade our software instead of our hardware. Law, like language, is built between us. We use it to work together. Law is language folded back upon itself: it uses narratives and cooperative fictions to talk about how we can develop even better narratives so that we can work together to solve the problems of the future. Law is the recursive form of language applied to human cooperation: it is rules for using language to refine language—rules about rules for how we live together. Or, as in this book, it is the discipline of how to work together to talk about what language we need to help us cooperate better.

---

[1] Fredric Jameson, *Foreword*, JEAN-FRANCOIS LYOTARD, THE POSTMODERN CONDITION: A REPORT ON KNOWLEDGE xi (Geoff Bennington and Brian Massumi, trans., 1984).

Law's strength is not empirical studies or logical rationalism. Law's strength is the telling of compelling stories of *why* we cooperate in a certain way, *why* we work together. Whether the cooperative narrative we create is that of the divine right of priests or kings, or the rule of law, or the sovereignty of the people, the cooperative fictions of law make it possible for us to cooperate in hundreds of millions and beyond. As Bob Cover notes, law is the projection of a sense of what *should be*—invisible, as yet unexisting—into the future.[2] It speaks new cooperative fictions of how we *ought* to live together into being, overwhelming old patterns of speaking.

Now more than ever, we need law's competence in crafting compelling cooperative narratives. We need a field skilled at and dedicated to the crafting of cooperative fictions, expressed through language, that will help us stay alive and adapt to changing technology. We need lawyers to help develop the twenty-first-century version of "all people are created equal," of "marriage equality," even of "the rule of law."

But before we can talk about how law does and can do that, we must survey the current terrain. Law has been colonized by some of the same myths that have infected science, and has forgotten and cast aside its primary method and tool of narrative. Legal academics, lawyers, legal theorists, and lawmakers are crippled by a debilitating sense of law's supposed inferiority to the so-called "hard" sciences, computer science and other forms of technological development chief among them. In the United States, and in other common law countries as well, the discipline of law has abdicated its responsibility to develop new cooperative fictions that respond to emerging technologies. Unpacking and addressing law's identity crisis and relationship to its core narrative tools is the project of this chapter.

LAW'S INFERIORITY COMPLEX

Law has an unwarranted inferiority complex that is holding it back from performing the deeply needed role of inventing and developing cooperative narratives. This inferiority complex is worth exploring, because like many of the governing myths of science, it is not scientific, it is not natural, and it is not accidental. It is an engineered, learned helplessness designed to keep people who study how human society can cooperate and thrive—lawyers—from raising valid objections to the underexplored narratives that drive the idea that technology must be developed regardless of human cost.

To start, let us examine the strange attitude of American legal professionals toward their profession. Americans hold law in contempt in no small part because American lawyers hold their profession in contempt. American

---

[2] Robert M. Cover, *Violence and the Word,* 95 YALE L.J. 1601, 1604 (1986).

lawyers collect lawyer jokes in self-defense. "What do you call a thousand lawyers at the bottom of the ocean?" "A good start." "Why won't a rattlesnake bite a lawyer?" "Professional courtesy." "Why don't lawyers go to the beach?" "Cats keep trying to bury them." These jokes are not entirely new; there's always the brutal and evergreen line from Dick the Butcher in *Henry VI*, which is trotted out anytime someone mentions lawyers: "First thing we do, let's kill all the lawyers."[3]

Of course, some lawyers have done some bad things, so have doctors[4] and pastors,[5] among others, but no other profession in American culture is so consumed by self-loathing. A society's attitude toward a profession impacts the quality of service. South Korea and Germany take teachers seriously, and the results show up in the quality of education. By contrast, American legal professionals' self-loathing produces a serious defect in the quality of their product, which creates a servile relationship between professional and client in the United States. Lawyers in other legal cultures—Germany, France, and Japan are all great examples—are valued professionals: their opinions are sought in matters of law; they use their training instead of simply employing it to subvert the rule of law and identify legal loopholes for their corporate masters.

Can you imagine if doctors were as routinely self-deprecating as lawyers? Can you imagine medical schools that teach doctors to subvert medical best practices, shortcut medical consent requirements, undermine medical expertise and authority, and teach hospitals to follow only the exact wording, instead of the spirit, of operation procedures? In the United States, lawyers are trained expressly to do all these things, and are further profoundly subservient to corporate clients in a way that far surpasses the range of normal professional relationships. An accountant is not expected to cook the books in inventive ways (and when they do, some people need to go to jail). A doctor is not

---

[3] WILLIAM SHAKESPEARE, HENRY VI, part 2, act IV, scene 2.

[4] *See, e.g.*, Alison Barrett, *Doctors Knew about Disgraced Surgeon Emil Gayed. What Else Do They Know?*, THE GUARDIAN, Feb. 18, 2019, www.theguardian.com/commentisfree/2019/feb /19/doctors-knew-about-disgraced-surgeon-emil-gayed-what-else-do-they-know; Greg Land, *Med-Mal Settlement Awards $140M to 255 Patients of Doctor Convicted of Fraud*, law.com, Feb. 20, 2019, www.law.com/newyorklawjournal/2019/02/20/med-mal-settlement-awards-140 m-to-255-patients-of-doctor-convicted-of-fraud/?; Amy Viteri, *Lawmaker Wants to Hold Disreputable Plastic Surgery Clinics to Account*, LOCAL 10, Feb. 20, 2019, www.local10.com /news/local-10-investigates/lawmaker-wants-to-hold-disreputable-plastic-surgery-clinics-to-account.

[5] *See, e.g.*, Jim Avila et al., *Preachers Accused of Sins, and Crimes*, ABC NEWS, https://abcnews .go.com/2020/story?id=3034040&page=1&page=1; Tim Funk, *Bishop Offers Apology to Clergy Sex Abuse Victims, but Still Not Releasing Priest List*, THE CHARLOTTE OBSERVER, Feb. 21, 2019, www.charlotteobserver.com/living/religion/article226523900.html.

expected to invent and perform entrepreneurial and untested medical procedures. But a significant part of the innovative and creative efforts of American
lawyers is aimed at circumventing and subverting existing law so that their
clients may do that which is questionable or clearly illegal. No other discipline
is so dedicated to its own destruction.

In my personal and professional experience, I have found that this problem
also infects the legal academy, where it ought to be weakest. Here, the problem
runs so deep as to create the current state of affairs in legal hiring, where
lawyers are only barely tolerated as academics: a young person wishing to
teach in a law school should get a PhD in any other discipline; the study of law
is optional, and the practice of law for more than a year or two is an active
minus.[6]

The legal academy lacks confidence in its own methodologies of narrative,
and goes begging from its neighbors. Legal academics borrow methodologies
(legal empiricism, law-and-economics, law-and-interior decorating, the list is
endless) from any non-law-based discipline in order to bolster chances of
publication. Most are some flavor of law-and-economics: the usual reaching
toward some other "science" that one perceives to be "harder." Others turn to
critical historical methods, yielding the modern critical legal studies movement and its varied progeny.

This deep unease about profession and method is particularly unfortunate
because it is scientifically unsupportable, and culturally disastrous. Lawyers
are master storytellers, and it is masterful stories that we need. Any lawyer
worth her salt knows that the framing of a legal issue is the most important part
of legal work. It is not the law that matters, but the frame. A lawyer can
understand what decision a judge has made in an eighty-page opinion by
reading the first sentence: it shows the frame, the narrative that the judge has
accepted.

Law fled its sense of methodological inferiority and subject-matter "impur-
ity" into the arms of scientism. But it is a case of "out of the frying pan and into
the fire." As we explored previously, scientism's devotees make two cleanly
false claims. The first is that all scientific truths can be expressed better, more
"purely" (purity in scientific disciplines is their god-awful made-up concept,
not mine) at a reduced and more atomistic level: love is explained as biochem-
istry; free will as physics. Second, and even sillier, is the claim that the
narratives of history, sociology, or cultural anthropology are not scientific or

---

[6] *See* Orin Kerr, *The Rise of the Ph.D. Law Professor*, WASH. POST, Oct. 22, 2015, www
.washingtonpost.com/news/volokh-conspiracy/wp/2015/10/22/the-rise-of-the-ph-d-law-professor
/?utm_term=.106861ifcae4.

factual. "Anyone who feels a longing to complete our knowledge in this way should try translating some simple historical statement into the deeper, physical truths that are held to underlie it," writes philosopher Mary Midgley.

What, for instance, about a factual sentence like "George was allowed home from prison at last on Sunday"? How will the language of physics convey the meaning of "Sunday"? or "home" or "allowed" or "prison"? or "at last"? or indeed "George"? (There are no individuals in physics.) The meaning of all these terms concerns very complex, far-ranging systems of social relation, not the physical details of a particular case.

For a translation, all these social concepts would have to vanish and be represented by terms describing the interactions of groups of particles moved by various forces. The trouble with this new version is not, as [chemist Peter] Atkins says, that it is "too cumbersome for everyday use", but that it does not begin to convey the meaning of what is said at all. The sentence as it stands does not refer only to the physical items involved. Indeed, most of the physical details are irrelevant to it. (It does not matter, for instance, where the prison is or by what transport or what route George came home.) What the sentence describes is a symbolic transaction between an individual and a huge social background of penal justice, power structures, legislation and human decisions. The words it uses are suited to fill in that historical and social background. Without such concepts, the whole meaning of the sentence would vanish.

This piece of history—this little narrative sentence—is not something sketchy or provisional. It is not a blueprint that needs scientific validation. It is not just an emotive expression or amateur "folk-psychology". It is solid information of exactly the kind that is needed. It is precise in the way that it needs to be, and if more precision is needed—such as why he is let out—that too can be supplied through concepts of the same kind. *And if anyone cares to try the same experiment with a sentence from the law, they will find themselves still more totally baffled.*[7]

Mathematics, physics, chemistry, biology, economics . . . none of these disciplines, as we climb the ladder from "hard" sciences to so-called "soft" ones (indeed, arranging these disciplines as a ladder is also part of the mythos of scientism), can provide any useful or coherent sense of a simple statement like "George was allowed home from prison at last on Sunday." And they certainly do not provide any account more factual or accurate than a reader who knows what the words mean interpreting the sentence in the normal way.

As much as lawyers may long for a discipline that reduces the language of law to logic or empirical reality, it doesn't work. And it doesn't work for the

[7]   MARY MIDGLEY, THE MYTHS WE LIVE BY 51–52 (2004). Emphasis added.

reasons Midgley lays out above: "George" is a node in a language network, not a description of an external phenomenon, and definitely not a logical proposition or statement. There is an unbridgeable gap between reality and any description of it. If you think, "ah, but 'George' is certainly an external person," ask yourself: In this context, what is George, really? We are talking fictions here, which let us cooperate in the task of making a point about the philosophy of language, law, and science.

George does not exist, he is a cooperative fiction, whose characteristics we are negotiating as I write and you read. Even the use of "negotiation" in this context is a cooperative fiction, because we are not presently face-to-face. As you read this, I ("The Author") am a fiction to you, and as I write it, you ("The Reader") are a fiction to me.

THE COLONIZATION OF LAW BY ECONOMICS

Attempts to explain phenomena at the wrong level—as happens when lawyers explain the language of law in the language of some other discipline—can lead to increased confusion and framing narratives that are flatly misleading. As one example, I would like to discuss the corrosive effects of the neoclassical law and economics tradition on legal thought. I touched on this example in the last chapter; I use it again here because law and economics has been the most successful attempt to colonize law with another discipline, to reduce the narratives of law to equations. It is the tool used most often by legal academics seeking to put their thought on a "more scientific" footing. It is also the idiom I have myself used most, having been being trained at the University of Chicago, and I think I have learned a few things for which the tools of neoclassical economics are well suited, as well as the many tasks for which using them is like conducting surgery with a chainsaw.

Any attempt to describe the field of neoclassical law and economics (NCLE) itself is doomed to draw criticism, because it's a bit of all things to all people, but the core of NCLE is the attempt to model human economic activity as the interactions of individual self-motivated rational actors. Of course, none of those words apply very well to the human condition: we are cooperative beings who reason in groups using language. Sure, individuals defect from group cooperation for individual advantage, and that's where most of the good thinking of law and economics comes from—but it is defection *against* the background of cooperation that is interesting in economics, not individual self-interest as the iron law of human action.

I don't mean to say that the fictions of NCLE, such as its ghostly "invisible hand" metaphor, offer no value. They solve many problems—and a reader familiar with law and economics will rightly point out that I use many of these tools and ideas in this book. They're decent tools. They are tools to solve certain problems in certain contexts (just like *all* science). NCLE produces simplified models of the world. Sometimes what they leave out doesn't matter. But just as studying physics can't tell you if you should marry the love of your life, law and economics tells us vanishingly little about how to build communities that develop language about the future. Ironically, NCLE is itself a reasonable attempt by a community to manufacture some good language—it just gets high on its own supply.

I have attended (and I'm afraid, given) many neoclassical law-and-economics talks. Many consist of a line of pseudo-mathematical econometrics, which translates a familiar phenomenon into unfamiliar and stilted relationships, with no testable hypothesis and no increase in understanding. It is the transformation of the familiar into the elitist arcane that seems to increase publishability. Earlier in my career I often received the advice to include a few tables or a line of mathematical pseudocode to increase the so-called sexiness of a piece and thereby its chances of publication. In short, the overwhelmingly common purpose, at least in practice, of neoclassical economic language in legal academic publication is to obscure the mind-bendingly obvious so that it appears more publishable. The reason that NCLE is so often used in shoddy legal academic work[8] is that lawyers are grasping at methods. They are not trained in economics or econometrics. Most are self-taught, or took a weeklong course. They make this effort because they feel that they have no methodology of their own, no way of determining correct from incorrect, or up from down. They feel that law is not a science, and economics is.

Scholars outside the law and economics tradition sense that something is wrong, and they often express it by saying that the law-and-economics assumption that humans are individual, atomic, rational actors is wrong: instead, humans are actually irrational. This is misguided too, and it gives NCLE too much credit. Consider the well-known tragedy of the commons, or indeed any other collective action problem. In a range of social problems the individual's self-interest cuts against the group interest. Neoclassical economics assumes that the individual will maximize her own self-interest, that is, will "behave rationally": individuals will choose to pollute even though we would all be better off if we all didn't pollute, or will keep overhunting or overfishing even though it means that the valuable pool of animals will be wiped out, to

---

[8]   To be clear: not all NCLE work is shoddy. Much is superb, or in the case of Ronald Coase's *The Problem of Social Cost*, 56 J.L. & ECON. 837 (1960), industry-changing.

everyone's detriment. Moreover, law and economics proposes the "unraveling" problem: even when a group is inclined to cooperate, if one person believes that others are likely to act selfishly in the future, that person will defect in the present, which chains back to the beginning, so that everyone will act selfishly in the very first round of a repeated game.

To put all of this in English, neoclassical economics predicts that humans can only maintain cooperation for the benefit of everyone in the group under very narrow and fragile circumstances. The mystery, for neoclassical economics, is *why humans stubbornly refuse to act that way in the laboratory.* Because here's the thing: humans cooperate under circumstances that neoclassical economics does not predict. When we actually bother to check patterns of human cooperation, a movement called behavioral law and economics, or more honestly, psychology, we find that humans in the laboratory routinely cooperate at rates and under conditions that NCLE cannot explain.

And of course they do. Cooperation at scale through language is humans' superpower, and it is the reason we (currently) rule the planet. That neoclassical law and economics can't reach this truth is a damning indictment of its guiding narratives. If we were scientists, and not scientism-ists, we would reflect that perhaps something was very wrong with the starting theory, and this turns out to be so. Consider the discussion of human eusociality in earlier chapters. The comparative evolutionary advantage of the human race is its ability to cooperate at the hundreds-of-millions scale using fictions like gods, nations, and laws. Why should we expect that humans, being humans, would not instinctively cooperate, and why would we expect them to not learn and value cooperation at very high rates?

Here we can begin to surface the nonsense of NCLE. In an attempt to appear "scientific," lawyers (and particularly legal academics) have adopted a language entirely unsuited to explaining human behavior, particularly our signature ability to cooperate through narratives and fictions. The biggest threat to group cooperation is managing the problem of individual defection. Bees and ants would not dominate the insect world if they acted individually—indeed, bees are threatened precisely because of "colony collapse syndrome." When bees stop cooperating, they all die. And so it is with us.

Neoclassical law and economics claims that humans are *irrationally* responding to evolved emotional precommitments to cooperate like empathy, and goodwill, that help humans manage defection. The NCLE movement labels individual selfish and ultimately self-destructive behavior "rational," and group cooperation "irrational." Then it has the gall to wonder why humans "irrationally" fail to fall into the trap of non-cooperative individual self-serving behavior at the rates that NCLE predicts. As Walt Kelly, author of the comic strip *Pogo*, once put it, "You're singing the wrong words to the wrong tune, and you sound like a platypus that just laid an egg."

Or, as E. O. Wilson puts it: "Authentic altruism is based on a biological instinct for the common good of the tribe, put in place by group selection, wherein groups of altruists in prehistoric times prevailed over groups of individuals in selfish disarray. Our species is not *Homo oeconomicus.*"[9] Why would a prominent biologist take a shot at silly economics? Because Wilson was struggling against the identical error in his own field: evolutionary biologist Richard Dawkins and others claim that there is no such thing as pure altruism, and that we only help our relatives to preserve the copies of our own genes that they carry. That this is dogmatic scientism is beyond question: if pure group altruism were incomprehensible, *Saving Private Ryan* would not make any sense to us.

The problem is not that humans are irrational, it is that the neoclassical movement within law and economics, and the kin-selection movement within evolutionary biology, proposes an identical stunted idea of the interests in play. Both movements start from the premise that defection is rational and cooperation is irrational, when the evidence is starkly to the contrary.

Neoclassical economics and "selfish gene" kin-selection evolutionary biology took turns into dead ends because they did not examine their metanarratives. Both relied on a sense of atomic, individualistic humanity that turns out to be observably untrue: neoclassical economics fails to account for rates of human cooperation, and kin-selection evolutionary biology fails to account for human altruism. In their focus on individual, atomic units, both fields failed to note the bonds and connections between those units. Both errors stem from the mythos of reductionism: only "atomic models," models based on the gene or the individual, were deemed "hard" science.

Reductive atomism often misses the forest for the trees—indeed, as Mary Midgley shows, atomism is a misguided mythology inherited from the disproven physics of several hundred years ago. Modern physics doesn't talk about individual atoms doing individual things; it talks about fields and relationships. NCLE is so reductionist that it's not even empirical: its predictions simply don't match what people do. Just as reducing physics to the movement of atomistic particles doesn't work, reducing human communities to atomistic individuals erases any insight from cooperative fictions, patterns, language: all the important stuff *between* us.

This claim of dominance by economic methods over legal narrative is inextricably bound up with the legal academy's abandonment of the tools of narrative and crafting cooperative fictions. As legal scholar Cass Sunstein has

---

[9] E. O. WILSON, THE SOCIAL CONQUEST OF EARTH 251 (2012).

written, "[E]conomic analysts sometimes claim that traditional legal reasoning is not reasoning at all, but instead is an encrusted system of unorganized and perhaps barely processed intuitions."[10] And through the dominance of NCLE on American legal thought, this attack has become a large part of the tendency of American lawyers to set aside their narrative powers.[11]

But the NCLE attack on narrative modes of law merely surfaces the weaknesses of NCLE as a normative system. NCLE claims to tell us what to do, and not how and why to do it. Sunstein writes, "In its normative form . . . economic analysis depends on too thin a repertoire for inquiry—that is, the notion that legal rules should be designed so as to maximize wealth."[12] Maybe legal rules should do something other than just maximize wealth? Furthermore, those words, "maximize wealth," cloak a world of hidden normative agendas: NCLE approaches attempt to maximize wealth in the aggregate, where adding $100 to the bank account of a billionaire counts more than adding $99 to the bank account of a starving pauper. This is lousy economics, especially given that economics got its start as a discipline by showing that you value money less the more you have, and value it more the less you have! Anyone struggling to make rent sees the lie in NCLE's devotion to "maximizing" wealth.[13]

The irony is that lawyers' tools, narrative and reasoning by analogy, are strong where NCLE is soberingly weak. Analogical reasoning, unlike economic analysis, doesn't require "that plural and diverse social goods . . . be assessed according to the same metric."[14] And this is clearer thinking than the fuzzy logic of economics. Judgments based on narrative analogy are "part of what it means to think well," writes Sunstein.

> Consider, for example, the view that we should see all of the following as "costs": unemployment, the loss of a species, higher prices for pencils, the adaptation of workplaces to accommodate people on wheelchairs, sexual assault, and chilling effects on speech. If we understand all these things as "costs," to be assessed via the same metric, we will disable ourselves from making important qualitative distinctions.[15]

Lawyers in the United States have been taught to distrust and disfavor their own methods of narrative and analogical reasoning, and quite often use worse

[10] Cass Sunstein, *On Analogical Reasoning*, 106 HARV. L. REV. 787 (1993).
[11] *Id.* at 741.
[12] *Id.*
[13] The math version of this argument is called the St. Petersburg Paradox.
[14] Sunstein, *supra* note 10, at 788.
[15] *Id.*

tools from other disciplines utterly unsuited to the job. The devaluation of legal narrative and analogical tools has been part of a systematic colonization of law by "harder sciences," which concept by this point should make the reader snort. Legal academics earn careers by dismantling legal methods and importing other, "more scientific" methodologies. If what a culture values drives the kind of science it produces,[16] then we can see why the social technology produced by American lawyers fails to serve human interests and is broadly subservient to ethics of productivity and efficiency that maximize wealth in the hands of a very few at the expense of billions.

Of course, we should not reject economic analysis, critical legal studies, evolutionary biology, empirical legal studies, or other "law and" traditions out of hand. I have used some of these tools extensively, including in this book. What is important is to suspect the hidden and often very unsatisfactory metanarratives that come with those tools, and in particular to suspect cases in which a driving need to use one tool inclines legal thinkers to use the wrong tool for the job. In particular, we should suspect such tools where the explanations they provide are of significantly less use than those produced by narrative and analogical reasoning.

Perhaps I have been too harsh with one or the other discipline: I mean for us to think about a number of their unfounded claims of superiority over narrative and analogical methods for the purposes of determining *what the law should be*. It is important for us to realize that a number of the metanarratives behind much of what passes for science in the "law and" movement are underexamined. In many cases they are observably false, or at least require a lot of mental gymnastics to come to a less clear picture than the one they started with.

REALITY BITES: LAW'S POWER OF NARRATIVE

As we've been discussing, the metanarrative of reductionist scientism is that certain methods are superior, or more scientific, because they drill down to "reality," that quaint linguistic construction. Many popularizers of modern science claim that the consciousness, or "self," is an illusion, merely because one can drill down to the level of neurons or molecular chemistry, or even further down to atoms, and so on. But there are better ways to describe the relationships between the different fields of human attempts to understand what we should do and how: as complementary lenses through which to view a world that we can never quite capture.

---

[16] JEAN-FRANCOIS LYOTARD, THE POSTMODERN CONDITION 13 (1979).

This drilling down is like explaining virtual worlds by studying the electric charge of computers' binary switches. The physical nature of the binary switches, their storage of state, and indeed, the degree to which a computer ignores the precise electric state of a given switch (electrical charge is continuous, after all, not a discrete on-off) is only very weakly related to the art, storytelling, language, point, and enjoyment of the game. Indeed, since the purpose of such games is to create an experience for the human mind, the medium is irrelevant to the message: a book can do the same thing as a video game with completely different technology. No one would produce a review of a video game like Skyrim or World of Warcraft by examining logic gates or the design of silicon chips. In the same way, "drilling down" on law using the language of economics, genetics, or chemistry can quite easily produce *less accurate* pictures of what is going on and *what should be going on* than would an educated interpretation of the law. The human mind is our best tool yet for interpreting human thought, and it is so odd that we keep using worse tools designed for other jobs in place of the tools of interpretive legal thought.

We'll talk further about how law's tools work, but first I want to talk about what law does. Every worthwhile legal invention builds up, away from amoral reality, away from a reality stripped of human cooperative instincts, empathy, and altruism, and toward a reality infused with those instincts. The reality is that we are, all of us, deeply different, with different abilities. Yet the law states, correctly, that "all people are created equal."[17] Even a cursory look at the real world shows that a person with a weapon can do whatever they want to a person without one. Mobs can lynch individuals. Autocrats and warlords can govern by fear and terror. Without law, there is one rule: force. The stronger can force the weaker to submit. Slavery was and is real. Rape is real. Cruelty and greed are real. But instead of enshrining these brutal facts, as the political strands of economics do for greed, for example, law as a system for building cooperative fictions pushes back. Law's task is not to represent reality, it's about bringing a new and better state of affairs into being by developing language—like "all people are created equal"—that helps us cooperate in the face of reality.

Brutalism is intolerable, and law sets about to change it. This is our standard story: humans set about fixing reality through cooperative fictions, and the cooperative fiction that addresses the reality of domination and force in human relationships is law. The law against murder doesn't stop reality; it

---

[17] Yes, it has been a journey from "all men" to "all people," and the official wording hasn't changed ("all men" doesn't even appear in a legally binding document). These are attributes of the narrative process.

does not restrain any murders. It merely sets in place a cooperative social reality: those who murder will be subject to group sanction.

Law has progressed further and further from brutalism through an ever developing set of fictions. The first fictions were extensions of naked force: a chieftain might rule by delegating power to underlings, or a king to vassals. But there remained a problem: Why would anyone submit to just another person? So kings developed the idea that they were *not* just other people, and the cooperative fiction of the divine right to rule was born. Never mind that the idea was nonsense on stilts: it was a powerful cooperative concept that permitted stability in government.

But law was by no means done. It developed further cooperative fictions. One major one was the development of contract law. Although we now see contract law as central to the discipline of law (as a Contracts professor, I must agree), it was a latecomer to the legal scene. Contract law was revolutionary because it changed the foundation of the legal basis of cooperation between people. Before the development of contract law, law enforced cooperation based on status.[18] Slaves built Pharaoh's pyramids not because they signed up to do so, but because they were forced to do so based on their status. In the feudal system in western Europe, people certainly worked together, but they did so based on status and coercion: peasants served knights, who served dukes, who served the king. Each relationship was between a lower-status party and a higher-status party.

Contract provided a basis for cooperation in law and language rather than by status. The parties literally wrote up a piece of paper, which the legal system then interpreted as if it were a special kind of law that just applied to the cooperative relationship between the parties. Contracts did not change all the elements of coercion: although few people in developed nations are now forced into slavery (other than in the US penal system, that is), the exigencies of capitalism force many to sign contracts, the terms of which reflect their desperate circumstances and bargaining position. Reality did not change: the fiction did. And that meant all the difference: we now work together under a myth of cooperation and collaborative design of mutually beneficial rules that apply to a cooperative relationship, rather than working together based on your status as knight and mine as serf, or your status as enslaver and mine as enslaved.

Relatedly, consider the change from the rule of men to the Rule of Law. I have capitalized it intentionally: let us always remember that the Rule of Law is a cooperative fiction, arguably the most important cooperative fiction ever

---

[18]   *See* Sir Henry James Sumner Maine, Ancient Law (1861).

devised. The Rule of Law is a claim that some set of rules and institutions, "Law," governs everyone, regardless of status. It is a claim that this abstract idea impacts the powerful as well as the powerless. Of course, the reality is that this is nonsense: drug cartels, authoritarian nationalist leaders, and wealthy spoiled rich kids infected with "affluenza" routinely escape the consequences of their actions. But every once in a while the system sacrifices a high-profile, high-caste person to the illusion that law applies to everyone. And the resulting increases in stability and acceptance of law—that is, the improvements to ordered society that the fiction of Rule of Law brings—mean it is a marked improvement over the prior iterations of cooperative legal fictions.

What is important to note is that in many cases, the more fictive an idea is, the better it works. It provides a cooperative fiction far from brutal reality. The early law codes were backed by the tax collectors and thugs of the local warlord: pretty real stuff. The divine right of kings, although one step removed from anything recognizable as reality, had at least this going for it, reality-wise: deny it, and the king will take your head off. But the idea that the Rule of Law applies to rich and to poor, or that a citizen may make a legal claim against a more powerful entity, indeed sometimes even against the sovereign itself, is a masterpiece of pure fiction. It is only true because we act like it is true, not because anything in the world outside of our own consensual hallucinations lends it an observable reality. And contracts are particularly miraculous: Why in the world should an entity in power lend the power of lawmaking to a pair of people just so they can write rules that only apply to themselves? Well, because it works: societies with robust freedom of contract use that capability to arrange local rules for local deals, rules that fit the transaction far better than whatever off-the-shelf rules for cooperation the society might provide.

The best products of modern law are highly fictive stories about how things *ought* to be, not descriptions of how things are. Few modern legal regimes deny the existence or importance of human rights, even though our daily newsfeeds are full of political torture, rape as a tool of war, and drugged refugee children warehoused in tents in the desert. Nor are our rights static. The rights we are currently developing are far removed from reality. We talk about a right to access information as a way of addressing reality, which is that information is carefully hoarded, controlled, and doled out to maximize profit for a few corporations under overreaching intellectual property laws. We talk about a right to data security and privacy in a world where data giants Facebook and Google commoditize data for sale to AIs that steal our consumer surplus. We talk about a right to be forgotten in a world that cannot forget anything. These rights are important, even vital. But they do not reflect reality as it is: they reflect our human sense of how things ought to be.

ANALOGY AND RELEVANCE

Thus far we have talked about why we need law to provide robust cooperative fictions. But how does it *do* so? Law's power and central method is narrative. Cases are narratives, not studies. Even in civil law systems, courts are places of storytelling, loci for competing stories of what happened and what should happen. Every lawyer tells a story, and wins or loses her case by the framing story she tells. If a judge accepts your story, you've won. If a judge rejects your story, you're done. Judicial opinions are acts of narrative. Good legal articles are narratives. The more powerful the story, the more the story is repeated. Powerful stories are picked up, and their names become synonymous for important debates: *Roe, Korematsu, Lochner*. Law adds language to language, just like other disciplines do. Just as a name becomes a symbol for a person's life and deeds (in academia, a name becomes the person's scholarship, for instance), names in law are transformed into shorthand for critical cultural discussions.

I want to talk about what is happening in this process of rejection or acceptance and greater acceptance. This is the process of analogical reasoning, and it's the method by which legal social technologies like human rights and marriage equality were delivered. We use forms of analogical reasoning all the time—*this* is like *that*, which tells me *this* and *this*; since I know *this* about *that*, I can expect *that* to be like *this*.[19] But even though thinking by analogy is common to human reasoning, it's a terribly misunderstood and maligned method of developing life-giving fictions in law.

This is part of the general malaise within the American legal culture about the value of what lawyers do. Cass Sunstein writes:

> Often lawyers themselves are unenthusiastic about analogical reasoning, urging that this way of thinking about law is unconstrained or not a form of reasoning at all. As a result, the legal culture lacks a sympathetic depiction of its own most characteristic way of proceeding. In the face of this odd combination of general indifference and critical attack, analogical reasoning maintains its status as an exceedingly prominent means by which both lawyers and nonlawyers think about legal and moral questions.[20]

---

[19] Sunstein provides the example of getting into a friend's car on a cold day: you have the same car, and since it your car starts when it's cold, you figure that your friend's will too. As you can imagine, that reasoning can leave you stranded! "[A]nalogical reasoning does not guarantee good outcomes or truth. . . . The major challenge facing analogical reasoners is to decide when differences are relevant" (Sunstein, *supra* note 10, at 745). In this case, perhaps you forgot to consider the difference between the ages of the two cars, or your friend's propensity to leave the lights on and drain the battery.

[20] Sunstein, *supra* note 10, at 741–42.

To be clear: this state of affairs would be like doctors rejecting germ theory, or mathematicians rejecting number theory. Analogical reasoning is how law *works*. That lawyers distrust, misunderstand, and often reject their own method has widespread practical consequences for the creation of decent law.

An analogy is a test of narrative resistance to language in the human mind and within human communities of meaning. The *proposal* of an analogy is one datapoint. The *adoption* of an analogy is a more important one, and the *broad adoption and further use* of an analogy within a linguistic community most important of all. Recall our review in chapter 4 of the findings of Steve Sloman and Philip Fernbach: humans think in groups through a process of proposal and evaluation. We are most highly evolved to attend to problems together, and to exchange stories of what might work. One human is a node in a network of analysis. When humans propose narratives to frame a problem, to set the landscape for what is going on, they do so passionately—they can see the connection between *this* current situation and *that* former one. Other members may adopt that language, that way of talking about things, or they may not. If they do, the community has a ground story to move forward on, and can draw on language developed in the prior scenario as a way to address the current one.

If this sounds familiar, it is because it is another way of describing the pattern we outlined in Part I of this book. At the center of law is the process of applying old narratives to new cases. New cases conjure old ideas. New scenarios remind us of things in the past. How are they different? How are they the same? What is relevant between the two?

Before we dig in further, let's examine what analogy is not. It is not formal logic. This does not mean it is inferior. It can do things that formal logic cannot. In fact, it can do the big thing that formal logic cannot. Formal logic cannot recurse, that is, talk about itself, without risking fatal contradictions. Analogical reasoning can refer to itself, can wrap back on itself, can tell stories about stories about stories, as we are in fact doing right now, without collapsing in the face of the inevitably arising contradictions. Ask Kurt Gödel if formal logic can do that! In mathematical parlance, formal logic may be consistent, but any system of formal logic sufficiently complex to be able to make basic statements about *itself* cannot be both consistent and complete. On the other hand, analogical reasoning can be complete—it can talk coherently about every situation—but it will not necessarily be consistent.

While formal logic takes some steps to avoid the incompleteness caused by rigorous consistency but never entirely avoids the problem, so narrative law-making by analogy takes some steps to avoid the most obvious inconsistencies, but can never entirely do so. Because it must able to address all questions, it must be able to step out of its own system and refer to itself. Stories about stories referring to stories is how we get better stories.

So what is analogical reasoning, really? Given two stories, what does it mean that a community of humans finds some similarities between the stories valid for some purposes, and irrelevant for others?

ON RELEVANCE

We develop language by telling stories. Let's try this with a basic language-game that I play with my wife each evening: "How was your day?" The one thing that is impossible to do is to play this game without telling a story. You might tell a mechanical, robotic story, trying to keep any subjectivity out. But there is no way to tell someone how your day was, or what happened, without a story. Let's be clear: "What happened" is an illusion. If you recorded your life for a full day and asked someone to watch the video and then craft a story about what happened to you, they would be quite likely to seize on utterly different facts to make up their narrative.

What we say happened today isn't really what happened that day, and indeed, we do not have the words or the information bandwidth to begin to describe the mass of data, the enormously complicated social interactions, the deep reservoirs of culture and understanding, that a human draws upon as they live for twenty-four hours. It in itself would take (at least) twenty-four hours, and those would be a different twenty-four hours. Any attempt to tell someone about our day involves pouring all that data through a funnel: the speaker, telling the story. From all the infinite experiences, and the infinities of infinities of facts that you could have mentioned, you will select a finite, discrete, four or five things that happened to you today. Things that *mattered* to you today.

Where does what matters come from? Ask yourself: What is good music? Good music cannot be anything other than what humans want to hear, what elevates them, enrages them, excites them, seduces them, calms them. Think of a harp (maybe you despise harp music, but that shouldn't threaten this analogy). Why is it built the way it is? There are some physical limitations: a nano harp is hard to hear; a thirty-foot harp difficult to carry. But theoretically, the particular shape and structure is arbitrary. At the same time, the strings and structure are also determined–cultural ideas of resonance and harmony determine what tones we choose. Sure, there's some math and physics behind which tones and which combinations we find pleasing, but that is not the *reason* we find them pleasing. We choose them because we find them pleasing. *We* are the reason.

There is no other existence for music. To reduce it to mathematics misses the point: even music generated by artificial intelligence is played on human ears and minds. It's the interplay between human expectation and the path the notes take that causes the human to enjoy the music. It's easy to hear the music of a completely different culture and notice that the foundations seem different in important ways. It's still music, recognizable, but the starting assumptions of tonality are important. But as anyone has listened to both Gregorian chant and Metallica will say, these base assumptions shift and change while remaining in relation to each other.

Your answer to what is good music comes from your mind. It's heavily programmed by culture and strongly influenced by physiology and physics (if dogs made music, much of it would be too high for our ears). It can change over time, and can include more than one type of music, or maybe even exclude all music. Yet in the end, it is your subjective response to the sounds you hear. What matters to you is what stands out. It's influenced by culture and physiology and physics. But what matters comes from your subjective experience. You can analyze and explain why you like the music. But *that* you like the music, and this music or that music, is objectively subjective.

So when you respond to the question, "how was your day?" you will share a story about the things that stood out to you. That a fact or a connection or a turn of phrase was *noticed and selected* by a human is both subjective reality and objective fact. Out of the infinity of potentially relevant facts to a human, some finite number of facts were actually relevant to them. Stories are built on the objective fact that some things *matter* to humans. The vast majority of facts are discarded by our visual processing systems before we even know about them. Of the smaller infinity of experiences that actually get to our minds, most are discarded as uninteresting. And even those interesting events are reworked into a narrative structure that shares almost nothing with the source material. The resulting narrative, "what I did today," is an objective fact, like a recording of a whalesong. It is evidence of what a human mind found relevant out of an infinite universe.

This is the key point: human minds, which are heavily programmed by language and culture, *objectively* experience the *subjective* reality of relevance. Or, to put it another way, you find that a story is relevant to another story, it "reminds" you of that story, or the two stories are connected in a way that matters to you. Or you don't. What is important here is that this is a subjective experience, and the fact that you have had this subjective experience is an objective fact.

The measure of the connection between narratives is the significance that the human found in the facts that ran the blockade of human perception and conception, and has now been produced by the human narrative impulse as "relevant." Relevant facts, relevant connections, strung into narratives, is how human minds structure information. It is how we build the language with which to answer the question while we are using language to answer the question.

And it is a question, after all. *You* don't need to know what you did today. Well, maybe you're a dedicated journaler who makes a habit of reflecting on your day. That's a different context, although still a useful one for thinking about how our minds decide what's relevant. And, really, the context is not so different. You may keep your journal under lock and key (or password), but what is that narration for, if not a future and not-present-you self? Furthermore, recall that the self-narration we do is an outgrowth of our need to narrativize *others*.

Still, let's step beyond own interiors and consider what happens when I present a narrative built on facts that seem relevant to me to other humans, to a linguistic community of meaning. When humans are presented with two stories, "I had a bad day too, honey, here's what happened," we begin to look for actionable similarities and dissimilarities. Let's say that my wife and I conclude our round of misery poker by sympathizing with each other: we both had bad days. (Or, my wife could decide that my day spent typing was fine despite a bout of writer's block, and hers was much worse, or vice versa.) Was my day the same as my wife's? Worse? Better? How would we know? My wife proposes a narrative, I propose a narrative, and then we try to find congruences, similarities, and connections between the narratives. The connections we discover reveal more about us than they do about the universe. But they are no less true: it is objective fact that my wife and I, who form a community of meaning, selected certain subjective similarities or dissimilarities between our narratives as being the ones that matter. Relevance consists of what *matters* to groups of humans when they are presented with multiple narratives. Relevant facts are those which the linguistic community finds relevant. Facts and connections are relevant when we decide they are.

We think in groups and build language in community with others. We tell each other stories, and try to link them. The links between the stories are subjectively created objective realities, just like words or music. Then we must negotiate with each other what constitutes relevance, or what is relevant. We do not discover relevance, we build it, as a language game. Out of what we each individually find relevant, we work out what is relevant to connect the stories together. Of course, we often do not agree, since each of us often has an immediate interest in our own interpretation of the stories or the meanings of words. Have you ever heard an argument as ferocious as that over game rules, or a fight as vicious as soccer parents over a referee's call, or even over basic facts once political juices start flowing over Thanksgiving dinner?

LEGAL ANALOGICAL REASONING

Earlier we discussed that there is good reason to believe that human rationality evolved not for thinking logically at the individual level, but for creating post-hoc justifications—reasons—for the purposes of social persuasion within the context of group deliberation. Here's the thing: that's not just what the most recent science shows about humans, language, and thinking in groups. It's also a pretty fair description of many court and legal processes. Legal analogical reasoning always has three key players: two speakers (the parties to the conflict, or their lawyers) and an audience (the judge, jury, or both). The speakers propose different sets of relevances between the stories in play in a given case. The audience represents the rest of the community of meaning. They accept or reject the relevances proposed by parties to the conflict.

Legal analogical reasoning is not failed or casual formal logic. It is instead a set of negotiated linguistic connections between situations and stories which have been found relevant by the legal community of meaning. We propose that one story is relevant to another, or that one element of a statute is relevant for the determination of another. Even the civil law system, with its rigid interpretive canons, is the same: those canons of construction do not exist in reality. They are ways of understanding language that have been worked out by a community of meaning. They are paths through a jungle of meaning, made passable by the footsteps of those before, and kept passable by present use.

A relevant fact is one that is relevant to a human and, when they make that claim to a community, is accepted by that community. We make analogical claims, claims that one story is relevant to another, by proposing that *this* is like *that* in a way that may matter to the hearer. Analogies work when the hearer, whether a judge or a jury (or your date or spouse or parent), agrees that the stories are analogous in ways that matter. Analogies fall flat when the hearer or broader community of meaning rejects the claim of relevance or, even more strongly, rejects the *idea* of analogy entirely. In that case (which is our current situation), the community is rejecting the idea that meaning can be negoti-ated. The courthouse, not just the case, is closed.

To address the problems of the future, we need to be able to analogize well, to say that *this* new technological situation is relevantly similar to *that* old traditional situation, and to honor the connections that we find, not because they are logically compelled, but because they objectively *matter* to us. This is not because *this* is or is not somehow factually similar to *that*. We construct the facts that matter culturally, and don't notice the other facts at all—nor should we. They are not relevant to us. We must instead notice what *is* relevant to us, and talk about the stories with the most salience. We must negotiate what connects stories of trains to self-driving cars when it comes to liability for accidents; what connects stories of email to those about snail mail for purposes of the government's ability to surveil citizens; what connects stories of the need for reproductive self-determination with the stories of genetic modification of offspring. Who we are is what we think of ourselves, collectively. To think of ourselves translated into a future context, we must be able to think analogically now more than ever.

TECHNOLOGICAL IRRELEVANCE

Technologists often claim that lawyers don't understand technical subjects. Fair enough: few lawyers are electrical engineers. But oddly, technologists don't have the same humility when it comes to their ignorance: they know nothing about the law, it shows, and they keep making policy proposals for the regulation of technology as if they were revealing holy scripture.

The problem is that most technological facts about a product are not relevant to human concerns. What happens "under the hood" of a technology is important to the technologist, not the lawyer. What humans *do* with the technology is relevant. I don't care if a car is propelled by gas, battery, fuel cell, or ghosts: it's how humans *use* it that is relevant. (Of course, how humans extract or harvest fuel is something that matters to humans; that's a separate conversation about use.)

Technologists often provide terrible policy recommendations because they think only technological features are "real" or "relevant." They make the wrong analogies, because they are relying on inapt relevances. Of course, if one technological solution is like another technological solution, the similarities there are relevant to solving the technological problem. But we can use nearly identical technologies for completely different purposes: blockchain technology (the tech underlying cryptocurrencies like Bitcoin and Ethereum) can be used to build an online currency or a voting system. Banking law and election law are quite different, and for good reason. Who cares that some of the underlying tech is nearly identical: that relevance is the wrong one for the community that is seeking to understand and guide how humans make use of a given technology. It's like regulating assault weapons and holiday fireworks under the same regime because of similarities in their chemical propellants (gunpowder and its cousins). Not all relevances are relevant to all communities for all purposes.

For example, when I was beginning my career, a budding legal issue was whether and to what extent the electronic objects and virtual goods in virtual worlds were a player's property, and to what extent they were merely pixels on a screen, controlled exclusively by the game designer, the intellectual property rightsholder. That question is still hotly debated in the era of Bitcoin, but what is interesting is that more than a decade after scholars seriously began considering these questions, there are still two basic kinds of answers presented by communities that have a very hard time understanding one another's languages.

Technologists thought the relevant features were the features of the underlying technology, not the affordances of human use. They noted that virtual items are just pixels displayed by a client, and a reference in a database—certainly nothing like their limited conception of the legal fiction of property. But, said the lawyers, that missed the point entirely. The question is not what the numbers in your bank account "are." It is what they mean, and how they are used by humans. Take a look at something you own. There is no mystical tag marking it as yours. Your ownership of it is a node in a network of meaning. Your ownership is virtual. There are no yellow lines between nations: the fact that one acre belongs to one country, and another to other, is all just a projection of negotiated meaning onto the ground.

Regulation based on technological similarities irrelevant to human use is a huge mistake when it comes to new technologies. We need to understand what the technologies mean to us, how they are relevant in terms of the similarities to things that people do. Dollar bills and Bitcoin don't use the same technology at all—paper versus encryption and game theory—but the relevant similarities are obvious in how they are used: try to bribe a police officer with dollars or Bitcoin, it doesn't matter, you're still going to jail. How the technology works under the hood is only of interest to those who work under the hood. (Obviously I'm exaggerating to make the point: of course some technological affordances, like what fuels a car, are critically important to how humans use the technology—but even then, we appropriately focus our legal attention on *those* affordances and not irrelevancies.) I could care less whether the packets for an email message are intercepted while they are in transit, or after they have arrived at the destination server, or before they have left the origin server (if you can believe it, huge distinctions in the law of electronic surveillance turn on such daft technicalities). What matters is whether we believe it is acceptable for someone to read another's private messages without consent. Generally, unless the interceptor is a government with a warrant, the answer has been no. But because of this shilly-shallying with the technological details of how technological systems function, rather than how they are used and understood by human beings, the regulatory framework is a fragmented mess.

In sum, then: narrative plays a critical role in explaining *why* we do something and *what we ought to do*, not the technical details of execution. Law reasons by analogy because humans reason best in groups. Analogical reasoning allows the parties to a legal conflict to assert different sets of facts as relevant, with some representative of the legal community (judge) and broader community (jury) acting as referee. The primary job is to sort what facts in a case are relevant to how humans act, not what technological similarities there might be hidden away from the user. The speed limit shouldn't be different for Teslas (it isn't), and the law governing whether the government can spy on your online communications without a warrant shouldn't be different from whether the government is permitted to open your mail without a warrant (it unfortunately is, to the point that the law in this area is infamous).

Analogical reasoning is an effective way of using groups of humans as a "relevance processor," asking humans—hey, between these two stories, what are the similarities that give us sufficient guidance to act? A modern example of failing to understand the reach and role of human relevance is our current techno-regulatory climate: it is rife with mistakes caused by continuing to ask technologists how to regulate their own products. At best, engineers provide the technological analogies that worked for them in developing the product, not the human analogies that work for groups of people trying to cooperate. More often, lobbyists offer spurious narratives to simply maximize profits regardless of damage done.

Analogy is how we discover what matters. It is not scientific, but science rests on it. After all, when a scientist decides whether an experiment worked, she is telling a story just as we tell stories about our day. The question is what narrative she constructs, and even more importantly, why she chose to conduct that experiment at all.

RESTORING LEGAL RELEVANCE

To solve the problem of rampant and toxic technology, we must use our words. The solution must come through narrative, some set of cooperative fictions that help us work tougher to fix a broken ecosystem, a broken political situation, and a broken economic system. Language, and in particular the ability to create legal cooperative fictions like temples, armies, nations, taxes, money, and California, is our only tool for cooperating in groups large enough to make a difference.

Science has failed, and will only fail, to produce any narrative powerful enough to tell us what kind of world we *should* build together. Science studies and talks about the world. It tells us how to do things, not why or whether to do so. It's error is in thinking those conversations aren't important, and dismissing—if not outright attacking—attempts to do so. Law, the social technology of interpreting and articulating how we wish to live together in a changing world, is the discipline we need to help us develop our goals. But it has abdicated its role and fallen sway to science's false narratives. And this is a terrible shame. The common law system, for one, could be an immensely powerful tool for creating new, resilient legal rules through an iterative, humble, experimental, creative process that revisits rules regularly, and updates them in the face of changing technology. Yet it is precisely that common law process that is now disfavored among American academics, who downplay analogic, metaphorical thinking in favor of the false uniformity of economics or other flavors of the moment. Legal abilities so well suited to anticipating technological change—assessing and building relevance between old and new—are seen as outmoded, incapable, and unnecessary. It's no wonder lawyers are known to evade the law rather than show their clients how to follow it. The profession, at least in the United States, has become so doubting of its own product that lawyers are doctors spreading the infection.

Language is the raw ore of cooperation. Law is language refined and forged into critically important cooperative tools. Legal fictions are our cooperative lifeblood: money, nations, corporations, inheritances, crimes, and human rights. When a nation takes an action in accordance with international law, it is a fiction proceeding according to a fiction. When a corporation buys stock in a bank account, it is a fiction purchasing a fiction using a fiction from a fiction. When a humanitarian organization asserts human rights, it is a fiction asserting a fiction. We might not survive as a species, but if we do, it will be because law stood up and took its place as a discipline, accepting the use of various empirical and mathematical techniques, but using them in service of a narrative of human thriving.

7

Shifting How We Think

It's all interpretation
To find the truth, you've got to read between the lines
Work out your own salvation
That narrow path is hard to define
Heaven's more than a place, it's a state of mind
         — Diamond Rio, *"It's All in Your Head"*[1]

I'm a combat epistemologist. . . . . . It's my job to study hostile philosophies, and disrupt
them.

         — Charles Stross, *The Annihilation Score*[2]

Lord Bertrand Russell, one of the preeminent scientists, philosophers, and mathematicians of his time, was asked in a 1959 interview what he would like to tell future generations in order to help the human race survive. Since that is the subject of this book, let's listen in:

> *Interviewer:* Suppose, Lord Russell, this film were to be looked at by our descendants, like a Dead Sea Scroll, in a thousand years' time. What would you think it's worth telling that generation about the life you've lived and the lessons you've learned from it?
>   *Russell:* I should like to say two things, one intellectual, and one moral. The intellectual thing I should want to say to them is this. When you are studying any matter, or considering any philosophy, ask yourself only: What are the facts? And what is the truth that the facts bear out? Never let yourself be diverted, either by what you wish to believe or by what you think would have beneficent social effects if it were believed. But look only and solely at what are the facts. That is the intellectual thing that I should wish to say.

[1]   Diamond Rio, It's All in Your Head IV (1996).
[2]   Charles Stross, The Annihilation Score 6 (2015).

The moral thing I should wish to say to them is very simple. I should say: Love is wise; hatred is foolish. In this world, which is getting more and more closely interconnected, we have to learn to tolerate each other, we have to learn to put up with the fact that some people say things that we don't like. We can only live together in that way. And if we are to live together and not die together, we must learn a kind of charity and a kind of tolerance, which is absolutely vital to the continuation of human life on this planet.[3]

What Lord Russell said was exemplary, precisely the kind of thinking we need. But: the opposite of a small truth is a lie. The opposite of a big truth is another truth, and Russell's is a big truth. This chapter is about the terrifically important truth that Russell failed to see.

Notice his mistake. The truth with which we are concerned appears in the paragraph break between Russell's two pronouncements, in the deadly division of the world into intellectual and moral. Put his big statements side by side. "Look only and solely at the facts." "Love is wise; hatred is foolish."

Do you see it? The first statement cannot lead to the second. In fact, the first statement contradicts the second. "Love is wise; hatred is foolish" is a cooperative fiction. It depends on the quality of its supporting narrative fictions, not on the quality of its supporting facts. The only defense of "Love is wise; hatred is foolish" is that, like "All people are created equal," it is obviously not factually true, and equally as obviously critically important for us all to accept as narratively true: to believe and act as if we did believe in order for the human race to continue.

Why is love wise? Why is hatred foolish? Where did these things, and the urgency with which we must believe them, come from? If, in studying all things, we are to rely only on the facts, what are the facts on which Russell relies, here? And even if there were any such facts, how could one determine that love is wise and hatred is foolish without interpreting those facts into a system of values? Would Genghis Khan, Charles Martel, or Joan of Arc agree? Why can Bertrand Russell, of all people, not see that his most treasured cooperative fictions—"Love is wise; hatred is foolish"—cannot be generated by his dogmatic logicism and empiricism? This separation, of removing the moral from the realm of the intellectual, this great divorce of thinking, is the root of why we can't think clearly, let alone talk, about what we should do to survive the future. So this is what I will call Russell's Gap: the gap between his two paragraphs, or why it is that logico-empirical scientism can never tell us *why* to do anything.

---

[3] PhilosophieKanal, *Bertrand Russell – Message to Future Generations*, YouTube, www .youtube.com/watch?v=ihaB8AFOhZo.

RUSSELL'S GAP

Russell's Gap goes very deep, both in the history of science in the twentieth century and in one of Russell's most profound and lifelong intellectual blindnesses, the one that caused the philosophical movement to which he made serious contributions—logical positivism—to founder. This failure is bound up with the foundation of modern interpretation-based social science, and its scientific disagreements with the logic- and empirics-based branches of science, and is therefore of enormous significance for our current conversation.

Russell's blindness was this: he never really understood what language was, or what it was for. The problem of language had teased at the edges of a revolution in scientific thought that had been building between Great Britain and Vienna, Austria. This is part of the same conversation we touched on earlier: the Vienna Circle of scientists and philosophers and mathematicians who sought to purge metaphysics from science by adhering to the principle of verifiability.[4] As you'll recall, verificationism dictated that only that which could be proven to be true would be accepted as scientifically valid. There were two kinds of statements that the Vienna Circle was prepared to accept as verifiably true: logical statements, which could be proved deductively true from axioms assumed to be true (here, the best example is mathematics), and statements verified from empirical observation. Logic and empirical observation were therefore established as the sole acceptable statements.

There were some real remaining problems (as Karl Popper would go on to show, you can only ever prove something to be false). For one, how could these scientists account for the very language they used to describe these scientific truths? Language *expresses* truths, but it itself seems to simply be generated by humans cooperating.

A decade or so earlier, Russell had finished, in his *Principia Mathematica*, a resoundingly successful attempt to connect logic to mathematics, and things were looking good for a comprehensive theory of science, in which logic, mathematics, empirical observation, and language could all be brought together under one unified theory of science. And precisely as these things were occurring, a young philosopher of language named Ludwig Wittgenstein made his appearance.

---

[4]   *See* Richard Creath, *Logical Empiricism*, THE STANFORD ENCYCLOPEDIA OF PHILOSOPHY, https://plato.stanford.edu/entries/logical-empiricism/#EmpVerAntMet.

Wittgenstein's earliest work, the *Tractatus Logico-Philosophicus*, appeared a godsend to both Russell and the Vienna Circle. Russell wrote the introduction for the book, and was instrumental in its publishing and dissemination.[5] The Vienna Circle took the book very seriously, and considered Ludwig Wittgenstein an important patron saint. Wittgenstein, however, felt that Russell's introduction misunderstood the book so badly that he nearly withdrew its publication. And the one time that Wittgenstein agreed to meet with the Vienna Circle, he turned his back on them and read poetry.[6]

What was going on here? Who was Ludwig Wittgenstein, why was he so important to Bertrand Russell and the Vienna Circle, and why did they so badly misunderstand his philosophy of language? To be clear, there are lots and lots of philosophers, scientists, poets, and cultural anthropologists who have picked up on the core themes that we will talk about here, but I will be (and have been) using the language Wittgenstein developed pretty heavily, so I want to talk about it here.

WITTGENSTEIN'S (FIRST) PHILOSOPHY OF LANGUAGE

Wittgenstein's problem was the meaning of language, how we develop it, and the relationship of fields like logic, mathematics, history, poetry, law (in our case), and philosophy (in Wittgenstein's), to the medium, language, in which they are expressed.[7]

His core idea was this: most problems of philosophy are problems of language.[8] Think back to your last philosophical debate with a friend (or enemy, if you have some). Did you get the sense that the two of you were using words slightly differently, and that if you would just agree to use words in the same way, the problem would go away?[9] I often find myself in "violent

---

[5]   *See* Anat Biletzki & Anat Matar, *Ludwig Wittgenstein*, THE STANFORD ENCYCLOPEDIA OF PHILOSOPHY, https://plato.stanford.edu/entries/wittgenstein.

[6]   *See* ALLAN JANIK & STEPHEN TOULMIN, WITTGENSTEIN'S VIENNA 215 (1973).

[7]   *See* LUDWIG WITTGENSTEIN, PHILOSOPHICAL INVESTIGATIONS (G. E. M. Anscombe trans., 3rd ed. 1974) (On pages 2–3, Wittgenstein poses his first question of language in the book by asking how a shopkeeper knows how to use the word "five" when you ask for five red apples. To Wittgenstein, the question is not "what does five mean?", rather it is "how is five used?".) [hereinafter WITTGENSTEIN, PHILOSOPHICAL INVESTIGATIONS].

[8]   *Id.* at 19. (In remark 38, Wittgenstein writes: "For philosophical problems arise when language goes on holiday." When language goes on holiday, it stops doing its job and is being misused, which can create philosophical dilemmas.)

[9]   An example of how two people may see the same word as not synonymous would be that of a scientist and a member of the general public. To a life scientist, "mutant" simply means "a change in the genetic coding," whereas a member of the general public may assume the word to mean "abnormal." In reality, the two definitions overlap in some aspects; however, the life

agreement" with people on a given subject—we agree on most things, except for how we are using words. Of course, we can also understand those we don't agree with—we recognize that they are using words within accepted meanings, simply not meanings we accept. Perhaps you have felt the problem in reading this book: you get what I am saying, but find that I am misusing words like "language," or "science," or what have you.

That was Wittgenstein's point: that almost all philosophical problems, such as Socrates's harping on definitional questions like "what does 'truth' or 'beauty' mean?" are better solved by attention to the mechanisms by which language acquires meaning than by any other means. "Truth" is not a transcendent concept with independent meaning, it is merely a word, used by humans, in a range of contexts. Pretending it is anything else causes endless muddle.

Wittgenstein at first thought he could solve this problem by restricting the role of language to making either true or false statements about reality. This was his project in the *Tractatus Logico-Philosophicus*. Essentially, the book said this: language either describes reality, that is, a word *corresponds* to an object, fact, or state of affairs observable in reality, or it tries to talk about how things "should" be.[10] (Yes, "reality" is itself a perceptual and linguistic construction, but this was Wittgenstein's early work. That part is coming.) In the *Tractatus*, Wittgenstein claimed that only the first use of language—the point-and-name part—made sense. He recommended we just stay quiet about things like love, justice, truth, beauty, privacy, freedom, tyranny—things you can't point-and-name.

Wittgenstein said that the first function of language could be expressed pretty simply, and that this fit very neatly with the logic and mathematics of Bertrand Russell's *Principia Mathematica*.[11] So, imagine we have some atomic facts, each fact consisting of a state of affairs. Fact: the *cup* is on the *table*.[12] Then we can tie statements together with logical connectors: the cup is on the table, *and* the coffee is in the cup. If either statement is false, then the statement of the state of affairs is false. If both sub-statements are true, then the statement of the state of affairs is true. Just as we put *and* in the middle of

---

scientist may view the word in a neutral light, while the general public does not. So, for this example, imagine a person from each of these categories arguing over a matter that involves the word "mutant." The two may ultimately agree on the overarching conclusion, but they may have conflict about what they perceive the word "mutant" to mean.

[10]   See Ludwig Wittgenstein, Tractatus Logico-Philosophicus (C. K. Ogden trans., 2010) [hereinafter Wittgenstein, Tractatus].

[11]   See Alfred Whitehead & Bertrand Russell, Principia Mathematica (1903).

[12]   See Wittgenstein, Tractatus, *supra* note 10 at 28.

the last sentence, we can introduce the other basic connectors of propositional logic: AND, OR, IMPLIES, NOT, EQUALS (as in statements such as "the cup is *not* on the table *or* the coffee is in the cup"), and we can evaluate the truth of the atomic facts, then examine the logical connectors, and thus decide if all statements are true or false.[13] If the cup *is* on the table.

That last bit was the important part: Wittgenstein believed we could determine whether all statements about reality were true, or false. He introduced (or at least popularized) the use of "truth tables," a way of logically tying together statements about reality so that we can see if a statement is true or not. Consider: "The cup is not on the table, OR the coffee is in the cup." If either statement is true (or both statements are true), because of the OR, the whole sentence is true.[14] However, if the cup in reality *is* on the table, AND the coffee is not in the cup, the statement is false.[15] And so on.

But here is where the wheels started to come off. Wittgenstein had no way of talking about narrative, about figurative language, about *why* statements like "but here is where the wheels started to come off" have meaning and are perfectly comprehensible. As noted above, Wittgenstein's first instinct was to argue that we should simply cease to make such statements. At the end of the *Tractatus*, he wrote:

> The right method of philosophy would be this: To say nothing except what can be said, *i.e.*, the propositions of natural science, *i.e.*, something that has nothing to do with philosophy: and then always, when someone else wished to say something metaphysical, to demonstrate to him that he had given no meaning to certain signs in his propositions.[16]

This leads to the famous—and often misinterpreted—statement at the end of the *Tractatus*: "Whereof one cannot speak, thereof one must be silent."[17] In short, we must shut up about statements like "we must shut up." Although these statements make perfect sense, Wittgenstein's first shot at thinking about language did not capture most of what language does.

It was the *Tractatus*'s devotion to logic and empiricism—the exclusion of all statements that did not precisely describe states of affairs observable through the methodologies of natural science—that drew Russell. What an enormous

---

[13] *See* Virginia Klenk, Understanding Symbolic Logic (4th ed. 2002). (This is an entry-level college logic textbook that details propositional logic and the truth tables in greater detail than will be discussed in this chapter.)

[14] *See id.* at 33–34.

[15] *See id.* at 32–33.

[16] Wittgenstein, Tractatus, *supra* note 10, at 107–08.

[17] *Id.* at 108.

relief for Russell, who wished to "look only and solely at the facts," that the rest of language, that part unrelated to empirical observations or logical propositions, could be swept into the trash heap of philosophy. Russell wrote in his introduction to the *Tractatus* that "[Wittgenstein] is concerned with the conditions which would have to be fulfilled by a logically perfect language."[18] If all "legitimate" language corresponds to reality, then Russell's focus on empirical observation and logical deduction can serve all the purposes we need.

Why, then, the ambiguity in Wittgenstein's reaction to Russell's introduction? Why did Wittgenstein literally turn his back on the Vienna Circle, whose entire project was to purge science of everything that could not be empirically observed or logically deduced, just to read poetry? Perhaps it was that, at that time, Wittgenstein believed he had solved all problems of philosophy by calling them all useless wordplay, and by isolating that part of language which was useful to the sciences, and quarantining the rest. Perhaps it was, as Wittgenstein scholars Allan Janik and Stephen Toulmin write, that Wittgenstein thought that everything which *could not* be said, that is, everything about how things, and we, ought to live and be, was the important part of philosophy.[19]

That latter idea is perhaps closer to the truth. After the *Tractatus*, Wittgenstein, convinced he had solved all problems of philosophy, became a schoolteacher. But within a decade he returned to philosophy, and Cambridge, and developed work on language which announced that the *Tractatus* was wrong about the subject of language's relationship to reality.[20] Wittgenstein wrote of "grave mistakes in what I wrote in the first book":[21] "In the *Tractatus*, I was unclear about 'logical analysis' and ostensive demonstration. I used to think that there was a direct link between Language and Reality."[22]

And, to return to the subject of this book, it is precisely this point that Russell failed to understand, and that currently we do not understand, about talking about how things *ought* to be when they *are not so*, both from a moral and from a futurist standpoint. It is precisely this link that Russell missed between his great statement of science: "Look *only* and *solely* at the facts," and his prescription for keeping us all alive in the future: "Love is wise, hatred is foolish. . . . If

---

[18] *Id.* at 7.
[19] *See* JANIK & TOULMIN, *supra* note 6, at 199. ("[F]or Wittgenstein considers that this "nonsense" is anything but unimportant.")
[20] *See* WITTGENSTEIN, PHILOSOPHICAL INVESTIGATIONS, *supra* note 7, at viii.
[21] *Id.* at iv.
[22] JANIK & TOULMIN, *supra* note 6, at 222.

we are to live together and not die together, we must learn a kind of charity and a kind of tolerance, which is absolutely vital to the continuation of human life on this planet."[23]

Russell's fierce logical positivism meant that he lacked the tools to bridge his paragraph break. The tools of logic and empiricism cannot get from "is" to "ought," or from "will be" to "should be."[24] Only the tool of interpretation, aimed at understanding language and culture, can do that. We can only get to statements like "we should love and help one another" by building linguistic instruments, ways of speaking, cultural complexes, in which those clearly fictitious statements are commonly accepted and acted upon in the language. "Love one another" is like money: a social fiction, albeit one that has an immense visible and practical influence on a society.

We need to be able to bridge Russell's Gap. We need to be able to understand, build, believe in, and act in concert upon cooperative fictive statements like "love is wise, hatred is foolish," without hand-waving about how the trick is done. "If we are to live together and not die together," we need to understand how it is that statements like "we must learn a kind of charity and a kind of tolerance, which is absolutely vital to the continuation of human life on this planet" can be created, evaluated, and acted upon within human communities. "Look only and solely at the facts" is not going to get us there. We need a different theory of language.

And we have one. Wittgenstein's return to philosophy produced a far more influential theory of language. It is influential not among mathematicians and empirical scientists, but among sociologists and cultural anthropologists, the people who work with human motivations, culture, and language. Indeed, it is largely the failure of the natural sciences to understand the deep challenges brought by this theory of language that today places law as a discipline in a backwater, the unloved and supposedly unscientific orphan left on the far side of Russell's Gap. Law calls to us to build a bridge across Russell's Gap, and indeed, to make that bridge the cornerstone of how we can live together and

---

[23] PhilosophieKanal, *Bertrand Russell – Message to Future Generations*, YouTube, www .youtube.com/watch?v=ihaB8AFOhZo.

[24] *See* David Hume, A Treatise of Human Nature, Book 3, Part 1, Section 1, 362–63 (2005) (Hume writes: "I am surprized [sic] to find, that instead of the usual copulations of propositions, is, and is not, I meet with no proposition that is not connected with an ought, or ought not. This change is imperceptible; but is, however, of the last consequence. For as this ought, or ought not, expresses some new relation of affirmation, 'tis necessary that it should be observed and explained; and at the same time that a reason should be given, for what seems altogether inconceivable, how this new relation can be a deduction from others, which are entirely different from it.").

build the kind of ways of talking we desperately need if we are to stay alive and thrive.

HOW TO BUILD A LANGUAGE

We have previously discussed the iron law of evolution: successful cooperative groups beat the pants off groups of uncoordinated individuals.[25] Humans cooperate at scale by creating cooperative fictions in language. A key element in the development of our eusociality is that our faculty of reasoning works best not to help us individually reach correct conclusions, but to justify ourselves to others and persuade them of our ideas. Our intelligence works best in groups, where we each make the best arguments we can, and others adopt successful language as their own. To understand how we cooperate and think at scale, we have to understand how we generate language.

The difference between Wittgenstein's early and later work lies at the root of Russell's Gap. We do not generate language by looking only and solely at the facts and describing the states of affairs we observe. Language is not point-and-click. (As noted, if this is sounding familiar, that's because we've touched on all this in earlier chapters. Wittgenstein's philosophy of language is the key with which the lock of language turns, and thus it warrants deeper discussion.)

Here is Wittgenstein's later and vastly better theory of language: words acquire meaning as humans use them within a linguistic community and context. Or more succinctly: meaning is use. Language does not get meaning from correspondence to objects, and language does not derive its structure from the structure of reality. Rather, language gets meaning from how humans use it.[26] The word "cup" does not derive its meaning from corresponding to, or pointing to, any particular cup. Rather, language is negotiated within a community of meaning, within a context, and in relation to a particular task. "Cup" means the thing you hand me when I make that noise. We do not make language by referring to objects in empirical reality, we make language by negotiating with each other to get things done, as anyone who has successfully used the phrase "pass me the thingummy" will know.

Wittgenstein makes this point with a "builder's language." Imagine we have two people, a builder and an assistant, who are trying to build something. The

---

[25] As Edward Wilson and David Sloan Wilson state: "Selfishness beats altruism within groups. Altruistic groups beat selfish groups. Everything else is commentary." *Rethinking the Theoretical Foundation of Sociobiology* 82 QUARTERLY REVIEW OF BIOLOGY 327, 345 (2007).

[26] *See* WITTGENSTEIN, PHILOSOPHICAL INVESTIGATIONS, *supra* note 7, at 20 (Wittgenstein refers to the use of language as "language-games," which consists of "language and the actions into which it is woven").

words they use, "here," "there," "post," "beam," and so on, derive their
meaning not from correspondence to reality, but from the nature of the task
at hand.[27] "Post" is an upright piece of wood, "beam" a horizontal one,
depending on how they are used.[28] As Roshan Ara points out, a word as used
is "not a description, but an order or an appeal."[29] I like the word *bid*. Each
time we use a word, we are making a bid on its range of meanings, a bid that
others may choose to accept or reject.

A community of meaning comes together when people try to communicate
with each other to do something—even something as simple as trying to
understand one another. Such a community can be as broad as the specialized
language used by any discipline (law's use of "legal language" among members of that community is legendary), or as narrow as asking your spouse,
"when you say pass me the thingummy, do you mean the doohickey, or the
widget?" If your spouse replies that thingummy means the widget, now the two
of you know what the other means and can accomplish that task. Those words
acquire meaning by use in a given context. And while people are part of many
different communities of meaning, they are never *not* part of one. Whenever
we speak, we are negotiating meaning with others.

Words become slippery and useless when we remove them from their
linguistic community and context of use. The words have no grip. In
a conversation at work, "thingummy" no longer means "widget." You have
perhaps experienced this in a political debate with someone from a different
political community of meaning: it is sometimes more as though you dis-
agreed about the meaning of the words than about anything else. It may feel as
if you are speaking different languages, because in a very real sense you are,
and you cannot see the world the other person is describing. The words they
link together don't link that way, to you. They don't make sense, and the
conclusions don't line up.

Wittgenstein's *Philosophical Investigations* tried to do what I hope that we
are doing in this text: to build language that will help us to talk about building
language. That is, his task and context was also a builder's language: he built
a language about building language. And so it is worth discussing some of the
tools he developed—words and phrases he created within the context of
talking about language and with the purpose of developing language, linguistic instruments like "builder's language" and "meaning is use"—because they

---

[27] *See* Wittgenstein, Philosophical Investigations, *supra* note 7, at 3.
[28] *See id.* at 4.
[29] Roshan Ara, *Wittgenstein's Concept of Language Games*, 26 Al-Hikmat 47, 49 (2006).

aid in our conversation of how we can build the kind of language we will need to talk coherently about the problems of the future.

Wittgenstein discussed a grouping of context, tasks, community, and words as a "language-game." For example, the context of builders building a house, the task of building, the community of builder and assistant, and the words that they negotiate between them, by using words like "bring me a beam" and "hand me the hammer," all are part of a language-game.

This neologism highlights the situatedness, the reliance on context, community, and task, that gives language its meaning. It helps us see language from the outside, as a shared, negotiated task of generating conventions of meaning. Imagine a greeting-game: you wish to greet and introduce yourself to someone with whom you do not share a language. Would you hold your hands out, empty, to show you are not a threat? Offer to shake hands? What if the other person places their hand on their chest and makes a sound? Would you do the same, interpreting that as the "this is my name" move in your greeting-game? What if the person placed their hand on their forehead and said a word? What would your countermove be? How would you interpret their move? Your responses to them, and their responses to yours, are worked out between you, in relation to and dependent on your context. A "hand-on-chest-and-make-a-sound" move has a completely different meaning in the greeting-game than it does in the "tell-the-doctor-I'm-having-a-heart-attack" game, for example.

The strength of the language-game idea is that it refocuses meaning as not what words refer to (i.e., the "correspondence" theory of language) but how they are used. Within the term "language-game" lurks a constant reminder that words have no core essential meaning by themselves. Furthermore, it reminds us that just as a ball or a deck of cards can be used in many different games, words can be used differently in many different games. Both language-games and "meaning is use" remind us that language is an activity. Words do not mean anything by themselves; they only draw meaning from the context, task, and community in which they are used.

The word "run," for example, has hundreds of distinct meanings in English, depending on how the word is used. I'd hazard that you could name a good three dozen uses right off the bat. Where did you learn all those meanings? I doubt you read through the dictionary entry (in the *OED*, it runs for pages). We learn these meanings by context, in community. If you're a cheesemaker, you know that you must make the cheese run—become solid—at the proper time and temperature. If you're a metallurgist, there is also a proper time and temperature for running metal—when it gets so hot it becomes molten. Yet if either cheesemaker or metallurgist is a stockings-wearing type, neither would be happy with a run in their tights.[30] (Unless one were a Brit, who would bemoan not having bought "ladder resist" nylons.) Do all these words seem unfamiliar or outdated? Our linguistic communities today are more likely to run an app than to run to the store for stockings or rennet. Our contexts and tasks have changed. Our language has too. All this is evidence of negotiated language. We know that language is nimble. Its dexterity is a reflection of its nature as an activity, a "form of life," as Wittgenstein described it.[31] This is what makes it our superpower.

GRAMMARS: PATTERNS IN SPACE

We often say that 2 + 2 does not equal 5. We also say that it is empirically true that the earth is not flat. Those statements are examples of how logic (math) and empiricism decide what is correct or incorrect. How, then, do we evaluate a statement in language like "love is wise, hatred is foolish," or even "the object on the table is a cup and not a mug"? How do we make those decisions?

We measure "rightness" and "wrongness" differently in language than in empirical observation or logical deduction. Empirical observation determines "wrongness" by reference to observable facts and the concept of falsifiability. If I want to test whether I can fly, I start with the null hypothesis (I cannot fly), and attempt to falsify it by attempting to fly. In logical deduction, the basis of mathematics, we start with axioms that we assume are true, and proceed by strict connectors, the AND, OR, NOT, IMPLIES, and EQUALS of propositional logic, to build a system consistent with its founding axioms.

Language does not determine rightness and wrongness in the ways that logic or empiricism does. I find Wittgenstein's idea of a "grammar" to be useful here.[32] A Wittgensteinian grammar is the set of legitimate moves made in a language-game such that an utterance makes sense. These grammars can and do shift, but they also give a speaker grounds to state that another speaker's

---

[30] *Run*, OXFORD ENGLISH DICTIONARY (2nd ed. 1989) ("To cause (milk, etc.) to coagulate or curdle"; "To flow as the result of melting; to become fluid; to melt and flow"; "A vertical strip of holes in a stocking, pair of tights, or other knitted garment, typically formed when the breaking of a thread causes the column of stitches immediately above or below the broken stitch to unravel").

[31] WITTGENSTEIN, PHILOSOPHICAL INVESTIGATIONS, *supra* note 7, at 8.

[32] A grammar, to Wittgenstein, is not what your high school English teacher taught about subjects, verbs, and direct objects, or those claims to universal grammar made by Noam Chomsky and more recently by Steven Pinker.

linguistic move is out of bounds. If I a sentence using the structure of German wrote, another speaker of English it notice would, and you me out-call could. Even though the preceding sentence is intelligible (and grammatical, using German's verb rules), it is also clearly ungrammatical for present purposes. So grammars in this sense have two traits: they are mutable and changeable, but only by agreement within a linguistic community. To use an analogy, a language is like a galaxy. It hangs together. Its parts move, to be sure, drawn by gravitational forces within. Indeed, the stars and planets may drift relative to each other, and have gravitational impact (and, very occasionally, actual impact) on each other. But the whole hangs and moves together, a pattern in space. It could be a different pattern, and the pattern does shift over time. But the pattern it happens to form is quite intelligible.

The key point of the concept of a Wittgensteinian grammar is this: words can change in meaning as the word's use by a linguistic community alters over time, yet anarchy and relativism do not reign—words can be used wrongly, despite their essential slipperiness. It is both true that *nice* used to mean something very different than it does now, and that "hitting your brother is not nice" is a sentence that makes sense. We must not give in to either definitionalism ("this" means "that" and nothing else) or relativism (anything can mean anything!). Language lives on this edge between theme and variation, between convention and innovation. Move it off the line, and it dies, quite literally: defined language implodes under the weight of self-reference, as proven by Kurt Gödel ("this statement is not a theorem of S"), and language with no context or constraint becomes nonsense that sounds oddly like sense, as explored by Lewis Carroll ("'Twas brillig, and the slithy toves / did gyre and gimble in the wabe: / All mimsy were the borogoves, / and the mome raths outgrabe").

THE PRIVATE LANGUAGE MISTAKE

Our understanding of Wittgensteinian grammar and "meaning is use" can be aided by one more term from Wittgenstein's toolbag.

Many of us experience language in our heads—subvocalization—so it is tempting to think that language lives and originates in our individual minds. But that idea, which Wittgenstein called "private language," is, if not entirely wrong (anyone with a four-year-old has heard new words be born), deeply misleading (the new word only becomes part of language if a parent accepts the term or turn of phrase, incorporating it into negotiated language). Language is born, lives, grows, and changes between us, externally, not in our heads, internally. This between-ness is the origin of language's stickiness, of the fact that we can change the meaning of words, but only by use, with others, in context. Stories matter: when we think about what words mean, the picture in our head should not be our minds, alone with the word hanging in space, but two or more people speaking, collaborating on meaning.

Words change with their community and context, but they do not mean whatever we want them to mean. They have to be accepted by some community of meaning: wherever two or three of us are gathered, there meaning arises. If I am the only one who thinks that the word "battleship" means "hippopotamus," I get no traction. No one agrees with me. If I think that "run," however, not only means to move rapidly on foot, but to run a bath, run for election, or run out of money, I am in good company.[33]

Language has meaning by convention, and acquires meaning by breaking old conventions and forming new ones within communities of meaning. These meanings then radiate outwards, like ripples from a pebble dropped in a pond. Some linguistic innovations are the equivalent of Cousin Fred doing a belly flop: they are sudden innovations that immediately swamp the pool. Take your pick of any of the hashtags that have dominated political debate in recent years: the phrase "Me Too" will never again have just and only its prior meaning. Others gain traction only slowly, and their glacial drift can only be noticed by scholars of language, who note that "Whan that Aprille, with his shoures soote / The droghte of Marche hath perced to the roote" has a few words that have drifted a bit in meaning, much less the praise for a good king in *Beowulf*: "Þæt wæs god cyning."[34]

Language is built on language, using language. The trick is to have enough convention so that words have meaning. If language changes too quickly, we lose the thread, as every generation which mourns the loss of its own youthful language can attest.

Language cannot exist just in our heads. Sure, we rehearse words subvocally, and anyone who has ever obsessed about a conversation at a dinner party (the French have a special word for this, *l'esprit d'escalier*, conjuring the perfect retort while on the stairs leaving an event) has in their own mind stretched, pulled, and tugged at the meanings of each word said, until the same words have completely different meanings to different people. But language resists our private meanings: it must take into account the interpretations of others, or else we cannot be understood. This is why we say of

---

[33] *Run*, OXFORD ENGLISH DICTIONARY, www.oed.com/view/Entry/168875?result=4&rskey=xe1naT&.

[34] Geoffrey Chaucer, prologue to THE CANTERBURY TALES; lines 1–2; BEOWULF, lines 11, 862, 2391.

someone whom we understand precisely that they are speaking our language. Here, the interpretations of the community of meaning are very similar, at least as far as the current subject of conversation is concerned. Or we might say of someone that they're speaking a foreign language, when what we really mean is that their interpretation of some terms is so far removed from what we understand by the meaning of those words that we can barely make out the point at all.

This is why conversations about religion, sexuality, politics, art, music, and most certainly law go so quickly astray. The communities that have gathered around those topics generate strong languages, and people speak those languages with thick intellectual accents that make it hard for others to understand what is generalizable and what is community-specific about the way they speak. This can make it hard for us to understand each other, precisely when what we are talking about is the most simple and important thing we can think to talk about: What is true, and what is false? It is the drift in the words "true" and "false," among others, that cause us to not be able to speak to one another clearly.

TALKING ABOUT TRUTH

Theologian Marcus Borg states the following about the truth of stories: "I don't know if it happened this way or not, but I know that it is true."[35] This uncovers the core ambiguity in how the word "truth" is used in a range of communities of meaning. "True" might mean that it accords with observed reality, or, more strongly, with our perception of repeatability and causation. Sometimes we might call this a fact.[36] A story can also ring true or ring false, just as a note in a chord can be in or out of tune. When a story rings true, it makes a normative claim consistent with and perhaps constitutive of an important set of normative beliefs. It fits with the rest of our beautiful cooperative fantasies.

"Meaning is use" dramatically shifts our sense of what happens when we talk. We see that "truth" is not a transcendent concept with independent meaning but rather a word we use in a range of contexts. Wittgenstein's philosophy of language places truth between us rather than imagining its frictionless drift "out there" on some or astral plane.[37] In doing so, we can

---

[35] MARCUS BORG, THE HEART OF CHRISTIANITY 51 (2003).

[36] As long as we are aware that facts, too, are created to some degree. *See* LAWRENCE ROSEN, LAW AS CULTURE (2006).

[37] *See, e.g.,* WITTGENSTEIN, PHILOSOPHICAL INVESTIGATIONS, *supra* note 7, 116 ("What *we* do," wrote Wittgenstein, "is to bring words back from their metaphysical to their everyday use").

begin to speak with precision. We can stop asking, "what is 'truth'?" and focus instead on how we use the word. We can ask, "how do we use it?" "How do we know what is true?" "What is our method for knowing?"

These questions are extremely important in the era of deep fake photos and videos, online disinformation spread by Russian artificial intelligence, QAnon and Pizzagate conspiracy theorists, "alternative facts," and fake news. A large part of the dangerous developments in modern society relates to the inability of humans to tell what is true and what is not. As anyone who reads the news may have noted, there seems to be a deep difficulty in how we come to understand what is true.

We are talking here about epistemology, which is a five-dollar word for the methods we use to decide together what is true. We are quite familiar with science's preferred methods: rationalism (or logic) and empiricism. But as we have seen, neither of these know what to do with our cooperative fictions. You cannot observe the United States of America, the nation, itself. You can certainly see people, buildings, and (certain) borders, but the social and cultural cooperative reality of a nation-state is in the power that humans give a set of cultural and linguistic signifiers of loyalty.

It is a deep error to think that empiricism and logic *find* truth. The rituals and language of logic and empirical observation are linguistic sub-games, social rituals that contribute some useful bids for what might be accepted as "true" in a language-game. When someone says, "$2 + 2 = 4$," we nod our heads and say, "true, because logic." When someone says, "the sun came up this morning," we nod our heads and say, "true, because we observed it." And when someone says, "all people are created equal," we also nod our heads, and say, "true, because that is how we speak."

How is this so? A cooperative fiction like "love is wise" is both subjective and meaningful. It is true not because it is factual or even logical but because it is part of what humans mean when we use the word "true." Our normative assertions—our language of *should*—is "the voice of a contingent human artifact."[38] It does not represent reality, but our response to it. If you agree with me, it is because you agree with the system of values in which the statement lives. There is nothing else on which it rests. It refers only to ideas humans have created.

Like any other word, "truth" is a word we breathe into being.[39] Or to put it more bluntly: we do not *determine* truth through epistemic methods. We

---

[38] RICHARD RORTY, CONTINGENCY, IRONY, AND SOLIDARITY 60 (1989).
[39] *See id.* at 5 ("Truth cannot be out there—cannot exist independently of the human mind—because sentences cannot so exist, or be out there. The world is out there, but descriptions of

negotiate it, as we negotiate the meaning of every other word. What we mean when we say "true" is complex, overlapping, and often conflicting, based on the linguistic sub-game used to generate the bid on the meaning of the word.

In the effort to define their territory, to separate "facts" from "fictions," the epistemologies of logic and empiricism forgot that they, too, are social constructions. It is this shift in perception that lets us not only bridge Russell's Gap but also see that the gap is one of our own making.

Redescribing facts as social constructions does not undermine them. It is an achievement of the twentieth century that the language-games of science have established their methods of empiricism and rationalism. Perhaps it is because these methods are so hard-won that they are so prized. And they should be. Empiricism has given us antibiotics. Logic gave us all of computer science and the information revolution. But we need to stop pretending these are the only methods for assessing truth. As we've been discussing, logic and empiricism cannot tell us why we might want to employ them, or why we might want this thing over that. Logic and empiricism capture the human desire to talk about certain things in certain ways. They do not capture the entirety of human language, human preference, human life.

This is the task of interpretation, which is this third way of knowing that I would like to discuss. Interpretation is the epistemology we use to understand what words mean, and how we create and communicate that meaning. It is the way of knowing that you used to understand this sentence. In the sciences, interpretation has been dismissed and denigrated as a valid source of truth. But it is our method for understanding and explaining human social constructions—that is, language, and the webs we build with it. Interpretation is the only way of answering certain questions about the world. What does the sentence "George will be allowed to come home from prison on Friday at last" mean?[40] It's a serious question, and has valid answers.

What I want is for the word "true" to encompass the interpretive results of natural language and cooperative fiction. I want us to recognize that we often say "true" to statements like "all people are created equal," too, and to include the ways that is done as legitimate contributions to our understanding of what is true.

Our current confusion is a crisis about what is true, whether that is an inability to parse out mis- and disinformation, believe vaccine science, establish consensus about democratic behavior, or even determine whether

the world are not. Only descriptions of the world can be true or false. The world on its own—unaided by the describing activities of human beings—cannot.").

40   *See* MARY MIDGLEY, THE MYTHS WE LIVE BY 51 (2004).

a public figure should be removed from office. As we will explore in the following sections, this confusion is caused by muddling these ways of knowing, and by more than occasionally relying on completely wrong ways of knowing. We need to understand the tools we use to study, understand, and live together in the world. And in particular, interpretation must be recognized, understood, and restored in order to build the language and narratives we need to survive and thrive.

WAYS OF KNOWING: NEGOTIATING TRUTH

Let's start with a few hypotheticals. Let's say that tomorrow at work, a coworker tells you he can fly. When you get home, your son claims in his math homework that the square root of -1 is -1. Your discouraged daughter comes home and states that "nobody likes her" at school. You have good reasons to believe that each of these statements is false. But the reason why each statement is false is completely different.

Your coworker cannot fly. How do we know? Because in a social ritual called an experiment ("oh? Show me!") he will not be able to falsify the null hypothesis, which is that he cannot fly. We observe no flight, the null hypothesis has not been falsified, and we conclude Mr. Kent cannot fly.

Your son is incorrect about the square root of -1. But here, the reason his answer is false is completely different. By convention, and to keep the math system consistent, we invent "imaginary" numbers (as if all numbers weren't already imaginary, but this is a different use of the word) to handle these cases. If 2 x 2 is 4, and 2 x -2 is -4, and -2 x -2 is 4, there is no regular number combination left to express the square root of -4, or any negative number. So we expand the logical system and create a category, imaginary numbers, to fill this void while keeping the system consistent.[41] There is no empirical experiment that will show that the square root of -1 is or is not -1. We could build a mathematical system with that as a starting assumption. It just wouldn't get very far, or be very useful, because it would immediately introduce logical inconsistency into basic arithmetic. Your son's answer is wrong because it makes a non-useful logical system, not because of any observable reality.

---

[41] *See, e.g.*, PAUL NAHIN, AN IMAGINARY TALE, 48–54 (1998) (Caspar Wessel was the first individual to determine the meaning of the square root of -1. He viewed the square root of -1 in a geometrical sense, simply rotating 90 degrees in a counterclockwise sense. Before him, other famous mathematicians, like Descartes, were posed with the question of what the square root of -1 was but knew it was not -1.); JOHN R. TAYLOR, CLASSICAL MECHANICS 67 (2005) (imaginary numbers, also called complex numbers, are commonly used in the realm of physics for the motion of a charge in a uniform magnetic field).

Your daughter is also quite likely wrong that "nobody likes her." Here, we might be tempted to say that, observationally, her best friend Elizabeth likes her very much. But how do we know that? This is not based on an experiment, or even observation—since what it means to "like" someone or "friendship" is not directly observable, but is instead a pattern in culture and language. Worse, the entire phenomenon of the mind, as separate from physical phenomena, is not observable, much less to like. Our determination of the truth or falsity of your daughter's belief is based on the cultural meaning of friendship, the linguistic meaning of the word "like," our interpretation and construction of Elizabeth's subjective intentions and state of mind. Yet based on your interpretation of the language, situation, culture, and people involved, you still have very solid reasons to believe that your daughter is wrong that nobody likes her. It is, in other words, untrue that nobody likes your daughter.

In the sciences, the typical white-lab-coated scientist is an empiricist. A mathematician is a rationalist. And a cultural anthropologist is an interpreter. An empiricist observes phenomena. A rationalist constructs a consistent system using rules of logic. An interpreter, as we'll explore, explains the cooperative fictions of culture using the cooperative fictions of culture.

An empirical scientist compares her projection under her theory to reality. If reality does not match her theory, her theory is falsified; if it does, her theory is (provisionally) confirmed. Empiricism looks to observable phenomena as the final arbiter of what is correct.[42] Under rationalism, correctness is determined by the regular application of logical rules to starting axioms.[43] Nothing is compared to reality. It is instead compared to itself, and to the ramifications of the starting principles through logical extension. A mathematical system has properties, that is all. Sometimes those properties help us get along in real life—arithmetic is pretty handy for most of us, for example—but the mathematical system is not compared to reality in order for mathematicians to determine that it is valid. Thus, rationalist scientific inquiry looks to consistency and features of a theoretical system, rather than reference to a separate empirical reality.

The third way that I have observed scientists quite rationally talking about reality is among students of cultural artifacts, from poets to sociologists. These people, when asked, "what is this book, Harry Potter and the Sorcerer's Stone, about?" interpret the book. To cultural anthropologists, the best practice of science involves intense subjective interpretation of language, culture, and

---

[42] Peter Markie, Rationalism vs. Empiricism, THE STANFORD ENCYCLOPEDIA OF PHILOSOPHY, https://plato.stanford.edu/archives/fall2017/entries/rationalism-empiricism/.
[43] See id.

other critical social components. In short, there is no mathematically rational or empirically observable answer to the question, "what is the meaning of this book?" The meaning of what a book is, and what it in turn is saying, takes place within the socially constructed web of meaning. To understand the book is to understand that web.

There are some key questions we simply cannot answer scientifically using the tools that are currently considered the most "scientific." No amount of observation through an electron microscope will tell you what a book means, or what the word "science" itself means. For those questions, interpretation is our only scientific method. The truth of the answer comes from the speaker's understanding of specific cultural, linguistic, and literary traditions. Should you encounter a curious alien, it is the method you would use to explain not just what a particular book is about, but what a book is. The only way to explain to a Martian what a book is, and what it means, is to explain what the relevant linguistic community calls a book, and why.

For those steeped in the language of empirical and logical methods, my claim that interpretation is a coequal way of knowing may not sit easy. How can cooperative fictions explain fictions? (Hint: It is not unlike how tools make tools.) How is interpretation judged? What makes an interpretation true, or at least more accurate than another interpretation? These are understandable questions, not least because the scientific community resists attempts to show that it, too, is at the mercy of these questions of language.

These questions, though, are more about how interpretation works than about its manifestation. My aim in this chapter is to demonstrate how interpretation works and how we negotiate truth. Interpretation is the method we use to understand the thoughts of others, and to have them understand our own. It's not logic that does that, nor empirical observation. It's a public activity that operates in and through language. (And remember, language is an activity for communicating meaning: shrugs and winks may be wordless, but they can still be understood.)

Furthermore, certain concerns about interpretation are not bugs but features: interpretation is circular and recursive. It does not offer what we perceive to be the solidity of empiricism or logic. It is fundamentally incomplete (any two interpretations of *Harry Potter* will be idiosyncratic). We will dig further into these implications, but for now it is important to see that there are certain and specific differences between empiricism, rationalism, and interpretation, as well as how epistemologies are used. When our way of knowing fails to match our subject matter, the way of knowing fails. An empirical scientist cannot observe mathematics. A mathematician cannot explain the meaning of the word "good." And the social and religious practices explained by a cultural anthropologist do nothing to explain particle physics.

When our way of knowing matches our subject matter, the way of knowing succeeds. An empirical scientist can provide a theory of gravity or evolution that, so far, seems to fit observed experimental facts. A mathematician can provide a useful, complex, and reasonably consistent logical construct that helps us leverage what we know—think those pesky word problems in math class. And a cultural anthropologist can explain why attitudes on marriage equality, race, gender, and sexuality are in flux in modern society.

Even the verbs of these approaches are different. An empiricist *induces*. That is, she looks at experimental results, and develops a theory drawn from the evidence. A mathematician *deduces*. She starts from axioms that are simply assumed, and then proceeds with logical rigor to try to find more rules that result from the starting rules. A cultural anthropologist *interprets*. She attempts to *understand and explain* the statements of other humans expressed in culture.

I am oversimplifying so that we can see the core epistemologies of these approaches. Almost everyone uses a bit of almost everything. A cultural anthropologist observes the subjective cooperative fictions of culture in a way that is reminiscent of, but *not quite the same as*, an empiricist. A mathematician is engaged in the cultural construction of a symbolic language of logic in a way that is reminiscent of, but *not quite the same as*, living language. And so on. A rum cake, a cherry mojito, and a rum-soaked cherry share the ingredients of sugar, alcohol, and fruit, but with a greater amount of sugar in the cake, alcohol in the mojito, and fruit in the cherry, resulting in three profoundly different (and delicious) dishes.

This mixing is valuable and good, but it results in profound confusion over what is *true* in each of the epistemological systems. This is because the way a human uses the word "truth"—and meaning is use, after all—is driven by the method, the social ritual, used. When the method of testing truth shifts, so does the answer to the question, "what is true?"

COMMUNITY AND TRUTH

If a scientist wants to conduct an experiment, how does she know to frame a null hypothesis, structure her question, set up observations, and report her findings in ways that others can replicate? How does she even talk about what it is she is doing? In what social ritual and language does the scientific method consist? To start, it may be helpful to think of epistemologies as tools: a piece of technology built to assess how we know something. Seen this way, we do not wonder how the painter opts for a brush and the electrician a voltmeter. We have a variety of tools for a variety of needs, and using the wrong tool gets us nowhere—or worse. If we perceive epistemologies as tools, we can stop insisting on using only certain tools and instead focus on whether we are using our tools efficiently.[44]

Furthermore, we can understand that these tools have come into being, have evolved, been retooled, and in some cases, discarded. As Richard Rorty writes: "Once we found out what could be done with a Galilean vocabulary, nobody was much interested in doing the things which used to be done ... with an Aristotelian vocabulary."[45] And just as the chariot was replaced by the carriage, then gasoline cars, then electric vehicles, and moderately soon, personal drones, we can see how new and different tools may be preferred to previous ones.

As you will recall, this is the process of paradigm shift that Thomas Kuhn illustrated in his *Structure of Scientific Revolutions*: the fundamental narratives of science shift as new ways of talking about science emerge.[46] Science is a linguistic process of selecting better guiding narratives, of inventing new tools that work better than the ones we have. They are "better" in the sense that most of us prefer matches to a flint. Beyond the chemical properties of phosphorus sulfide, nothing about matches in particular was foreordained, but once we began to have a use for fires, we were bound to figure out better ways to make them.[47]

This brings us back to the efforts of the Vienna Circle to expel metaphysics—spiritual woo—from the philosophy of science. They argued that only two things could count as true: logical truth (i.e., a theorem correctly deduced from axioms), and empirical truth (observations based on reality). In time, they developed the idea of verificationism: only that which could be verified could be true.

---

[44] See, e.g., Rorty, *supra* note 38, AT 12 ("This is a question about whether our use of tools is efficient, not a question about whether our beliefs our contradictory"); MIDGLEY, *supra* note 40, at 87 ("The forms of thought we need for understanding social dilemmas are distinct from those that we need for chemistry and those again from historical thinking, because they answer different kinds of questions. They are bound to have different standards of validity. . . . The sort of unity that thought actually needs . . . is a unity that flows adequately from the fact that we are studying a single world—the one we live in—and that our thought arises from a single source, namely, our joint attempt to live in that world.").

[45] Rorty, *supra* note 38, at 19.

[46] THOMAS KUHN, THE STRUCTURE OF SCIENTIFIC REVOLUTIONS (1962).

[47] *Id.* at 171 ("Products of a process that moved steadily from primitive beginnings but toward no goal.").

As we've noted, their work did some good—it was a solid and practical way of thinking. But it did not last. Karl Popper convinced the scientific community that one can only ever prove a theory false, and not true, since further experimental evidence might contradict even the most well established theory.[48] So within the scientific community, the narrative of "falsifiability" replaced that of "verifiability" as the gold standard of scientific experiments, and scientists now set about proving things false rather than proving them true.

What I want to point out here is that the shift from verifiability to falsifiability was a shift in language and social practice within the scientific community. It then changed the practice of the scientific method, by, for example, leading scientists to propose their hypotheses using the "null hypothesis," the theory that their idea is *not* true. This little social ritual, in which my experiment to show that sneezing causes hair loss is framed with a hypothesis that sneezing does *not* cause hair loss, is a social and linguistic change within the community of meaning.

Empiricism is a colossally crafted term. So are logic and tautology. The scientific method does not exist outside our heads. Science does not exist outside our heads. There is nothing empirical about empirical method. There is nothing verifiable about verificationism. Falsifiability itself cannot be falsified. This is not a criticism, but a description. Epistemic methods are linguistic endeavors. We depend on community and language to create the language and rituals for determining how we will use the word "true." That is, we rely heavily on each other to determine not only what is true, but *how to determine* what is true. We invoke systems of people to determine both what we think— we rely on knowledge held in the heads of trusted others—and how to decide what we think.

When a group seeks to understand something, that undertaking provides a context and a goal, leading to the development of a grammar (as Wittgenstein would say) of truth. The group determines how it will assess what it is seeking to understand. Some of these rituals are long established, and the community can be massive. Consider the weight of the scientific method, and how many people practice it.

Different communities of meaning have different social rituals to determine what that group of people will accept as true, from peer review and replication to leaving fleeces out in the morning dew. If you've ever had the feeling of being "between worlds" when passing from one group of people to another, particularly when those groups hold radically different ideas about

[48] KARL POPPER, THE LOGIC OF SCIENTIFIC DISCOVERY (1959).

how the world works on ostensibly the same facts, you have felt the power and weight of these shifting grammars of truth.

Our deep failures to understand one another come from the fact that we often speak completely different languages for the linguistic sub-game of "what is true?" One person looks to one system of symbolic structure and meaning, with its attendant high priests (of technology, politics, or faith); another to another. These rituals can be so entrenched that we forget they are social constructions. For example, looking someone in the eye is a symbol of truth-telling in many cultures; in others it's a sign of anger. Thus, the antidote is not merely to realize that we are speaking different languages and practicing different rituals. We must be able to understand each other. If we are to live and work together, we must be able to talk to each other. Our social ways of knowing are collapsing because of our lack of engagement with the science of interpretation: of our skills at reading and explaining the minds of others.

IT'S ALL INTERPRETATION: SORTING WINKS FROM TWITCHES

The Vienna Circle and Karl Popper established new standards and methods for doing science, which the community adopted because they were persuaded that it was a better way to do science. And it is: alchemy was never going to give us gold, but modern medicine has given us antibiotics. However, in trying to extract itself from narratives of the supernatural, which of course needed to happen, science got its feet tangled in the idea that narrative had to go as well. Science—oblivious to the fact that science, too, is a social construction—embraced the false belief that statements about cooperative fictions like law were somehow unscientific or unnecessary.

This is ironic, of course, because as Thomas Kuhn demonstrated, you can't get to any discipline without going through its paradigmatic stories, without interpreting its narratives and language. Empiricism cannot do without it: otherwise, how would we understand what a scientist means when she describes why an experiment should be done in a certain way? Logic cannot do without it: we have to interpret words to understand the meaning of the mathematician and the meaning she ascribes to her signs and symbols.

Interpretation is the method of knowing that lies nearest to our cognition. If we think of ourselves as reasoning in groups, interpretation is a method internal to our own cognition. It is so close to us that we fail to see it.[49] We

---

[49] *See, e.g.*, WITTGENSTEIN, PHILOSOPHICAL INVESTIGATIONS, *supra* note 7, § 129 ("The aspects of things that are most important for us are hidden because of their simplicity and

must be able to interpret others' words, motivations, and intentions to be able to think and work together. We interpret each time we ask ourselves, "why did she say that?" or "he did this, what does that mean?" It is the truth discerned when someone shuts a door and we think, "they want privacy." It is the understanding gleaned when we offer someone a cookie and they say, "I'm good."

Of course, behavior can be misunderstood—perhaps it was the wind that closed the door. And because interpretation is a study of behavior, it is inherently incomplete. Your guest may decide they want that cookie after all. Or perhaps they were joking in the first place. Interpretation is not an empirical or rational source of truth, and as we will see, it is subject to exploitation and misunderstanding. Even so, the methods of linguistic interpretation can make as strong a claim to having contributed valuable meaning to the word "true" as have the distinct and different sub-games of logic and empirical observation.

Because interpretation is so close to us, it is useful to triangulate off another point rather than try to see beneath our own nose. The field of cultural anthropology models how a discipline that must deal with words does deal with words. Cultural anthropologists are by no means the only practitioners of interpretation, but they are a core example of scientists who answer real and valuable questions about the world using interpretive methods. As Clifford Geertz, a godfather of cultural anthropology, writes, they are experts in "alien turns of mind."[50] In other words, anthropology's engagement with the subjective gives us a perch to watch interpretation at work.

Anthropology is a profession "obsessed with worlds beyond our own and with making them comprehensible first to ourselves and then, through conceptual devices not so different from those of historians and literary ones not so different from those of novelists, to our readers."[51] The anthropologist observes, records, analyzes, describes, and explains. These tasks might hint

---

familiarity. [One is unable to notice something—because it is always before one's eyes.] The real foundations of his enquiry do not strike a man at all. Unless that fact has at some time struck him.—And this means: we fail to be struck by what, once seen, is most striking and most powerful.").

[50] Clifford Geertz, *The Uses of Diversity*, 25 MICH. Q. REV. 1, 118 (1986). Note: I'm not here to defend those who have called themselves anthropologists but were merely defenders of ethnocentrism. Many anthropologists made their way among the "savages," "natives," or "primitives" and only ended up revealing the savagery of their own nativist worlds and the crudeness of their approach. Perhaps if we'd been less focused on a sense of inherent connection among "our people," we might have seen more clearly that foreignness, as Geertz writes, starts not "at the water's edge but at the skin's" (*Id.* at 112).

[51] *Id.* at 118.

at empirical observation (the subjects did this, or said this), but the anthropologist seeks meaning, not a transcription. Tasks like transcription are in service of the interpretation, and are themselves a result of interpretation.

All this is to say, interpretation is recursive: it articulates the entire enterprise. An interpreter follows the "flow of social discourse" and describes and explains what it means, a process they must "contrive somehow first to grasp and then to render."[52] Anthropologists weave stories based on their understanding of the cultural and linguistic traditions in which they are immersed. "Man," writes Geertz, "is an animal suspended in webs of significance he himself has spun" (and, I ask, what more precise account of language could there be?). Culture is those webs. And the analysis of culture is "not an experimental science in search of law but an interpretive one in search of meaning."[53]

Let's zoom in on some threads in these webs of significance. Geertz outlines a scene where two children are contracting their eyelids. The movements are identical, but one happens to be an involuntary twitch, while the other is a wink. Although the action is the same, the meaning is not. We have all observed such behavior, and have all understood (or confused!)[54] the difference.

Imagine further that there is a third child, who parodies the first child's twitch. He contracts his eyelid with feigned and repeated effort. His aim is not conspiracy but ridicule. How would the anthropologist explain the scene? "Flicking his eyelid up and down" falls woefully short—it describes the action but is too thin to capture its meaning. We need instead a thick description: "Practicing a burlesque of a friend faking a wink to deceive an innocent into thinking a conspiracy is in motion."[55] This dense account of context and activity sketches the web of meaning within which this "fleck of culture" lives. A wink has no meaning beyond this web of meaning, and its meaning is understood by sorting through these "piled-up structures of inference and implication."[56]

Following Wittgenstein, we can understand that these behaviors are public (what is a wink for, if not another's eyes?). They are clothed in context. They are telegraphed to others for one purpose or another, based on the task and the commonly understood context in which the action or word is enmeshed. The

---

[52] CLIFFORD GEERTZ, THE INTERPRETATION OF CULTURES 10 (1973).
[53] *Id.* at 5.
[54] The *Seinfeld* episode "The Wink" (October 12, 1995) is one such example.
[55] Gilbert Ryle, *The Thinking of Thoughts: What Is "Le Penseur" Doing?*, quoted in Geertz, *supra* note 52) at 7 (Geertz borrows Ryle's concept of "thick description," as well as his narrative example of winkers and twitches).
[56] Geertz, *supra* note 52, at 6–7.

point, which the anthropologist arrives at by understanding, analyzing, and explaining the webs of significance, is deciphering what it is that is being said.

The children comprehend all this in an instant—so quickly, in fact, that the first may laugh at the third before he realizes, if he ever does, that he is the one being parodied. If so, he has misinterpreted the joke. As anyone who has been the object of a joke will recognize, the power of parody is in its ability to exploit interpretation.

Interpretation can be exploited; information can be misinterpreted. Those fields which deal with words have the unenviable task to "seek complexity and order it."[57] But here our understanding of our own quotidian misinterpretations can inform our understanding of methodological ones. If I misunderstand what someone says, my interest in understanding will be marked not by protesting or pulling away, but by drawing closer to their words, to their use. "A good interpretation," writes Geertz, "takes us into the heart of that which is the interpretation." It "sorts winks from twitches and real winks from mimicked ones."[58] This is the truth that interpretation seeks and claims. It does not reveal reality or prove logic; it renders comprehensible human subjective experience.

INTERPRETIVE METHODS AND THE LAW

Anthropology is by no means the only field that employs interpretive theory. Myriad volumes in sociology, cultural anthropology, semiotics, literary criticism, and music theory, to name just a few fields, deal with the question of how one interprets the statements of others. We do not have space or time here to cover all these fields and their widely differing methods for determining meaning. But from their variety we can see one easy truth: interpretive methods are constructed in communities as a way of both creating and communicating meaning. They are linguistic community bridges, strategies for helping one person or group understand another. The key way that humans communicate is by reaching out to form a community of meaning. "Me Tarzan; you Jane" is how some of those attempts at building a common vocabulary might start—by naming the members of the emerging community. It is an attempt to bridge different languages. It is not unlike translation, as long as we keep in mind that the object of interpretation is not simply to understand what the other party said, but to converse.[59]

---

[57]   *Id.* at 34.
[58]   *Id.* at 18, 16.
[59]   Translation, at least as we use this word today, is also problematic in the sense that we think of it as falling only to Italian or Urdu or Klingon. Foreign languages abound, and the degree to

In that sense, the science of interpretation is the skill and methodology of developing language that not so much perfectly represents what the other person or community said, what their precise position is, as provides a series of bridges, paths between worlds, that help us understand what other people from other communities mean when they speak. Interpretation makes the unintelligible intelligible by bridging, or negotiating a path between, linguistic communities and contexts.

So when we are talking about interpretive methods, we are talking about specific linguistic communities that grow up around the task of understanding what other people are saying. That explains our different fields, from sociology to literary criticism. Those methods differ, and one could take a class in each to learn to speak the local language of interpretation. But having learned that language, one would enter a rich world of meaning.

Legal interpretation is no different. To learn the law is to learn a language, or a locally practiced dialect. And because law is the language of human cooperation, law has often been concerned with narratives of interpretation, with stories about *why* interpreting things a certain way is a good idea or a bad idea. One could (many have) write a treatise on how to interpret legal texts. It would be full of Latin interpretive guides like *expressio unius est exclusio alterius*, which means that when a statute says one thing, it excludes the things it doesn't say, or reads on power and context like *contra proferentem*, the maxim that instructs courts to interpret contracts against the party who wrote them.[60]

Those specific interpretive rules are the relatively uninteresting output of a very interesting process. They are encodings in language of useful ways to approach reading a statute or a contract. And they provide guidance for how to write a statute or a contract, knowing that judges may read them in that way.

which another person with whom you share a language makes sense to you is reflective of the degree of correspondence among your respective linguistic communities. If math is not your strong point, the example of the son who concluded the square root of -1 is 1 is an example of what I mean. Or perhaps you might spend the afternoon with a group of teenagers. You will, I suspect, recognize implicitly what Wittgenstein meant when he wrote: "We do not *understand* the people. (And not because of not knowing what they are saying to themselves.) We cannot find our feet with them" (WITTGENSTEIN, PHILOSOPHICAL INVESTIGATIONS, *supra* note 7, 225).

Of this point Geertz notes, "Finding our feet, an unnerving business which never more than distantly succeeds, is what ethnographic research consists of as a personal experience; trying to formulate the basis on which one imagines, always excessively, one has found them is what anthropological writing consists of as a scientific endeavor." (GEERTZ, THE INTERPRETATION OF CULTURES, *supra* note 52, at 13).

60 In other words, the consequences of ambiguity fall to the one responsible for setting the words down.

Law cranks out little bits of interpretive interface like that, and society gets a way to formalize agreements by speaking through legal language.

There is a further significant payoff in seeing law in this way. If we wish to change not only specific legal rules, but the actual nature of law itself, then we realize that we must look at the linguistic community of people making bids on how legal language should be interpreted, and must consider how to negotiate better legal language within and outside of that community. We must actively negotiate cooperative fictions that serve as healthier touchpoints for us to discuss the question of law: how to live together and cooperate. Interpretations bridge communities of meaning—creating a version of the "fusion of horizons"[61] that happens every time two people communicate—and creating key touchpoints for interpretation will help us talk clearly about the problems we are facing.

It is the process we are after, not just the product. The product is of course significant (it gives us insight; it adds to the record "of what man has said").[62] But we must remember always that we do not engage in interpretation so as to say definitively, "we have conversed." We interpret because we wish, in the present-progressive sense, to converse, to understand and be understood. It is not a conclusive process; it is, till death do us part, endless.

Law is interpretation, of course, and so everything a lawyer does follows some theory of interpretation. When legal scholarship tries to work with theories of interpretation, it often sounds like this book: getting into how we can know what words mean. Law, though, has a strong solution. Because law *must* interpret language and must render a decision—after all, not interpreting the language isn't really an option—it creates interpretive links: saying something in *this* way is legally effective, even though saying it *that* way is not. Despite attempts to modernize the interpretation of contracts and statutes, for example, creeping formalism is the hallmark of legal language, because it *sets it apart from natural language* as having legal power and effect. The "wherefore-s" and "howsoevers" of legal language mark a different mode, a language of formality and authority. Think of legal language like lifeforms evolving. Legal language survives if it is read to have legal effect, and thus is reused by the legal linguistic community. Legal language dies if it is read to have no legal

---

[61] *See* HANS-GEORG GADAMER, TRUTH AND METHOD 301, 305 (1960) ("The horizon is the range of vision that includes everything that can be seen from a particular vantage point.... A person who has no horizon ... does not see far enough and hence over-values what is nearest to him. On the other hand, 'to have an horizon' means not being limited to what is nearby, but to being able to see beyond it"; "Understanding is always the fusion of these horizons supposedly existing by themselves").

[62] Geertz, *supra* note 52 at 30.

effect, and thus is discarded by the legal linguistic community. Legal language is no less effective for having evolved. To the contrary, the field of law is a rich soup of linguistic ferment, constantly tossing up couplings of language and interpretation, such that when parties agree on language and how to interpret it, they can come to legal agreement. Once we understand that interpretive methods are created within quite small communities of meaning, we see how much of the work of the law is in generating the context in which legal speech will be heard and acted upon.

Law's essential purpose is to talk about how we ought to live together. Life is not static, nor is negotiation over how best we should live together. If an anthropologist is a student of human cultures generally (via the observation and interpretation of specific, contextual behaviors), lawyers are students of human preferences generally (via the reading and interpretation of cases, statutes, precedents). A trained legal mind is a cultural harp upon which theme and variation in rules for human cooperation are played. Cases are thick descriptions of facts and interpretations of the meanings of speech-actions. The flow of social discourse is about life together. The anthropologist and lawyer share a kinship as students of the cultural-linguistic webs we weave as we live in the world together.

The task of legal interpretation is to build interpretive bridges that permit humans to use their superpowers of linguistic cooperation. For example, many of us work together in corporations. The set of legal language around our modern social practice of working together in corporations makes that form of cooperation, for better or worse, one of the most widely practiced in human history. One simple measure for the success of interpretation, then, is the actual observable fact of cooperation: Are the humans working together? If the humans aren't talking, something is amiss with our interpretation. Recognizing this, the lawyers are not to grasp for less well suited tools because they are socially constructed to be more "scientific." They should draw their ears and eyes closer to the flow of social discourse and strengthen their grip on the sturdy and effective tools of analogical reasoning, narrative construction, and interpretation.

The linguistic output of legal communities is cooperative fictions called laws. Laws are negotiated results to specific contexts. Not all rules survive or are encoded in law: the inputs to the legal system are that minute fraction of cases in which the community has failed to negotiate a rule that works for everyone and must turn to an arbiter under a community rule of decision. These laws collect and collate human preference.

Laws are much more than statutes and case decisions, they are convincing (or unconvincing) narratives that tell us how to manage the intricate fictive dance of human cooperation. A bee dances to tell other bees where to find food. A human lawyer consults political and legal stories (perhaps a story called "The Social Contract" or one called "The Leviathan" or one called "The United States," hatchets, cherry trees, slavery, and all) to help us coordinate. These cooperative fictions of law store in our common language what we have learned about living with each other. They make our lived experience part of our language, and we can turn around and use that language to craft further cooperative fictions. It takes a fiction of a United States grounded in equality and liberty (a fiction established by slaveholders and colonizers, to be sure, but narratives can and often do contradict themselves) to create concepts like marriage equality. It takes a fiction of a United States founded in rebellion to sustain modern concepts of gun ownership.

The core barrier to developing laws that handle technology—consensus about what we should do—has been a strange intellectual handicap, an odd ashamedness, on the part of those who teach or practice law. They cannot see that their field has just as much grounding and justified existence as the methods and communities of laboratory scientists.

Qualitative interpretation, no matter the field, takes culture, language, and narrative seriously. It doesn't offer thin facts (the child's eye closed five times). It looks at, analyzes, and explains the tapestry of negotiated meaning. It gives a rich description that brings us to a closer understanding of the context and aims of specific and diverse communities. It makes the unintelligible intelligible and gets to the heart of what is being said. It tells us why those humans did what they did. It is the tool we need when we want to talk about why and what we want to do.

COMBAT EPISTEMOLOGY: FIGHTING BAD WAYS OF KNOWING

Our confusion about truth and epistemologies has led to bad ways of knowing. In particular, there are two big epistemological errors that I would like to focus on.

The first is using interpretive methods to establish observational truth. For example, among certain religious groups, a standard truth-seeking move is to pray about whether something is true, and then consult one's feelings.[63] If a powerful positive emotion results, this is taken as a "spiritual confirmation" or "spiritual witness" of the truth of the statement.[64] If a negative emotion or

---

[63] See, e.g., *Spiritual Witnesses* (Oct 22, 2015), www.youtube.com/watch?v=UJMSU8Qj6Go.
[64] *Id.*

no emotion results, this is taken as disconfirmation. The difficulty is, feelings and other subjective perspectives are not a reliable method for determining scientific or logical reality. When this method is used to confirm statements of fact, it regularly fails.

It is easy to see this error in a religious context: pick someone who is a faithful member of a religion you do not share. They will very often tell you they have received a powerful spiritual witness that their religion is true. Now, pick someone of a different religion: same method, same result. Their method of truth is to examine and rely on the feelings of elevation produced by religious language, and multiple modes of religious language create feelings of elevation.

There is a reason, though, that Bertrand Russell cautions us to look for this error in considering "any philosophy," and that in doing so, to "never let yourself be diverted, either by what you wish to believe, or by what you think would have beneficent social effects if it were believed."[65] The error is epidemic: mistaking our feelings for facts, our gut-level read for how the universe is, navigating by the lights of the ideas we like, that fit with our existing worldview, we are likely to deeply misunderstand the world around us. So, for example, a person who believes that white people are superior on the basis of their ground-level perceptual-cognitive bias against people of other races is unlikely to be disconfirmed in her racism. Some people "are good, decent people," others "aren't," and people "just know it in their gut."

The second epistemological error dismisses interpretive accounts as unscientific, or "softer" science. As discussed, the claim that interpretive approaches are less scientific than logical or empirical approaches is nonsense. Again, consider the method of a religious believer reading a scriptural story and experiencing a powerful emotional response. How is one to understand what the story means without interpretation? Interpretation is necessary for any understanding of the meaning of the story, the socially negotiated position of scripture, the language used, and the subjective state of mind that results from reading the story.

To illustrate these two errors, let us take a concrete example. I will use my own background and namesake. The Old Testament scripture of Joshua 10 reads:

> Then Joshua spoke to the Lord in the day when the Lord delivered up the Amorites before the children of Israel, and he said in the sight of Israel:

---

[65] PhilosophieKanal, *Bertrand Russell – Message to Future Generations*, YouTube, www.youtube.com/watch?v=ihaB8AFOhZo.

"Sun, stand still over Gibeon;
And Moon, in the Valley of Aijalon."
So the sun stood still,
and the moon stopped,
till the people had revenge
upon their enemies.

Is this not written in the Book of Jasher? So the sun stood still in the midst of heaven, and did not hasten to go down for about a whole day.[66]

If one were to receive an emotional confirmation that the sun actually stood still on this day, one would be of course quite wrong. And if one were to read this passage as one of empirical fact rather than cultural storytelling, thereby excluding interpretive methods from the understanding of the passage (which might include questions like "what is the book of Jasher?" and "what was the role of such myths in binding a community together?"), one would be equally wrong. Treating the statement as one of empirical fact is wrong. Attempting to understand the story, its quoted poetry, and its role within that society, as well as its meaning within modern cultural traditions, without interpretative methods, is also wrong. Both lead to clear and ascertainable error.

The first error betrays our tendency to see the world only as we wish. The second dismisses our subjective accounts entirely. The problem lies with the relationship between the branches of science that encompass chemistry and mathematics and are guided by logic and empiricism, and the branch of science that encompasses linguistics and the study of culture and is guided by interpretation. Because the core function of legal thinking is to construct and interpret cooperative fictions, this confusion about epistemology has gutted our ability to take on the task of building the kind of fictions we need. We have downgraded the study of law along with the other interpretive sciences, and precisely because of foolish and verifiably false claims that interpretive methods can reveal anything other than what is in our heads and language. What interpretation does, only it can do. What it can't, it really can't.

THE WAR ON TRUTH

The breach between logical and empirical methods and interpretive ones could not have come at a worse time. Or, perhaps more accurately, the breach has caused this time to be worse. The technologist manifesto that only more technology can help with the problems created by technology is every bit as

---

[66] Joshua 10:12–13 (NKJV).

dumb now as it was in the 1950s, when apostles of scientism claimed nuclear power would only help humanity. Scientism-ists then and now dismiss normative, interpretive truths. And the epistemological error of attributing fact to narrative with which one passionately identifies is hardly limited to fringe religious groups. We are often likely to be wrong about subjects on which we are the most powerfully convinced: political opinions, for example. The curse of "what we feel in our gut is correct" is that we are often very wrong, and the method isn't a reliable one for producing results that help humans thrive. For example, measuring truth by conviction results in a significant portion of the population simply unable to respond to existential threats by acting on climate change or vaccinating their children.[67]

But the worst of the matter is that the divide between branches of knowing what is true have been exploited by apologists and trolls. Consider the misleading apologetic statement that "evolution is just a theory." Like all effective lies, it states a surface truth. Evolution *is* just a theory: it just happens to be the best theory we have that fits the available evidence, and has not been falsified despite every effort being made to do so. Some parts of the scientific community have good reasons to rely on falsifiability as their standard, and to not ever say that anything is true. If a future experiment were to falsify the theory—a possibility that must be kept open for science to progress, no matter how unlikely it seems[68]—another would be proposed. Even if the theory were tweaked to account for new experimental results, no theory now offered by apologists is a candidate. There is no evidence, and in every case the null hypothesis is sustained. The lie is contained in the subtle linguistic switch between the scientific meaning of a theory and the common, street meaning of a theory, along with the misleading "just." The two communities—scientific and street—have two different ways of using the word, and the war on truth launches attacks into the breach.

Truth warriors attack the scientific method because their own epistemology is as unconvincing as the coworker who claims without evidence he can fly. Apologists are therefore devoted to attacking valid epistemologies to cover for the failures of their own way of knowing.[69] Trolls exploit a similar weakness in

---

[67] *See, e.g.*, Eli Saslow, *'Nothing on This Page Is Real': How Lies Become Truth in Online America*, WASH. POST (Nov. 17, 2018), www.washingtonpost.com/national/nothing-on-this-page-is-real-how-lies-become-truth-in-online-america/2018/11/17/edd44cc8-e85a-11e8-bbdb-72fdbf9d4fed_story.html.

[68] *See* POPPER, *supra* note 48.

[69] Why, for example, does science so commonly come under attack in fascist or authoritarian revolutions? Because it provides a way of deciding what is true that is not reliant on party loyalty.

interpretive methodology. "In finished anthropological writings," writes Clifford Geertz, "what we call our data are really our own constructions of other people's constructions of what they and their compatriots are up to."[70] There is no other way to construct what other people's intentions are than to construct what other people's intentions are. How do we tell the difference between a wink, a twitch, a wink with a particular message, a wink to parody another wink? No other instrument has ever been as good at this as ours is: remember, our intelligence is essentially the ability to mirror the social intentions of others.

Yet even the human mind, the best of tools evolved to engage with and interpret other minds, can be fooled by irony, by inversion. We know that it is quite possible to say one thing and mean another. We know that a wink can be an invitation or a mockery. This is why bullies claim they were just kidding, why harassers claim their victims "can't take a joke," and why, online, Nazis drape themselves in ironic fig leaves. Their use of white supremacist symbols and rhetoric is ironic, until it isn't, until it is, but of course it isn't really. This is not merely an observation, it is a community strategy openly espoused by the publisher of the Daily Stormer, a dark web neo-Nazi publication. Irony shields the ironist by permitting the expression of horrifying symbols while protecting the speaker from repercussions.

Irony is an attack on interpretation's Achilles heel. Just as the empiricist must admit that we can never know whether something is true (the fact that the sun has risen every day does not prove it will rise tomorrow—it just lets us predict that the chance of it not doing so is vanishingly small), so an interpreter must admit that she can never truly know what is in the mind of her interlocutor. Just as apologists exploit honest use of the scientific epistemology of falsification, so trolls exploit honest use of the scientific epistemology of interpretation of motives.

Here's an example drawn from the online communities I study. Online radical free speech website 4chan is often a center for the generation of language that supports the white supremacy and neo-Nazi movements. The generation of the language is cloaked behind the claim of baiting outrage from "social justice warriors" or "libtards" (more pieces of ironic-nonironic language generated by the same methods) or whomever the perceived target of the day happens to be. In a recent instance, 4chan denizens decided to "troll" media outlets by claiming that the OK hand-sign stood for "white power," since the three extended fingers supposedly form a W and the looped index and thumb form a P. The results were predictable: white supremacists

---

[70] Geertz, *supra* note 52, at 9.

promptly started using the OK symbol unironically as a White Power symbol because, as one weary internet commenter noted, "of course they did."

We can develop responses to apologist attacks on the empirical method, and troll attacks on interpretation. For one, these attacks identify their users. The "just a theory" argument, presented without observational evidence, is immediately dismissible: Why should we abandon a theory consistent with all available evidence for theories backed by none? And the ironic attack on interpretation is eradicated once we realize that private meanings neither matter nor exist, per Wittgenstein's private language argument. It does not matter what you claim to have meant privately when you use language that has a different meaning in the culture. Use harassing language, welcome to #MeToo. Use racist language, lose your spot in the incoming class at Harvard.[71] We can confidently claim that ironic assertion of Nazi symbols by trolls is an adoption of those symbols, despite the flickering claims to irony and humor. (After all, after World War II, Nazis hid their affiliations too, in the "zero hour myth": immediately after the surrender of Nazi Germany, there were mysteriously no Nazis to be found anywhere in Germany.) The phenomenon for switching meaning to avoid repercussions is not one that should work. Claims of trolling or humor in the use of Nazi symbols should be met with rejection and whatever consequences can be brought to bear. The apologist or troll has done us the favor of hiding under a very identifiable bridge.

Ultimately, our defenses lie in cultivating our understanding of language. We must be able to articulate a vision of the rule of law that can survive a blizzard of inaccuracies and intentional assault, and we must be able to recognize the linguistic markers of communities that actively seek to undermine the rule of law. Belief in mere words to bind a society together on any kind of equal footing is a fragile trick: it needs to be attended to.

A final assault focuses a perceived weakness in truth itself. If truth is constructed and tested in different ways, how is that any different from saying that truth is relative? "That's your truth; I'm entitled to mine." This impulse toward relativity is very much afoot these days. As Hannah Arendt theorized, totalitarian propaganda is much less about a particular message and more about getting people to "believe everything and nothing, [to] think that everything was possible and that nothing was true."[72] The word "truth" can

---

[71] Isaac Stanley-Becker, *What Leads Harvard to Rescind Admission? Racism, Plagiarism—and Killing Your Mom*, WASH. POST, June 18, 2019, www.washingtonpost.com/nation/2019/06/18/what-leads-harvard-rescind-admission-racism-plagiarism-killing-your-mom/.

[72] HANNAH ARENDT, THE ORIGINS OF TOTALITARIANISM 382 (Harvest Books 1976) (1968).

take on a range of meanings, particularly on the basis of the underlying mix of epistemologies used to test it, but there are some uses of the word that fall clearly beyond any sane meaning of the word. Words can be used incorrectly, that is, to Wittgenstein, ungrammatically. When, as a toddler, one of my daughters pointed at a dog and said, proudly, "duck," we let her know that the animal was, in fact, a dog.

In the war on truth, lies are proudly asserted as true under the incorrect assumption that everyone is entitled to their own tailored version of "alternative facts." But we do not have to cave in to the liars. We can say, for example, that anti-Semitic conspiracy theories are untrue: no valid epistemology, no respected linguistic community, holds those things to be true. And this renders stark the startling rise of online fascist-ironist communities: they are literally attempting to speak a different system of "true" into being, to develop the language of white supremacy, to create languages in which humans say "true" to the most terrific falsehoods. The presence of such sick languages highlights what we are doing: trying to speak into being systems of cooperative fiction that help us "live together, and not die together."

WHY, NOT HOW: VIABILITY AND THRIVING

Our goal is to build a language that will help us survive the future. Wittgenstein built a language to help us to talk about building language. How do we create life-giving language like "love is wise; hatred is foolish" or "all men are created equal"? It's not just any old language that will do—as we've seen, many of today's fictions are wearing us and the world thin. We need *life-giving* fictions. How do we know which ones are good? How do we know if our cooperative fictions and interpretive bridges are sturdy?

To skip to the end, the answer is that we must choose the cooperative fictions and interpretive bridges that lead humans to thrive. We must choose the interpretive bridges that work to permit humans to link up and use their superpowers of linguistic cooperation. We must choose the fictions that do the kind of good for society that "all men are created equal" has done for the cultures that use that cooperative fiction, and avoid the kind of fictions espoused by white supremacists or neo-Nazis, for example.

In particular, we need to evaluate our stories of *why* we do something. Why do we do so much junk science? Why do we do so much work that makes so few people so rich and so many people so sick and poor? The answer for why we conduct most science is simple: the bulk of research scientists are corporate employees, and are directed to learn ways to make a profit for a very few people, which is a terrible proxy for human thriving.

Science has been barely treading water in the post-truth era because scientists take their metanarratives, their reasons why, for granted. They shouldn't. The meta-narratives of maximizing production and increasing efficiency with an eye toward maximizing profit is an unconvincing governing story for science, and one that leads to the kind of science that cooks the planet in pursuit of making things no one needs.

Similarly, the discipline of law is in dire need of a *why*. My sense is that the best *why*, for both science and law, is the promotion of human thriving, and must be at the very least the protection of human viability. Law must help humans continue as a species. A human system, like law, will do nothing and be nothing if the underlying systems on which it runs—human communities, human minds, and most of all, human language—collapses.

Science has developed verification and falsifiability as ways to guide empirical questions: a non-falsifiable question is not a good one for empirics. In a similar vein, I believe that viability and thriving are useful guides for the *kinds* of legal and scientific questions we ought to be asking and the language we ought to work out to enable us to work together. If a narrative of science stops science because it ends the existence of all questioners, then it is a bad science. The discipline of what questions to pose assumes the value of asking questions. If answering a given question stops questions, it was a bad question. It does not let us do more of what we want to do.

Good stories help us use our superpower of language. They help us cooperate at scale. Bad stories divide us; they divide our language and destroy our ability to communicate. Good stories tend toward our survival, and toward more stories and questions about the world. Bad stories plunge us into silence. *Great* stories use our superpower to maximize our capabilities.

Bad stories abound. We need to build better ones, and part of that is getting better at identifying the ones that do not promote viability and thriving. And this can be done in a more "scientific" mode than we might suppose. We have valid ways of asking humans how well they are doing, and other measures of thriving. When cooperative fictions and narratives increase human thriving, we say that they are good ones. When such fictions and narratives increase human suffering, we say they are bad ones.

Our current inability to take language, culture, and narrative seriously—the exiling of the tools of cooperative fiction and interpretation from the toolbox of science—seems to be the place to work on for improvement. We badly need good, cooperative narratives that will help us stay alive, but at the same time we have (except in the disciplines of linguistics, cultural anthropology, sociology, and the fields they influence) thrown narrative to the side of the road. In working out twenty-first-century ways of knowing, we must return narrative to our toolbox. If we cannot craft human cooperative fictions that orient us to the *why* of life with emerging technological affordances, we cannot begin to understand *how* to live together with technology.

Unfortunately, the discipline of law has been badly damaged by the pseudo-scientific exclusion of interpretation from the canon of scientific methods. I don't think it would surprise anyone to learn that lawyers for the most part create and interpret language. But law's self-perception, its guiding meta-narrative in the twentieth century, has wavered between the logical-rationalist perception, where law is understood as a sort of closed system of arbitrary rules given by a lawgiver—the legal positivist position—and the empirical perspective, where law is understood as a system of social statistics backed by experiments, as encompassed by the current American trend of empirical legal studies. But neither law-as-closed-ruleset nor law-as-experimental-outcome help answer the question: In what direction should our law-making efforts be directed? What is our narrative? That question has disastrously been left to demagogues and denialists.

There are very real consequences to these differences in approaches that one can observe in the various sciences. My proposal is to take the tools of cultural anthropology, of linguistic interpretation, and philosophy of language seriously. Or, more simply, to help lawyers, lawmakers, and law teachers to understand the importance of their own narrative-generating and narrative-testing tools, such as analogic reasoning, and their central importance to helping humans accept the rules of cooperative behavior that they desperately need to thrive.

We'll talk about what that might look like in chapter 9, but a little fore-shadowing never hurt. Law as a discipline should attend to the conditions that cause humans to develop innovative solutions to complex problems. Certain kinds of groups outperform others on complex nonroutine tasks that require innovation. Building those kinds of groups, those kinds of legal communities, will take us the furthest in developing the kind of language we need to describe and adapt to the problems of the future.

LIVING TOGETHER: LAW'S CENTRAL ROLE IN HUMAN THRIVING

How should we live together? And how will we know if our decisions about how to live together are the right ones? It seems reasonable to believe the field of law might have something to do with that question. We might also consider the fields of economics (particularly behavioral economics), religion, psych-ology, history, and many more. Yet law claims pride of place. Law shoulders aside other fields when it comes to the question of what rules actually come into being and are enforced with state violence. Since that is so, law should explain itself, and most of all should have a solid answer to the question of what it is doing: the interpretive work of creating cooperative fictions that help humans cooperate and thrive at scale.

Or, to put it more simply. Question: "How should we live together?" Answer: "Under a system of laws, cooperative fictions that help us work together." Question: "Why?" Answer: "Because living under a regime of raw force or random chance or superstition is not attractive to humans. Most of us do not prefer to live that way."

Human preference is a scientific fact, an answer to a scientific inquiry. Humans prefer the rule of law to warlordism. The idea of law is the "rule of law" itself: the idea that some sort of abstract human linguistic social construct called "law" ought to govern our relationships with each other at some level of society above the family, rather than personal power, or random chance, or a supernatural God, or some other principle. Very few ideas have been so overwhelmingly accepted by humans as helping them thrive as the idea that we want to be governed by rules, rather than each other.

The idea of the rule of law is one really good answer to the question of how we should live together. It's an answer that history and culture as well as the more analytic sciences have confirmed. Humans powerfully adhere to the idea that there are rules between humans that apply to everybody. To be clear, those rules appear nowhere in the real world, other than in the actions of the humans themselves. For us to believe in such a phantom thing as law, the very fact that all of us, from the most law-abiding citizen to the jailed outlaw, means we are all hallucinating. All of us are acting as if these laws existed somewhere other than purely in our own behavior. So don't let us miss a big truth precisely because it is big. Law and the rule of law is a great answer to the question of how we should live together. As far as I know, no other field of inquiry has produced a better answer or more important result.

PART III

LAW AND THE LANGUAGE WE NEED

8

Why We Fail

I have a foreboding of an America in my children's or grandchildren's time—when the United States is a service and information economy; when nearly all the key manufacturing industries have slipped away to other countries; when awesome technological powers are in the hands of a very few, and no one representing the public interest can even grasp the issues; when the people have lost the ability to set their own agendas or knowledgeably question those in authority; when, clutching our crystals and nervously consulting our horoscopes, our critical faculties in decline, unable to distinguish between what feels good and what's true . . .

— Carl Sagan, *The Demon-Haunted World*[1]

Thus far we have focused on law's ability to keep up with technology and the critical role it plays in creating an interface between human social technology and natural science–based technology. Law is a social technology that runs on words. We can harness our cooperative linguistic power to develop resilient law that enacts our preferences about how we should live together within an increasingly technological world.

But asserting that law can keep up does not mean that it is. Indeed, the question we should be asking is not "can law keep up?" but "why does it not?" The United States, the world's most technologically advanced nation, is a failed state when it comes to technology regulation. While some other countries manage to address emerging regulatory problems quickly and effectively, the United States neglects to do anything at all. I would like to look at the elements that fuel our inability to do anything about technology, despite widespread public support for doing so and the growing evidence that

---

[1] CARL SAGAN, THE DEMON-HAUNTED WORLD: SCIENCE AS A CANDLE IN THE DARK 25 (2011).

unregulated behavioral advertising and social media giants are damaging democracy worldwide.

It is not as if the Silicon Valley tech-bros awoke one day with a Machiavellian plan to dismantle the democratic structures that surrounded them. Their stated dangerously naive motto was "move fast and break things." Well and good: they moved fast, broke democracy, and have immeasurably advanced the cause of authoritarian nationalism, for the sake of simple profit. Innocence or ignorance are hardly believable defenses when mounted by those who profit from the model they defend—and who have increasingly embraced methods that undermine or disregard democratic values and institutions.

Furthermore, such defenses dissolve in the light of the larger context of digital technology. Social media and big tech, believing themselves to be a democratizing force—despite their lack of electoral legitimacy or democratic oversight[2]—happily defeated the old gatekeepers of media and information flow. The *New York Times* lies at Facebook's feet. The information ecosystem that emerged is one that equates *good* with *popular.* "The best stuff spreads," said Mark Zuckerberg in a 2010 interview.[3] What has grown increasingly popular during the ascendancy of Facebook and other social media companies? Extremist content, conspiracy theories, false information, and misinformation.

It is unsurprising that misogynists, authoritarian nationalists, and trolls seized the opportunity to exploit the vulnerabilities of social media. Bigotry and bad faith are always seeking a toehold. But this overlooks and comes close to excusing social media's business model: promote maximum content, regardless of the damage that content produces. Zuckerberg makes money from clicks and likes. And the most engaging material is stuff that inspires "activating" emotions like awe, anxiety, and anger.[4]

Facebook claims to merely be a technology company, not a media company or publisher, insisting that they create tools, not content. This assertion paves the way for the inclusion of any and all content. Twitter has been unabashed about the link, calling itself, at least informally, "the free-speech wing of the free-speech party."[5] But regardless of particular companies' attitudes about

[2] See SHOSHANA ZUBOFF, THE AGE OF SURVEILLANCE CAPITALISM: THE FIGHT FOR A HUMAN FUTURE AT THE NEW FRONTIER OF POWER 127 (2019).

[3] Quoted in ANDREW MARANTZ, ANTISOCIAL: ONLINE EXTREMISTS, TECHNO-UTOPIANS, AND THE HIJACKING OF THE AMERICAN CONVERSATION 48 (2019).

[4] *Id.* at 79.

[5] Josh Halliday, *Twitter's Tony Wang: "We Are the Free Speech Wing of the Free Speech Party"*, THE GUARDIAN (Mar. 22, 2012), www.theguardian.com/media/2012/mar/22/twitter-tony-wang-free-speech; Laura Sydell, *On Its 7th Birthday, Is Twitter Still the "Free Speech Party"?*, NPR:

their roles, Zuckerberg and his tech-bro imitators have espoused a mutant strain of thought: the idea that anyone ought to be able to say anything at any time—even things like advocating genocide or denying the Holocaust. By framing themselves as advocates of "free speech," their platforms were free (some might say duty-bound) to host ever more content. Mark Zuckerberg doesn't necessarily share ideological alliances with Nazis, but he certainly shares financial ones. And that is evidenced by the cause célèbre of both modern-day Nazis and social media tycoons: the idea that any speech should be free from consequence.

This online mutant strain of "free speech" is a complete misunderstanding of the already fairly exceptionalist American legal thinking around the First Amendment. The First Amendment dictates that the US government may not censor speech. By comparison, online and in the hands of content-profiteering social media tycoons, "free speech" has become the idea that racists, authoritarians, misogynists, chauvinists, and religious fanatics ought to receive a free pass for their bigotry. That has nothing to do with government censorship whatsoever. When provocateurs like Richard Spencer or Mike Cernovich whine about "free speech," what they really mean is that they ought not suffer any consequences for their anti-Semitism, nativism, and misogyny.

"Free speech" ought not mean speech free from consequence. We moderate our speech all the time. If someone wishes to express a vicious sentiment, they are likely to be careful about where and how they do it. If not, they are right to expect repercussions. People are always free to impose costs on racists, misogynists, and authoritarians for their hatred of minorities, women, and democracy. The same ought to be true online.

Internet pseudonymity and physical remove embolden vicious sentiments, which are given free rein by hiding behind this incorrect and unfaithful use of "free speech." The irony of online pseudonymity is that online bigots, racists, and authoritarians *are in fact identified*: Facebook, Google, and Reddit know enough about them to write a dissertation on how they act (the "behavioral" in "behavioral advertising") and what they like to buy. They certainly know enough to identify them and stop their spread of vicious ideology. Instead, the illusion of pseudonymity is carefully fostered by surveillance capitalists to minimize the impact of their spying, and to maximize the creation of the activating content that drives their bottom line.

It is worth talking more broadly about digital technology's profit model. Clicks and likes serve as direct pathways for advertising and invite further

MORNING EDITION (Mar. 21, 2013), www.npr.org/sections/alltechconsidered/2013/03/21/1748 5868i/on-its-7th-birthday-is-twitter-still-the-free-speech-party.

engagement. Zuckerberg is correct that Facebook does not produce content. Many tech services are in many ways repackagers of content: Google does not (yet) operate an airline; its flight searcher merely gathers flight info and makes it readily searchable. And it is that information that is valuable: what we search, when we search, how often we search.

Business scholar Shoshana Zuboff identifies this as surveillance capitalism; the harvesting and exploitation of human behavior as "free raw material for hidden commercial practices of extraction, prediction, and sales." This is not merely a twist on capitalism as we have known it; rather, it is a new, unprecedented economic logic that threatens freedom and autonomy.[6] The goal is to automate us, to predict and shape our behavior for other's ends. Just as the mutant form of "free speech" contorts free expression and corrodes the system of values that free speech supports, so surveillance capitalism co-opts human sovereignty, a foundation of democratic society.

There are no laws of science, economics, or history that demand that Mark Zuckerberg be permitted to undermine liberal democracy to increase advertising revenue and profit from data sales to election hackers like Cambridge Analytica. Twitter need not be a vector for authoritarian nationalism, or serve as a megaphone for conspiracy theorists and disinformation mongers like Alex Jones.[7] Reddit—for all the powerful good it does in building online communities—does not need to provide a coordination platform for Nazi and incel violence.[8] Search engines do not have to collect and collate our data in order to subtly influence the information we see.[9] As Zuboff writes, "Search engines do not retain, but surveillance capitalism does."[10] These are assertions parading as inevitabilities.

It is shockingly simple to do something about election hacking profiteering, rampant data breaches, hidden sales of data, or online threats of violence: pass a cautiously worded law against them, provide for reasonable consequences, and let the legal system do its job. Plenty of nations do, and it works. This does not fix everything, of course, but we cannot let the perfect be the enemy of the good enough. We need to do something, and the American legislative position

6   Zuboff, *supra* note 2, at 7.
7   *See* Tucker Higgens, *Alex Jones' 5 Most Disturbing and Ridiculous Conspiracy Theories*, CNBC, Sept. 14, 2018, www.cnbc.com/2018/09/14/alex-jones-5-most-disturbing-ridiculous-conspiracy-theories.html.
8   *See* Christine Lagorio-Chafkin, *How Charlottesville Forced Reddit to Clean Up Its Act*, The Guardian, Sep. 23, 2018, www.theguardian.com/technology/2018/sep/23/reddit-charlottesville-we-are-the-nerds-book-extract-christine-lagorio-chafkin.
9   *See generally* Eli Parisier, The Filter Bubble (2012).
10 Zuboff, *supra* note 2, at 15.

of learned helplessness in the face of technological change is simply not viable.

There are three particularly virulent and interrelated trends that I would like to explore here. The first is the success of laissez-faire surveillance capitalism propaganda: regulation is bad, law can't possibly keep up, and technological development is inevitable. Second is the mutated concept of "free speech": the idea that the value of free expression is the right to say anything, regardless of content or context. As we will explore, acquiescence to these demands—which are falsely presented as unobjectionable facts—is seriously undermining our democratic institutions. And they are amplified and reinforced by a third factor: the rising tide of hardball constitutionalism, that is, the exploitation of loopholes, tolerance, and norms in democratic society that corrodes the rule of law.

SURVEILLANCE CAPITALISM TRIUMPHANT: GOVERNMENT OF, BY, AND FOR THE CORPORATIONS

Why does technology regulation fail in the United States, but succeed elsewhere in the world? The short answer is that the United States does not try to regulate. Just as it has remained paralyzed on gun control at the behest of the NRA even in the face of a constant stream of dead schoolchildren, so the US Congress takes its marching orders on technology from its big-tech donors and lobbyists. And its standing orders are "do nothing."

To put it plainly, the context and goal of the current regulatory conversation in the United States is maximization of private corporate profit, not the long-term viability, sustainability, or health of democratic institutions. The supposed failure of law to regulate technology in the United States is not a fact, but an argument, propaganda advanced by surveillance capitalists whose profits are threatened by attempts to stop them from stealing our data against our will and weaponizing that data against our economic and political self-interests. Social media and big data analytic companies hope to teach us helplessness. They chant that we can do nothing to stop them because they are very aware that we can.

Framed as it is in terms of Silicon Valley propaganda, technology policy in the United States is ineffective by design. We are concerned here with two historically interconnected narratives that have birthed the modern narrative of technological inevitability. The first narrative is that government must be reduced in order to avoid totalitarian state power.

The second narrative is that law only hampers technological development, and that the answer to our problems is more technology. The first
narrative was born out of the reaction to twentieth-century totalitarianism.
The second narrative is an offshoot of the first. Companies used the
language developed to resist totalitarian political control of citizens to
claim that companies should be free of all commercial regulation—not at
all the same thing. Together, these two narratives gave rise to the current
state of affairs, the mythical narrative of technological inevitability, the
idea that technology will "just happen," and that human objections, like
privacy or decency, must wither away.

In *The Age of Surveillance Capitalism*, Shoshana Zuboff describes in
exquisite detail the historical path that led to the first myth of surveillance
capitalism: law is bad and wild-west unregulated markets are good.[11]
Totalitarian state power, in its fascist and communist forms, was the great
evil of the twentieth century. To resist, reduce, and hollow out the totalitarian
state, Austrian economist Friedrich Hayek and the German ordoliberals
argued that decisions must be permitted to flow from the market.[12]
Necessary to the idea of hollowing out totalitarian power was the idea that
the state must have as little control as possible over the market. In other words,
the idea was that keeping the state's hands off the market would sharply curtail
state power and maximize citizen autonomy.

This was a strong turn from the usual reasons for appreciating a free-market
economy: the efficiency and social-welfare-maximizing effects of enabling
trade at low transaction costs. Realizing welfare gains from trade depends on
fair rules of the road. Markets have always been regulated, because a truly
unregulated market becomes a robber's war zone: it disintegrates in the face of
power asymmetries, force, fraud, and simple theft.

But the ordoliberals were undeterred: they believed that the market offered
not only a rationale for enabling low-cost, welfare-maximizing trade, but also
a principle of organization that would weaken the state.[13] And it did. A wave of
deregulation starting in the 1970s and 1980s destabilized financial markets,
leading to crises in lending,[14] cyclical corruption in financial markets (which
led to events like the 2008 Great Recession),[15] privatization of national

---

[11]   See ZUBOFF, *supra* note 2.
[12]   *Id.*, at 42.
[13]   *Id.*
[14]   See Timothy Curry & Lynn Shibut, *The Cost of the Savings and Loan Crisis: Truth and
      Consequences*, 13 FDIC BANKING REV. 26 (2000).
[15]   See, e.g., Lynn A. Stout, *Derivatives and the Legal Origin of the 2008 Credit Crisis*, 1 HARV.
      BUS. L. REV. 1, 38 (2011).

infrastructure,[16] and the evisceration of labor,[17] environmental,[18] and consumer protection laws.[19]

One thing the turn to markets did *not* do was intrinsically or necessarily limit state power. China (and Singapore and others, but China is the best example) embraced markets without democracy quite successfully. The anti-law narrative therefore did nothing to limit totalitarian states. But it did set the stage for the hollowing out of liberal democracies by shifting power from public to private hands, thereby shifting the potential for abuse and exploitation of citizens from the now debilitated and enfeebled democratic governments to unregulated corporations.[20] Ironically, the only states that deregulation limited were democratic ones.

These corporations cheerfully repurposed the social technology of democracy into a direct attack on the institutions of democracy. The First Amendment was thoroughly reworked, for example. Instead of protecting the power of citizens to vote and control democracy, the US Supreme Court turned the First Amendment into the basis for unlimited corporate election bribery.[21] This replaced the voting citizen with the contributing corporation as the basis for political decision-making. The political economy of votes was rendered subservient to the financial economy of corporate slush money at the direction of one-percenter owners.

Similarly, surveillance capitalists repurposed the First Amendment to protect their ability to extract and exploit citizens' personal data without their consent.[22] In one poignant example, the US Supreme Court struck down a Vermont law that prevented pharmacies from reselling some of customers'

---

[16]   See, e.g., The World Bank, *Privatization and Deregulation: A Push Too Far?*, in ECONOMIC GROWTH IN THE 1990S: LEARNING FROM A DECADE OF REFORM 163 (2005).

[17]   See Janus v. AFSCME, Council 31, 138 S. Ct. 2448 (2018) (holding that requiring public employees to subsidize a union violated the first amendment).

[18]   See Nathan Rott, *Trump EPA Proposes Major Rollback of Federal Water Protections*, NPR, Dec. 11, 2018, www.npr.org/2018/12/11/675477583/trump-epa-proposes-big-changes-to-federal-water-protections.

[19]   Matthew S. Schwartz, *Net Neutrality Goes Back to Court*, NPR, Feb. 1, 2019, www.npr.org /2019/02/01/690609162/net-neutrality-goes-back-to-court.

[20]   See Ellen Dannin, *Crumbling Infrastructure, Crumbling Democracy: Infrastructure Privatization Contracts and Their Effects on State and Local Governance*, 6 Nw. J. L. & Soc. Pol'y 47 (2011).

[21]   Citizens United v. Federal Election Committee, 558 U.S. 310 (2010).

[22]   See ZUBOFF, *supra* note 2, at 109 ("[S]urveillance capitalists vigorously developed a 'cyberlibertarian' ideology. . . . Their legal teams aggressively assert First Amendment principles to fend off any form of oversight or externally imposed constraints that either limit the content on their platforms or the 'algorithmic orderings of information' produced by their machine operations. As one attorney who has represented many of the leading surveillance capitalists puts it, 'The lawyers working for these companies have business reasons

most intimate medical data: their drug purchases.[23] Drug companies wanted to be able to buy doctors' prescribing records to improve their ability to lobby doctors. This is the kind of behavior that precipitated the opioid crisis, for example: perks and bribes to doctors induced them to increase their prescriptions of certain drugs.[24] Vermont certainly had good reason to require corporations to seek the consent of doctors before buying the doctors' prescription records from pharmacies. But the Supreme Court showcased its corporatized view of the First Amendment, holding that a corporation's right to sell personal medical information trumped citizens' rights to privacy, self-determination, and expression.

Just as corporations repurposed key elements of liberal democracy, like the First Amendment, so too they repurposed the post-war narrative of market freedom into a kind of techno-libertarianism. The idea here is that just as the market must be allowed to hollow out the state (keep in mind, it only hollowed out democratic ones), so technology must be permitted to advance free of regulation. Plainly stated, the idea seems nonsensical, but it forms the cornerstone of much bad thinking about technology. Go to any policy conference and propose the most modest regulation possible of a technology that has clearly detrimental effects. The responses will be an automated horror at any form of regulation, combined with an instinctive attack on law invoking both institutional competence (the argument that technologists must be better at law than lawyers) and false humility (it is *always* too early to regulate in Silicon Valley).

Here we must be careful. There are good ideas at stake. It is often a good idea to hold off on regulating a new technology when it is new so that we can see how the technology shakes out. But initial prudence has been repurposed into permanent paralysis. The idea that one must not rush to judgment of new technologies does not mean that one should not act when detrimental effects of a technology or business model become clear. Consider Facebook. A recent UK parliamentary report commissioned in the wake of Facebook's provision of data to election hacker Cambridge Analytica stated bluntly that Facebook is a group of "digital gangsters" whose profiteering compromised the 2016 UK

for supporting free expression. Indeed, all these companies talk about their businesses in the language of free speech.'").

[23] Sorrell v. IMS Health Inc., 564 U.S. 552 (2011).

[24] *See, e.g.*, United States v. Babich, 301 F. Supp. 3d 213 (D. Mass. 2017); United States v. Gurry, 2019 U.S. Dist. LEXIS 16176 (D. Mass. 2019); *Founder and Owner of Pharmaceutical Company Insys Arrested and Charged with Racketeering*, U.S. Department of Justice, Oct. 26, 2017, www .justice.gov/usao-ma/pr/founder-and-owner-pharmaceutical-company-insys-arrested-and-charged-racketeering; Nate Raymond, *Billionaire Insys Founder Charged in U.S. Opioid Bribe Case*, YAHOO NEWS, Oct. 26, 2017, www.yahoo.com/news/billionaire-insys-founder-charged -u-opioid-bribe-case-020312521 — finance.html.

Brexit referendum vote and US presidential election.[25] Yet any claim that these technologies ought to be subject to even the most light-handed regulation—for example, requiring Facebook to get actual permission before extracting contacts, telephone calls, texts, geolocation data, app usage, and many other forms of data from every single mobile device on which it is installed[26]— is met with the same numb chorus: "Law *bad*. Technology *good*."

It is time to see these claims for what they are: naked, self-serving power grabs. Data firms make their money by paying nothing for the data they extract and exploit. Their lifesblood is avoiding even the lightest possible regulations requiring them to ask permission before they use our smartphones, televisions, cars, thermostats, and fitness trackers to spy on us for the purpose of selling us more things at a higher price.[27] The claim that technologists make the best technology regulators is even more contrary to common sense. Industry lobbyists, who write many of these laws for the lawmakers their companies have sponsored, of course do not write them with the public's best interests at heart.[28] But even technologists of a seemingly neutral mien have next to no idea how law actually works as a discipline, and have no access to the bank of experiential learning stored in legal texts, communities, minds, and language. Worse, those who work in the data parsing and extraction industry by and large cannot afford to understand the damage they are causing, and fear the consequences to their work if any safeguards are put in place. As Upton Sinclair wrote: "It is difficult to get a man to understand something, when his salary depends upon his not understanding it."[29]

Together, these narratives have produced markets in technology that are anything but free. Go ahead, buy a smartphone from the "free" market that does not spy on you. I'll wait.[30] The narratives of surveillance capitalism have

[25] Laurel Wamsley, *Facebook Has Behaved Like "Digital Gangsters," U.K. Parliament Report Says*, NPR, Feb. 18, 2019, www.npr.org/2019/02/18/695729829/facebook-has-been-behaving-like-digital-gangsters-u-k-parliament-report-says.

[26] *See* Andrew Griffin, *Facebook Admits Collecting Phone Calls and Texts from People's Phones, But Claims It Had Consent*, INDEPENDENT, Mar. 26, 2018, www.independent.co.uk/life-style /gadgets-and-tech/news/facebook-cambridge-analytica-data-my-download-phone-calls-text-messages-contacts-history-a8274211.html.

[27] ANNA BERNASEK & D. T. MONGAN, ALL YOU CAN PAY: HOW COMPANIES USE OUR DATA TO EMPTY OUR WALLETS (2015).

[28] LAWRENCE LESSIG, AMERICA, COMPROMISED (2018).

[29] Paul Krugman, *The Undeserving Rich*, N.Y. TIMES, Jan. 19, 2014, www.nytimes.com/2014/01/ 20/opinion/krugman-the-undeserving-rich.html; UPTON SINCLAIR, I, CANDIDATE FOR GOVERNOR AND HOW I GOT LICKED (1994).

[30] *See* Jennifer Schlesinger & Andrea Day, *How GPS Can Track You, Even When You Turn It Off*, CNBC, July 14, 2018, www.cnbc.com/2018/07/13/gps-can-spy-on-you-even-when-you-turn -it-off.html.

ensured that technological progress relies not on mutual benefit and trade but on unilateral extraction. Worse, the data that is extracted as the raw material of surveillance capitalism is used to undermine the value to the consumer of purchasing goods and services.[31] When you bargain against an online company who knows the maximum you are willing to pay, you are literally getting the least possible benefit from the transaction.[32] This cuts directly against the reason for markets in the first place. In a normal trade, both sides are better off. In the new behavioral advertising economy, the overwhelming majority of the surplus from the trade goes to the corporation, not the consumer. These are anti-markets built on extraction and exploitation, not surplus.[33] Our current technology markets are the data equivalent of high-seas piracy. Value changes hands, to be sure, but this is not a trade model to be celebrated.

The twin narratives of market over state and industry over regulation have now generated a third, mutant offspring. This is the myth of technological inevitability, which merges the narratives of robber-market fanaticism and deregulatory zealotry with tech-bro utopianism: technology should not and cannot be fettered. Consider one of Silicon Valley's favorite aphorisms: "Privacy is dead. Get over it."[34] This is not a fact, it is a move in a game. The reason that privacy is, as they say, "dead," is that Zuckerberg and the like wish to kill it. Their argument is looter's logic: "You can't say no, because I won't take no for an answer." It is an argument intended to demoralize, to teach helplessness: don't bother to try to secure your private information, we will get it anyway.

Although this argument is particularly infuriating, it is worth seeing past it to the core problem: the so-called facts about technological development are not facts at all. They are moves, claims, demands for surrender. The goal is to convince us that, to quote the Borg, resistance is futile.[35] But these claims have nothing at all to do with how the world has to be, but merely with how the data

---

[31] See Neil Howe, *A Special Price Just for You*, FORBES, Nov. 17, 2017, www.forbes.com/sites/ neilhowe/2017/11/17/a-special-price-just-for-you/#14b24c0390b3.

[32] This procedure is sometimes referred to as differential pricing. *See* RUTH MACKLIN, DOUBLE STANDARDS IN MEDICAL RESEARCH IN DEVELOPING COUNTRIES 166 (2004).

[33] See Catherine Rampell, *The Wedding Fix Is In*, N.Y. TIMES, Dec. 3, 2013, www.nytimes.com /2013/12/08/magazine/the-wedding-fix-is-in.html

[34] *See, e.g.*, Bobbie Johnson, *Privacy No Longer a Social Norm, Says Facebook Founder*, THE GUARDIAN, Jan. 10, 2010; Mark Rasch, *Privacy Is Dead. Long Live Privacy*, SECURITY CURRENT, June 29, 2018, https://securitycurrent.com/privacy-is-dead-long-live-privacy/.; Roger Aitken, *Is This the Proof That Facebook's CEO Mark Zuckerberg Wants "No Privacy"?*, FORBES, Mar. 20, 2019, www.forbes.com/sites/rogeraitken/2019/03/20/is-this-the- proof-that-facebooks-ceo-mark-zuckerberg-wants-no-privacy/#256528a7436b.

[35] *Star Trek: Enterprise: Regeneration* (UPN television broadcast May 7, 2003) ("[Y]ou will be assimilated. Resistance is futile.").

abusers want it to be. "Surveillance capitalism is not technology; it is a logic," writes Zuboff. "Most significantly, it makes surveillance capitalism's practices appear to be inevitable when they are actually meticulously calculated and lavishly funded means to self-dealing commercial ends."[36] The myth of inevitability is the "this will be our little secret" of technology policy: no fact, but a desperate attempt to hide exploitation from disinfecting sunlight.

These three myths have hollowed out democratic institutions to the point that studies have begun to seriously question whether and to what extent the United States remains a democracy. In one influential Princeton study, researchers followed US policy issues for over two decades, tracking policy outcomes preferred by citizens with those preferred by corporate interests.[37] Their results were sobering: citizen preference made little difference in whether a given policy goal was enacted into law. Only where citizen and corporate interests were aligned did popular policies become law. Meanwhile, corporate interests became law even when opposed by a significant majority of the citizenry.[38]

A recent example of this phenomenon would be the debate over net neutrality. Briefly, network neutrality is the idea that internet service providers must not discriminate against traffic.[39] All traffic must be given equal priority on the network. Thus, mom-and-pop (and any) websites can be assured that their content is accessible to their customers without needless delay. Without net neutrality, internet service providers can bottleneck traffic in order to hold content providers' business models hostage: "Such a nice video-streaming service you have. It would be a shame if something happened to it." So, for example, internet service providers throttled Netflix at key points during negotiations, trying to force extra payments.[40] Without net neutrality, video sharing sites like YouTube would never have gotten off the ground.

Net neutrality was grounded in longstanding common law traditions of common carriage: the idea that the railroads could not be permitted to discriminate in terms of what freight they would carry.[41] As noted in chapter

---

[36] Zuboff, *supra* note 2, at 15.

[37] Martin Gilens & Benjamin Page, *Testing Theories of American Politics: Elites, Interest Groups, and Average Citizens*, 12 Perspectives on Politics 564 (2014).

[38] *Id.* at 576.

[39] Jan Kramer et al., *Net Neutrality: A Progress Report*, 37 Telecommunications Policy 794 (2013).

[40] *See, e.g.*, Olga Kharif, YouTube, *Netflix Videos Found to Be Slowed by Wireless Carriers*, Bloomberg, www.bloomberg.com/news/articles/2018–09-04/youtube-and-netflix-throttled-by-carriers-research-finds (Sept. 4, 2018).

[41] To the lawyers in the room: relax. I am talking here about the tradition of common carriage, not its telecommunications law definition.

3, common carriage helped first Great Britain[42] and then the United States[43] come to terms with the fact that unlike public roads, the lifeblood infrastructure of the industrial revolution was privately owned.[44] To move industrial freight overland, one was obliged to use privately owned railroads. The question was how to balance that fact with the public need to communicate, move, and so on.[45] It was as if the roads had been suddenly sold into private hands. Common carriage was an elegant solution. It limited the ability of railroad owners to turn their monopoly on motion into strangleholds on other areas of industry, commerce, politics, and culture.[46]

Although telecommunications technology has nothing in common with railroads as a matter of engineering, it has a similar shape as far as the relationship between public and private sectors.[47] It is a monopoly on the motion of information rather than merely people or goods. And so it made

[42] *See, e.g.*, Robert J. Kaczorowski, *The Common-Law Background of Nineteenth-Century Tort Law*, 51 OHIO ST. L.J. 1127, 1134 (1990) (Although other bailees were held to varying standards of care, the common carrier was strictly liable "against all events but acts of God, and of the enemies of the king.") (quoting Coggs v. Bernard, 2 Ld. Raym. 918, 92 Eng. Rep. 112 (K.B. 1703).); An Act for the better Regulation of the Traffic on Railways and Canals, 17 & 18 Vict. ch. 31 (1854) [sic] ("[No railway or canal company] shall make or give any undue or unreasonable preference or advantage to or in favour of any particular person or company, or any particular description of traffic, in any respect whatsoever, nor shall any such company subject any particular person or company, or any particular description of traffic, to any undue or unreasonable prejudice or disadvantage in any respect whatsoever . . .").

[43] *See* N. J. Steam Navigation Co. v. Merchants' Bank of Boston, 47 U.S. 344, 381 (1848) ("The general liability of the carrier . . . [includes being] an insurer of the goods, and accountable for any damage or loss that may happen to them in the course of the conveyance, unless arising from inevitable accident, — in other words, the act of God or the public enemy.").

[44] *See* Phil Nichols, *Redefining Common Carrier: The FCC's Attempt at Deregulation by Redefinition*, 1987 DUKE L.J. 501, 507–09 (1987) (explaining that the doctrine of the common carrier was first developed by Lord Hale in the United Kingdom as the intersection between *jus privatum* (i.e., proprietary rights in privately owned property) and *jus publicum* (i.e., the common interest), and was later adopted in the United States in the 1800s for regulating railroads, communication, and interstate commerce).

[45] *Id.*

[46] *Id.* (citing the Interstate Commerce Act of 1887, ch. 104, 24 Stat. 379); *see also* id. at 508 (quoting T. CHITTY & L. TEMPLE, A PRACTICAL TREATISE ON THE LAW OF CARRIERS OF GOODS AND PASSENGERS BY LAND, INLAND NAVIGATION, AND IN SHIPS *14–*15 (1857)) ("To render a person liable as a common carrier, he must exercise the business of carrying as a "public employment," and must undertake to carry goods for *all persons indiscriminately*; and hold himself out as ready to engage in the transportation of goods for hire as a *business*, and not as a casual occupation *pro hac vice*.") (emphasis in original).

[47] *See* 47 USC § 153(11) (2019) (Federal statute defining common carrier as "any person engaged as a common carrier for hire, in interstate or foreign communication by wire or radio or in interstate or foreign radio transmission of energy"); see also Mann-Elkins Act, Pub. L. No. 61–218, 36 Stat. 539 (1910) (classifying telephones and telegraphs as common carriers for the first time).

sense that the telecommunications regulations of the mid-twentieth century would enshrine common-carrier-like protections in telecommunications law as well.[48]

We are passing over some law and history here, but it is the broad contours that I would like us to see. If any issue should be held sacred to democracy, it would be the principle that private owners may not discriminate against traffic on their networks. The modern incarnation of that idea is net neutrality.

With this background, the controversy around net neutrality should take on a new light. Railroad robber barons, not known for democratic commitments, lost this fight. Ma Bell,[49] in all her pre-breakup monopolistic glory, lost this fight. The needs of the citizenry to use these key infrastructures on a fair and equal basis were simply too important to democracy. Unsurprisingly, network neutrality was one technology issue on which the otherwise divided American population had a strong common view.[50] In one widely viewed plea, comedian and newscaster John Oliver implored people to resist the Obama administration's determination to create internet fast and slow lanes.[51] The uprising seemed to work. Industry lobbyist Tom Wheeler, who was then Chairman of the Federal Communications Commission, famously reversed course, leading the FCC to finally reclassify internet services so that they could be subject to net neutrality regulation.[52]

And, just as famously, after the 2016 election, Ajit Pai—another telecommunications lobbyist—appointed chair of the FCC, himself reversed course, in a blizzard of dishonesty.[53] Public attempts to express opposition to the FCC's

---

[48] See 47 USC § 202(a) (2019) (Provides that "undue or unreasonable preference or advantage to any particular person, class of persons, or locality, or to subject any particular person, class of persons, or locality to any undue or unreasonable prejudice or disadvantage" is unlawful).

[49] Ma Bell, or Mother Bell, is a colloquial term that refers to the conglomerate of telephone services that was split by the US Justice Department. This note is for my Gen Z research assistant who had never heard this term before. *See generally* John Pinheiro, *AT&T Divestiture & the Telecommunications Market*, 2 BERKELEY TECH. L.J. 303 (1987) (explaining the entire history of the antitrust suit and breakup of AT&T's telecommunications monopoly).

[50] See ALDOUS HUXLEY, BRAVE NEW WORLD (1931).

[51] See Amanda Holpuch, *John Oliver's Cheeky Net Neutrality Plea Crashes Fcc Website*, THE GUARDIAN, Jun. 3, 2014, www.theguardian.com/technology/2014/jun/03/john-oliver-fcc-website-net-neutrality.

[52] See Rebecca R. Ruiz & Steve Lohr, *F.C.C. Approves Net Neutrality Rules, Classifying Broadband Internet Service as a Utility*, N.Y. TIMES, Feb. 25, 2015, www.nytimes.com /2015/02/27/technology/net-neutrality-fcc-vote-internet-utility.html?login=email&auth=lo gin-email.

[53] See Jon Brodkin, *Ajit Pai Grilled by Lawmakers on Why FCC Spread "Myth" of DDoS Attack*, ars technica, Aug. 14, 2018, https://arstechnica.com/tech-policy/2018/08/ajit-pai-must-answer-for-fccs-lies-to-congress-about-ddos-senators-say/.

planned course of action were buried in astroturfing.[54] Hundreds of thousands of comments were spammed to the FCC website opposing network neutrality: these were traced back to botnets.[55] Many dead people apparently opposed network neutrality, their identities stolen in a modern artificial intelligence–fueled update to the time-honored tradition of voting the graveyard.[56] The FCC lied about the astroturfing, claimed agnosticism as to what the people wanted (since there were so many comments "on both sides"), ignored the techno-logical muting of the democratic voice of the citizenry, and carried out the corporate agenda against the overwhelming and demonstrable democratic will of US citizens. Ajit Pai and his agenda are widely reviled by the American voting public[57] but it doesn't matter: politicians in the United States answer to corpor-ations, not citizens.

The example of network neutrality is a snowglobe miniature of the hollow-ing out of democratic institutions by corporate control. The story has it all: artificial intelligence astroturfing muting democratic outcry, fake news propa-gated by Russian-funded social media hacking firms, raw lobbying power, and above all, the demonstration of the present futility of democratic expression in the United States. The present American system of government can only responsibly be termed a corporate oligarchy. Net neutrality is not the only example; it is merely a powerful and recent one. The Princeton study indicates that this has been going on for decades.[58] When it comes to technology policy, the United States is no democracy. The laws are not of us, by us, or for us.

THE RISE OF EXTREMIST CONTENT

Thus far we have discussed how surveillance capitalists push narratives of technological inevitability to maximize content, engagement, and the profit to be made from spying on their users. To do this, they championed a newly born version of "free speech," which, as explored earlier, is the idea that everyone must be permitted to say anything without consequence. This made social

---

[54] See Emily Birnbaum, *FCC chairman Acknowledges Russia Interfered in Net Neutrality Public Comments*, THE HILL, Dec. 5th, 2018, https://thehill.com/policy/technology/419846-fcc-chairman-acknowledges-russia-interfered-in-net-neutrality-public.

[55] See Chris Baraniuk, *"Bots" Spam FCC Website over Proposed Net Neutrality Reversal*, BBC NEWS, www.bbc.com/news/technology-39950399 (May 17, 2017).

[56] See *Net Neutrality: "Dead People" Signing FCC Consultation*, BBC, May 26, 2017, www.bbc.com/news/technology-40057855.

[57] Andrew Rice, *This Is Ajit Pai, Nemesis of Net Neutrality*, WIRED, May 16, 2018, www.wired.com/story/ajit-pai-man-who-killed-net-neutrality/.

[58] Martin Gilens & Benjamin Page, *Testing Theories of American Politics: Elites, Interest Groups, and Average Citizens*, 12 PERSPECTIVES ON POLITICS 564 (2014).

media giants money, of course, and it's worth noting that the people spouting the free speech credo were usually not those who would stand to suffer from increases—which there have been—in bigotry, racism, homophobia, and so on. The tech bros only saw themselves as saviors of supposedly neutral values, but really only ended up profiting from speech that harms vulnerable groups and individuals.

The "free" for the surveillance capitalists was exactly that: they needed users to provide free labor. The contents of the content didn't matter, only its costs and effects did. The perfect content was highly activating, drawing users into more time spent on the site or service, whether out of a sense of enjoyment, outrage, or fear of missing out.

In its purest form, internet sites would lay out flypaper for vicious content, and then make money from the flies. The crudest business model was to attract some sort of negative activating content, like defamatory stories about university students (JuicyCampus, which operated between 2007 and 2009, would be an example)[59] or businesses, and then charge a fee to "mediate" the dispute: Don't like that an angry ex posted a porn video to a website? Pay the website to take it down.[60]

The key to the "attract and profit from activating negative content" model, in the US legal framework, is an early internet law called the Communications Decency Act.[61] Originally drafted to censor internet content, the law was held broadly unconstitutional. One subpart, however, the (in)famous Section 230, essentially protected online sites and services from liability for the statements of their users.[62] The statute was instrumental in

---

[59] Mark Milian, *JuicyCampus Shuts Down, Kills the College Grapevine*, L.A. TIMES (Feb. 4, 2009), https://latimesblogs.latimes.com/technology/2009/02/juicy-campus.html.

[60] *See, e.g.*, Doe v. Bollaert, No. 2:13-CV-486 (S.D. Ohio May 21, 2013); cf. Samantha Schmidt, *This Site Will Remove Your Mug Shot–For a Price, Authorities Say. Its Owners Are Charged with Extortion*, WASH. POST (May 18, 2018), www.washingtonpost.com/news/morning-mix/wp/2018/05/18/this-site-will-remove-your-mug-shot-for-a-price-now-its-owners-are-charged-with-extortion/.

[61] 47 U.S.C. § 151 et seq. (Chapter 5 of the Telecommunications Act of 1996).

[62] 47 U.S.C. § 230(c):
"Protection for private blocking and screening of offensive material:
(1) Treatment of publisher or speaker. No provider or user of an interactive computer service shall be treated as the publisher or speaker of any information provided by another information content provider.
(2) Civil liability. No provider or user of an interactive computer service shall be held liable on account of—
(A) any action voluntarily taken in good faith to restrict access to or availability of material that the provider or user considers to be obscene, lewd, lascivious, filthy, excessively violent, harassing, or otherwise objectionable, whether or not such material is constitutionally protected; or

helping companies build an open internet: a single statement by a user could otherwise threaten a site or service. But this freedom has proven costly: internet companies are now like neighbors who take garbage from the entire city onto their property, then charge the neighbors to keep the stench under control.

Extreme content drives engagement on social media platforms, whether through outrage or echo-chamber agreement. The new social media tycoons therefore keep the doors for extreme content propped as wide open as possible: they cannot be liable for anything anyone says, and they profit enormously from internet dumpster fires, whether the onlookers are warming their hands or can't look away.

In turn, then, extremists have taken to social media to drive their own shift in narrative. Their window of opportunity is that the new media giants are allied with them in terms of profit. *New Yorker* journalist Andrew Marantz spent several years interviewing and observing the rise of the alt-right movement surrounding the 2016 election. His observations are damning: as we've discussed, alt-right propagandists like Alex Jones and Richard Spencer monetized their delusions by driving content to and through Facebook, Twitter, YouTube, Reddit, and many others. The more outrageous the statement, the more traffic it generated, the more profits the extremists reaped, and the happier the surveillance capitalists were. The resulting radicalization of online communities has been startling, rapid, and extreme: gamers openly celebrating Nazi ideology and symbols, incel misogynists built into a movement with its own murderous terrorist heroes, and bigots developing their own language of dog-whistles.

For someone who observes online radicalization at a distance, it can look like a failure of intelligence. It is not: it is an intentional perversion of language. Here, Marantz's work offers a clear example of how communities develop language, and how that language provides the ground for reason, such that people who adopt extremist language don't detect that shifts in their linguistic community are profoundly altering the way they view the world.

In his book *Antisocial*,[63] Marantz charts the intentional crafting of toxic language within alt-right communities. He notes that language provides a surface for thought; its use compels agreement in the sense of what he terms internal assent to a proposition, and more than that, it creates communities even where there have been deep disconnects in the underlying

---

(B) any action taken to enable or make available to information content providers or others the technical means to restrict access to material described in paragraph (1)."

[63] Marantz, *supra* note 3.

investments of community members in the actual racist or bigoted ideas.[64] In particular, Marantz draws on the work of philosopher Richard Rorty to illustrate this process. Rorty used the term "vocabularies" to describe the language we use to talk about something, the linguistic system a society uses to talk to itself. He believed that a transition from one vocabulary to another happens roughly the way a paradigm shift happens in science: by a change in the guiding narratives. So, Maratz writes:

> Why, after almost a century of legalized apartheid, did the United States start to pass antisegregation laws? It was not the result of the inevitable arc of history, or of white Americans finally living up to their inherently noble character. Rather, it was made possible by decades of political and intellectual work—by organizers and preachers and artists and all sorts of other people, many of them perceived as fringe, who gradually pointed the way toward a better moral vocabulary. And yet the arc could also bend in the other direction. How did Weimar Germany, one of the most progressive societies in modern Europe, descend into barbaric madness? It was possible, in part, because Germans spent a long time treating barbaric madness as inconceivable, and then their sense of what was conceivable began to change.[65]

The alt-right is engaged—they talk about this openly—in speaking fascism into being. Their approach is simple and shockingly effective: make "jokes" and ironic "edgy" statements to move sick ways of speaking back into common parlance. It's the process that removed horrible racist words from general parlance, in reverse. By constantly claiming that it's a joke—but not—but a joke—but not, the words still enter the language. Useful innocents bleat about "free speech" to protect the jokers, but by further engaging, by further giving the language use validity, they further strengthen it. This is quite literally how the word "alt-right" entered the mainstream, by encouraging "ironic" use (and think about the irony of scare quotes around that word), by aligning profit models of the new media with their radicalization agenda, and by fostering pearl-clutching, pageview-selling, constant breathless coverage by the few traditional media outlets still extant.[66]

---

[64] *Id.*, at 324.

[65] *Id.*, at 60.

[66] *See, e.g.*, Jason Wilson, *Hiding in Plain Sight: How the 'Alt-Right' Is Weaponizing Irony to Spread Fascism*, THE GUARDIAN (May 23, 2017), www.theguardian.com/technology/2017/may/23/alt-right-online-humor-as-a-weapon-facism; Katie Notopoulos and Ryan Broderick, *A Glossary of Far-Right Terms & Memes*, BUZZFEED NEWS (Mar. 3, 2017), www.buzzfeednews.com/article/katie notopoulos/a-normal-persons-guide-to-how-far-right-trolls-talk-to-each.

Marantz shows how this works with a series of profiles of members of alt-right communities. As the language they were engaged with changed, they did as well. The change he describes isn't what we think of when we think of how humans change. It was a sort of ambiguous drift in and out of linguistic communities. The person's engagement with a community drove their language, how they spoke with that group. That language was, of course, toxic, but was also a marker of membership in a tribe, the way that that group spoke. This aligns with the phenomenon of code-switching, in which the way we speak depends on the group to whom we are speaking. Such switching isn't an edge phenomenon of language, it is the only phenomenon: we use words in ways understood by a linguistic community so we can be accepted into that community, honored for carrying its water, and understood in the narrower constructed language of that group.

Watching members of the alt-right slip in and out of positions as a function of their membership in linguistic communities and their use of language is a different model from that which we often assume: that people's beliefs are determined entirely by some set of internal precommitments. Marantz describes one woman who became central in a white supremacist identitarian organization after she became immersed in racist language in order to understand a boyfriend who had become, to her shock, an avowed fascist. At first she was appalled. But as she read up on (and listened to) everything she could, her language began to shift. It was not so much a process of ideological or logical conversion as a change of vocabulary. "All day, in her car or through her earbuds, she listened to alt-right podcasts and videos and livestreams. At first she found them shocking; then she found them engrossing; eventually the dialogue started to merge with her internal monologue, until she could hardly tell the difference between what they said and what she thought."[67] What is interesting is that similar undertones of language, narrative, vocabulary, and story attended her exit, a couple of years later, from the white supremacist movement as well. After a falling out with an abusive ex-partner who was a rising member of the community, her lived experience of contradictions led her to question the language in which she was immersed. As Marantz describes it,

> She'd spent months convincing her friends, and herself, that the movement was more innocuous than it seemed.... But what if the ironic racism really was just racism? ... Once she saw this possibility, she couldn't unsee it.... She'd told herself that she was waiting for the mask to slip and reveal actual hatred; by the time the hatred was there

[67] MARANTZ, *supra* note 3, at 325.

in plain sight, she'd been so turned around by movement propaganda that she somehow made herself look past it.[68]

Her exit from the community was disorienting, traumatic, and not easily explainable as a matter of individual self-determination. Marantz's description of her deconversion is as inexplicable from the perspective of thought as an individual exercise as it is clear and comprehensible from the perspective of our language determining our thought structure by locating us within a linguistic community: once she no longer spoke the language, she dropped from the community.

This linguistic element of online extremism explains why the alt-right is obsessed with "free speech." It is the vector by which they can speak the language of fascism back into common parlance. Meanwhile, that the trolls' speech comes from no particular values beyond enjoying the pain their language causes—many eschew attachment to values other than radical free speech—should serve as cold comfort. Their irony takes earnestness as its enemy: the way to damage is to argue speciously, to move the goalpost, to make the other party scramble to defend against absurdities. Distress, not truth, is the goal of the conversation.

Rorty's analysis—his analogizing the evolution of moral vocabularies to the development of science by changing the dominant scientific paradigm—also contains the seed of hope, a thread that we have pursued throughout this book. The arc of progress, of kindness, of cooperation is not inevitable. But neither is a resurgence of the barbarity of open racism, anti-Semitism, misogyny, and classism. If liberal democracies have learned that they benefit from no particular protection against the vicissitudes of history, that they can decline and fall like any other government, and that if the arc of history sometimes bends toward justice, it can also bend toward authoritarian nationalism, there must be at least as much hope as horror. If the alt-right can speak fascism back into everyday language through their coward's irony, people of good faith and good conscience can speak a language of decency, pragmatism, and technological realism into being that will help us thrive and survive the problems of the future.

HARDBALL CONSTITUTIONALISM

We've been discussing the hollowing out of US democratic institutions at the hands of surveillance capitalists and the alliance between content

---

[68] *Id.*, at 333.

peddlers and producers of extremist content. A third element completes a feedback loop between surveillance capitalism and online extremism: the rising tide of hardball constitutionalism. Hardball constitutionalism is the practice of subverting liberal democracy's unwritten rules of civility and fair play, abusing loopholes in the system, and generally throwing sand in the gears of democracy where there was once oil to help the system function.[69] The gears grind on, but soon grind down.

Hardball constitutionalism shares several important parallels with the "truths" of surveillance capitalism and the rise of extremism: there is a refusal to play the game (I'm stating facts, not negotiating with you). There is a willingness to co-opt rules (demanding "free speech" while rejecting its very meaning, or the ironist's demand that their targeted counterpart answer earnestly), and an overall unwillingness to cooperate and recognize the legitimacy of others.

Hardball constitutionalism is how totalitarian regimes hatch from liberal democracies. Authoritarians come to power through technically legitimate means, although the path to the seizure of power is filled with double standards. Authoritarians seek to hold their democratic opponents to norms of tolerance and the spirit of the law, while they themselves smash the norms that had kept the democracy functioning.

Following the letter against the spirit of the law is a longstanding political habit, but we are now seeing something different. Hardball constitutionalists do more than merely toe the line of the law, they scuff it, using the institutions of law to erase the rule of law. In a recent interview, Chuck Hagel, a Republican who was Secretary of

---

[69] The term "constitutional hardball" was coined by professor Mark Tushnet in a 2004 law review article. *See* Mark Tushnet, *Constitutional Hardball*, 37 J. MARSHALL L. REV. 523, 523 (2004). He defined the term as "political claims and practices—legislative and executive initiatives—that are without much question within the bounds of existing constitutional doctrine and practice but that are nonetheless in some tension with existing pre-constitutional understandings." *Id.* In other words, political parties play constitutional hardball when they disregard the "goes without saying" assumptions that underpin working systems of constitutional government." *Id.* at 523 n. 2. Tushnet provided as a prime example the Senate Democrat filibuster against President George W. Bush's judicial nominations in 2003. *Id.* at 524.

In a 2018 article, Joseph Fishkin and David E. Pozen provided more recent examples of constitutional hardball, such as the Senate Republican blockade of President Barack Obama's nomination of Merrick Garland to the Supreme Court, the retaliatory Senate Democratic filibuster of President Donald Trump's nomination of Neil Gorsuch to the Supreme Court, and the eventual "nuclear option" exercised by Senate Republicans to change cameral rules so that Gorsuch could be nominated by a simple majority vote. *See* Joseph Fishkin & David E. Pozen, *Asymmetric Constitutional Hardball*, 118 COLUMBIA L. REV. 915, 917–18 (2018).

Defense under President Obama, spoke about the challenges of foreign policy in a world racked by hardball constitutionalism:

> I would mention another [important worldwide security threat]: the destabilizing of Western democracies. Start with the obvious, Brexit. But every one of those Western democracies is not very stable. France. Germany. Italy. They're all in a state of flux and uncertainty. And you look at our country. We are as divided politically, in many ways polarized. I don't think like anytime since the Civil War.... . I was a young chief of staff to a Republican congressman during Watergate, and that was a bad time. But it was not near as bad as what we've got today.
>
> And when we're off-balance, the United States is off balance, the world's off balance. The world has keyed off of us. We made plenty of mistakes, but the world has always been secure in knowing there is a centerpiece to global leadership. And if we walk away from that, a vacuum will surely occur. Something will fill that vacuum. It'll either be China trying to fill the vacuum, or we'll go back again to a decentralized world.[70]

I had the enormous privilege to host a small conference several years ago. Some of the scholars at that conference had a strange story to tell. The United Kingdom, United States, Germany, France, Italy, and other traditional bastions of the liberal democratic tradition have either been so compromised in their political ecology that they do not function as democracies (the pattern we've been discussing) or have seen an unprecedented upswing in participation and influence of avowedly authoritarian nationalist parties, like the German Alternativ für Deutschland or the French Front National (and its successor): parties once at the racist and anti-Semitic fringe now have a seat at the table. Nor is the effect limited to Western democracies. Liberal democracies the world over are failing or falling.[71] Turkey, once a secular democracy, is now neither.[72]

---

[70] See Stephen J. Dubner, *Speak Softly and Carry Big Data*, FREAKONOMICS (2019), http://freakonomics.com/podcast/chicago-live/.

[71] *Freedom in the World 2019: Democracy in Retreat*, Freedom House (n.d.), https://freedomhouse.org/sites/default/files/Feb2019_FH_FITW_2019_Report_ForWeb-compressed.pdf ("In 2018, Freedom in the World recorded the 13th consecutive year of decline in global freedom. The reversal has spanned a variety of countries in every region, from long-standing democracies like the United States to consolidated authoritarian regimes like China and Russia. The overall losses are still shallow compared with the gains of the late 20th century, but the pattern is consistent and ominous. Democracy is in retreat.").

[72] See Peter S. Goodman, *The West Hoped for Democracy in Turkey. Erdogan Had Other Ideas.*, N.Y. TIMES (Aug. 18, 2018), www.nytimes.com/2018/08/18/business/west-democracy-turkey-erdogan-financial-crisis.html.

Hungary,[73] Brazil,[74] the Philippines,[75] and many other once at least nominal democracies have shifted from liberal democracy toward authoritarian nationalism.[76]

We do not have unlimited time to develop a new vocabulary. The optimism of the mid-1990s, that liberal democracy had an end-of-history advantage over other forms of government, has proven as false as the now-devastated optimism of the Arab Spring. In a span of four years, the Arab Spring turned to the Arab Winter, a return to religious fundamentalism and authoritarian nationalism.[77]

The loss of US soft power has been particularly devastating to the desperately hard task of maintaining democratic institutions worldwide. Many regimes that at least pretended to uphold democratic ideals in a world when the United States had soft power influence have abandoned the pretense when cozying up to China or otherwise finding their way in a post–Pax Americana political climate. It is worth recognizing that US soft power has often been wielded in a corrupt manner, and that it has been a wildly ineffective champion of democracy. But vast US economic and military power meant that

---

[73] Patrick Kingsley, *On the Surface, Hungary Is a Democracy. But What Lies Underneath?*, N.Y. TIMES (Dec. 25, 2018), www.nytimes.com/2018/12/25/world/europe/hungary-democracy-orban.html; see also Orbán: *"Liberal Freedom-Based Democracies Can No Longer Give Sense to Europe"*, HUNGARY TODAY (Sept. 16, 2019), https://hungarytoday.hu/orban-liberal-freedom-based-democracies-can-no-longer-give-sense-to-europe/.

[74] Anthony Faiola and Marina Lopes, *Bolsonaro Wins Brazilian Presidency*, THE WASH. POST (Oct. 28, 2018), www.washingtonpost.com/world/the_americas/brazilians-go-the-polls-with-far-right-jair-bolsonaro-as-front-runner/2018/10/28/88odd53c-d6dd-11e8-8384-bcc5492fef49_story.html; see also Jake Spring, *Brazil's New Right-Wing Government Asks Schools to Read Out Bolsonaro Slogan*, REUTERS (Feb. 25, 2019), www.reuters.com/article/us-brazil-politics-education/brazils-new-right-wing-government-asks-schools-to-read-out-bolsonaro-slogan-id USKCN1QE2PJ.

[75] Jim Gomez, *Philippines' Duterte Threatens Authoritarian Rule over Relentless Criticism of Presidency*, THE STAR (June 6, 2018), www.thestar.com/news/world/2018/06/06/philippines-duterte-threatens-authoritarian-rule-over-relentless-criticism-of-presidency.html; *see also* Chad de Guzman, Duterte: I Will Ignore Supreme Court, Congress on Martial Law, CNN Philippines (May 28, 2017), https://cnnphilippines.com/news/2017/05/28/duterte-ignore-supreme-court-congress-martial-law.html (quoting Philippine President Duterte as saying: "Until the Armed Forces and the police say that the Philippines is safe, this martial law will continue. I will not listen to anyone else, be it the Supreme Court, congressmen. They're not here.").

[76] *See generally Democracy Index 2019 Whitepaper: A Year of Democratic Setbacks and Popular Protest*, THE ECONOMIST: Intelligence Unit (n.d.) (reporting that the average global score for democracy in the world dropped from a 5.48 rating in 2018 to a 5.44 rating in 2019, the lowest score recorded by the Democracy Index since its 2006 inception).

[77] *See, e.g.*, Mohamed Elshinnawi, *Arab Spring Became Brutal Winter, Analysts Say*, VOICE OF AMERICA (Jan. 19, 2016), www.voanews.com/middle-east/arab-spring-became-brutal-winter-analysts-say.

countries around the world often adopted a posture of lip service toward democratic ideals, and that lip service sometimes translated into real democratic successes. Now that the United States has given up the pretense, much of the rest of the world has stopped using the language of democracy, causing a massive uptick in authoritarian language, politicians, and regimes.

Different cultures have different weaknesses, different vectors by which authoritarian nationalists exploit democratic tolerance and the need to accommodate plural voices. The core historical example is the Weimar Republic, mentioned earlier, which ended in a democratically elected (at least as democratically elected as modern elections are) authoritarian nationalist regime. The Weimar Republic's own commitments to debate, diversity, and pluralism were precisely the wound in the skin that permitted the fascist infection.

Modern attempts to stave off infection have proven largely ineffectual: the problem is a sort of jejune sense of fairness. The Western democratic tradition is gravely infected with the sense that it must tolerate intolerance—that "free speech," for example, must include those who advocate silencing others by terror and genocide—even though that's as stupid as saying that defending oneself is the same as attacking others without provocation.

In the American context, hardball constitutionalism has profoundly changed the nature of one end of the political spectrum, from constitutional conservativism to authoritarian nationalism. Compare President Obama's regular practice of appointing Republicans to prominent positions and focus on securing bipartisan support (which crippled his administration in the early years of his presidency) to the Republican Senate's hardball constitutionalist takeover of the US Supreme Court, long a goal by certain religious groups and sympathetic politicians focused on controlling women's reproductive choices. Senate Majority Leader Mitch McConnell essentially forced the Senate not to do its job for over a year in order to secure an imbalance in Supreme Court nominations, or led the Senate to vote not to convict a president.[78] There was no technical rule saying the Senate must do its job, either in permitting President Obama to make nominations or for McConnell and the Senate to actually hold more than a show trial, and so McConnell exploited the law to undermine it in classic hardball constitutionalist fashion.

As the British will confirm, it is the unwritten laws of civility and the spirit of the rules that allow a democracy to function. When laws become only the

---

[78] *See* Amita Kelly, *McConnell: Blocking Supreme Court Nomination "about a Principle, Not a Person"*, NPR (Mar. 16, 2016), www.npr.org/2016/03/16/470664561/mcconnell-blocking-supreme-court-nomination-about-a-principle-not-a-person.

mechanism of an authoritarian coup, they lose any legitimacy. Laws can be entirely lawless: there is no use following rules for rules' sake, especially when the goal of following the law is the abolition of the rule of law. Authoritarian nationalists first use, then dismantle, the legal systems they exploit to come to power. And that is how lawless regimes can lawfully come to power, from the genocidal fascism that followed the Weimar Republic to the authoritarian nationalists of the United States, the Philippines, Britain, Hungary, and Brazil, as well as the former-fringe right-wing parties lurking in Germany, France, and in many other countries worldwide.

The infection vectors are different for each country. Here, let us bring our discussion full circle. We have been exploring why people have the perception that law cannot regulate technology. My suggestion has been that the perception of legal inability is actually caused by the United States' failures as a political and legal institution. A key reason is the decline of democratic impact in the United States: privacy and data security laws would be effortless at this point, since everyone else has moved forward with them, and wildly popular with the American people, but all government movement on issues like net neutrality and privacy directly serve corporate donors rather than voters.

The US precommitments to laissez-faire surveillance capitalism complete a loop from the extremist content creators for social media to congresspeople influenced by corporate donations. That means that any attempt to regulate social media's vicious exploitation of extreme content for profit goes nowhere. And the bizarre mutation of the US First Amendment into the internet ideal that says racist, anti-Semitic, misogynist, bigoted, and pro-genocidal speech ought to be actively tolerated, almost promoted in a masochistic sense, ties the bow up neatly. Extreme content drives engagement. Social media giants need free and engaging content, and are not willing to pay for the blood their business model spills. So they pay off congresspeople, through campaign contributions, to keep things that way. They influence elections to ensure they won't be held responsible for the damage they cause. And they do it through the rhetoric that law cannot impose effective limitations on their data strip-mining. This rhetoric, especially that surrounding free speech, is then championed by politicians because it sounds law-ish, and because it provides them with dog-whistles to activate their constituents who have been radicalized by extreme content.

The American cult of rampant technological progress is a cooperative fiction: it is one that causes us to unite against our own interests, to put the profits of data billionaires above the bullying and deaths of children, to value a cultural norm of "free speech" as including statements supporting murder, threats, bombing, and genocide, whether political or ecological. American law is united by a series of guiding narratives: precommitments that stop us from building the legal systems necessary to reasonably regulate technological change. They are framing stories, not facts. The idea that law cannot keep pace with technological change is provably false, but as long as we believe that the marketing message is somehow a description of reality, we will remain victims of learned helplessness. We can develop laws that provide a reasonable and livable interface between technological capability and human needs. The first step is deciding to do so.

IT CAN'T HAPPEN HERE

Between January 2009 and February 2020, there were 226 mass shootings in the United States, resulting in 1,292 people shot and killed, and an additional 938 people shot and wounded.[79] So far, the United States has done nothing about the problem worth writing about. So is law somehow incapable of doing anything about the problem of mass shootings? Or, is the answer that regulators in the United States dance to the drum of the NRA?[80]

Five days after the Facebook-promoted alt-right shootings in Christchurch, New Zealand, in March 2019, Prime Minister Jacinda Ardern announced that, under laws passed in those five days, "[We will ban] all military style semi-automatic weapons, we will also ban all assault rifles, we will also ban all high-capacity magazines."[81] Those bans went into effect three weeks later. Within four months of the shootings, the New Zealand legislature had instituted a buy-back program. By the end of the year, 32,000 people had turned in 56,000 guns, out of a population half that of the state of Virginia.[82]

In addition, New Zealand initiated the "Christchurch Call," a series of international, worldwide reforms to handle the streaming of extremist

---

[79] *Mass Shootings in America, 2009–2020*, EVERYTOWN FOR GUN SAFETY (Feb. 20, 2020), https://everytownresearch.org/massshootingsreports/mass-shootings-in-america-2009-2019/ (defining "mass shooting" as "any incident in which four or more people are shot and killed, excluding the shooter"). *But see* Jason Silverstein, *There Were More Mass Shootings Than Days in 2019*, CBS NEWS (Jan. 2, 2020), www.cbsnews.com/news/mass-shootings-2019-more-than-days-365/ (defining a "mass shooting" as "any incident in which at least four people are shot, excluding the shooter" and reporting that there were 417 mass shootings in the United States in 2019 alone).

[80] *See, e.g.*, Elisabeth J. Ryan, *Firearms and Physicians: Finding A Duty to Discuss*, 11 NE. U.L. REV. 155, 163–64 (2019).

[81] Jacinda Ardern, N.Z. Prime Minister, Public address (March 20, 2019).

[82] *See* Karen Zraick, *New Zealand Ban on Most Semiautomatic Weapons Takes Effect* (Dec. 20, 2019), www.nytimes.com/2019/12/20/world/australia/new-zealand-gun-ban.html.

content.[83] The Christchurch Call drew attention to the gold-star white-glove treatment that the Christchurch shooting video had received at Facebook's hands: it was promoted, streamed, and pushed to millions of viewers to drive engagement, views, and advertising dollars in the social media giant's boundless appetite for extremist violence voyeurism. When New Zealanders looked to Twitter to find out what was happening during the shooting, Twitter had auto-played video of the massacre. So enthusiastically did Twitter's system push murder porn as its prized engaging content that people saw the first few deaths before they even knew what was happening.[84]

In the face of Twitter- and Facebook-promoted mass murder, New Zealand enacted gun laws in a matter of days and took positive action to handle sewage-peddlers like Mark Zuckerberg within a few weeks. New Zealand's neighbor Australia imposed fines of $2.1 million AUD or three years in prison for not quickly taking down extremist violent content.[85] The United States, by way of comparison, merely continues to serve as a breeding ground for further obscenities, clutching its pearls and tweeting thoughts and prayers with each new massacre.

The response to the Christchurch shootings and social media streaming is an example of legislatures doing something fast. There are also examples of countries that can do things slowly, carefully, experimentally, iteratively, humbly, and to enormously powerful results. That's fine, too: ultimately, it's doing *nothing* that's the problem.

---

[83] *See* RT Hon Jacinda Ardern, *Christchurch Call to Eliminate Terrorist and Violent Extremist Online Content Adopted*, Beehive.govt.nz (The Official Website of the New Zealand Government) (May 16, 2019), www.beehive.govt.nz/release/christchurch-call-eliminate-terrorist-and-violent-extremist-online-content-adopted; *see also* Christchurch Call (May 15, 2019) (available at www.christchurchcall.com/christchurch-call.pdf).

[84] Jason Abbruzzese & Brandy Zadrozny, *Streamed to Facebook, Spread on YouTube: New Zealand Shooting Video Circulates Online despite Takedowns*, ABC NEWS (Mar. 15, 2019), www.nbcnews.com/tech/tech-news/streamed-facebook-spread-youtube-new-zealand-shooting-video-circulates-online-n983726 ("Some Twitter users reported seeing the video through the platform's autoplay feature, which begins playing videos without user interaction. Others pleaded with people not to spread the video.... Videos of the shooting continued to spread on Twitter [into the afternoon], with one such example having been online for more than 11 hours."); *see also* Nikki (@randomlilnikki), Twitter (Mar. 14, 2019, 11:49 pm), https://twitter.com/randomlilnikki/status/1106401934506758147 ("There's graphic video of the #Christchurch shooter's livestream footage circulating, so now would be a good time to disable autoplay on your feed. Twitter disabled the account, but some people unburdened by a sense of common decency have been sharing it.").

[85] Damien Cave, *Australia Passes Law to Punish Social Media Companies for Violent Posts*, N.Y. TIMES, April 3, 2019, www.nytimes.com/2019/04/03/world/australia/social-media-law.html.

Consider the example of the current world-dominating privacy law, the European General Data Protection Regulation.[86] When US law students study privacy, they don't much bother studying US law—there isn't any worth the candle. US privacy students and professionals instead study the GDPR, a European Union law that went into effect in 2018. The GDPR is an overhaul and upgrade of the 1995 Data Protection Directive, which drew worldwide best practices of data protection, including many from the US experience, into a single directive to EU states to pass data protection laws under their own power. The directive lasted the better part of a quarter century before it was substantively revised and overhauled, discussed and litigated, weighed and measured, and finally iterated and upgraded into the version passed in 2016 as the EU GDPR. Go to any US digital privacy conference and you will notice that the GDPR is absolutely the center of everyone's attention. It is *the* law, worldwide, on digital privacy.

By contrast, in the same twenty-five years, the United States has done very nearly nothing worthy of attention or emulation on privacy. The United States had even more time than everyone else: the issues became clear in the States well before they became apparent in the rest of the world. Of course US thinkers have played a leading role; standards like the influential Fair Information Practice Principles[87] were in no small part developed by US actors. This thought-leader position has not translated into US law, however. Despite having more time and greater clarity, the United States has squandered its world-leading position in technology and has become the butt of the joke as far as technology regulation is concerned.

Sinclair Lewis's novel about American apathy and the embrace of fascism is titled *It Can't Happen Here*.[88] Since the rise of American authoritarian nationalism is now a matter of historical record, we might as well use the phrase differently. The United States cannot currently serve a leadership role in technology policy: it lacks the functioning legislature, the soft power, and the ideas to do so. The geographical, cultural, and linguistic center of the effort to find responsible regulatory principles for technology must gather elsewhere. American soft power is at a disastrously low ebb, and US ideas about technology regulation are not respected on the world stage. More, the United States has done nothing that can be exported; having assiduously

---

[86] General Data Protection Regulation (EU) 2016/679.
[87] OECD Guidelines on the Protection of Privacy and Transborder Flows of Personal Data, Organisation for Economic Co-operation and Development (OECD) (Sept. 23, 1980) (available at www.oecd.org/document/18/0,2340,en_2649_34255_1815186_1_1_1_1,00.html) (memorializing the eight Fair Information Practice Principles).
[88] SINCLAIR LEWIS, IT CAN'T HAPPEN HERE (1935).

prevented any ideas from coming to fruition, it has produced vanishingly few worthy of emulating. Even if the United States does reverse the erosion of its former democratic principles, the damage to its ability to command respect on questions of corporate and government surveillance is simply too deep, and the continued role of companies in writing US tech policy make that policy unpalatable to other countries.

IF NOT THE US, THEN . . . ?

Europe is a potential candidate for serving as the center for fostering a new language of how law might engage with technology to promote human thriving. Europe has serious problems, to be sure: Brexit and Greece each in their own way might herald grim things for the future of the European experiment. But those challenges are not disqualifying, merely disheartening. Europe has other advantages as a locus for the kind of forward-leaning thought necessary to craft new language to help us deal with the emerging problems of technology.

In writing this book, I spent time at the Max Planck Institute for Innovation and Competition in Munich, Germany, and at the European University Institute in Florence, Italy. I spent months traveling to different institutions and conferences, studying, interviewing, and exchanging ideas with European legal scholars. Through those conversations, I developed a sense of some of the ways in which the European legal system deals with technological change, and how those systems might help fill the leadership gap.

My pragmatic sense is that Europe may be able to act as a nexus and a facilitator for a badly needed conversation around responsible technology regulation. Europe's legal culture has several distinct advantages. There is a profound commitment on the part of multiple European states—most notably Germany—to data privacy. This serves as a bulwark against the corrosive efforts of surveillance capitalists to undermine effective legislation limiting their exploitative business model. And as far as extremism and authoritarian nationalism are concerned, the democratic bona fides of many of the most important European member states are, although far from spotless, nowhere near the debacle of US democracy. Lastly, the EU has an established track record of imposing real controls and consequences on both surveillance capitalists and right-wing extremists.

A particularly important element in EU legal culture is its relative freedom from corporate domination. Several of the core legal cultures in the EU do not believe the goal of law ought to be maximizing corporate profit, and many more Europeans than Americans are suspicious of corporatism, especially of massive US technology companies. The geographical and cultural differences have given European legislatures some remove from the hegemony of surveillance capitalists, and the result is an imperfect, often bumbling, but quite effective and impactful set of laws regulating Silicon Valley robber barons.

And while the EU does have a robust tradition of open civic discourse, it does not share the United States' commitment to "free speech." For historical reasons, Germany is not at all unclear on the need to protect democracy from authoritarian nationalists. France has robust laws banning Nazi speech. And the EU broadly has strong laws and effective redress against Holocaust denial. This is not to say that the rise of right-wing authoritarian nationalism hasn't been felt in France and Germany as it has worldwide: as noted, the Front National and Alternativ für Deutschland have moved from extreme fringe movements to winning major elections, and former East Germany in particular is a hotbed of racist, anti-immigrant, and nationalist sentiment. But the most prominent EU member states do not have a self-sacrificing commitment to tolerating the speech and organization of those who seek to abolish the rule of law and promote anti-Semitism, Islamophobia, and at the edges, ethnic cleansing. As horrible as it is to say, that is a start, and is better than the United States currently manages.

The EU has a legal culture of publicly funded intellectual endeavor. In Germany, for example, a robust network of foundations and institutes—most notably the flagship Max Planck Institute's many different centers, on subjects ranging from psychology and behavioral economics to innovation to physics—provide input for legislative endeavors. Europe-wide academic networks like the European University Institute provide a strong public-supplied context for public-focused academic debate. A conference promoted by a public foundation with the goal of exploring how new technologies impact society has a completely different atmosphere and outcome than one sponsored by Google, Facebook, and Palantir.

Relatedly, and although I am painting with a broad brush, EU legal cultures rely on expertise to a greater extent than does the United States. The United States has a broad cultural tendency toward anti-intellectualism. Many of the constituent EU cultures have not yet given up on knowledge, facts, and experts who can make use of them. Experts are still regularly consulted for their expertise, rather than for their willingness to parrot a political line (although, again, the EU's political elites are far from immune to the temptation to handpick fringe science as a political bargaining chip).

Of course, I've been talking thus far about Europe as a unit, which hides the massive differences in legal cultures and regulatory approaches espoused by individual EU member states. Those internal differences are greater in many senses than the differences between the United Kingdom, a soon-to-be former

member, and the United States. For example, the differences between northern and southern Europe are profound, as the perennial conflicts between
Germany and Greece demonstrate. The Netherlands and Italy, just to pick
a random example, have profoundly different cultural emphases, and embed
expectations about law and legal orderings in different ways.

That diversity is not a weakness, however. As we will see in the next chapter,
diverse groups systematically outperform monoculture groups on complex
and innovative, problem-solving tasks. Moreover, although nationalism is on
the rise in Europe as it is worldwide, it plays less of a role in EU lawmaking,
since experts and legislators come from very different traditions. This avoids
the pitfalls of American exceptionalism and techno-libertarian monoculture.

Nor should the fact that EU member states predominantly follow civil law
traditions, rather than the common law, matter much. I have described the
process of development of the law as an organic process, as illustrated by
Robert Cover, and as an analogous progression of narratives—the paradigm
shift model championed by Thomas Kuhn and applied to language by
Richard Rorty. It is easy to see how such a model applies in common law
countries. The cases are literally narratives, and the reasoning in the cases
constitutes direct law. The methods are different in civil law jurisdictions, but
the results are the same. Civil law jurisdictions rely on judges more than juries,
on interpretation of law codes more than analogy between cases, and on
treatises more than the legal instinct of the presiding judge. But these differences aside, civil law cultures do a strong job of managing progress in the face
of technological change. For example, in Germany, although cases are not
precedent, cases are collected by well-known professors, who then breathe life
into the direction of the law by including the cases as examples of the overall
rules they are meant to embody. An academic finds the pattern and tells the
stories based on their view of the overall rule and its proper interpretation, and
individual cases are examples that prove the rule. Judges, then, often turn to
the treatises in which new cases have been fitted into chains of legal theory and
jurisprudential traditions.[89]

The diversity of the EU proves an asset on this point as well. EU-level courts
follow common law traditions. This matters, because many of the most
pressing questions of emerging law and technology fall to these courts.
Much critical harmonizing legislation, particularly on data, privacy, and
electronic commerce, is at the EU level. For example, the famous "right to
be forgotten" case, in which a Spanish citizen sued Google for failing to de-list

---

[89] I'm indebted for this analysis to my colleague Professor Russ Miller, a constitutional law
scholar and leading German legal specialist.

outdated and irrelevant information, was heard by the Court of Justice of the European Union.[90] The well-known *Schrems* cases, brought by an Austrian attorney and privacy advocate, started most recently before the Irish Data Protection Authority (many US surveillance capitalist firms use Ireland to avoid paying taxes), and has ended at multiple *reprises* in front of the CJEU.[91] Thus, when it comes down to it, the European-level legal system has input from extremely different cultures and very different legal traditions, while still retaining the ability to bring a new question of law and technology promptly before judges for development of new legal norms. And the process has worked: CJEU decisions on privacy and data security are without a doubt the most carefully read and influential legal decisions on the intersection of data, privacy, and commerce worldwide.

Of course, Europe is no techno-regulatory Shangri-la; it is just the cleanest dirty shirt in the closet. There are challenges worth acknowledging. In particular, several of the core EU legal cultures ascribe to various degrees of legal formalism. EU attorneys are trained in what the law is—positive law—and in highly developed methods of interpretation. This can be a mixed bag. Formalism can lead to a certain hidebound sense of law. European lawyers often specialize into narrow silos. While I was conducting research in Germany and Italy, EU lawyers and legal academics often had trouble understanding the subject matter of this book. They asked, was it about intellectual property? Competition law? Constitutional law? My response was that the book was about the future of all law, of how the institution of law adapts to technological change. European lawyers struggled with finding a mental home for the concept, because it fell outside of the concerns of any given silo of positive law.

And yet that structure and formalism has served EU lawyers well. What appears to be hidebound formalism—a belief that the law *is* something ascertainable—also yields a strong belief in the rule of law, one that has been undermined in the US context by lawyers trained to skirt and rewrite rules for their clients' benefit. And while civil law systems' reliance on broadly shared rich interpretive tools can, again, seem formalistic, it is precisely the development of shared interpretive tools that we need. If European legal cultures can be pried away from their conviction that the law *is* something—that is, the

---

90   *See* Case C-131/12, Google Spain SL v. Agencia Española de Protección de Datos, Mario Costeja González, 2014 EUR-Lex CELEX 62012CJ0131, P 99 (May 13, 2014).
91   *See* ECJ, Case C-362/14, Maximillian Schrems v. Data Protection Commissioner, ECLI:EU: C:2015:650, judgment of Oct. 6, 2015 ("Schrems I"); Opinion of Advocate General Saugmandsgaard Øe, Case C-311/18, Data Protection Commissioner v. Facebook Ireland Ltd., Maximillian Schrems (Dec. 19, 2019) ("Schrems II").

conception that it has a formal existence separate from human language and negotiated meaning—without sacrificing the love for the law as an equal and valuable field of human inquiry (in Germany, lawyers are called scientists, *Rechtswissenschaftler*), European reverence can be melded with American innovation to build cooperative fictions that really may give us a shot at surviving the future.

Indeed, although the conversation can't be centered here in the United States, many of the components for that all-important conversation will be made in the United States. American legal entrepreneurialism, for all its profound corrosion of legal institutions and norms, does generate a vibrant panoply of ideas. It is nearly a truism that the United States innovates legal ideas and solutions that other legal cultures then turn into reality. The United States is the equivalent to the eponymous start-up maven: someone who is full of ideas and can start many successful companies, but cannot stay the course to build a stable business. As we will see in the next chapter, cognitive diversity is key to building new languages and new solutions to complex and hard innovation problems. The US perspective will contribute far more once those who speak the language of unbridled innovation are freed from the suspicion that they are merely techno-libertarian shills for US technology companies. US-generated ideas need to be tested for corporate corruption, for payoffs from Google to researchers, for Facebook or Palantir's domination, for rote subservience to Silicon Valley, to be taken seriously. They cannot be so tested in their home context.

The best US-generated ideas have always formed the basis for European data and technology regulation. As with the Fair Information Practice Principles, ideas grow in the United States and are harvested in Europe. The intellectual locus of the effort to survive the future thus hovers somewhere over the Atlantic. It is a gulfstream of ideas: life-giving ideas flow from the United States, receive polishing, definition, and details in Europe, and then gain a worldwide stage and impact.

Finally, although the discussion here is admittedly Eurocentric, I want to stress that Europe is just one example. The point is to look for places where diverse currents of ideas can come together without the hegemonic lobbying influence of American surveillance capitalists or the bullying of American authoritarian nationalists. Europe is one such place, at the moment. The GDPR is an example of political possibility. A polity faced with an emerging major technological issue thought about the future, took action, tested, fixed errors, rinse, repeat. The EU was not paralyzed by lobbying dollars and spurious claims that corporate surveillance was required for technological progress. The law served citizens rather than corporate profits. And those conditions can be found elsewhere in the world as well.

There are other places where diverse legal communities with still-effective democratic institutions come to effective and timely grips with the changes technology has wrought. We started this section with a discussion of New Zealand's and Australia's timely and influential efforts to handle Facebook's and Twitter's (and Reddit's, and YouTube's) peddling of vicious lies and lurid racist violence for corporate surveillance profit. There are other bright spots around the world, from Canada to the democracy protestors in Hong Kong. Liberal democracy—one of the best, most complex, and contingent libraries of cooperative fictions ever created to forward human thriving—need not surrender to surveillance capitalists and authoritarian nationalists.

It is not enough, however, to find such bright spots in the wild. We must learn to *create* communities that can generate the kind of language—the kind of law—we need to survive the future. Recent studies demonstrate that those sorts of communities will have the characteristics we have associated with the more successful regulation of technology in this chapter: freedom from domination and coercion, rich cognitive diversity, and shared goals and purposes. Figuring out how to build the kind of language-generating communities we need is our next step, and the focus of the next chapter.

9

Jurisgenesis

To live in a legal world requires that one know not only the precepts, but also their connections to possible and plausible states of affairs. It requires that one integrate not only the "is" and the "ought," but the "is," the "ought," and the "what might be."

— Robert Cover, *Nomos and Narrative*[1]

When we talk about the future and what might or should be, we cannot help but talk about things that do not yet exist, or exist only in our minds and language. We do so because they are not so. "We inhabit a *nomos*— a normative universe," writes Robert Cover in a best-beloved law review article.

> We constantly create and maintain a world of right and wrong, of lawful and unlawful, of valid and void. . . . No set of legal institutions or prescriptions exists apart from the narratives that locate it and give it meaning. For every constitution there is an epic, for each decalogue a scripture. Once understood in the context of the narratives that give it meaning, law becomes not merely a system of rules to be observed, but a world in which we live. . . . In this normative world, law and narrative are inseparably related.[2]

To develop the kind of law that we need to thrive under conditions of technological change, we will need to adapt our normative language. Genetic evolution is simply too slow compared to progress based on selection of ideas. Because language is our competitive advantage as a species, only a study of language, and a method of improving language, will help us cooperate well enough to survive rapid evolution of our environment, bodies, and minds.

---

[1] Robert Cover, *Nomos and Narrative*, 97 HARV. L. REV.4, 10 (1983–84).
[2] *Id.* at 4–5.

We will need the best cooperative fictions that we can create to survive technological change. Belief in human rights, Wednesday, money, the nation-state of South Sudan, or any number of gods is not a belief in nothing, or in something ephemeral: it is a belief in the power of cooperative fictions suspended in language. Or, as Yuval Harari would put it, these represent a range of cooperative fictions that help us do our human thing—cooperate in communities to solve the question of how we should act toward one another.

But we have not intentionally pursued the creation of social technology, through language, that helps us deal with the future. What artifacts we have generated, like #MeToo, or the expanding vocabulary and language around gender and identity, have been haphazard, and the language of liberal democracy has lagged the intentional language generation of authoritarian nationalists. This has been our mistake: to believe that our cooperative fictions are less real and less valuable than the products and services of natural science. We have chosen to underdevelop our ways of living together. That's a problem we'll have to fix, if we are to survive the future.

THE LANGUAGE OF COOPERATION

To survive radical technological and environmental change, we must take care to develop better things to which to commit. We need our language of *should* to grow, to develop, to spread, and above all to give life—to promote viability and human thriving. As Cover writes: "This *nomos* is as much 'our world' as is the physical universe of mass, energy, and momentum. Indeed, our apprehension of the structure of the normative world is no less fundamental than our appreciation of the structure of the physical world."[3]

I do not know what ideal, what kind of language, what combination of normative beauty and social rituals for observing empirical reality (like the scientific method itself) will give us the opportunity to live together in peace in such a way that we can show reverence to the Earth, wonder and curiosity about the universe, kindness to our neighbors, hospitality to strangers, generosity to the poor, and mercy to our enemies. As those images imply, I believe that viability and thriving should have much to do with it. But I am a single node in a network, and if I am right about anything, it is that none of us is as smart as all of us. And how should we best live together is a decision, not unironically, that we must make together.

---

[3] *Id.*

Even though I cannot say what ideals—what language—we should give our lives to, I think I know where that language comes from, and that is what interests me here. I think that if we gave the same attention to robust communities of language as we have to the theory of the firm,[4] for example, we might find that groups devoted to developing life-giving language will produce good language, just like a strong theory of the firm contributed to producing better products and services.

In sum: language comes from communities of meaning. Thriving communities of meaning produce thriving language. To grow the right kind of language, we need the right kind of community garden. By the "right kind," I mean those gardens that grow language that help humans cooperate at scale to thrive. These communities are the seeds of law. They are the generative core of culture. They are, in Cover's parlance, *nomoi*:[5] worlds governed and shaped by a normative order, a system of commitments that make sense of life. They are the center of Cover's jurisgenerative principle of creating legal meaning. These gardens are where law grows.

We make our normative universe by developing language between us. We speak this normative universe into being, this *nomos*, this orientation toward life together, these cooperative fictions, this language-game of living and working together. We craft all of this, languages, *nomoi*, for the task of living together in harmony. Like music, math, art, and language, our norms, our shoulds, are no less real or less powerful for having been human-made.

Law is our method of bridging the *is* of science and the that which is not yet, the future, as determined by our *nomos*, our common language of cooperation. As Cover writes, "Law may be viewed as a system of tension or a bridge linking a concept of a reality to an imagined alternative—that is, as a connective between two states of affairs, both of which can be represented in their normative significance only through the devices of narrative."[6] Law is a form of language in which humans discern together, in community, how to build a bridge from what is to what should be. It is both intensely subjective, because it is language, and intensely objective, because it can only occur between speakers, and is not created inside any one person's head. It is an objectively verifiable subjective bridge between the state of things that are and the state of things to come. Of course, how things *should* be has a fraught relationship with how they *will* be. Nobody expects even the near future. But it

---

4   *See* R. H. Coase, *The Nature of the Firm*, 4 ECONOMICA 386 (1937); *see, e.g.*, Ning Wang, *The Legacy of Ronald Coase*, 4 THE J. OF THE COASE SOCIETY (2017).

5   Plural of "nomos."

6   Cover, *supra* note 1, at 4, 9.

is undeniable that our normative worldview is constitutive of both how the world is for us and what it becomes for us. "Thou shalt not steal" is a bridge between a known world—where theft undeniably exists—and a normative world, in which Wal-Mart does not routinely commit wage theft.

Law is the fundamental linguistic art of handling the future itself. In its currently impoverished and weakened state, this language cannot do its job. It has been mulcted as useless in the discourse of progress, when it is in fact the discourse of progress itself. No wonder, then, that we cannot keep up: we have hobbled the horse we must ride in the race.

BUILDING GARDENS OF LANGUAGE

Language develops between us, in community. To generate better language, we need better linguistic communities. The way to develop better language faster is to create communities that foster vibrant, life-giving language, that create cooperative fictions, norms we can hang our hats on, language like "all [people] are created equal" or #MeToo. And given some of the cognitive science and studies of linguistics we have already discussed, we are beginning to see ways in which we can evaluate communities for the characteristics that cause them to generate the language of human thriving.

When I speak of linguistic communities, I mean any gathering of humans for the purpose of talking together about how to do something complex and nonroutine, for which new words and a new way of thinking may offer new solutions. Such a gathering can range from a jury in a courtroom to a cross-disciplinary scientific team on a research grant, from scholars around a conference roundtable to a corporate research and development team. When a group like this gets good at its task, it develops language and concepts to help us grapple with the issues that technology surfaces. A jury may determine the privacy concerns about a new technology, because it is the trier of fact in a case where the edges of the interests have not yet been determined. A multidisciplinary team of quantitative computer science PhDs may team up with cultural anthropologists to find extremist leaders in virtual worlds. A corporate R&D team might blend the social elements of design and choice architecture with ongoing A/B testing to craft new products à la Apple—products that don't just work, but work *for* the consumer.

Since our heavy lifting in the crafting of future language will be performed by groups, it is worth noting that technology has fundamentally changed group formation, incentives to cooperate, information flow, and other group cooperative institutions. Take blockchain technology, for example. Vaunted as a money substitute, blockchain is really a decentralized database technology. It solves a big problem of cooperation—the Byzantine General's problem—whereby groups have to cooperate even knowing that some members are undermining the group project. Here's the point: the technology doesn't solve a technological problem, it helps with a fundamentally human one: trust. With blockchain, we have enhanced abilities to cooperate even knowing that some supposed cooperators are defecting. Other technologies have other effects on groups and group cooperation, from Facebook groups to subreddits. And these effects feed into each other. Humans design technology in groups, technology changes the affordances of those groups, and groups using the technology advance the ball further, in an accelerating cycle.

The work of building better jurisgenerative communities—communities that build life-giving cooperative fictions—is more important than developing any one solution or right idea for the problems of the future. A solution lasts for a day. A system for constantly and dynamically upgrading our language with rich sets of cooperative fictions provides us with a process for dealing with the future on an ongoing basis, rather than a solution for right now. So the following sections look at what we now know about the art and science of building the kinds of linguistic communities that systematically create better ideas, better cooperative fictions, better solutions to the problems of the future.

Linguistic communities capable of building the kind of normative language we need have certain critical features. There are three broad themes, which we will explore in turn. Recent studies on how groups approach innovation problems—complex unprecedented nonroutine tasks—demonstrate that the most successful groups are highly cognitively diverse, are noncoercive, and have shared goals. These characteristics are melded and balanced in the most successful groups, and part of the trick is dealing with the pull of these elements in different directions—diverse groups may have diverging goals, for example, and coercion is a favorite method for creating unity. But there is no question: groups that do negotiate this balance are at an enormous advantage in brainstorming innovative solutions to complex nonroutine problems.

DIVERSITY

We have been talking about how communities can develop language that allows their members to live together in peace and prosperity, and to develop new rules for handling the impact that new technologies have on the social fabric. We have also talked in prior chapters about the nature of human rationality and how it serves social functions of justification and persuasion, rather than logical rigor, as well as of the nature of language as our means of cooperating to think better together and upgrade our social software to outpace evolution. It should come as no surprise, then, that groups of humans equipped with a wide variety of cognitive tools for approaching a problem outperform groups that lack such variety.

To recap the literature, studies of group rationality and social intelligence show that humans solve some problems better in groups. Individual rationality—the part of us that suggests solutions—seems to suggest solutions that secure our place in the group and persuade others to increase our social capital. Our individual rationality does not systematically find correct answers.[7] Each of us is a social-reason-producing node. It takes other humans to error-check our passionately proffered and myside-biased reasons.[8]

The science on diversity takes a related tack.[9] Here the idea is that different people bring different cognitive tools to bear on a problem. A common tendency in building groups to solve hard problems is to try to find the "best" people. The problem is that the "best" people tend to have done well on the same metrics, which means they have redundant cognitive toolsets. This means that groups comprising the "best" people can have fewer cognitive tools at their disposal than groups composed of people who can bring diverse (but, individually, fewer) cognitive tools to bear.[10]

Because diversity is a contested term in our current language, I offer a few points on how I use it here. This section follows the approach of leading diversity scientist Scott Page in focusing on cognitive diversity.[11] Cognitive diversity is distinguishable from (although never entirely separable from) demographic or identity diversity, which tends to be the more common meaning of the term. However, the two have a strong relationship, and it is without question true that demographic diversity contributes to the development of cognitively diverse tools.

Page describes cognitive diversity by reference to cognitive tools.[12] Suppose six tools are relevant to getting a job done: an Arc welder,

---

[7]   *See* Martin G. Kocher & Matthias Sutter, *The Decision Maker Matters: Individual Versus Group Behaviour in Experimental Beauty-Contest Games*, 115 THE ECONOMIC J. 200 (2005). For a nonhuman example *see also* Takao Sasaki & Stephen C. Pratt, *Emergence of Group Rationality from Irrational Individuals*, 22 BEHAVIORAL ECOLOGY 276 (2011).

[8]   HUGO MERCIER & DAN SPERBER, THE ENIGMA OF REASON 7 (2017).

[9]   *See generally* SCOTT E. PAGE, THE DIVERSITY BONUS: HOW GREAT TEAMS PAY OFF IN THE KNOWLEDGE ECONOMY (2019) [hereinafter, PAGE, DIVERSITY BONUS].

[10] *Id.* at 8 ("When diversity bonuses exist, the best group will not, as a rule, consist of the best individual performers according to some criterion. Instead, it will be diverse. I am not saying that an organization should hire less talented people. The claim is that talent is multi-dimensional.").

[11] *Id.* at 8.

[12] *Id.* at 16–17.

Bandsaw, Cutting torch, Drill, Electric screwdriver, and Framing hammer (A–F). Let us assume three builders, Ruth, Sam, and Tammy. Ruth has four tools, B through E. Sam has three: A, B, and C, and Tammy has three: D, E, and F. The question is, which team of two people will bring the most tools to bear on the situation?

It is clear that Ruth has the most tools, and thus is in that sense is the "best" of the builders. But the overlap between her tools and those of the others means that a team made of Sam and Tammy will have more tools than would a team made up of Ruth and either of the other two. Each has fewer tools, but because there is no wasted overlap, Sam and Tammy will be able to bring all six tools to bear. A team of Ruth and Sam would miss tool F. A team of Ruth and Tammy will miss tool A. Thus, any team with Ruth on it will have five tools. A team made up of Sam and Tammy will have six.

Worse, let us now say that Ruth, Sam, and Tammy are not individuals, but types. We can test and find multiple Ruths, multiple Sams, and multiple Tammies. This is the hiring trap so many employers fall into. If they hire only the best—Ruths: people who score best on a neutral metric testing how many tools a person has—they will build teams of Ruths, and those teams will have four tools because the overlap between team members is so very high: they all scored the best, they all have the same tools. Groups of Sams and Tammies will trounce the best-in-class Ruth groups: six tools to the Ruths' four.

From this tool analogy, Page builds his core ideas: cognitive repertoire, and diversity in tools.[13] A cognitive repertoire is the set of tools that an individual brings to the team. These tools might be a matter of training, of field, of perspective, of life experience, or so on. What matters is not just the size of an individual's tool chest, but their diversity to other team members, the degree of overlap with other members of the team: a measure of diversity in the cognitive tools group members can bring to bear.

So when diversity bonuses exist, the best group will not, as a rule, consist of the best individual performers.[14] Measurement by any single metric causes overlap in cognitive toolsets, reducing the overall number of tools available to the team. By cognitive diversity we therefore mean reducing cognitive toolset overlap. A person who possesses different—diverse to the existing team— cognitive tools for attacking a problem is a better addition to a team than someone who has the best or the most cognitive tools. Page's research is full of examples in which social scientists are the best addition to teams of computer

---

[13] *Id.*
[14] *Id.* at 8.

scientists; psychologists to teams of economists, linguists to teams of algorithm designers, and so on.[15]

Page recognizes but brackets the normative values of social inclusion, pipe-lining, and historical injustice that often inform the diversity debate. I find the need for such strong bracketing to be overdone. Identity and life experience drive differences in cognitive repertoires. And while there are likely problems for which the diversity driven by identity and life experience yield fewer cognitive differences relevant to the task at hand (where, Page argues, inclusion based on identity diversity is more likely to yield a "dog's breakfast" than an iPhone),[16] his point does not hold when the relevant question is how different people from different groups ought to live together under the rule of law. Identity-driven differences in cognitive repertoire include, but are not limited to, understanding how certain policies (say, policing, insider trading laws, drug policy, or incar-ceration rates) impact different communities, which is a primary concern of good legal thinking. Law and legal policy are precisely those tasks in which a core problem is the differential impact a legal rule has on different popula-tions. So although the discussion here centers on cognitive diversity, for a range of problems of legal innovation, identity diversity will both directly and indir-ectly (through development of differing cognitive tools) contribute to the development of better rules for living together.

THE KINDS OF PROBLEMS COGNITIVE DIVERSITY SOLVES

Not all tasks are best performed by diverse groups. Some tasks are best performed by groups composed of the best performers—that is, "best in class" monoculture teams. Page uses the analogy of a relay race. Here, the best team is composed of the fastest runners: a single metric. There is no use including a fast swimmer on the team. In a footrace, a diverse team of fast runners and fast swimmers will not beat a team of the fastest runners.

If all one needs to do is drive a nail, hammers work best. Having a team with access to screwdrivers and wrenches won't help drive a nail better. So routine, repeated, one-dimensional tasks do not benefit from diverse teams.[17] Multidimensional, complex tasks do. Teams with diverse cognitive repertoires trounce teams with overlapping cognitive repertoires on tasks that involve innovation, creativity, or predicting the future.

---

[15] *Id.* at 102–04.
[16] *Id.* at 210.
[17] *Id.* at 105.

Updating law for the challenges of the future is a complex, multidimensional, nonroutine task. It involves elements of innovation, creativity, and prediction, each themselves areas that benefit from cognitive diversity. Developing effective language to help us talk in a clean and clear way about the problems of the future is precisely such a task. We need input from a range of approaches; we need a broad range of lived experience to even get close to making a reasonable guess about how a rule will affect a population.

Page provides reams of evidence supporting his thesis that cognitively diverse groups are necessary in order to effectively address complex nonroutine tasks. He notes studies of patents, where team-created patents outstrip single-inventor contributions, giving the lie to the myth of the brilliant solo inventor.[18] Influential academic papers, as measured by citation count, are not only much more likely to have been drafted by a team, but also show signs of internal diversity.[19] A paper is more likely to be influential when it represents two (or more) diverse but deeply researched fields. Page reports measures of consistency—that is, how often two papers are cited together—and diversity— that is, how unlikely two papers are to appear together in the literature. Influential papers are both consistent and diverse: they represent the coming together of two or more in-depth fields.[20]

Together, these metrics give evidential teeth to the anecdotally well-known Medici effect, coined by Frans Johansson in his award-winning book on innovation by that name.[21] The neologism is inspired by the House of Medici, a noble family famed for bringing thinkers of different disciplines together in European Renaissance patronage culture (and for the innovative political use of poison). The Medici effect stands for the principle that many important breakthroughs come from putting people who look at problems in radically different ways in the same room together.[22] Breakthroughs don't tend to occur when people deeply rooted in the same tradition pool their efforts to double down on their familiar approaches: innovation is not a matter of brute-forcing the same approach. Nor does the effect occur when groups splash on a bit of a different discipline—as legal academics tend to do with badly understood economics, for example—to gain a bit of interdisciplinary sex appeal.

---

[18]   *Id.* at 176–77.
[19]   *Id.*
[20]   *Id.* at 176–77, 219.
[21]   Frans Johansson, The Medici Effect: Breakthrough Insights at the Intersection of Ideas, Concepts, and Cultures (2004).
[22]   *Id.*

Rather, the Medici effect appears when team members are deeply grounded in different traditions; problems intractable to one are solvable as a matter of course to the other. That is the pattern which Page's evidence describes: the coming together of grounded but deeply different traditions and perspectives through teams of people, each of whom is fully read-in to their own discipline. These results also hold true in the finance sector. Team-managed wealth has become the norm on Wall Street, and Silicon Valley venture capitalists look for teams, not ideas. But for all Page's efforts to make the business case for diversity, the evidence in that context is not unequivocal. As he puts it, compliance-driven token nods to diversity can result in loss of experience and may not increase the cognitive repertoire of the group. For example, laws in Scandinavia that required a certain percentage of corporate board members to be women did not yield immediate performance results for those companies. It didn't help that the firms took a mercenary approach. Many named family members with little experience. Highly qualified women, on the other hand, were in such demand that some were members of multiple boards, making the likelihood that they would be able to contribute to any one enterprise vanishingly low.[23]

Rampant corporate tokenism of this sort was designed to meet percentage goals, not to produce diversity benefits—so it is little surprise that it did not. This is not to say that rules or laws mandating gender or other forms of diversity on corporate boards are not wise policy, merely that their positive effects, if any, will become apparent only after pipeline effects increase the number of skilled candidates and reduce tokenism. Page calls this planting a "golden carrot." We will have to see.

DIVERSITY HELPS LAW KEEP UP

Imagine you are assembling a team to answer a hard question of law and technology. For example, let's consider whether and how to integrate the multitude of sensors (smartphone cameras, smart television microphones, and so on) that are now seeded throughout our environment, with our social norms of privacy and human need for retreat and solitude. Ubiquitous sensors have destabilized privacy, and despite assertions that "privacy is dead" by surveillance moguls, this intrusion is deeply felt by everyone from seventh graders bullied on Instagram to police officers who feel threatened by being recorded on the job. The seventh graders should probably be afforded some

---

[23] PAGE, DIVERSITY BONUS, *supra* note 9, at 167–70.

space and privacy; the cops need to understand that public servant means public.

A diverse team will likely generate better insights. Perhaps the best team combines technologists, public interest lawyers, entrepreneurs, psychologists, union representatives, and economists. Your ideal team composition may differ. What is clear is that a diverse team will develop better language about the problem of ubiquitous sensors than will the usual group of industry lobbyists.

If it is true that diverse groups can help law keep up, we must address why "representative democracy" doesn't deliver the goods. The problem is that "representative democracy" is now neither. It is currently designed to have the *form* of diverse collaborative decision-making, while the function of rulemaking resides in corporate hands. Larry Lessig's damning indictment of congressional dependence on corporate funding provides a clean example.[24] From the perspective of diversity, congressional dependence on corporate cash reduces whatever diversity the representative might have brought to the table in favor of what the congressperson's handlers prefer.

Whereas two people might come to the table with two opinions, they can both be paid to voice the same perspective. Anyone who has dealt with a lobbyist in a deliberative setting knows how frustrating it can be to work with a paid parrot. Because the lobbyist takes his position for pay, there is no diversity bonus to his inclusion, and the inclusion of paid shills—especially when they are in the majority, or control the parameters of discussion—reduces the value of cooperation for cognitively diverse voices. This is of course not to say that team members cannot be paid for their time, just not for a predetermined and predefined policy outcome favoring one party over the other interests at the table.

This is why Lessig's account of formerly democratic institutions compromised by lobbyist cash is so damning from a diversity perspective.[25] Staffers are beholden to lobbyists because of the revolving door, lobbyists are beholden to their paying clients, and congresspeople to the same firms. There is no diversity anywhere there, just strings and marionettes. What appears diverse on the surface is merely mutual congratulation. A system that may once have worked to gather diverse voices representative of various constituencies now actively excludes those voices as a threat to the bought consensus.

---

[24] Lawrence Lessig, Republic, Lost: How Money Corrupts Congress—and a Plan to Stop It 143 (2011).
[25] *Id.*

As grim as all this is, there is a bright silver lining. The failures of compromised democratic institutions are precisely that, failures of those institutions to live up to their own aspirations, not failures of the aspirations: gathering members with a diverse and non-overlapping set of tools. On the contrary, the failure of formerly democratic rulemaking institutions to produce good laws can be directly traced to the unifying influence of paying off all members with campaign contributions or promises of lobbying jobs. Restoring democratic principles to compromised democracies will do much to restore the diverse nature of representative democracy.

Adapting law to changing technology is a perfect example of a complex, nonroutine, multidimensional problem. Gathering team members with diverse life experiences will increase the quality of social technology developed by the group. As noted in an earlier chapter, "the life of the law is experience, not logic."[26] In questions of legal design, the law of unintended consequences is a constant. Humans actively respond to their regulatory framework. They are the definition of a dynamic system. What this means is that knowing how humans will respond to a situation because of knowledge of how they did respond to a similar situation is invaluable to sane lawmaking. Humans do not respond as they ought, they respond as they do.

Consider a practical example. Suppose we are trying to develop rules about mobile bandwidth. Such rules will affect different groups very differently. City-based users may benefit from municipal broadband, whereas rural dwellers may rely more on satellite access. However, both are likely to depend on cell phone networks as a core source of information for daily life, and may make far less use of the suburban cable home-by-home broadband model.

For these kinds of problems—and when it comes to adapting law to technology they are almost all these kinds of problems—people with diverse lived experience can help address the dynamic problems of law and technology. In our mobile bandwidth example, it helps to have input on or from people with experience in living at the last mile of the cable as well as from those who navigate urban environments with just a smartphone for internet access.

DIVERSITY'S POSITIVE FEEDBACK LOOP

Thus far our discussion has been about how cognitive and identity diversity in groups improve outcomes and make better law. We must also acknowledge a feedback effect. Making law inclusively not only improves outcomes, it

---

[26] OLIVER WENDELL HOLMES, JR., THE COMMON LAW 1 (1881).

improves the process itself. Authoritarian rulemaking not only creates worse rules, but worsens the process.

Here's why. Law is cooperative fiction, with the emphasis on cooperation. In the previous chapter we discussed the advent of hardball constitutionalism, whereby authoritarian groups turn constitutional structures against themselves.[27] The idea of the rule of law is itself fictive: any victim of war crimes or back-alley bullying knows that when others choose to not cooperate, we can terrorize each other on a whim. As with any of these ideas, the rule of law only has the strength we give it. It has power purely through human groups committing to and giving action to the norms of cooperation and consent. We can revert back to naked power as the driving principle of human social organization anytime we wish. Those who play constitutional hardball prey on the good graces of those who still wish to cooperate and who still act as if our actions were constrained by law. But the spirit of the law is a wasting resource, as is the spirit of cooperation in which all good social technology takes root and grows.

How we do things matters. When we go about producing law inclusively and cooperatively, we not only create better rules but also strengthen the norms of cooperation that help us think better in groups. We become not only more free and fair, but smarter and faster, the very characteristics we will need to keep up with technology. Authoritarians seek dominion, not thriving. They seek to silence voices and seize power for a minority—the rich, the race, tribe, or creed traditionally in power, or whatever. In the short term, their reliance on brutal power politics and violence may well triumph. In the long run, it will get us all killed, whether by pandemics, wars, ecological disaster, or conflicts over water and the like, as factors combine geometrically. Cognitive diversity in group decision-making is, therefore, not merely a matter of social justice (and when did those words become pejorative?), it is a matter of survival.

So, to summarize: jurisgenerative communities must be cognitively diverse. Helping law keep up with technology is a multidimensional, complex, non-routine cognitive task. Groups will need both field depth and diversity of cognitive tools. And while we ought not to expect immediate diversity bonuses from random groupings of identity diverse individuals, we ought to expect life experience and the different learning paths traveled by different identity groups to yield useful insights, particularly where the dynamic interaction between social and hard technologies has distinct impacts on distinct groups. Finally, doing law in this way will yield not only better rules and insights for

---

[27] *See generally* Mark Tushnet, *Constitutional Hardball*, 37 J. MARSHALL L. REV. 523, 523 (2004).

cooperation in the face of technological change, but will also have critical and cumulative effects on our ability to keep coming up with rules that keep us one hop ahead of extinction.

NONCOERCION

Noncoercion is the second key attribute of communities that produce thriving language and law. Communities dominated by one person or a few people systematically create terrible law. Noncoercive gardens may produce terrible law, too, but the terrible law created by a noncoercive garden does not spread, because no one is forced to adopt it. The terrible law produced by coercive groups is an aggressive, invasive species. Force breaks the normal mode of cultural transmission, in which rules are adopted when they benefit the adopter.

I am not arguing here that coercion is bad in the enforcement of laws. Once we agree what the rules should be, then the state may use its traditional monopoly on force to enforce the law—and indeed, that state monopoly on force is intended to restrict coercion's role within a society to the enforcement of laws agreed upon by that society. The coercion I am talking about is deadly at the *generative* stage: when we are talking together about what rules to adopt. When coercion is used at that stage, such as when a puppet parliament accedes to the force-backed demands of a dictator, the group loses the advantages of thinking in groups and of integrating diverse viewpoints. The group is merely enslaved to the dictator.

At the generative stage, coercion is the opposite of law. For a trivial example, that's why legislators are often somewhat immune from arrest while acting in their legislative capacity. A norm, a story, a narrative, a way of "acting as one should," runs on human minds either as a matter of conviction or as a matter of force. Force permits no progress: a worse rule can survive against a better rule through force. In the famous series *Roots*, an enslaved man named Fiddler approaches Master Reynolds to ask that he call off the brutal whipping of the protagonist Kunta Kinte. It is not lost on the viewer that Reynolds is reading the Bible at the time. And it is clear to anyone watching the scene that Fiddler's idea, that the whipping should not happen, is the better way for these humans to live together. Reynolds refuses to stop the murderous beating.[28]

Coercion at the language-generation stage destroys ideas. It suffocates new ways of relating. Coercion is to law—the determination of how we *ought* to live together—what an acid attack is to the life of a young woman attending

---

[28] Part 2, ROOTS (1977).

school under a repressive or lawless regime: vicious, destroying, life-ending.[29] And the public association of law with coercive power is the heart of what has gone wrong.

Too many lawyers mistake power for the rule of law. They think state power is synonymous with law. On the contrary, it is only the rule of law that legitimizes state power. Without the rule of law, force is just force, and laws aren't really laws. They're just words on a page that are erased under the shadow of violence.

Now we can begin to see why noncoercion is a key ingredient for linguistic gardens. Agreement is only possible in the absence of coercion. Coercion renders our hand-wringing about law, or what the rules are, moot. Who cares what the law is, or what "law" is, when the powerful simply pull guns and do as they will? This gives the final lie to positivist pretensions to any serious description of law. If all they have been saying is that the powerful do what they have the power to do, everyone ought to yawn, then spit.

A claim of coercive power is never a legitimate claim of legal norm generation. It is just more base force attempting to assuage its guilt and acknowledging that it has no common narrative worth the candle. It is just lawless force, pretending to respectability. Let us pick the very worst rule: slavery. Slavery is nothing but force. There is no ideal worth following, no convincing anecdote, no possible coherent defense of the vile practice. It is force, defended by force, propagated by force, and dependent on force. There is nothing life-giving there, because no one would seek slavery absent force. It is easily detected as a terrible way of living in community. Nothing the subjugator "gains" is worth more than what the subjugated loses. This isn't rocket science.

Let us compare a different rule: trade. When trade is not accompanied by force, it is often pure gain. Trade without force makes both parties wealthier. If I have four cookies but no milk, and someone else has a jug of milk but no cookies, we are both better off if we trade some cookies for a glass of milk.

The more coercive trade becomes, the less it is worth considering as a principle. As Anna Bernasek and D. T. Mongan write, when the price of a good or service is "all you can pay," the value of trade for the exploited party is nearly nil.[30] Why trade, if you know the value of the exchange goes entirely to

---

[29]   *See, e.g., Acid Attacks Keep Afghan Girls from School*, N.Y. TIMES, Oct. 14, 2008, www .nytimes.com/2008/11/14/world/asia/14iht-15acid.17826269.html; Allie Torgan, *Acid Attacks, Poison: What Afghan Girls Risk by Going to School*, CNN, Mar. 17, 2016, www.cnn.com/20 12/08/02/world/meast/cnnheroes-jan-afghan-school/index.html.

[30]   Anna BERNASEK & D. T. MONGAN, ALL YOU CAN PAY: HOW COMPANIES USE OUR DATA TO EMPTY OUR WALLETS (2015).

the other party, or so nearly so that you are just serving as a resource to be exploited?

A forced trade is no trade at all. Here is the basic coercive trade: "Your money or your life."[31] We reject this trade (I would, however, suggest giving the nice person with the gun your money) because the overwhelming presence of force in the trade means that the entire concept of trade is corrupted by the presence of coercion.

As force increases within a *nomos*, the value of the rules generated by that *nomos* approaches zero. If force ever becomes the norm, the value of the rules generated by that *nomos* are zero. They have no validity. We cannot tell why they were adopted, because there is always the explanation: people adopted this rule at gunpoint.

Noncoercion takes many forms. It is of course no accident that Bob Cover, in "Nomos and Narrative," selected nonviolent communities as the standard bearers of his discussion of jurisgenerative communities.[32] Cover selected the Amish because he wanted readers to share his vision of law bubbling up from below, of law as an everyday incidence of people talking to each other about how to live together without worrying that one's neighbors might force their rules on people who were not part of the discussion.

In Cover's piece, the Amish were the poster children for permitting a religious group to build its own jurisgenerative unit, even when that unit decided (as in the case of my uncle's family, *Wisconsin v. Yoder*)[33] that children should not be educated beyond the eighth grade. The Amish got top billing because of their religious precommitment to nonviolence. Indeed, the brief on behalf of the Amish in *Bob Jones Univ. v. United States*[34] indicated the risk that an "old" and "innocent" culture could be wiped out.

But add notions of force and coercion to the equation, and all our intuitions change. Amish communities are rife with the sexual abuse of children, and the vaunted separation of the community from the "English" serves as a superb barrier against stopping this horror.[35] Or consider the practice known as shunning. A member of the Amish community must follow the community's

---

[31] *See Batman Begins*, Warner Bros. Pictures (2005) (Excellent example of a "your money or your life" scenario in the beginning of Batman's origin story by Christopher Nolan).

[32] *See* Cover, *supra* note 1, at 4.

[33] Wis. v. Yoder, 406 U.S. 205 (1972).

[34] Bob Jones Unv. v. United States, 461 U.S. 574 (1983).

[35] *See, e.g.*, Malcolm Gay, *A Crisis in Amish Country*, N.Y. TIMES, Sept. 2, 2010, www .nytimes.com/2010/09/03/us/03amish.html; Sarah McClure, *The Amish Keep to Themselves. And They're Hiding a Horrifying Secret*, TYPE INVESTIGATIONS, Jan. 14, 2020, www .typeinvestigations.org/investigation/2020/01/14/amish-sexual-abuse-assault/.

group determination, or risk exclusion from their entire social network, the list of people who help keep each of us alive.[36] How do we feel now?

I do not mean to laud or attack the Amish in particular, but to help us observe our reactions as we think about the relationship of coercion to the development of rules about how we ought to live together. Cover understood this point exquisitely. Coercion at the moment of norm generation destroys the effectiveness of the norm. The more coercion is involved, the less we can have any sense that the rules generated by a given garden, a given *nomos*, is worth a second look.

And this leaves us in a worrisome place: much of what we call law, worldwide, is incurably infected with coercion. It is anti-law, created solely by force, sustained by asymmetries of power. This infection runs so deep that some legal scholars actually identify law only with state force. What nonsense! The only thing we can know about an idea adopted at gunpoint is that it is a terrible idea. Otherwise it would not need the gun.

SHARED GOALS

To create good language, we need group members who have diverse cognitive toolsets working together in a noncoercive environment. But unless those group members share goals, the teams will disaggregate, with members wandering off to join other like-minded people to further their common agendas.

The third and in many ways the most challenging characteristic of groups that successfully generate creative and innovative solutions to the problems of the future is that of shared goals. There is an inherent tension, although not a logical opposition, between the prior two characteristics and this one. Coercion is often the method of creating and enforcing unity, but such force-induced unity no longer permits good ideas to rise to the top: whatever the person with the gun says goes. Without coercion, we are left to find other, less intuitive ways to create shared goals than forcing everyone to work together. Similarly, if cognitive diversity does not pull against the ideal of shared goals, it at least tugs against it. The cognitively diverse will likely have different backgrounds, different perspectives, and ultimately, different goals.

The key to creating shared goals within cognitively diverse and noncoercive groups is to realize that the shared goals are themselves norms. A group must build a shared world, a shared description of the task in which it is engaged:

---

[36] See, e.g., Associated Press, *Amish Shunning Is Central to Ohio Hate Crime Trial*, Sept. 15, 2012, www.usatoday.com/story/news/nation/2012/09/15/amish-shunning-is-central-to-ohio-hate-crime-trial/1572615/.

a language-game. A group working together on the task of producing shared goals is like a factory producing the tools it needs to build the machines it needs to finally make the products the factory workers want to produce. There is a recursive, ramping-up effect. So one of the key elements of creating shared goals is for a group to talk about shared goals, to craft language about shared goals that works for the group, that induces public commitment within the group to those goals. Group members will have to desire to work together, and will have to desire the creation of a sufficient level of abstraction in describing their common problem and the range of its solutions so as to make group activity generative of good language, rather than descending into partisan bickering.

The creation of shared goals as a starting norm serves a valuable sorting function. Group members will have to value cooperation to be any use in creating cooperative fictions anyway, and if they are unable to publicly commit to shared goals or cooperation in the group context, then they are the wrong addition to the group. But more: mediators, facilitators, and other people whose job it is to bring together humans with wildly differing incentives and views of the world find that conversations about shared goals, and group commitments to those goals begin the lovely recursive process of shared language. Once the goal of a linguistic community is specifically set to the creation of shared goals, the language that is generated shares that goal. Moreover, the successful artifacts of language—the themes picked up by other speakers that make it into the general parlance of the group—will be those that command the most support as shared goals. The bootstrapping of shared goals from suggestion to group-adopted norm is therefore less problematic than our current polarized situation might otherwise suggest.

Since I have said we need to craft common goals through the processes of narrative described in this book, I will again mention my own ideas on the subject of what shared goals we ought to organize our thinking around when coming at various issues of law and technology. My proposed shared goals are the same as my tests for valuable cooperative fictions: human viability, and human thriving.

Viability, because the only way we can wonder at and keep asking questions about the universe is for us and our descendants to stay alive. I really cannot see a way around viability as a core measuring stick for cooperative fictions. If certain guiding narratives—climate change denialism, for example—lead us to extinction, we can say with confidence that they fail our test for good narratives.

But the measuring stick of our cooperative fictions should not merely be to secure the lives of questioning beings, but to make those lives worthwhile. We should want humans to thrive, and the question is how to best do that. Here, I have followed at least two broad ideas. The first is that a clear understanding of our language of cooperation—law—is indispensable to securing the benefits of human cooperation under changing circumstances. The second is that, broadly speaking, systems that maximize what people can *do* with their lives tend to be pretty pleasant societies to live in: Amartya Sen's capabilities theory, which we discussed earlier. I agree: I think it's a good goal to help humans to be able to do as many of the things that make their existence worthwhile, from their own perspective, as possible. Within broad limits that again humans can talk about and agree on, maximizing human capability is a strong way of looking at our cooperative fictions. If a cooperative fiction helps more people do more of what they deem makes life worthwhile, it passes our narrative litmus test. Just as a scientific experiment must pose a falsifiable hypothesis in order to mass muster within the guiding narratives of science, so a cooperative fiction must tend to maximize human capability, satisfaction, thriving, even welfare (not aggregated, however).

As always, though, the conversation is more important than any given answer. The goal is to do what humans do best—cooperate—on developing the thing that we need most to be able to cooperate: our language.

CONTEXT AND PRESENCE

The problem of polarization has some other solutions, as well. I note two here: the first, context and physical presence (or online technology that mimics both) serves to reduce conflict and generate a sense of shared goals. Maroon a progressive and a libertarian on a desert island, and they begin to work together. Do the same with a monster to slay in a virtual world, and watch cooperation similarly emerge. There is a reason certain online environments breed cooperation, moderation, and complex governance structures, and others are cesspools of racism, anti-Semitism, and authoritarianism. Platforms that encourage cooperation engender a strong sense of continuity and presence. They provide tasks at right angles to any ideology, the completion of which require multimember diverse teams.

The second solution draws from cognitive science research to address the root cause of polarization: the fact that individually we do not know much about the world around us, but rather believe in knowledge stored in other people's minds as a matter of weighted and discounted conviction.[37] Piercing

---

[37] *See generally* STEVEN SLOMAN & PHILIP FERNBACH, THE KNOWLEDGE ILLUSION: WHY WE NEVER THINK ALONE (2017).

the illusion of explanatory depth—the misconception that we know what is best because we think we understand how things work—can do much to reduce myside bias and engender shared goals. This is because one of the major ways to reduce myside bias is to ask someone to explain precisely how something is supposed to be done. Asking clean causal questions ("exactly how would you make that work?") both maintains a shared goal of creating ideas that can be put into actual practice and reduces the polarizing impact of our implicit reliance on the reliance of others. Asking us how we feel about policy one versus policy two won't change our minds. But asking us to describe precisely how we would execute one policy or another may. Let's consider each of these phenomena—context and presence, and polarization—in turn.

Humans are genetically predisposed to cooperate through language with other humans in their immediate presence. Context is, as Wittgenstein showed, how language is generated. So it is no surprise that presence and context are drivers of the ability and desire to create common languages. If isolation and alienation separate and corrode language, context and presence are key building blocks.

One clear factor that emerges from the study of online communities is that of presence. Physical presence is one strong social institution that has sustained cooperation over time: we really are in the same space, together. Humans are built to cooperate, but online, where there are no social institutions to constrain antisocial behavior, outrage has become a habit of mind.[38] When we are far away from each other, and unlikely to encounter each other personally, social institutions and norms of kind behavior break down. This is one of the reasons that developing such social technology—through law—is of such paramount importance. The system of interaction can change the humans who interact through it: we become more cooperative when channeled by a system to successfully cooperate.[39] Public goods experiments strongly support this view: when humans successfully cooperate in round one of a public goods experiment (one in which players must contribute their money to a central pot that is doubled, or keep their money and free ride on other players) are more generous in later rounds. By changing our legal environment, we can potentially smooth the cliff in social institutions between online and off.

Humans act differently when face-to-face with other humans than they do when they are striking at their ideological foes from the depths of their

---

[38] See Gaia Vice, *Evolution Explains Why We Act Differently Online*, BBC, Apr. 3, 2018, www .bbc.com/future/article/20180403-why-do-people-become-trolls-online-and-in-social-media.

[39] *Id.*

grandparents' basement. Perhaps you have felt the effect: when speaking directly to someone with whom you discover a deep-seated ideological difference, perhaps you have felt the urge to moderate your statements, to extend a bit more grace to the other side. Daryl Davis, a Black man who is a blues musician, befriends white supremacists. He connects with them over shared points of interest. Some renounce their racism. Some, including former KKK grand dragon Scott Shepherd, become strong friends. Davis has a collection of Klan robes given to him by former Klansmen friends who have renounced their Klan affiliation; he hopes someday to open a museum.[40]

The evil of racist ideology is never to be doubted, but the behavior of virulent racists in such one-on-one encounters often changes slightly. It is as if the ideology becomes slightly less real than the person seated across the table from the ideologue. I do not mean to say that making friends with avowed racists will magically convert them, or that this is the best way to address either patent or structural racism. The point of the story for present purposes is that personal presence and relationship can play a role in moderating even the most pernicious ideologies. Personal presence and personal relationship operate below the level of logic. No matter what you believe, the person with whom you are personally speaking is a factor in how you speak. Of course, where there is no relationship, personal presence does not solve all problems: members of the Westboro Baptist Church are certainly physically present, but they have sanitized their contacts by refusing to engage with anyone as an actual human harmed by their bigotry.[41]

Presence is a problem, online. The most vicious communities are marked by an absence of presence: people post, but they can hide behind usernames and change those names at no cost.[42] The creators of pseudonymous services manage their users' sense of visibility carefully. The system designers can, of course, identify their users precisely. By using and combining a range of

[40] Rachel Chason, A *Black Blues Musician Has a Unique Hobby: Befriending White Supremacists*, Wash. Post, Aug. 30, 2017, www.washingtonpost.com/news/morning-mix/wp/2017/08/30/a-black-blues-musician-has-an-unique-hobby-befriending-white-supremacists/.

[41] *See, e.g.*, Larry Keller, Women of the Gay-Bashing Westboro Baptist Church Say They're Just "Loving Their Neighbor" When They Predict He'll Burn in Hell, Southern Poverty Law Center, Feb. 26, 2009 (available at www.splcenter.org/fighting-hate/intelligence-report/2009/westboro-baptist-church-debates).

[42] *See, e.g.*, Jonathan Mahler, *Who Spewed That Abuse? Anonymous Yik Yak App Isn't Telling*, N. Y. Times, Mar. 8, 2015, www.nytimes.com/2015/03/09/technology/popular-yik-yak-app-confers-anonymity-and-delivers-abuse.html; see also Cecilia Kang, *Seeking Privacy, Teens Turn to Anonymous Messaging Apps*, Wash. Post, Feb. 16, 2014, www.washingtonpost.com/business/technology/seeking-privacy-teens-turn-to-anonymous-messaging-apps/2014/02/16/1ffa583a-9362-11e3-b46a-5a3d0d2130da_story.html?noredirect=on.

metrics, they can determine who is who, linking either to real-world identities or to advertising profiles that are every bit as complete. The structures encourage a carelessness of speech fostered by "the amoral openness of the social web," as journalist Andrew Marantz describes it, homogenizing opinions into marketable "likes," and simplifying complicated emotions into outrage or even desensitization.[43] Even "social" ecosystems like Facebook, which ostensibly exist to amplify community and connection, don't do so—and don't by design. Personal information is constantly extracted for exploitation outside the context in which it was offered, and presented to parties whom users did not intend to receive it and for purposes that do not benefit them. The connected feel of the Facebook interface does not foster closeness, but disclosure.

Facebook's design decisions aren't a natural law of online interaction. Some online communities have characteristics that draw people together, that make connections first, that value communal context and task over disclosure of marketable personal information. Consider a strong relationship in your own life with someone whose values and perspectives are very different from your own. For some of us, it's a family member. For some, a spouse. For some, it's a member of a religious community or a club. What seems to happen is that humans form relationships first on some point of commonality—do we share an interest in gardening? model train building? philosophy? keeping a family going?—and only afterwards do we begin to take the person's point of view into consideration. Think of the last time someone changed your mind. It is quite unlikely it occurred within a single conversation, exchange, or argument. Rather, what can cause us to reexamine our points of view is the presence of someone in our lives who is there for *reasons unrelated to the particular perspective*.

Consider a family with homophobic beliefs that learns one of its members is LGBTQ. (For greater clarity, let's say a young adult child has just come out to their parents.) The point of contact, of commonality, is the family. In a sense, we are stuck with our family. Of course, many families split over such questions, but what is surprising is the number of cases in which people change deeply held beliefs in order to love a family member.[44] The relationship comes first, then the change in perspective.

Families are not the only groups that cause relationships to form across ideological precommitments. I will call these kinds of groupings—of families,

---

[43] Andrew Marantz, Antisocial: Online Extremists, Techno-Utopians, and the Hijacking of the American Conversation 127 (2019).

[44] By surprising number, I mean a third. *See* Sabra L. Katz-Wise et al., *LGBT Youth and Family Acceptance*, 63 Pediatric Clinics of North America 1011, 1017 (2016).

churches, clubs, whatever—*orthogonal.*[45] The point of commonality of the group stands apart from any ideological commitment: model train enthusiasts know no politics, they're just into trains. A group that shares a political identity, and has self-selected because of that political identity, will become an echo chamber. A group that has a tribal signifier, a group purpose beyond a given political identity, seems to be able to form relationships first, and foster kindness and understanding on issues of difference later. For example, in his book *Us Plus Them: Tapping the Positive Power of Difference,* Todd Pittinsky speaks of cultivating pride, which can enable group members to reinvest in the group.[46]

Orthogonal groups may be a way to challenge online echo chambers. Many online groups are, of course, echo chambers. But many others are orthogonal: people share an interest in dieting, or exercising, or finally conquering Blackwing Lair (I know, I'm dating myself). Groups in online games cooperate toward game goals. Groups in some online fora do not cause echoes, but resonance. Such groups come at a problem such as financial management, or weight loss, or travel, from different directions, and the resulting hive-mind is diverse and engaged, rather than hollow, overlapping, and a viciously reinforcing cycle.

Orthogonal groups have a number of characteristics worth noting, although of course not all orthogonal groups have every feature. To simplify the discussion, I propose we consider opposing paradigms: a family, on the one hand, and a political discussion forum, such as a political subreddit, on the other. I understand there are problematic associations with family—not everyone has the same experience, and many have experiences of alienation and separation— but even in those negative experiences one can detect the underlying social sense of what a family has been constructed to be: the social technology of the family, if you will. It is that which I am talking about, rather than any one person's experience of family.

Families are persistent over time. Echo chamber associations are often short-term. Families are random—you can pick your friends, the saying goes, but you can't pick your family. Echo chambers are self-selected. Families often involve personal presence. Echo chambers are intermediated: the faces of those who are harmed are hidden from the trolls—and other members of the group. Families have costly exits: the cultural and legal

---

[45] *See Orthogonal,* OXFORD ENGLISH DICTIONARY ("Relating to or involving right angles; at right angles (to something else).")

[46] *See* TODD PITTINSKY, US PLUS THEM: TAPPING THE POSITIVE POWER OF DIFFERENCE (2012).

technology surrounding them makes it difficult to pick up and leave. Echo chambers are self-selected with zero exit costs—no one in them is required to deal with and get along with people with different points of view.

Families involve repeat play—knowing that you will interact with the people in the group again has a strong and sustaining effect on cooperation in the behavioral economics literature. Echo chambers have less repeat play: members are pseudonymous and do not directly impact each others' lives. Repeat play in the echo chamber context does not yield decency. Rather, each member competes with the others for extreme positions along the ideological axis that identifies the group. The more extreme the position, the more accolades.

What can we make of this comparison? Groups that use telepresence technology can create a sense of personal presence. Experiments in virtual worlds have shown that looking at a family member or loved one's virtual image triggers brain chemicals similar to those released in their actual presence.[47] And a number of online communities use apps like Marco Polo to create a sense of physical there-ness, which facilitates relationship building.[48] These relationships can then serve as a vector for understanding and tolerance of diverse opinions.

Online groups can also take other steps to be more like families and less like online echo chambers. Groups that take steps to include diverse voices will have taken a big step. Groups whose leadership ban dissenting voices are intentionally creating echo chambers: these groups are dangerous sinkholes. Groups focused on orthogonal goals—clearing a virtual world dungeon, finding the right balance of nutrition for maximum exercise gain, and so on—will have an easier time attracting a diverse community, one not self-selected for a single ideological perspective. Communities with orthogonal goals are often more healthy, and create the kind of relationships that, again, can sustain people who are otherwise tempted to extremes in the search for community.

A final note: many of the people who are attracted to online echo chambers are doing so because of real world failures of community.[49] Of course, many of the people attracted to online extremist groups come from loving families and homes. But among those who have exited online extremist groups—as among

---

[47] *See, e.g.*, Mar Gonzalez-Franco, *The Neurological Traces of Look-Alike Avatars*, 10 FRONTIERS IN HUMAN NEUROSCIENCE 392 (Aug. 2, 2016).

[48] *See* Our Story, Marco Polo, www.marcopolo.me/our-story.

[49] *See* Shan-Mei Chang et al., *The Mediation Effects of Gaming Motives between Game Involvement and Problematic Internet Use: Escapism, Advancement and Socializing*, 122 COMPUTERS & EDUCATION 43 (2018).

those who have exited extremist groups generally—there is a common thread of seeking for community. Thus, not only can community and relationships serve as a vector for tolerating and perhaps eventually adopting kinder and more understanding positions, but they can also serve as a buffer against the pull of community within extremist groups.

DEPOLARIZATION AND CAUSAL REASONING

One of the things we are going to have to do to create common ground and shared goals in groups is to deal with myside bias. The very source of strength of diverse, noncoercive communities is that they contain natural ideological opponents. The problem is that polarization quickly sets in, turning myside bias into a source of weakness in the very contexts—contact with others with diverse cognitive tools—in which it should help us think clearly. To create shared goals and contexts in jurisgenerative groups, we will need the best possible tools for handling the natural polarization that comes from our tendency to think in like-minded groups. Fortunately, we have fairly good tools for doing so.

As we discussed earlier, cognitive scientists Philip Fernbach and Steve Sloman found that most of what we think we know is actually what we trust others to know. The problem is, when so much of what we think we know is stored in others' minds, we often believe we understand things much better than we do. (This is the illusion of explanatory depth we explored in chapter 4.) Think of some everyday invention, like a toilet or a zipper: Can you explain exactly how it works?

How can we break free from the illusion of explanatory depth? Fernbach and Sloman's best answer is causal reasoning.[50] Causal reasoning relies on the fact that human minds have evolved to pay attention to what causes what. We seek cause everywhere, because figuring out what causes what is key to survival.

Causal reasoning helps us think more clearly about situations in which causal relationships both exist and matter. Consider the classic four-card logic test, which we discussed in chapter 4. Assume the standard four cards: [E], [2], [K], [7]. As a reminder, the test is this: Given a rule, which is that "*if* there is a vowel on one side of the card, *then* there is an even number on the other," which two cards must the participant turn over to verify the rule? Most participants turn over the E and 2, not E and 7. This is incorrect, because the rule says *if* [vowel], *then* [even number]. It does not say *if* [even number],

---

50   SLOMAN & FERNBACH, *supra* note 37, at 181.

then [vowel]. So turning 2 over doesn't help you determine whether the tested rule is true.

But let's try the same test with causal relationships. Again, let's have two states of affairs: snowing / not snowing (taking the place of vowel / consonant) and cold / not cold (taking the place of even / odd). Then, we ask participants to test the rule *"if* it is snowing, *then* it is cold."[51] Recall that most participants flubbed the letter-number variant by flipping over 2. That is the equivalent of asking, "if it is cold, must it then follow that it is snowing?" No. Causal reasoning clears our head. Whereas most participants get the letter-number version wrong, almost nobody gets the same question phrased causally wrong. This is because cold is causally connected with snowing, whereas snowing does not cause cold (except when it does, by reflecting enough light and slowly triggering an ice age, but that's a different book). If it is snowing, it must be cold. If it is cold, it is not necessarily snowing.

Causal reasoning is the tool to shake us out of our illusion of explanatory depth. Explaining how things work can clear our heads when our rationality is overwhelmed by our motivation and our often misplaced trust in the know-ledge stored in other people's minds. "People often have strong positions on issues, positions that are generally based on very little, certainly very little that they can articulate," Sloman and Fernbach write. "Our research shows that shattering people's illusion of understanding by asking them to generate a detailed causal explanation also makes them less extreme."[52]

How is this so? Causal explanations make speakers think about and name consequences. First it makes them realize they don't know as much as they thought they knew. (*How* does a toilet work, again?) When this process is applied to a proposed idea or policy, it makes them imagine and think through the implications. (What happens if we require everyone to replace their toilets with low-flow ones?) "Causal reasoning takes explainers out of their belief systems," write Sloman and Fernbach.

> You can't consider the implications of a policy by ruminating on how you feel about it. You are forced to think about the policy on its own terms, how it would actually be implemented and by whom and what would happen next in the world. This kind of thinking beyond yourself may be critical for moderating political opinion. Getting people to think beyond their own interests and experiences may be necessary for reducing their hubris and thereby reducing polarization. Causal explanation may be the only form of

---

[51] *Id.* at 54–56.
[52] *Id.* at 181.

thinking that will shatter the illusion of explanatory depth and change people's attitudes.[53]

If causal reasoning reduces bias and commitment to incorrect ideas by shattering the illusion of explanatory depth, motivated reasoning that appeals to what Sloman and Fernbach term "sacred values" is a tried and tested way of increasing the knowledge illusion and further biasing thought. Our values are not usually based on causal analysis. Values voting, for example, is rational kryptonite. Sloman and Fernbach observe, "[O]ur argument that causal explanation is an easy and effective way to moderate opinion applies only to certain issues, issues that elicit opinions based on outcomes as opposed to opinions based on values."[54]

Our task, then, is to develop outcome-oriented groups that favor causal explanations. In groups, motivated reasoners, who know that their reasoning will be discounted if their motivation is discovered, do their best to hide. Everyone claims to be just focused on results, even while arguing from moral precommitments. Financially motivated reasoning can be uncovered if the payments are made clear, but other types of motivated reasoning can be harder to detect.

One approach might be to bake outcome-based thinking into a group's procedures. This could mean policy proposals would have a concreteness requirement, something like the environmental impact statements that have been moderately effective in environmental regulation. Simply requiring that arguments be put into a certain causal form might help community members benefit from the sobering effect of causal thinking.

Citation can also be an effective means of helping dispel the illusion of explanatory depth. Although a citation norm will sound drably familiar to anyone who has been a student, the value lies as much in the deliberation and reflection involved in thinking through what parts of the knowledge represented actually resides in other minds as it does in avoiding plagiarism, for example. Of course, a citation norm also helps listeners identify the other minds that undergird a speaker or author's assertions, which helps listeners evaluate the credibility of the statement by looking at its intellectual pedigree.

If a citation norm sounds too bookish for the often rough-and-tumble discussions that generate norms in online communities, consider that it is precisely these spaces where credibility and trust are sufficiently low that cries for "source!" or "link pls." or even "pics or it didn't happen" are small bits of linguistic technology that establish an online citation norm. Wikipedia is the

---

[53]   *Id.* at 178–79.
[54]   *Id.* at 184.

fruit of that norm. Indeed, the driving innovation of the Web (that old, dead word) was the hyperlink—a social technology that was utterly unnecessary for the computers that formed the backbone of the network, but invaluable for humans who need to know sources and connections between information as much as or more than the information itself. If the fundamental action of computers across networked systems is to store and transfer information, the fundamental act of a thinking being on such a system is to examine the network of related information itself for reliability and relevance. Computers are about data. Humans are about data about data—metadata.

BY THEIR FRUITS YOU SHALL KNOW THEM

If we are going to invest in building linguistic communities—churches, subreddits, boardgaming clubs, debate societies, juries, corporate research teams—how can observers tell fruitful communities from rotten ones? The answer is fairly simple: observe the quality of the experience of the humans in and in contact with those communities. Subjective experience is as objectively observable as anything else humans do science on. We can observe how humans react to the language that governs their interactions. Are the humans angry, frightened, hopeless, hungry? The garden in question bears rotten fruit. Do the humans in and in contact with a community react with support, honesty, understanding, increases in knowledge, and above all compassion? The garden in question bears good fruit.

We are not just the authors of culture, we are its measuring instrument and its end. "Are the humans thriving?" is the right question, and we can measure it by looking at how the humans respond to the language and culture in which their minds swim and which their minds produce together. The human mind is the instrument that creates and interprets human-facing words, symbols, actions, and other behavior.

We understand symbols by interpreting them with a human mind. There is no other way, not even with computers, to determine what something means to a human other than to check with the human. But somehow along the way, some mistakes in how we do science have caused us to doubt the objective reality of our subjective experience, to disfavor the entire study of what badly must be studied —language and culture—merely because our established ways of doing science do a terrible job of studying them. Ask a scientist where the mind is: the fact that she cannot tell you has no bearing whatsoever on our measurable, observable, objective reality of subjective experience. The bigotry of the "hard" sciences toward the "softer" sciences has yielded this meager harvest: we have left off the practice of interpreting, of explaining what we and other sentient intelligences *mean*, precisely when the concept of meaning is under vicious attack.

In sum: we can know good communities because they produce healthy, thriving, happy human beings. Sometimes we hear claims that we cannot tell who is healthy and thriving; maybe raging incels are doing very well! But this is nonsense. We can ask people how they are doing, handle the most obvious lies and deceptions, survey respondents employ through strong experimental design and tools, and get as good an understanding of the quality of their subjective experience just as well and as empirically as we observe any other phenomenon.

We can and most often do successfully interpret the subjective experiences of other people—nothing remotely unscientific about it. In fact, hearkening back to the middle of this book, that is precisely what our intelligence does best! Humans are pack animals, and we must guess what the other humans are thinking, both to cooperate with them and to compete with them. There is, therefore, no other instrument for measuring the objective reality of a human's subjective experience than the mirroring of that experience by a human who objectively consults her subjective experience. Of course we can get things wildly wrong, every measuring instrument can. But the way to solve that problem is to more finely tune the instrument, and to build better communities of meaning that build better instruments. And as we do so, as in any good science, we will further improve and expand our language for doing so.

There are of course slightly challenging cases: What do we make of a cult, for example, whose members claim to be deliriously happy? The guiding stories and language of that community would ring true to cult members, of course, but that does not mean that those narratives are good ones for humans to orient to. The story could ring true to those members because the community has bad norms: perhaps there is an undercurrent of coercion, or a pull toward slavish unity of experience. Both are not uncommon in cults, leading members to find truth in dangerous and deadly stories. But these concerns are not difficult to address. We can detect coercive and deceptive grammars by their need for isolation, for their failure to survive in proximity to other normative grammars. We can judge a cult, or internet echo chamber, or political cult of personality, thus: members separate themselves from other communities that call their stories into question.[55]

By way of contrast, groups that produce thriving language have the same external facing qualities that they possess when looking inward: they value diversity in approaches, they spread their norms by persuasion, not coercion,

---

[55]   *See id.*

and they build bridging language, the language of shared goals, to expand their pool of potential linguistic contributors. As groups link, as successful normative language spreads, we see the virtuous cycle of language again at work, linking humans in filaments of language that become thicker and richer as they connect to more contexts, more uses, more ways of being, more ways of growing and living together.

10

TL;DR

Hello, babies. Welcome to Earth. It's hot in the summer and cold in the winter. It's round and wet and crowded. On the outside, babies, you've got a hundred years here. There's only one rule that I know of, babies—God damn it, you've got to be kind.

— Kurt Vonnegut, *God Bless You, Mr. Rainwater*[1]

As I was writing the end of this book, I was thinking about taking a friend around Washington, DC. One thing I've always loved to do is visit the National Air and Space Museum, where you can walk through some of the spacecrafts. You can see the incredible blend of design and function, the absolutely amazing advances in wildly different fields that had to come together by raw human ingenuity to make machines like that achieve their purpose.

Humans can cooperate to build amazing things. But in Washington, DC, right now it's clear something's gone wrong with our ability to cooperate to build a language of how to live together so that we thrive under the new circumstances that technology generates. This book was written in the hopes of helping us look at law, and language, with enough clarity to help us build better law and better language.

Let us put the entire book together at once. Stansilaw Lem wrote: "Technology is the domain of problems proposed and the methods of solving them."[2] Law is a technology. It is a means of solving the problem, "How can we cooperate fruitfully? How should we live together?" Linguistic cooperation is humans' superpower—with bees and ants we are one of only a few truly eusocial species on the planet—but while ants and bees accomplish cooperation through genetic evolution, humans do so through language, through the

---

[1] KURT VONNEGUT, GOD BLESS YOU, MR. RAINWATER 129 (2007).
[2] STANISLAW LEM, IMAGINARY MAGNITUDE 135 (2012).

creation and evolution of symbols, cooperative fictions, and networks of meaning. Language is thus the raw stuff of law, and emerges within groups of humans as they negotiate meaning within the context and task of life together. And here is the seed of the answer to our question of "can law keep up?" Unlike genetic evolution, language allows us to upgrade our cultural software at terrific speed, without having to wait for our genetic hardware to upgrade. Evolving language is how humans have always managed technological change, and it is our only hope now.

For law, the context is life together, and the task is helping humans thrive. Law, like language, evolves. Solutions that don't work die off, or are killed off by judges. The better narratives survive because they are better adapted in the face of the challenges of how to live together. They are resilient. They offer rich, memorable, adaptable stories that speak to different constellations of human needs. This gives law its narrative, organic, lived, often experiential, and contradictory qualities.[3]

This is the same process of narrative evolution by adverse selection that drives scientific progress: advancement by paradigm shift. A scientific community works together to craft language—paradigms, stories about how the world works—that responds well to the current problems faced by the community. Paradigms that do not address these problems fade as incongruities accumulate. Paradigms emerge that better respond to the accumulated problems with the current dominant narrative of a scientific field, and the linguistic community slowly (or suddenly) shifts over. Science does not advance one accumulated disproven theory at a time (*pace* Karl Popper), but rather one funeral at a time, as the old guard that still speaks the old language dies off. We no longer speak of "phlogiston" or "ether." Now we tell new stories of new spirits, of quarks, of subatomic players in a narrative structure: "up," "down," "charm," "strange," "truth," and "beauty." We know that these stories are also not definitive; they just let us approach and solve certain hard problems by thinking of things that way.

Law and science do not differ in this respect: both are driven by a process of selecting better guiding narratives, measured by the success of the narrative in solving problems faced by the linguistic community of lawyers or scientists. The difference is one of method. The tools of law are, like the tools of linguistics and cultural anthropology, interpretation, analogy, and narrative: telling stories and

---

[3] One example is the recently repealed North Carolina statute 18B-308. See N.C.G.S. § 18–308 (2019). The law made it "unlawful to consume or sell alcohol in any room where a bingo game is being conducted." Alexandra Drosu, *Bye, Bye Bingo*, RALEIGH MAGAZINE, Mar. 13, 2017, https://raleighmag.com/2017/03/bye-bye-bingo-bars-face-scrutiny/. Shortly after some scrutiny, a repeal was passed.

stories about stories. This is fully scientific, if one is objective: in fact it is the only scientific method of understanding and explicating cultural artifacts like Mary Midgley's sentence "George was allowed home from prison at last on Sunday."[4] Interpretation is the only method for understanding certain things. Indeed, interpretation is the only way of understanding the language of empiricism or rationality/logic, as attested by anyone who has ever been confused by what a teacher in a math class is trying to say. But because of cultural chauvinism among empiricists and rationalists, interpretive methods remain in a strange gray zone. The philosophical fallout of reductionist scientism and Vienna Circle verificationism, which only allowed empirical or rational (mathematical) methods to count as true "science," interpretive methods are sneered at as "soft," "qualitative," or "less pure" to this day. Of course, all these narrative descriptions of interpretive methods are themselves interpretive and qualitative (and frankly nonsensical)—a fact that escapes adherents of scientism entirely.

Law is the art (or science, if one rejects scientism's silliness) of crafting cooperative fictive narrative. It has been significantly hampered in its ability to do its job by the modern trend of training lawyers to eschew legal narrative and analogical reasoning and focus instead on armchair empiricism (the current fad is for "legal empirical studies") or rationalism (usually in the form of the law and economics movement). The problem with this development is that law then swaps the vital and living methods of narrative production for the deeply under-theorized narratives of empiricism or economics: "What shall we observe and why should we do so?" is not a question empiricism can answer, and neoclassical law-and-economics' disastrous meta-narratives about the nature of humans are both demonstrably false (in the lab, humans cooperate at rates that defy the assumptions built into neoclassical economics math about individual selfishness) and narratively corrosive (studies regularly show that the only people who act as selfishly as economists predict are students of economics or those who have otherwise been taught the narrow rules of the game presented to them in the lab). Lawyers have done a great disservice in abandoning their task of crafting coopera-tive fictions that help us work together and stay alive, in exchange for the almost entirely unacknowledged meta-narratives of verificationist science.

But now that lawyers know better, we can do better. We can challenge and defeat corrosive guiding narratives like "law cannot keep up with technology." Properly understood, the statement is nonsense: "technology cannot keep up with technology." We can understand that those sentences are not true, but are asserted as an unacknowledged meta-narrative behind "science" by surveil-lance capitalists who do not *want* our law to keep up with technology. The

---

4   Mary Midgley, The Myths We Live By 51 (2011).

statement "law can't keep up" is properly interpreted as "it would hurt our profits if it did." We are not helpless, we are being taught helplessness by companies that have hijacked our democracy and are looting our private data in the great gold rush of the twenty-first century: learn all about us so that companies can extract "all we can pay."[5]

And this is seen in the worldwide response to the uniquely American assertion that law cannot keep up. Other countries disagree, and it is obvious enough that they are right: when they do something about technological challenges like Facebook's election hacking[6] or the rapid rise of Nazi and white supremacist narratives online,[7] that something works: Facebook suddenly discovers the ability to deplatform hate speech,[8] just as Yahoo suddenly discovered the ability to stop sales of Nazi memorabilia some twenty years ago.[9] Google couldn't possibly comply with the European right to be forgotten, until it had to, and it suddenly could[10]—whining all the while, but corporate whining doesn't have the same impact when one doesn't own enough legislators.[11]

The American experiment of self-induced paralysis in the face of incredible damage wrought to democracy and the middle class has no persuasive power in the rest of the world. American surveillance capitalism is dismissed with amused contempt in Europe, and China has profited from the utter abdication of the United States as a believable advocate of democracy to build out massive systems of social influence technology in the form of an Orwellian "social credit system."[12] Russia, of course, has merely jumped at the

---

[5] *See* ANNA BERNASEK AND D. T. MONGAN, ALL YOU CAN PAY 15 (2015) (describing "the consumer surplus" as "the ultimate prize for firms").

[6] See Alissa de Carbonnel & Robin Emmott, *Fearing Election Hacking, EU Leaders to Ready Sanctions*, REUTERS, Oct. 18, 2018, www.reuters.com/article/us-eu-summit-cyber/fearing-election-hacking-eu-leaders-to-ready-sanctions-idUSKCN1MS2N3.

[7] Germany Approves Plans to Fine Social Media Firms up to €50m, THE GUARDIAN, Jun. 30, 2017, www.theguardian.com/media/2017/jun/30/germany-approves-plans-to-fine-social-media-firms-up-to-50m.

[8] Barbara Ortutay, *Facebook Bans 'Dangerous Individuals' Cited for Hate Speech*, AP NEWS, May 3, 2019, https://apnews.com/7825d0df3fda4799a78da92b9e969cdc.

[9] *Yahoo! To Stop Auctions of Nazi Memorabilia*, THE GUARDIAN, Jan. 3, 2001, www.theguardian.com/technology/2001/jan/03/internetnews.

[10] Sean Keane, *Google Forced to Remove Search Results in EU "Right to Be Forgotten" Case*, CNET, Jan. 22, 2019, www.cnet.com/news/google-reportedly-forced-to-remove-links-in-right-to-be-forgotten-case/.

[11] An example of corporate legislative ownership is Purdue Pharma's payments to lobbyists and the campaigns of Massachusetts state legislators as recently as 2018. *See* Christine Willmsen, *How OxyContin's Maker Sought to Influence Mass. Legislators*, WBUR, Apr. 25, 2019, www.wbur.org/commonhealth/2019/04/25/purdue-pharma-state-house-lobbying.

[12] *See* Robert Hockett, *When Is "Social Credit" Orwellian?*, FORBES, Jan. 3, 2019, www.forbes.com/sites/rhockett/2019/01/03/when-is-social-credit-orwellian/#2e3b86a53674.

opportunity to weaponize American unwillingness to protect its democracy when doing so conflicts with corporate data profiteering and advertising revenue. And all of this occurs against the backdrop of a worldwide collapse of liberal democracies in the face of national authoritarianism (Brazil, Hungary, United States, the Philippines, the United Kingdom, and others) and successful now-mainstream authoritarian nationalist movements in France, Germany, Italy, and many, many other countries worldwide.

What, then, is to be done? We need a better guiding meta-narrative for our goals of living together, as well as a better meta-narrative for our development of technology. I have proposed in this book both my own individual (and thus lesser) ideas about what that meta-narrative should be and (as a better idea) a model for coming up with much better solutions together, by using our cooperative superpower.

My own individual (and thus lesser) idea for a better meta-narrative than a science directed toward the ends of maximizing corporate profit is a model of technological and legal development that is focused on human survival and thriving. The better and broader idea is that we form the kind of linguistic communities, which studies routinely show produce better cognitive outcomes by leveraging our ability to think more clearly in groups under conditions of noncoercion, shared goals, and cognitive diversity. These linguistic communities, which I have termed "gardens," will then become jurisgenerative centers, centers that produce rich shared language and create meaning that then can be iteratively used to create more meaning. We need linguistic gardens that can create the twenty-first century's version of foundational cooperative fictions like "all men are created equal," money, or Tuesday. Maybe those cooperative fictions will look like "we are made of starstuff,"[13] cryptoledgers, or the European Union. Probably not: we have not thought of the language we need to survive the future, yet.

So: "Can Law Keep Up?" Yes, without any doubt. The story of rampant technological progress and stumbling trailing legal regulation is paid marketing nonsense. But to do so, we must change our understanding of what law is (language, not rules), where it comes from (communities, not courts), how we do it (experimentally, not by providing definitions), and most importantly, what we hope to get from it (human thriving, not corporate profit). If we make those shifts, we will make it. Life in the twenty-first century might even look like some of the utopian projections: more prosperity, more free time, less work, with benefits broadly distributed. But if we do not make these shifts, we

[13] Carl Sagan & Jerome Agel, The Cosmic Connection: An Extraterrestrial Perspective 189–90 (1975).

will continue to automate humans out of vast sectors of the economy, shrinking the proportion of goods and services that most humans can earn with their labor, and increasing the proportion ever fewer people receive merely by owning and inheriting more and more of the output of automated processes. We will threaten our children with starvation if they do not outproduce automation. I hope we get it right.

Law can keep up if we want it to. If we don't, we may not survive, and we will certainly not thrive. If we do want law to keep up, we will find that solutions which are better than the current nothing come quickly to mind, and that through experience and honest discussion within noncoercive and cognitively diverse communities of meaning focused on shared goals, we will be able to iterate and experiment with solutions, to see which meta-narratives guide us best. Those ideas will come quickly: there are very, very many humans, and at least one of us is bound to have the right idea, and others of us will recognize good ideas when we see them—that's how our intelligence has evolved to work. Human language is massively parallel—it links human minds together to help us all hammer on problems—and is capable of developing solutions to technological problems at terrific and accelerating speed. It is more than capable of crafting a language for dealing with the problems of the future.

Can law keep up? Yes. Let's talk.

Index